88

HISTORY OF ZANZIBAR
FROM THE MIDDLE AGES
TO 1856

HISTORY OF ZANZIBAR

FROM
THE MIDDLE AGES
TO
1856

JOHN GRAY

LONDON
OXFORD UNIVERSITY PRESS
1962

Oxford University Press, Amen House, London E.C.4

GLASGOW NEW YORK TORONTO MELBOURNE WELLINGTON
BOMBAY CALCUTTA MADRAS KARACHI LAHORE DACCA
CAPE TOWN SALISBURY NAIROBI IBADAN ACCRA
KUALA LUMPUR HONG KONG

Printed in Great Britain

CONTENTS

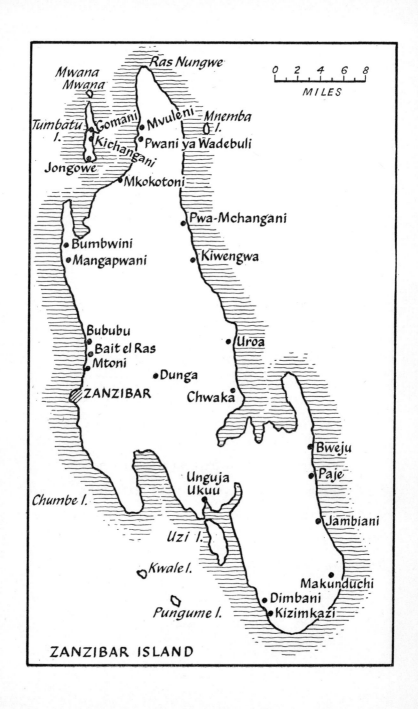

MILES
0 2 4 6 8

Mwana
Mwana

Ras Nungwe

Tumbatu
I.

Gomani

Mvuleni

Mnemba
I.

Kichangani

Pwani ya Wadebuli

Jongowe

Mkokotoni

Pwa-Mchangani

Bumbwini

Kiwengwa

Mangapwani

Bububu

Uroa

Bait el Ras

Mtoni

Dunga

ZANZIBAR

Chwaka

Bweju

Paje

Unguja
Ukuu

Chumbe I.

Jambiani

Uzi I.

Kwale I.

Makunduchi

Pungume I.

Dimbani

Kizimkazi

ZANZIBAR ISLAND

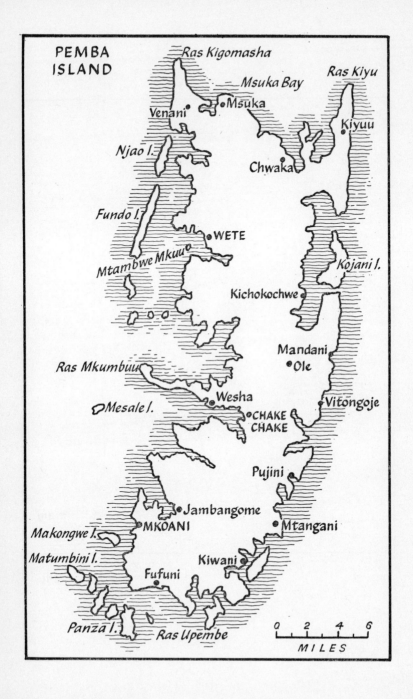

PEMBA
ISLAND

Ras Kigomasha

Msuka Bay

Ras Kiyu

Venani • • Msuka

Kiyuu

Njao I.

Chwaka

Fundo I.

• WETE

Kojani I.

Mtambwe Mkuu

Kichokochwe

Ras Mkumbuu

Mandani
• Ole

• Wesha

Vitongoje

Mesale I.

• CHAKE
CHAKE

Pujini

Jambangome

• MKOANI

• Mtangani

Makongwe I.

Matumbini I.

Kiwani

Fufuni

0   2   4   6

Panza I.   Ras Upembe

M I L E S

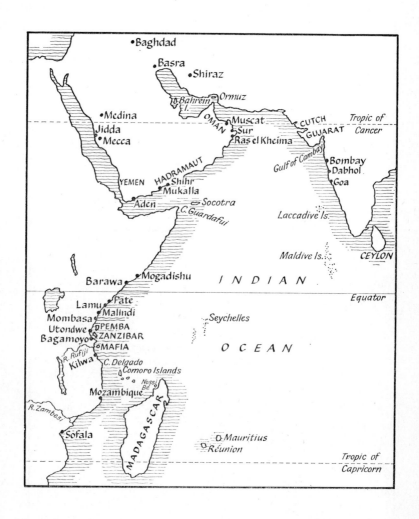

CHAPTER I

INTRODUCTORY

IT is safe to say that the history of every country has been affected to some extent by its geographical and geological features. Its climate, rainfall and soil have very often had a most important influence on that history. If the country in question is an island or an archipelago prevailing winds and currents may also have a like influence. In the case of the present Protectorate of Zanzibar all these matters have very profoundly affected its history.

The present Protectorate comprises the islands of Zanzibar and Pemba with a number of islets adjacent thereto, of which the most important is that of Tumbatu.

The island of Zanzibar is separated from the mainland of East Africa by a channel a little over twenty miles wide. It lies between latitudes 5° 40′ and 6° 30′ south. It is about fifty-three miles in length and twenty-four miles in breadth at its broadest point. Its area is about 640 square miles, or a little more than the area of Hertfordshire.

The island of Pemba lies about thirty miles NNE. of Zanzibar between latitudes 4° 80′ south and longitude 39° 35′ and 39° 50′ east. It is separated from the main continent by a channel some thirty-five to forty miles wide and has an area of about 380 square miles, or, about that of Huntingdonshire.

The channel separating Zanzibar from the mainland has been likened to 'a somewhat shallow, wide, sickle-shaped valley' for the most part barely twenty fathoms deep. In Mr. G. M. Stockley's opinion 'it is probable that this convexity of the sea floor is due either to material brought down by rivers and deposited in recent times or to the incomplete marine erosion in ancient times, the sea carving out the channel simultaneously from both directions'. In contrast to this, the Pemba Channel is described by Mr. Stockley as 'a deep gorge with steep sides' which suggests to him that at one time Zanzibar was more intimately connected with the mainland than Pemba. It further suggests to him 'either that Pemba had no connection with East Africa and Zanzibar, or that a separation was brought about by some structural dislocation'.

In past times winds and currents have had their influence in shaping the history of the two islands. The principal winds are the south-west and north-east monsoons, each of which sets in with almost clock-like regularity each year and then continually blows in varying degrees of strength over a period of several months after which they cease almost with the same regularity as they first set in. The south-west monsoon begins to blow in March. During its first two or three months are the greater rains or *Masika*. The lesser rains or *Mvuli* fall in October and November, after which the north-east monsoon sets in. Between each monsoon there is a short period of variable winds. Close to the land the wind is inclined at all times of the year to be somewhat variable with a tendency to become easterly in the afternoons. Until the days of steam all navigation in the Indian Ocean was dependent upon these winds. Ever since the earliest days when men of the East first began to go down to the sea in ships and to occupy their business in great waters, they have learnt that sailing vessels bound to East Africa from India or, the Persian Gulf, or Southern Arabia must avail themselves of the north-east monsoon, by setting out before that wind begins to die down and is followed by variable winds rendering navigation uncertain. Similarly, the return voyage can only be made whilst the south-west monsoon is blowing. A striking example of the truth of this rule of navigation occurred in the case of the British squadron under Commodore Blankett which tried to make its way up to the Red Sea in December 1798, and had to put back to Zanzibar owing to the strength of the north-east monsoon. Similarly, one reads of many instances of Portuguese and British ships bound for India which had to 'winter' at Mombasa, Pemba or Zanzibar because of that monsoon. Conversely, in April 1841, the south-west monsoon carried Captain Atkins Hamerton, the first British Consul at Zanzibar, past his destination to Pemba. Finding that 'we could not reach Zanzibar unless we stood out to sea for about eight degrees to the eastward and that even then we were not likely to reach Zanzibar under twenty or five and twenty days', Hamerton landed on Pemba and had to make his way thence by boat to Zanzibar.

As seen, currents also have their influence on navigation. On the east of the two islands and also in the Zanzibar and Pemba channels there is always a current which sweeps northward from Mozambique. The *Africa Pilot* tells us that it also runs out through the channel between Zanzibar and Pemba 'with great velocity'. During the south-west monsoon its rate is about two to four miles an hour, which is reduced to about one to three miles an hour during the other monsoon. When therefore both this current and the wind were operating together, navigation in the days of sail often became extremely difficult, if not at times impossible.

Topographically, the two islands present a number of contrasts as well as other points of resemblance. On the western and southern shores of Pemba the most striking features are the numerous creeks and inlets, which indent the coast line. Some of the creeks penetrate a long way inland; for example, the end of the Chake Chake inlet is barely six miles from the eastern shore. On the other hand, the east coast is much less indented. The low coralline cliffs on this coast contrast strongly with the steep sandy cliffs of the west coast.

With the exception of Kojani there are no islets of any size off the east coast, whereas the western and south-western shores are protected by archipelagos consisting of jagged, honeycombed coral platforms rising for the most part some twenty-five feet above sea level. Many of these have springs of water and with few exceptions all of them have at one time or other been inhabited and others, if no longer inhabited are still given over to cultivation or pasturage. The thing which probably impresses most visitors to Pemba by sea, is the steepness of the immediate ascent from the shore to a level platform about fifty to one hundred feet in altitude. Proceeding about half-a-mile further inland the visitor will find another step taking him about another fifty feet higher. Altogether there are four such terraces each some fifty to sixty feet above the other. The highest point on the island is 311 feet. On the west coast the first three of these terraces are very noticeable. A visitor landing at Mkoani on the south coast will ascend all three within one mile of the shore. In about the middle of the island, running more or less north and south, is a central ridge. Descending thence to the east coast the terraces are further apart, and accordingly less obvious, though just as well developed.

Another remarkable feature about Pemba consists of its deep valleys and meandering drainage. Generally speaking, the streams drain to the east and the west from the central ridge. The valleys have flat floors, in which there are generally sluggish streams, which as often as not eventually lose themselves in marshy swamps.

The sides of the valley are covered with vegetation. At the present time many of them are studded above with clove trees, but these have been introduced during the last hundred years. Previously the hillsides were given over to the growing of timber, which was in great demand for local shipbuilding. The floors of the valleys contain a rich alluvial sand and are given over to the cultivation of rice, cassava and other food crops.

Pemba has an annual rainfall which exceeds that of Zanzibar by about fifteen inches. This is to be accounted for by the fact that Pemba has a higher average altitude and that the south-west monsoon first reaches Pemba and intercepts the moisture laden winds. This rainfall and the great fertility of the soil has given the inhabitants of Pemba advantages which the people of the opposite mainland have never enjoyed. In the past not only was the island self-sufficient in regard to its food supplies, but it also exported quantities of fruit and grain to the mainland.

The island suffers from the disadvantage that it has few satisfactory deep-water anchorages. Most of the creeks are extremely shallow and dry to considerable distances off shore at low water. Wete, which is protected by the natural breakwater formed by Fundo Islet and has a good anchorage in depths of from four to five fathoms, is the best of these harbours. Mkoani likewise has the partial protection of the Makongwe islet, but suffers from the disadvantage that the water dries out for a considerable distance at low tide. As the creeks leading to Jambangome and Chake Chake dry out to an even greater distance, they have rarely been used except by dhows of shallow draught. Chake Chake, which is the capital of Pemba, is still used as a dhow port, but Jambangome, which at the beginning of this century was a flourishing trade centre, has ceased to be used for that purpose. Msuka Bay, which lies to the east of Ras Kigomasha, the northernmost point of the island of Pemba, is protected by reefs on nearly all sides. During the north-east monsoon it has a troublesome swell, but even then it is a safe anchorage, which was fairly extensively used by slave dhows in the last days of the slave trade. The east coast of the island is for the most part exposed to the extreme force of the Indian Ocean. It therefore has few safe anchorages, though existing archaeological remains show that from time to time attempts have been made by immigrant races to establish settlements at the heads of several of the creeks along this shore.

As already said, the topography of Zanzibar presents a number of marked contrasts to that of Pemba. In the first place, the shores of the island are less indented. The drainage is chiefly towards the west, but a number of large streams debouch to the north and south, but other streams disappear into the ground in the *uwanda* or waste lands in the north.

The *uwanda* lands are found mainly in the eastern and southern parts of the island, though occasional patches of such land are also to be found in the more fertile regions in the west. The highest point in Zanzibar is at Mazingini on the ridge of that name which reaches 440 feet. The step-like topography of Pemba is repeated in Zanzibar, where the main ridges run north and south. The central and highest ridge has ridges running parallel to them on either side.

Off the north-west coast of Zanzibar lies the islet of Tumbatu. It is about six miles in length and little over a mile across at its widest point. It lies about a mile and a half from the main island, but at low water the channel dries at an average distance of about a mile, thus considerably shortening the passage from the main island. The channel between it and the mainland affords a large and sheltered anchorage in depths varying from four to nine fathoms. Today there are three villages on Tumbatu, but until very recently there was no local water supply and the necessary supplies had to be fetched from the main island.

Proceeding southwards from Tumbatu one comes to the harbour of Zanzibar, which is protected by a number of off-lying islets and reefs. Here there is a good anchorage anywhere off the town of Zanzibar in about eight to ten fathoms. There are actually two anchorages, one to the north and the other to the west of Shangani Point. During the south-west monsoon the northern anchorage is the preferable one, but during the north-east monsoon landing from boats on the north shore of the town could at one time be difficult, and embarkation and disembarkation was easier to lee-ward. In the *Africa Pilot* of 1887 it is suggested that 'in this season it is better perhaps to anchor to the westward of Shangani Point, (so) that boats may land on either side'. Since the date of that publication the more recently constructed harbour works have rendered this advice more or less superfluous, but in the days before steam one of the inestimable advantages, which the harbour of Zanzibar had over other harbours on the East African coast, lay in the fact that one or other portion of the roadstead afforded a safe anchorage at all seasons and could therefore be once used for purposes of 'wintering' by vessels proceeding round the Cape of Good Hope to India or the Red Sea.

In addition to the harbour works, other reclamation work at the back of Zanzibar town has largely effaced what was at one time a very important asset to the roadstead. The best description of this topographical feature as it appeared before that reclamation is given by James Christie, writing in 1876 in his *Cholera Epidemics in Zanzibar:*

Zanzibar city is built on a triangular spit jutting into the sea, and during high water and spring tides, it is very nearly converted into an island by the flow of sea into the creek. At low water the creek is quite dry. . . .

A considerable extent of ground is covered by water during high tides, and this plain and the slightly elevated neck of land separating it from the sea is called Mnazi Moja. . . . The narrow neck of land at Mnazi Moja connects the city with the main portion of the island, but not directly with that portion of the city lying to the west of the creek, called Ngambo. . . .

There is no shipping at Ngambo, but the shelving sea bank is utilized by native craft for the purpose of careening. The dhows are placed in position during high or spring tides, and, supported on each side by poles, they are allowed to remain until they have undergone the necessary repairs, or till the season arrives when they must enter the harbour to take in cargo for the voyage. . . .

The triangular spit on which the principal portion of the town is built may be described as foot-shaped, the sole being exposed to the north-east monsoon, and the ankle to the south-west monsoon, the arch representing that portion separated from the main part of the island by the creek.

In his annual *Report on the Zanzibar Dominions* for 1860 Colonel Rigby stated that in this creek 'vessels of 300 to 400 tons can be careened in security. With very little expense it might be converted into an excellent dock'.

To continue with Dr. Christie's description:

Zanzibar has thus, in addition to the natural dry dock, two harbours, the one being safe to shipping during the north-east monsoon, and the other during the south-west monsoon. The two harbours are separated by the heel, or the angle. . . . The northern harbour being sheltered from the powerful and long continued south-west monsoon is the more important of the two, but both are filled with native craft during the respective seasons. While the south-west monsoon blows hard, vessels cannot ride with safety in the southern harbour, and during the north-east monsoon, native craft are not safe in the northern harbour, and vessels cannot discharge and load owing to the surf on the beach. There being no jetty or pier, the loading and the discharging of ships is accomplished by cargo boats only. . . .

The slope of the land on which the town is built is towards the lagoon and the seashore, and the superficial drainage is natural and easy. During the heavy monsoon rains the streets are torrent beds, but when the rain ceases they become dry in a very short time. . . .

In the days before steam few vessels exceeding 400 tons burden ever visited Zanzibar. Few other places along the East African coast could provide such good facilities for careening and 'dry-docking'. Moreover, except in the case of islands such as those of Kilwa and Mombasa, few places on that coast were so easily capable of defence by alien settlers against attacks by the local inhabitants as this foot-shaped peninsula.

The town also had a plentiful water supply. It is true Burton spoke badly of the quality of the water in describing the place, when it had grown in 1857 to be a large and populous town, but in earlier days it was sufficient and good enough for the needs of a much smaller population. Good water could be obtained by digging wells twelve to fifteen feet deep. As Burton said, 'below the old sea beach, and near the shore it is only necessary to scrape a hole in the soft ground' to obtain drinking water.

Proceeding further southwards down the west coast of Zanzibar Island, one comes to a large inlet, now known as Menai Bay, which is about twelve miles in length and on an average a little over three miles in width. The head of the bay is lost in a mangrove swamp. The western arm of the bay is formed by a peninsula at the southern point of which is the present village of Fumba. Extending about eight miles to the southward of this peninsula is a chain of reefs and islets ending with Pungume islet, which protect Menai Bay from the south-west monsoon. On the eastern shore of the bay almost due east of Fumba is the village of Unguja Mkuu, the first portion of which name is the Swahili name for the whole island and its capital. There is a good holding ground for ships in from twelve to fifteen fathoms in the outer parts of the bay. Smaller vessels can anchor further up the bay off the islet of Sumi in about six fathoms. Here, however, the bay commences to be shallow and the navigation becomes somewhat intricate. Moreover, when the south-west monsoon begins to gather strength, the only sheltered anchorage is under the lee of the chain of protecting islands.

As in the case of Pemba, the east coast of Zanzibar is exposed to the full force of the Indian Ocean. Nevertheless, small vessels proceeding up that coast can in two places find suitable temporary anchorages. Chwaka Bay, which lies more or less due east of the town of Zanzibar is a case in point. This bay is protected by a coral reef and a temporary anchorage can be obtained in five fathoms close to this reef. Most of the bay is, however, so shallow as to be nearly useless to anything but small canoes.

Proceeding northwards up the east coast one comes to Mnemba islet, which lies abreast of a point some six miles to the south-east of Ras Nungwe, the most northerly headland of Zanzibar Island. It stands inshore of a coral reef and is separated from the main island by a deep channel about a mile wide. At the present time the islet possesses a good supply of water in a masonry well in the centre of the island and is resorted to by fishermen at certain seasons of the year. There is a good anchorage three-quarters of a mile north of the islet in ten fathoms, where shelter can be found during the period of the south-west monsoon under the lea of the extensive coral reef.

Though the rainfall of Zanzibar is somewhat less than that of Pemba, there is little or no difference regarding the fertility of the soil. Today cloves and coconuts are the two stable economic crops, but before their introduction Zanzibar, like Pemba, was noted for its grain and fruit crops, of which the island produced such an abundance as to be able to supply not only visiting ships but also places on the mainland with a less productive soil.

As is shown at the present time by a number of scattered giant trees and a few patches of forest, Zanzibar was at one time well afforested and its timber was in great demand for shipbuilding. Pemba timber was also at one time in great demand for the like purpose.

CHAPTER II

EARLY HISTORY OF ZANZIBAR AND PEMBA

AN eminent geologist once defined history as being 'pre-history encumbered with documents'. Adopting that definition for our purposes, we may say that, in so far as Zanzibar and Pemba are concerned, there is little need to discuss the early pre-history of the two islands for the very simple reason that at the present time we have no local discoveries upon which to work. All that can be said is that the pre-history of the two islands must in all probability have been of the same, or much the same, pattern as that of the adjacent mainland.

If, as Mr. Stockley has suggested, the two islands at one time formed part of the main continent, primitive man may have settled in them before they were cut off by the sea. But this point is of no great importance. After the islands became separated from the main continent, early man began to cross over from the mainland in dug-out canoes, which he was able to fashion with the aid of stone tools and of fire. This exploit was in no way remarkable. In other parts of the world primitive man has made some remarkable voyages in equally frail and primitive craft across far wider expanses of water than the Zanzibar Channel. It is not suggested that these immigrations were at any given time or on any very large scale. A dug-out canoe can carry very little in the way of passengers, crew and cargo, but a few such vessels could in the course of a few hours' paddling easily ferry parties of one or more families over the very short distance which separates the two islands from the mainland. Very probably, when pre-history or proto-history began, by the encumbrance of documents, to be merged in history, the inhabitants of each island could still be numbered in thousands rather than in tens of thousands.

Who these original settlers were can only be a matter of guess work. They may possibly have been of the primitive type of the 'strandlooper', whose remains have been found in South Africa, that is to say, a long-headed type of negro with protruding jaws and a small brain capacity, but in the absence

B

of any archaeological finds this cannot be asserted as a positive fact.

All that can be said with any possible certainty is that at a remote date, which it is not easy to fix with any degree of proximity, Bantu speaking races began arriving in the islands and either exterminated, expelled or else absorbed any African communities, whom they may have found there. In Pemba there is a tradition that the island was once inhabited by a race of gigantic stature called the Magenge. It is true that certain of the local traditions ascribe the building of certain mosques to these Magenge and allege that their conquest took place at a relatively recent date. But archaeology does not bear out this ascription of the mosques, and the traditions as to the date of their vanquishment are contradicted by other traditions. Without saying that the theory has been conclusively proved to be correct, it may not be unreasonable to infer that these Magenge were vanquished by Bantu invaders. In this connection it is interesting to note that the *Periplus* asserts that 'along this coast live men of piratical habits, very great in stature, and under separate chiefs for each place'. At the same time it has to be borne in mind that in many parts of the world the traditions of the invading race often seek to magnify their exploits by attributing gigantic stature to their opponents. The sons of Anak of Hebrew tradition and the Titans of Greek mythology are notable examples of this tendency. Accordingly, in the absence of any anthropological evidence, the allegation that the aboriginal Magenge were giants must be regarded with caution.

The so-called Bantu peoples belong to one language family, but there is a great diversity in outward appearance, shape of head, and other physical characteristics amongst the members of that family. There is at present, moreover, no certainty as to the exact birthplace of the Bantu, or as to the particular group of dialects or languages from which the language sprang. The legends and traditions of most Bantu peoples almost invariably point to a northern origin. From their first home they made their way to the Central African lakes and thence to the south as well as eastwards to the shores of the Indian Ocean. Tribal legend and tradition suggests that their arrival at the great lakes was at a date not wholly removed from their racial remembrance. It is not possible to assert how many centuries ago it was that Bantu-speaking peoples first reached the East African coast and thence crossed over to

Zanzibar and Pemba. They may have arrived there after the first discovery of the islands and coast by people of non-African origin – possibly many centuries after that event.

The East African coast was certainly known to the people of Arabia in the eighth century before Christ. The Arab state of Ausan, which came to an end about 700 B.C. traded with, and possibly held a portion of the coast. Some centuries later, in about A.D. 60 an unknown Greek compiled a treatise known as the *Periplus of the Erythraean Sea*. In his description of the East African coast the author tells us that

the Mapharitic chief governs it under some ancient right, that subjects it to the sovereignty of the state that has become the first in Arabia. The people of Muza (? Mocha) now hold it under his authority, and send thither many large ships, using Arab captains and agents, who are familiar with the natives and intermarry with them, and who know the whole coast and understand the language.

He also refers, but obviously with no knowledge of first hand, to an island called Menouthias, which is described as lying about three hundred *stadia* (about thirty-five miles) from the mainland and which has been identified with Zanzibar by a number of geographers.

Whether that identification be right or wrong, all that the writer of *Periplus* would appear to show is that in the first century of the Christian era trade relations between Arabia and East Africa were already established. But the 'ancient right' under which the Arabs of that day claimed sovereignty would appear to have been somewhat nebulous. Apparently, Arab merchants and sailors were in the habit of taking up their abode, either permanently or temporarily, at various places along the coast and on the islands adjacent thereto and in their intermarriage with the women of the local tribes we can see the genesis of the present Swahili race and language. But Arab colonization such as that organized by the Greeks, Carthaginians and Romans on the shores and islands of the Mediterranean Sea was either something yet to come or else still very much in its infancy. According to one version of the Pate Chronicle the earliest recorded attempt at organized colonization originated from Persia, and not Arabia. According to the chronicler, Abdulmalik, the fifth of the Umayyad Caliphs (A.D. 695–705) heard of East Africa 'and his soul longed to found a new Kingdom'.

Accordingly, he sent 'Syrians' to build cities along the coast. One of these cities was on the island of Zanzibar. But the chronicler further tells us that after Abdulmalik's death 'his sons did not care for the work of founding towns, and so they left them' – a story which, as archaeological remains along the coast prove to us, has been more than once repeated in East Africa. The famous Abbasid Caliph, Harun el Rashid (A.D. 786–801) is said by the same chronicler to have attempted to revive Abdulmalik's projects and to have sent Persians to East Africa, but there is no mention of Zanzibar or Pemba as having been settled by his people.

The Arabic version of the Kilwa Chronicle tells us of a large scale emigration from Shiraz in Persia to East Africa about a century later. The story goes that a certain Sultan of Shiraz, named Hassan bin Ali, dreamt that he saw a rat with an iron snout nibbling and gnawing at the walls of his house. He interpreted this dream as foretelling the downfall of his kingdom. Accordingly, he and his six sons embarked in seven dhows and sailed for East Africa. The father and his sons eventually settled in seven different places along the coast. One son settled in Pemba. Another, named Ali, settled at Kilwa Kisiwani in what is now Tanganyika in about A.D. 985.

There is also a somewhat mutilated chronicle from Pemba, which gives another account of an emigration from Persia. The leader of this party of colonists was a certain Sultan of Shiraz, named Darhash bin Shah, who left his country, because of famine, in company with two brothers, his sister, and three sons of an aunt, and a number of neighbours and slaves. As in the other chronicles, the members of this expedition settled in different places on the East African sea board. Shahame bin Ali, a cousin of Darhash, settled in Pemba. Another cousin, Daud bin Ali, and Darhash's sister, Kazija binti Shah, landed on the island of Zanzibar and Kilwa and the Mrima (mainland). Kazija had an illegitimate child, who settled with one of her slave girls named Tanu binti Shah on the islet of Tumbatu. There is no indication as to the approximate date of the arrival of these immigrants, but the story bears a number of points of resemblance to that in the Kilwa Chronicle and may possibly be assignable to the date of the arrival of the first Shirazian colonists in Kilwa.

Our next information regarding Zanzibar also comes from the Kilwa Chronicle. In about A.D. 1035 Hassan bin Suleiman became

Sultan of Kilwa, After he had reigned for about twelve years he was driven out of his country by an African tribe called the Matamandalin, who put in as *Amir* (governor) an Arab, named Muhammad bin Hussein el Mendhri. Hassan bin Suleiman had in the meantime taken refuge in Zanzibar. Kilwa remained in enemy occupation for twelve years, during which time the inhabitants were constantly planning the restoration of their exiled Sultan. Eventually, they managed to seize the person of the alien Amir and placed a son of the exiled Sultan in charge of Kilwa. After that

they sent an embassy to Zanzibar to bring back the exiled Sultan so that he might hand over the land to his son. Then the exiled Sultan came back from Zanzibar with six dhows. When he arrived at Kilwa, the Amir went to the shore to meet the Sultan and to oppose his landing, but he was slain by the followers of Hassan, who thus returned again in triumph to his kingdom.

This story of the Sultan's flight from Kilwa to Zanzibar, his lengthy sojourn in the latter island, and his eventually triumphant return to his own country at the head of a fairly considerable naval expedition points to the fact that by this date there was some firmly established Asiatic colony in Zanzibar, the members of which were of a race closely akin to that of the rulers of Kilwa.

We have definite proof that such a settlement existed near Kizimkazi at the southern end of Zanzibar some sixty years later. The mosque at Kizimkazi-Dimbani stands close to the seashore. As an inscription on one of the pillars of the *kibla* arch shows, much of the present fabric belongs to the eighteenth century, but the kibla itself is a little architectural gem, the features of which, as Professor Flury has said 'exhibit such a degree of technical skill and feeling for style as is not likely to be the work of a provincial craftsman'. On the wall of the kibla is a Cufic inscription, which Professor Flury translates as follows:

'This is what has been ordered by the high and very great Sheik Es-Said Abu Imran Musa, son of El-Hassan, son of Muhammad – may God grant him long life and destroy his enemies – on a Sunday in the month of Dhul Haj in the year five hundred' (corresponding to August 1107 of the Christian era).

About a hundred yards to the south of this mosque are the ruins of a walled enclosure about forty yards square. It immediately overlooks the landing place and at the south-west corner thereof is a rectangular turret-like chamber, which suggests that the enclosure was intended as a fort. Just outside the mosque are a number of graves, which are in all probability of much later date than the kibla of the mosque. The local inhabitants say that two of the graves are those of a woman named Mwana Mwatima daughter of Mfalme (Sultan) Madi el-Shirazi and of her son Mfalme Ali Sharifu.

A local legend agrees with Professor Flury's opinion that the kibla arch at Kizimkazi was not the work of a local craftsman. According to that story the mosque was ordered to be built by Mfalme (Sultan) Kiza, the founder of the settlement, who employed a slave named Kizi as his architect. The work so excited the envy of a neighbouring chieftain that he asked Kiza to hand over the slave to him. Kiza refused to do so, whereupon his neighbour resolved to obtain the slave by force of arms. He embarked his troops on dhows and approached Kizimkazi by sea. Kiza was at the time engaged in building operations, and on catching sight of the flotilla, prayed for divine assistance. His prayers were answered and swarms of bees drove the enemy away. The chieftain thereupon prepared a second expedition, which came overland from the north by way of Muyuni. This time Kiza was not warned of the approach in sufficient time. With a premonition that defeat was inevitable, he cut off the craftsman's right hand and then proceeded to the shore, where he prayed that he might be removed from the face of the earth. Once more his prayer was answered. The ground was opened beneath him, engulfed him, and then closed over him and covered his grave with a rock. Both crevice and rock are pointed out by the local inhabitants to this day. The invader reached Kizimkazi to find the craftsman with his hand cut off and no Sultan to be seen. So he and his following returned to their homes.

The legend of the killing or maiming of a craftsman so as to render him incapable of working for any other person is of course common to many other lands. The story of the 'Prentice Pillar' in Roslin Chapel, near Edinburgh, is a notable example. A like story also told regarding the fate at a much later date of a master and slave is clearly a local attempt to solve the etymology of a place name. Nevertheless, the archaeological evidence goes to prove that the legend probably contains a substratum of actual fact. The person responsible for the building of the mosque was clearly a non-African, who was in a position to obtain the services of a craftsman with a knowledge of Persian architecture. It is also clear that the Sheikh Es-Said Abu Imran Musa (the Kiza of the local legend) claimed to be an independent ruler of the immediate locality in which Kizimkazi is situated. The prayer engraved on the wall of the kibla of his mosque and the walled enclosure adjacent thereto do tend to suggest that, as the legend asserts, he did not live entirely in peace and amity with his neighbours.

Local tradition asserts that at one time the southern portion of the island of Zanzibar was an independent sultanate with its capital at Kizimkazi. In this connection it is interesting to note that Mwana Mwatima, whose grave is said to be just outside the mosque, was the daughter of a certain Mfalme (Sultan) Madi el-Shirazi. She evidently married into a family called Sherifu, who apparently became successors to the Sultanate once enjoyed by her father. Her son, Mfalme Ali Sherifu, is said to be buried in a grave close to hers. Other members of the Sherifu family, who are said to be buried in the same graveyard, are a certain Seyyid Abdulla bin Seyyid Almada and a certain Sheikh Ali bin Omar, a one-legged and one-armed carpenter, who despite his infirmities was endowed with legendary powers and enjoyed a great reputation for piety. The title Seyyid, it should be noted, is commonly conferred upon persons of royal blood. Seyyid Abdulla is said to have been related to the Sultans of Kilwa, from whom he received a milk gourd and a drum. This latter gift, which often comprises part of a sultan's regalia, is still in existence and shown at Kizimkazi. The fact that it is associated with relatives of the Shirazian Sultans of Kilwa is interesting.

It is also interesting to note that tradition in Pemba likewise attributes the erection of certain mosques and other buildings to Shirazi immigrants and that archaeologists are of the opinion that some of these remains are more or less contemporary with the mosque at Kizimkazi.

Mtambwe Mkuu is an islet opposite to Wete on the west coast of Pemba. It is connected with the main island at low tide. There are at least five sets of remains of stone buildings. On the southern shore, at the point where access is obtained to the islet, there are

also the ruins of what the present inhabitants say was once a gateway. Finally, there is a masonry well, which now yields only
brackish water. Little more than the foundations of these ruins at
present survives, but strewed along the seashore is a mass of broken
pottery dating from the tenth century to modern times.

On the west coast about six miles to the south of Ras Kigomasha,
the most northerly point of Pemba, there are some extensive
ruins standing on a cliff about eighty feet above sea level. They
include a mosque and some pillared tombs. The ruins bear many
points of resemblance to and are probably contemporary with
those at Ras Mkumbuu, to which further reference will be made
later.

The Portuguese version of the Kilwa Chronicle tells us that
Suleiman bin Hassan, who was Sultan of Kilwa from about 1178
to 1195 'conquered the great part of the coast, and having his
father's inheritance he made himself lord of the commerce of
Sofala and of the islands of Pemba, Mafia, Zanzibar, and of a great
part of the shore of the mainland'. Confirmation of this statement
appears to be forthcoming from the Arabic geographical dictionary
Mu'jam al Buldan which was compiled by the Greek ex-slave
Yakut bin Abdullah Ur-Rumi and which first saw the light of day
in 1224. Yakut calls Zanzibar, Languja, that is, by its Swahili
name Unguja. He tells us that it is

a large island in the land of Zanj, where their king lives. The vessels
which trade on this coast come there to careen. There are some vines,
which bear fruit three times a year. The inhabitants have been removed
from this island to another called Tumbat, the inhabitants of which
are Muslims.

Though Yakut does not say as much in so many words, it
seems reasonable to infer that the migrants from the main island
to the islet of Tumbatu were fugitives from invaders hailing from
Kilwa.

As mentioned earlier in this chapter, Tumbatu is said to
have been colonized by a son of one of the immigrants who
reached East Africa from Shiraz in the latter half of the tenth
century.

According to a manuscript history of Tumbatu in the six
hundredth year of the Hijra (A.D. 1204) there arrived in that islet
a certain Sultan Yusuf bin Alawi of the Abdali or Alawi tribe.

He is said to have come from Tudi, in the country of Basra and twelve days' journey from Bushire. According to local tradition he built the now ruined town of Makutani (place of walls). At about the same time an African named Chongo crossed over from the mainland and settled at the southern end of Tumbatu at a place called Chongowe (the Jongowe of modern maps). Sultan Yusuf wanted to kill him, but Chongo received timely warning and hid himself. Soon afterwards disaster overtook Sultan Yusuf and the people of Makutani. They were raided by Arabs, who destroyed the town and put most of the inhabitants to the sword or else enslaved them. A few of the inhabitants managed to escape. After the departure of the raiders they built a new town at Gomani. Being weak in numbers, they joined forces with Chongo's party and from their progeny sprang the present tribe of Tumbatu. Sultan Yusuf was succeeded as Sultan by his brother, Ali, who in his turn was succeeded by Yusuf's son, Abdulla. The manuscript history alleges that Sultan Abdulla bin Yusuf's son, Ismail, became Sultan of Kilwa and married the daughter of a neighbouring Yao chief, named Koranda. Neither the Portuguese nor the Arabic version of the Kilwa Chronicle has any record of a Sultan Ismail bin Abdulla and the story is on the face of it somewhat improbable. What may have happened is that the Persian family of Tumbatu Sultans left that islet and took refuge in Kilwa from attacks by pirates.

The traditional accounts of the rise, decline and fall of Tumbatu may perhaps be taken as representative of the history of the majority of the early Asiatic settlements in Zanzibar and Pemba. Their settlements at Tumbatu and Mtambwe Kuu were on islets. Kizimkazi, Mkia wa Ngombe, and Ras Mkumbuu, as well as other ancient sites traditionally ascribed to the Shirazi, are all of them close to the seashore. Many of them show evidence that they were at one time fortified. The settlers had to guard against three types of assailant, namely, the local African inhabitants, pirates and rivals of Asiatic stock who either sought to settle some old vendetta or else coveted what their neighbours possessed. If the general pattern of the history of Kilwa and Mombasa was followed these latter may at times have called in African tribes to fight their battles for them.

More interesting still is Yakut's description of Pemba, which he says he obtained at first hand from a visitor to the island from

Basra. The following is a translation of the relevant extract from *Mu'jam al Buldan*, leaving blank for the moment two all important place names:

The Green Island is also a large island in the land of Zanj in the Indian Sea. It is long and broad. The salt sea surrounds it on each side. There are two towns in it. The name of one is. . . and the name of the other. . . . In each of these there is a sultan. Each is independent of the other. There are also a number of villages and market places. Their sultan says he is an Arab and belongs to that race and came to settle here from Kufa. I was told this by Sheikh As Salim Abd Al Malik Al Halawi from Basra. He had with his own eyes seen this and known this; and he is reliable.

Arabic script omits vowels. The consonants in the two blank spaces appear to equate with MTNBJ and MKNBLU respectively. There are different opinions as to what are the vowels to interpolate between these letters. In his *Berichte Arabischen Geographen des Mittelalters über Ost-Afrika* (Berlin, 1914) Friedrich Storbeck transliterates these words as being Metenebbi and Mekenebulu respectively. This latter name is strongly reminiscent of Kanbalu of the Arab geographer Al Masudi. On the other hand Ernst Damman in *Bieträge auf Arabischen Quellen zur Kenntniss des Negerischen Afrika* (Bordesholm, 1929) with Matumbi(ni) and Mkumbuu respectively. The first named is an island, which is shown on Yakut's map and lies to the south-west of the modern town of Mkoani on the main island of Pemba.

The ruins at Mkumbuu lie at the extreme point at the head of a long and narrow peninsula, which forms the northern arm of an inlet on the west coast of Pemba leading up to the present town of Chake Chake. These have recently been excavated by James Kirkman.

These ruins include a mosque, which Kirkman considers to be the second finest Jami or congregational mosque in the territories of Tanganyika, Kenya and Zanzibar, and also a number of pillared tombs and some dwelling-houses. Some Islamic yellow sgraffiato have been found below the level of one of these tombs. In his *Early Islamic Wares* (pp. 26 and 34) Arthur Lane attributes such wares to the late twelfth and early thirteenth centuries of the Christian era, that is to say to about the date at which Yakut was writing. For reasons, which he sets out in detail, Kirkman, on the other hand, is reluctant to assign an earlier date to the foundation of the settlement than the late thirteenth or early fourteenth century.

As Kirkman says, the dating of the early levels at Mkumbuu, as at all other ancient sites in East Africa, offers great difficulties and doubtless the final word on the subject still remains to be said. The present writer makes no claims to being an archaeologist. He can therefore do no more than hazard a guess which may hereafter prove to be wrong. As one opinion is that the remains on the site of Mkumbuu date back to the time at which Yakut was writing and as Yakut was writing on information obtained by him at first hand, it would appear that he was describing a settlement at Mkumbuu which had very recently been established by an Arab from Kufa. This settlement was never a large one and came to an end in the middle of the fifteenth century. The cause of its abandonment can only be a matter of conjecture. The inhabitants may have migrated to some other place, which offered better trading facilities, or they may have been driven out by pirates, trade rivals, or as the result of some family or tribal feud.

No doubt these early settlers on Tumbatu Island and at Mkumbuu brought a number of slaves with them and there may well have been a certain amount of miscegenation, but the impression that one gets is that generally speaking these early immigrants at first kept themselves aloof from the local inhabitants and that a constant influx of fresh immigrants enabled them to keep their stock more or less pure. But later, when the stream of immigrants became little more than a trickle, and when for purposes of self defence the colonists had to have recourse to alliances with the local African tribes, racial barriers began to break down and miscegenation became fairly widespread.

At the present time a number of the inhabitants of the two islands call themselves Shirazi in assertion of their claim to be descended from these early immigrants. In a certain number of cases this claim would appear to be fully justified, but that is by no means so in every case. Of recent years a great aversion had been shown by many members of the aboriginal Hadimu tribe in Zanzibar to being called by their traditional tribal name owing to its resemblance to the Arabic word *Khadim*, meaning 'slave'. Like many other tribal names, 'Hadimu' appears to be a nickname given to them by members of other races or tribes and, like many other nicknames, is intended to be the reverse of complimentary.

In actual fact the Hadimu, as a tribe, never were enslaved, but their dislike of the name has led many of them to style themselves Shirazi in assertion of a supposedly free Persian origin. For a somewhat similar reason many of the aboriginal Wa-Pemba of Pemba have adopted the name in assertion of their origin as freemen of a long established indigenous group, who now seek to establish their right to preferential treatment as original owners of the soil, in contradistinction to the numerous later African arrivals, who very often were of servile origin. The result has been that at the present time it is difficult to say how many soi-distant Shirazi are genuinely entitled to that name.

Apart from any results of miscegenation this closer association between the early Asiatic settlers and the African inhabitants enabled the former to bring certain cultural influences to bear upon the latter. It is to these settlers that undoubtedly must be attributed the spread of Islam amongst the original inhabitants of Zanzibar and Pemba. They also brought with them their Zoroastrian solar calendar of 365 days, which has persisted in Persia despite the introduction at the time of the Arab conquest of the Muslim lunar calendar of 354 or 355 days. The local name for first day of this solar year is *Nairuzi*, an adaptation of the Persian word *Nauruz*. *Nairuzi* is celebrated in Zanzibar and Pemba on the same day every year as is *Jamshid Nauruz* in Persia. In each country part of the ceremonial on that day is a purificatory bath, which in East Africa is known by the name of *Kuoga Mwaka* and takes the form of bathing in the sea just before daybreak. As once was the case in Persia, so also in Zanzibar and Pemba, the day was formerly given over to general licence and rough horse play, which at times had fatal results. Each new year is called after the Swahili name of the Muslim seven-day week on which it begins *e.g. Mwaka al hamis* (Thursday year). In this connection it is interesting to note that, when he condescends to dates, the Muslim, who wrote the Arabic version of the Kilwa Chronicle at the beginning of the sixteenth century, employs the Swahili names for the years as well as giving the Muslim years of the Hijra.

As might also be expected, one consequence of intercourse between sailors, traders, and settlers from Persia and the peoples of East Africa has been the introduction into the Swahili language of a number of words of Persian origin. Many of the nautical terms in that language are derived from this source. Most interesting of all are perhaps several words connected with local adminis-tration. *Sheha* and *Diwani*, the titles bestowed in Zanzibar and Pemba respectively upon the local chief are two such examples. *Serkali* (government) and *boma* (fort) are other notable instances.

It is difficult to say when this one time intimate connection between Persia and the two islands came to an end. In course of years it dwindled considerably, but even at the time of the first advent of the European it would appear to have been still continu-ing. In the Zanzibar museum is a modern manuscript called the Ndagoni II MS. It purports to be 'copied from an old paper of the people of Ndagoni (Ras Mkumbuu), who bought the land of Mkubwa in the island of Pemba'. The land is stated therein to have been bought on

Friday, the first day of Muharram 910 A.H. (June 14, 1504) from the son and daughter of Sheikh Omar el-Shirazi by two sons of Mgwame el-Shirazi for the consideration of twenty slaves, that is ten males and ten females, and two bars of gold and one bar of silver and also one mortar of gold.

A footnote is appended to this deed, which informs us that

Mwijaa (one of the two purchasers came with forty-two slaves. Out of these he paid twenty as consideration for the shamba (plantation) of Mkubwa; and twenty-two slaves remained with him in the land of Ndagoni, who later multiplied. Three slaves out of the twenty-two were removed to the land of Ngalama in Pemba.

Admittedly, despite an injunction in the Koran, Muslims did not often at that early date put transactions such as this into writing. Admittedly also deeds were sometimes fabricated at dates later than those stated in the documents themselves in order to bolster up a claimant's title to land; but none the less intrinsically the document has all the signs of being a genuine one. If it is genuine, it suggests that Shirazi immigrants were still arriving in Pemba at the time of the arrival of the Portuguese. It may well be that it was the subsequent Portuguese domination of East Africa which finally put an end to migration from this source.

So far this chapter has dealt almost entirely with immigrants from Shiraz and other parts of Persia, but it must not be assumed that in these early days immigration was only from that country or even that the majority of such immigrants hailed from those regions. Local traditions and chronicles centre very largely round

Shiraz and rather tend to overemphasize that place as the home-
land of these early colonists from Asia. It is, however, clear that
there was also a considerable amount of emigration to East Africa
from the north-eastern and southern shores of Arabia. Immigrants
began to arrive in East Africa from Oman at a very early date.
The el-Harthi tribe from Oman claims to have founded colonies
at Mogadishu and Barawa in Somaliland as early as A.D. 924.
When Hassan bin Suleiman (fl. 1005–17) was driven out of
Kilwa, the invaders installed as Amir (governor) of Kilwa a certain
Muhammad bin Hussain el-Mendhri, whose tribe likewise belonged
to Oman. As Hassan bin Suleiman took refuge in Zanzibar and
led an expedition thence to recover his dominions, it may possibly
be inferred that at that date there were no Omani colonies in
Zanzibar. What, however, appears to be evident is that by the
eleventh century of the Christian era the Shirazi were having to
fight to defend their East African colonies from Arab attacks and
were at times finding themselves hard put to hold their own.

After the Asian settlers in Zanzibar took refuge from invaders
from Kilwa on the islet of Tumbatu, neither chronicles nor local
traditions have anything to tell us regarding Zanzibar and Pemba
for close on a century and a half. At the end of that period the Pate
chronicler tells us something of a somewhat negative character.
That chronicler sets out in detail the exploits and prowess of
Omar bin Muhammad, who was Sultan of Pate from about 1331
to 1348.

> He became powerful and smote the whole of the Swahili towns. . . .
> He gained possession of all the towns from Pate to the Kerimba Islands
> (south of Cape Delgado). . . . On the eastern side he extended his
> dominion as far as Warsheikh (on the Somali coast) by war. . . . He
> lived, and all these lands were subject to him, except Zanzibar; he did
> not rule over Zanzibar at this time; it was not a country important
> enough to have a king.

One at once asks why, if the island was so unimportant, did the
chronicler go out of his way to refer to it. King or no king, the
island's fertility, which greatly exceeded that of most of the other
places which the Sultan of Pate claimed to have subdued, ought
to have attracted the covetous eye of this 'ever victorious' ruler.
One cannot but feel that this is a case of Aesop's fox and the sour
grapes and that behind this slighting reference to Zanzibar lies

hidden the story of a military reverse at the hands of the islanders, which the Pate chronicler was anxious to conceal.

Another century passes before a chronicler makes any further reference to Zanzibar. Then the Kilwa chronicler tells us of certain events which followed the death of the Kilwa Sultan, Suleiman bin Muhammed, which occurred in about 1442. There was a dispute regarding his successor. One of the claimants was Said bin Hassan, the son of a former Sultan. We are told that,

as he had no supporters, he thought it better to proceed to Zanzibar and ask for help. When he arrived in Zanzibar, he found Sultan Hassan bin Abibakar on the throne. He asked for his help to recover Kilwa and the Sultan agreed to give it to him. He then got married to the mother of Sultan Hassan. In Zanzibar there was an Amir, whose name was Zubeir and who prepared an expedition to go to Kilwa in order to help Said. When news of this reached Kilwa, Amir Muhammad (of Kilwa) sent him one hundred mithkals of gold and told him that the gold was sent by Sultan Ismail so that he might drop the idea of waging war against him. This measure worked and no further preparations for war were made.

We also know the names of what appear to have been three other Sultans in Zanzibar, who must have lived very near in point of time to Sultan Hassan bin Abibakar. They are Al Hassan ibn Ali, Al Hassan ibn Ahmad and Ishak bin Hassan. These last two would appear to have been father and son. All we know about them is that coins bearing their names have been found in Zanzibar. These coins have rhyming couplets inscribed upon them and resemble similar coins issued in the fifteenth century by the Sultans of Kilwa. It is not out of place to add that the greater quantity of the coins of these rulers have been discovered buried only a little way below the surface at Kajengwa and Uroa on the east coast of Zanzibar.

The rhyming couplets upon these coins suggest that the Sultans in question belonged to a mysterious people, who are known in Zanzibar tradition as the Wadebuli. Writing of the Zanzibar and Pemba, Archdeacon Godfrey Dale of the Universities Mission, tells us that according to local tradition

there arrived off the coast of the island people whom they called the Wadebuli. I have heard them spoken of constantly. . . . They are said to have come in sailing vessels and to have possessed cannon. I have also heard it said that their sails were not made of canvas or of cloth but of some kind of palm leaf. . . . They had towns on the coast, planted coconuts and dug wells. They also built places of worship. The ruins of those places of worship are found all over the island of Zanzibar and Pemba. . . . They have never been forgotten. They treated Wahadimu (natives of Zanzibar) most cruelly, using men as beasts of burden. . . . The Wahadimu have never forgotten the Wadebuli.

In his *Land Tenure amongst the Wahadimu* Mr. R. H. W. Pakenham tells us that Zanzibar legend has it that the Wadebuli never remained long in any one place.

According to other traditions, the Wadebuli gained a footing in Mafia and the islands adjacent thereto and also on the mainland at divers places between Kilwa Kisiwani and the regions of Vumba near the present Tanganyika–Kenya boundary. The Arabic version of the Kilwa Chronicle tells us that at the beginning of the sixteenth century there was dwelling in Kilwa Kisiwani 'one Haji Muhammad ibn Rukn al Din al Dabuli who was together with his brother treasurer of the Kilwa during the time of Muhammad Kiwab. These two brothers were very wealthy people and the whole city of Kilwa was indebted to them for their kindness and hospitality', but, as the same chronicler also tells us, Haji Muhammad 'had grudge against Kilwa long before'. Portuguese records, which call him 'Mohammed Anconi', show that after the arrival of the Portuguese he became a quisling.

Though Haji Muhammad and his brother began their careers at Kilwa in the role of peaceful citizens, elsewhere on the mainland tradition makes the Wadebuli armed invaders. In the vicinity of Pangani, which lies opposite to the southern end of Pemba, those traditions speak of what appear to have been somewhat prolonged 'wars of the Wadebuli'. Further to the north the Wadebuli would appear to have established colonies in the vicinity of Vumba. In the course of time intermarriage with the members of neighbouring tribes resulted in these colonies becoming to a large extent Africanized. They were finally subdued by Sultan Mwana Chombi Chandi Ivor of Vumba in about 1630.

In Pemba tradition appears at times to confuse the Wadebuli with the Wadiba, who despite the similarity of the two names appear to have belonged to a different race. It is therefore not possible to say with any certainty what sites in that island are attributable to the Wadebuli.

In Zanzibar many of the remains attributed to the Wadebuli are masonry wells, which are almost invariably close to the seashore. One such well is on the islet of Mnemba which lies about one mile off the north-east coast of Zanzibar. Early Portuguese charts describe it as having a good anchorage off the islet during the south-west monsoon. At the present time the islet is the resort of fishermen at certain seasons of the year, but it is not permanently inhabited. With one other exception, which is about to be mentioned, all the other remains attributed to the Wadebuli are to be found on the rather inhospitable eastern and southern shores of the main island. They include a mosque at Makunduchi. The one exception to this general statement is a ruined building near Mvuleni on the north-western shore of the island facing the islet of Tumbatu. It stands near a portion of the beach known as Pwani Wadebuli. Until the site has been scientifically excavated, the purpose of the building must remain a mystery. It is loopholed and has the appearance of a fortified farm. The position of all these traditional Wadebuli sites confirms the tradition that these people did not stay long in any one place in Zanzibar. It also suggests that they and the people whom they found in the island profoundly mistrusted one another. The number of wells attributed to them, and in particular that on the islet of Mnemba, gives the impression that their occupation was more or less limited to the establishment of protected ports of call for their shipping. On the other hand, there is other evidence tending to show that they at times gained territory by force of arms. For example, the ascription to the Wadebuli of a well at Kizimkazi suggests that they either evicted some earlier colonists or else that they took over a site which such settlers had abandoned. Another such well exists at Chwaka which is evidently the port 'on the outer side' of the island to which the Portuguese chronicler Barros refers in describing certain events which took place in 1503. Barros describes this port as 'the port of the town of Zanzibar from which the island takes its name'. The ruler of the town of Zanzibar lived somewhere inland and Barros describes him as a 'lord' (*senhor*), who was styled a 'king' (*rey*). His residence in the interior suggests that part of the southern portion of the island was under his sway. Lastly, the fact that tradition asserts that the Wadebuli treated the inhabitants as beasts of burden points to some sort of conquest. Albeit, the facts that the sole survivals of the Wadebuli are a few scattered archaeological remains and reputation for cruelty and

c

oppression tend to show that they did not gain so permanent and lasting a foothold in Zanzibar as they apparently did on the adjacent mainland.

Who were these Wadebuli? Archaeological evidence would appear to show that they were 'the people of Dabhol', a port on the west coast of India about one hundred miles to the south of Bombay. During the fourteenth and fifteenth centuries this place was one of the principal ports of the Deccan, which was then ruled by the Bahmani dynasty. The coinage of this dynasty had rhyming couplets of the same pattern as those to be found on the local coinage of Kilwa and Zanzibar. Several of the Bahmani rulers were responsible for the building of Muslim places of worship, of which the mosques at Gulbarga and at the *Madrasah* (school) at Bidar are outstanding examples and remarkable for their elaborate use made of the pendentive. There is the same use of this style of architecture, though on a much less pretentious scale, in the fifteenth century mosques at Kilwa Kisiwani on the mainland and the Msikiti ya Chiroko ('the pea mosque') at Chwaka in north Pemba. The first mention in Indian history of the use of artillery is in 1336 in connection with the wars of Muhammad, the second of the Bahmani dynasty, against his Hindu neighbours. From Barros we learn that in 1503 a number of Zanzibar vessels were carrying artillery and that bombards were used at that date against a Portuguese commerce raider. Finally, the close association between East Africa and the Deccan is shown by the presence in the latter country of a large population of Africans or persons of African descent, who were known as Siddis and who played a prominent part in the political dissensions which eventually led to the fall of the Bahmani dynasty and the disruption of their kingdom. In other words, there is a considerable volume of evidence tending to show cultural and other contacts between East Africa and the port of Dabhol during the days of the Bahmani dynasty.

Studded up and down the east coast of Pemba are a number of ruined buildings, for the most part on the infertile and inhospitable seashore. In the locality known as Vitongoje there is a solitary grave near by a stone wall, which at the present time is about one hundred yards in length and, instead of proceeding in a straight line, consists of a series of angles, suggesting that it was constructed for purposes of defence. Local tradition says the tomb and wall were the work of strangers, who came from a distant unnamed land, and started to build a city. Before the work was completed, their chief or ruler died. They buried him on the seashore and then sailed away in ships to an unknown land. The tradition may be true. Possibly the unknown strangers were of the same race as those who built the fortified settlement at Pujini a few miles further to the south. The remains at Pujini are at the head of a winding creek. There are the ruins of stone-built houses within the walls which are crowned by a rampart walk. Approached from the interior on the side facing inland there is a keep which is crowned with pinnacles. Porcelain, which has been found on this site and is now in the Zanzibar Museum, belongs to the sixteenth century. It is very probable that Pujini is the place, to which the Portuguese historian Barros refers, in his account of a Portuguese expedition to Pemba in 1510. He describes how a landing party, crossing the island in search of cattle, was

able to find tracks and thus to reach some dwellings which were fortified in the manner of a fortress in a deserted village, where the Sheikh had collected his treasure because he was afraid to keep it in the vicinity of the sea. As it appeared that he had taken nothing with him except what he could carry, our soldiers and sailors found some property which paid them for the trouble of their journey.

The building of Pujini is traditionally attributed to one Muhammad bin Abdulrahman, who is better known by his nick-name of Mkame Ndume ('the milker of men'). He is said to have got the stone for his fortress from the north end of Pemba and to have inflicted the most sadistic cruelties on the porters who carried it to Pujini. It is somewhat significant that the pinnacles on his 'keep' are loopholed and that these loopholes point landwards, and not out towards the sea. Many other stories are told of the Mkame Ndume's cruelties and oppression, but he is also credited with being a builder of mosques and a great stickler for the forms and ceremonies of religious worship. He is also said to have been highly proficient in the building of *mitepe* (sewn vessels). There are differing accounts as to his place of origin, but at least one account says he was one of the Wadiba. According to some traditions he was killed by the Portuguese; according to others he died a natural death, but no man knows the place of his sepulchre until this day.

The Mkame Ndume is said to have had two sons. The eldest of these was named Mjawili and was buried in what is now forest country a few miles to the west of Pujini. His burial place may have been on the site of the Sheikh's 'place', to which according to Barros, the Portuguese landing party set fire in 1510 whilst on their way to Pujini. The tomb of the Mkame Ndume's other son Haruni, is pointed out at Chwaka at the north-east end of Pemba. It appears to be of much the same date as the ruins at Pujini. Haruni's nickname was Mvunja Pao (the breaker of rods) and his reputation for cruelty rivalled that of his father.

If therefore tradition has any basis in fact, the Mkame Ndume or his family, or his compatriots must have ruled at one time over most of the east coast of Pemba. If the tradition is true which says that the members of the family were Wadiba, invaders of that race must at one time have made fairly extensive conquests in Pemba.

It would appear that the Wadiba, like the Wadebuli, came from the East. They evidently had a good deal of Arab blood in their veins and hailed from the Maldive Islands, which were known to fourteenth century Arab geographers as the Diba Islands. According to the well-known traveller Ibn Battuta, who officiated as a Kathi in the islands on two occasions in the middle of the fourteenth century, they exported great quantities of cowries to the African continent. He also tells us that they exported coconuts and in this connection it is interesting to note that one of the few virtuous acts which Pemba tradition credits to the Wadiba was the introduction of the coconut tree. Writing in 1335 the Arab geographer ad-Dimashi refers to the trade between the Diba islands and Mogadishu 'in the land of Zinj'. Ibn Battuta also gives an interesting account of the manufacture of coir in the Maldive Islands and its use for sewing together the planks of ships. As already said, the Mkame Ndume was credited with proficiency in the construction of mitepe in this manner. Moreover, there is a tradition that it was the Wadiba who first introduced this method of shipbuilding into East Africa. In *Man* (1919) p. 46, Mr. G. J. W. Lyddeker records a tradition which comes from the region of Lamu. According to that tradition a number of people, whom the local inhabitants call the Wadiba, were blown out of their course and their vessels became total wrecks off the island of Kiwayu, which lies off the Kenya coast about thirty-five miles to the north of Lamu. This catastrophe is said to have occurred some time before the arrival of the Portuguese. The local inhabitants gave the castaways a friendly welcome. The Wadiba intermarried with the people of the country and began to build vessels after their own fashion. Hitherto the local inhabitants had only had dug-out canoes, but were so attracted by the new design that they copied it. As Mr. James Hornell points out, there are a number of similarities between the East African mitepe and the smaller Maldive sailing craft. Each type carries a square sail rig and the lines of the East African mitepe resemble the open decked Maldive craft.

Like the Wadebuli in Zanzibar, the Wadiba do not appear to have sojourned long in Pemba. If the fortified village to which Barros refers was in fact Pujini, the Mkame Ndume fled to Mombasa in 1510 and may never have returned. The impression one gains from local tradition is that both Wadebuli and the Wadiba were relatively newcomers to Zanzibar and Pemba at the time of the first advent of the Portuguese and that the flow of immigration from Dabhol and the Maldive Islands came more or less to an end after the Portuguese had arrived. Consequently neither set of immigrants was in sufficient numerical strength to enable them to leave any extensive mark on the two islands, culturally or otherwise.

Events which followed the arrival of the Portuguese must be left to subsequent chapters, but before bringing this chapter to an end it may not be out of place to summarize briefly the political situation in each of the islands at the time when Europeans made their first contact with Zanzibar and Pemba. In 1506 Pedro Ferreira, Captain of Kilwa, reported that he had ascertained that the island of Pemba was divided into five kingdoms. Local tradition says these kingdoms were called Twaka, Mkumbuu, Utenzi, Ngwana, Pokomo or Ukoma. At the present time there are no names corresponding to these just given except the first two. Each of the kingdoms was said to contain seven towns. It is possible that this division of the island owed its origin to the colonization by settlers arriving from different parts of Asia.

Portuguese records suggest that there was only one 'king' in Zanzibar, but local traditions state that at certain dates the southern portion of the island was divided into two or more kingdoms. There is also good ground for believing that the northern portion of the island was at a very early date occupied by the surplus population of the islet of Tumbatu, who even to this day insist that they are a race apart from the Hadimu dwelling to the south of them. To judge from Portuguese writers, by the beginning of the sixteenth century Asian colonists and their descendants no longer dwelt exclusively in fortified settlements on the coast, but had so far gained the good will of the local inhabitants as to be able to acquire plantations in the interior of the island. The centre of the islands was, however, still dense forest.

In so far as commerce was concerned, both islands were carrying on a thriving coastal trade, carrying their surplus produce to the mainland and exchanging it for cloth and other commodities from the East. Many centuries were to elapse before piracy was eradicated and after the arrival of the Wadebuli many of their ships were carrying light cannon for their protection.

Despite occasional piratical raids and internecine quarrels, storm, fire, tempest and other set backs, the two islands appear to have been in a flourishing condition at the opening of the sixteenth century. Writing in 1512, Duarte Barbosa tells us that

They are very fertile islands, with plenty of provisions, rice, millet and flesh, and abundant oranges, lemons and cedrats. . . . The inhabitants trade with the mainland with their provisions and fruit. . . .

In these islands they live in great luxury and abundance; they dress in very good clothes of silk and cotton which they buy in Mombasa of the merchants from Cambay (Gujarat) who reside there.

Their wives adorn themselves with many jewels of gold from Sofala (near Beira), and silver in chains, earrings, bracelets and annl rings, and are dressed in silk stuffs.

There was of course another side to the picture – that of the slave and the primitive agriculturist living in the interior of the two islands. Though the slaves might wear chains, they were not of silver, and the wife of the ordinary tiller of the soil was far from gloriously apparelled. Nevertheless, the fact that early Portuguese visitors were impressed by the opulence and luxury of the leading persons with whom they came in contact shows that at this date the two islands were places where fortunes could be made.

CHAPTER III

THE PORTUGUESE IN ZANZIBAR, 1498–1698

THE Kilwa Chronicle records that in the early days of 1498 in the Christian era news was brought from Mozambique that certain ships, belonging to the Franks and commanded by a person, named Almirante (Admiral), had reached that place.

It was expected that they would call at Kilwa, but they sailed past that island and also the islands of Zanzibar and Pemba and finally dropped anchor outside Mombasa harbour, where, as the said Chronicle tells us,

the people of Mombasa at first were very happy to receive the strangers, but later an informer told them that the Franks were bad people and that they had come to spy out the land and finally wage war against its people and capture the city. On hearing this the people of Mombasa tried to cut their anchors so that they should drift ashore in order that they could then plunder and destroy the ships. The trick was discovered by the people of the ships and they sailed away to Malindi. The people of Malindi were afraid of these Franks. They gave them water, firewood and all that they wanted. Then the people of the ships asked for a pilot who would direct them on the way to India and then from India they would go back to their own accursed country.

That 'accursed country' was Portugal and 'Almirante', the commander of the fleet, was Vasco da Gama, who incidentally gives a somewhat different version of the facts to those set out above. On their way home from India the Portuguese sailed from Malindi down the coast of East Africa to Mtangata opposite to Pemba where, as he had not enough men to man his three ships, Vasco da Gama proceeded to dismantle and to burn the *Saint Raphael* after distributing its crew and stores between the two remaining ships. This operation appears to have occupied sixteen or seventeen days. After completing it, the Portuguese crossed over to Zanzibar, where they arrived on February 28 or March 1, 1499. Here, as Goes tells us, 'the Lord (*Senhor*) of this place sent people to visit Vasco da Gama with provisions and to ask for his friendship'. But da Gama was anxious to press on so as to round the Cape of Good Hope before the weather turned unfavourable. He therefore stayed only one day off Zanzibar and then weighed and made sail to the southward.

Though other Portuguese ships soon followed in the wake of da Gama up and down the East African Coast, it was four years before another Portuguese ship called at Zanzibar. In 1503 a single ship, commanded by Rui Lourenço Ravasco arrived off the island. He subsequently alleged that on arrival he asked for provisions, but 'instead he had been received with many guns and arrows' (*ante achara muita bombarda e frecheda*). In retaliation he cruised up and down in the channel off Zanzibar, 'between which and the mainland there is so little distance that no ship can pass, which cannot be seen from both sides' and captured more than twenty vessels laden with provisions. Goes, who was the official archivist to the Portuguese Crown, tells us 'that, the greater number of these vessels were ransomed for money but he had no cause for what he did and for this tyranny, which offended against the rules of war, because the Lord (*Senhor*) of Zanzibar was at peace with us and we had never received any harm from him'.

After some time Ravasco shifted his cruising ground and in the words of Barros 'went round the island to the outside and came to the port of the town of Zanzibar, whence the island gets its name'. Standing by themselves, the words 'to the outside' (*per fora*) would appear to suggest that Ravasco sailed to the east coast and arrived at the anchorage in Chwaka Bay, but the ensuing reference to the port 'whence the island gets its name' rather suggests that what he did was to sail round Fumba peninsula and anchor in Menai Bay off Unguja Kuu, the port whence the island gets its Swahili name. The sun was just setting as he arrived, but there was enough light for Ravasco to see a number of vessels lying at anchor. According to Goes this port 'was very large and had many fine houses'.

The next day 'the King (*el Rey*) for thus they called the Lord (*Senhor*) of this town of Zanzibar', which would appear to have been somewhere in the interior of the island, sent a message to Ravasco asking why he had seized so many ships, but offering to let bygones be bygones, provided that Ravasco restored the artillery and other things which he had taken from the ships. Ravasco replied that he had been attacked, when he had asked for provisions, and he had done what any man in those circumstances was entitled to do. Nevertheless, he was prepared to overlook the past, provided that the King now gave him a more fitting welcome and agreed to receive the friendship of the King of Portugal.

In reply a number of boats set out to attack Ravasco's vessel, but the Portuguese ship's boats successfully routed the attackers and captured four of their boats. By this time the inhabitants had mustered in considerable force on the seashore. Barros gives their numbers as 4000, but this is almost certainly an exaggeration. Ravasco was not deterred by their numbers, whatever they may have been, and despatched three boats with a party of armed men to effect a landing.

The Moors all collected together at the spot at which they thought our men wished to land. This crowding together added to their destruction; because when the boats had come close to the shore under the pretence of landing there, the crowd of people gave the artillery a much better opportunity so that at the first discharge they laid low five and thirty of them, amongst whom was the son of the lord (*Senhor*) of the land, who commanded them.

After this carnage the islanders fled from the shore, but not before they had succeeded in wounding a number of their assailants and killing one of them. Ravasco next proceeded to hold a council of war, but whilst he and his officers were still deliberating, a Moor appeared on the shore, carrying a standard on which was emblazoned the Portuguese royal emblem of the Five Wounds, and calling out in Arabic 'peace! peace!' We are told that when Ravasco saw the flag, 'as one who sees a sacred thing, worthy of veneration, he removed his helmet from his head, and fell on his knees, and did reverence to it, as though he saw his King, and all the rest of our people who were with him followed his example'. This act emboldened the standard bearer to approach the Portuguese and to inform them that the 'king' of Zanzibar was suing for peace.

Negotiations then took place on board Ravasco's ship and eventually peace was granted on condition that the King of Zanzibar became the vassal of the King of Portugal and agreed to pay a yearly tribute of one hundred golden meticals and thirty sheep 'to the captain who should come to receive them'. In confirmation of all of which things the king 'gave his charter on a leaf of gold, and at the same time paid one hundred large, fat sheep, with tails half-as-fat as themselves'.

During the negotiations it transpired that one of the vessels which the Portuguese had captured belonged to the nephew of the 'king' of Malindi and that the Portuguese flag, which had been displayed when seeking for peace, had been given to this nephew two years before by a certain João da Nova so that he might sail the seas without molestation. As at this date the inhabitants of Malindi were almost the only people who had shown themselves friendly to the Portuguese, Ravasco realized that he might get himself into trouble at Lisbon. He momentarily tried to smooth matters over by explaining to the king's nephew that he had done wrong in not displaying the banner earlier. In reply the nephew said that, as he was 'in another man's port', he could not display this emblem of Christianity there. After receiving the tribute Ravasco handed over two of the vessels which he had captured to the nephew and then made his way to Malindi. Whilst at Malindi, he managed to pacify the 'king' by seizing a number of ships belonging to the 'king' of Mombasa, the hereditary enemy of Malindi. On his subsequent return to Portugal he was censured for 'having caused the greatest offence to the country and alienated the goodwill of many people'. Nevertheless, despite this indignation, King Manoel readily accepted the tribute, which Ravasco had wrung from the 'king' of Zanzibar, and treated the king's submission to himself as valid and binding.

In 1505 two Portuguese vessels under the command of João Homem and Lopo Chanoca reached Zanzibar. After his recent experience the 'king' of the island decided that he had better agree with his adversary quickly. We are told that he did Homem and his men great honour, and made them many professions of friendship, sending them presents of fruit and the delicacies of the country, cows, sheep and hens, 'thus showing himself to be a very noble servant of Dom Manoel'. Though many lowing kine and more than thirty fat-tailed sheep may have been conveyed on board Homem's ship, neither a single golden metical nor a single nugget or bar of gold changed hands. Homem went on his way to India rejoicing and highly gratified by the traditional hospitality of an oriental ruler, but no tribute had been paid to his royal master.

In 1510 Duarte de Lemos was sent to collect the arrears of rent due from the 'king' of Zanzibar. An attempt was made to prevent him from landing on the island, but the defenders were driven off with loss. The inhabitants then retreated into the thickets and bush country amongst the hills in the interior of the island. In the meantime their Sheikh (*Xeque*), who had incited the islanders to oppose the Portuguese, not trusting his life to the conqueror, and not daring to remain on the island, passed to the mainland in a vessel, which in case of necessity he had stationed at another port, where he embarked. The Portuguese were thus enabled to occupy the king's 'town' without opposition. They were, however, much disappointed to find little in the way of plunder, 'which showed the poverty of the island'. They set fire to the place, but had to return to their ships without any golden meticals.

In 1522 two Portuguese vessels set sail from Mozambique for Cape Guardafui. Correa tells us that,

as they were going along the coast, they met a vessel with messengers from the Kings of Zanzibar and Pemba taking letters to the Alcaide Mor (Governor) at Mozambique, because, as vassals of the King of Portugal, they wished for help against the Kerimba Islands, which had rebelled because of the aid given to them by the King of Mombasa.

In support of their claim to Portuguese co-operation, the emissaries alleged that the recalcitrant inhabitants of Kerimba 'denied the tribute of those of Zanzibar and Pemba, whereby they were disabled from paying theirs to us' (the Portuguese). This plea of *quominus* had its effect. Portuguese vessels and soldiers were sent to Kerimba. A number of villages were destroyed, but it is not without interest to note that one such village was spared from the flames, 'as it belonged to the King of Zanzibar'. After seeing their property thus destroyed, the inhabitants of Kerimba made their submission.

In 1528, after a stormy voyage from Lisbon as far as Madagascar, Nuno da Cunha decided to winter on his way to India at Mombasa. On their way up the east coast of Africa his vessels lost their bearings and eventually found themselves at the dead end of one of the inlets on the south-west shores of Zanzibar. When Nuno da Cunha sent a landing party to get in touch with the local inhabitants, the party was driven off with the loss of one man killed and several others wounded. Nuno, however, managed to capture a fisherman who was returning to the island after nightfall. This captive piloted the Portuguese to what is now the anchorage of the modern port of Zanzibar. Nuno da Cunha then got in touch with the 'king' of the island, who lived at a place some distance inland and who readily arranged for the Portuguese to be supplied with refreshments and provisions.

Some of Nuno da Cunha's vessels had been wrecked on their way out and the survivors had been transferred to other ships. Many of the vessels were consequently overcrowded and the crews were suffering from the effects of a long voyage. In the circumstances Nuno da Cunha decided to leave 200 sick men behind at Zanzibar with instructions that they should rejoin him at Mombasa after their recovery. He also left behind

Manoel Machado, their factor, who knew the trade well, and the nature of the land, and something of the language, as he had been stationed at Mozambique for four or five years and had transacted all kinds of business. Nuno da Cunha also left money and wares with his factor.

It is not known whether Nuno da Cunha left Machado in Zanzibar with the idea of establishing a permanent factory on the island or whether this venture was purely of a temporary or experimental character. What we do know is that a few months later Machado and the 200 invalids rejoined Nuno da Cunha at Mombasa after having been entertained with the utmost hospitality by the ruler of Zanzibar, who also sent some of his people to assist the Portuguese in making war on the people of Mombasa. Those operations were somewhat desultory and quite inconclusive. Eventually in April, 1529, Nuno da Cunha evacuated Mombasa after having set fire to the town.

After Nunho da Cunha's departure Portuguese chroniclers have little to say regarding Zanzibar for some forty years. What little mention is made in those records goes to show that the inhabitants remained on good terms with the Portuguese. In 1542 a small Portuguese squadron, which had conducted some none too successful operations against Turkish raiders at Mogadishu, spent some forty to fifty days at Zanzibar and was given a friendly reception. Three years later a Portuguese vessel was wrecked in the vicinity of Zanzibar and the crew were well treated by the inhabitants.

In 1569 Francisco Barreto, who had been Governor and Captain-General of India from 1555 to 1558, returned to East Africa with the title of 'Governor of Monomotapa and Conqueror of the Mines' and with express instructions to take possession of the gold mines in what is now Rhodesia in the name of King Sebastião of

Portugal. He was also commissioned to take charge of the East Africa coast. As the people of Pate had been causing trouble to the Portuguese, Barreto proceeded there in 1571 with a number of small vessels. On his way he called at Zanzibar. He was accompanied on this expedition by Father Francisco Monclaros of the Society of Jesus, who subsequently wrote an interesting and valuable description of the whole coast.

The Father tells us that on reaching Zanzibar they found there

some Cafre rebels from the mainland, and they kept the land in a great state of disturbance and the inhabitants were so weak that they did not dare to go to their farms (*fazendas*) because of them. We penetrated some seven or eight leagues into the country and our men made war on them and drove them out without any resistance, so that, in addition to the homage which he owed to the King of Portugal the king made a donation to him of the island with full solemnities and playing upon musical instruments at the time of delivery of it to us.

The information given by Monclaros suggests that in the interval since Nuno da Cunha's visit Zanzibar had fallen upon evil days. He tells us that 'the island has a city, which once was as large as Kilwa, but is now destroyed and mostly in ruins'. This, coupled with the information that the settlers, who presumably were 'Moorish' settlers, were afraid to go to their farms suggests either that there had been a large scale and well coordinated invasion of some African tribe from the mainland or else a mass migration from the mainland, which led to the outnumbering and the ultimate overpowering of the Moorish settlers, including the ruling family. Of the island itself Father Monclaros had this to say:

The island is very fertile and has many farms, fruit, and produce of the soil. It frequently rains here. There is much sickness both here and also on the whole of this coast. . . .

The soil is very productive, and if they built the town in another place, it would be healthy, but it is situated in a very sickly spot. There is a large quantity of timber and a forest of trees, which are so exceptionally tall, that we passed through it for two leagues and for the greater part of the time never saw the sun. Here I saw for the first time areca trees, which are shady Indian trees held in much esteem for their fruit, which is eaten with the betel, which twines round the trees like ivy. They are like palm trees, but are more shady; and they grow

beside a stream of water. The trees are the best and yielded the most
beautiful timber that I have ever seen.

They have much produce here, which in case of necessity could
assist India. In this forest there are many apes and forest pigs, but not
much other vermin. There are some small oranges, which are very
yellow and are eaten with their skins, but though they are very sweet,
they are very unhealthy. There is also the tamarind, a drug which is
much valued in apothecaries' shops, and other foodstuffs of divers kinds.
The land and trees very much resemble Portugal. There are hills, but
they are not very high. The harbours are not safe, being small bays and
roadsteads.

From Zanzibar Francis Barreto passed on to Pate. On his
return voyage he made straight for Mozambique without putting
into Zanzibar. Thereafter his attention was entirely devoted to the
affairs of Monomopata and its gold mines. He died at Mozambique
in 1573.

The fact that Monclaros makes no reference to the existence of
a factory at Zanzibar would appear to show that any factory set
up by Nuno da Cunha in 1528 or by any other person at any subsequent date was no longer in existence in 1571. Very probably
the first permanent factor arrived very shortly after Barreto's
visit. The King had donated the island to his brother in Portugal
and owed his safety to Portuguese arms. There was also the rather
awkward question of many years' arrears of tribute. In the circumstances it was desirable to place himself on the same footing as his
brother King of Malindi and become the ally of the King of
Portugal and to consent to the establishment of a Portuguese
trade enclave in his dominions. If the factors and other merchants
were accompanied by a few soldiers, that caused him no serious
alarm. Not only could the soldiers help to repel any future African
invaders from the mainland, but they could also assist him in
case of piratical raids by vessels from Mombasa and the Lamu
archipelago, which were still holding out against the Portuguese.

One great advantage about this factory was that it was established on the foot-shaped peninsula which has since become the
stone town of Zanzibar. At a later date there was a fishing village
at Shangani Point the 'heel' of the peninsula described in Chapter
I. The Portuguese factory was established some five hundred
yards to the north of the 'heel' so that fishermen and Portuguese
could live and let live without intruding upon each other's domains

or affairs. Apart from fishermen, there would appear to have been no other inhabitants of the peninsula. The Portuguese therefore evicted nobody and could live their own lives without intruding on those of the local inhabitants.

As already said, no precise date can be fixed for the arrival of the Portuguese. From information given by the first English visitors to the island we learn that in 1591 the factory was already in existence. The visitors were travelling in the *Edward Bonadventure*, commanded by Sir James Lancaster which 'wintered' off the island during the period of the north-east monsoon from November 1591 to February 1592. The story of that sojourn is best told 'as written from the mouth of Edmund Barker of Ipswich', Lancaster's Lieutenant, by Richard Hakluyt.

At length a Portugal *pangaia* coming out of the harbour of Zanzibar, where they have a small factory, sent a canoe with a Moor which had been christened, wherein they brought us a letter wherein they desired to know what we were and what we sought. We sent them word we were Englishmen come from Don Antonio upon business to his friends in the Indies, with which answer they returned, and would not come any more at us.

Don Antonio was one of the claimants to the throne of Portugal after the death in 1580 of the Cardinal Henry without issue. Philip II of Spain had then seized the throne and after vain efforts to oust him Don Antonio had taken refuge in England, where Elizabeth I had espoused his cause. As will be seen, the Portuguese at Zanzibar either were not supporters of Don Antonio or else were not satisfied with the Englishmen's credentials.

Whereupon [Barker told Hakluyt], not long after we manned out our boat and took a *pangaia* of the Moors, which had a priest of theirs in it, which in their language they call *Sherife*; whom we used very courteously which the king took in very good part, having his priests in great estimation, and for his deliverance furnished us with two months' victuals, during all which time we detained him with us. These Moors informed us of the false and spiteful dealings of the Portugals towards us, which made them believe that we were cruel people and maneaters, and willed them, if they loved their safety in no way to come near us. Which they did only to cut us off from all knowledge of the state and traffic of the country.

While we rode from the end of November until the middle of February in this harbour, which is sufficient for a ship of 500 tons to ride in, we set upon a Portugal *pangaia* with our boat, but because it was very little, our men were not able to take the said *pangaia*, which was armed with 10 good shot like our fowling pieces.

This place for the goodness of the harbour and watering, and plentiful refreshing with fish, whereof we took a great store with our nets, and for sundry sorts of fruits of the country, as cocos [*sic*] and others, which were brought us by the Moors, also for oxen and hens, is carefully to be sought for by our ships, as shall hereafter pass that way. But our men had need to take good heed of the Portugals; for while we lay here the Portugal Admiral of the coast from Malindi to Mozambique, came to view and betray our boat if he could have taken at any time the advantage, in a galley frigate of ten guns with 8 or 9 oars on a side. Of the strength of which frigate and their treacherous meaning we were advertised by an Arabian Moor which came from the King of Zanzibar divers times unto us about the delivery of the priest aforesaid, and afterwards by another which we carried thence along with us; for wheresoever we came, our care was to get into our hands some one or two of the countries to learn the language and the states of those parts where we touched.

Moreover, here again we had another clap of thunder which did shake our foremast very much, which we fished and repaired with timber from the shore, whereof there is a good store thereabout of a kind of trees some forty feet high, which is a red and tough wood, and as I suppose, a kind of cedar.

Here our surgeon Arnold, negligently catching a great heat in his head being on land with the master to seek oxen, fell sick and shortly died, which might have been caused by letting the blood before it had been settled.

Before our departure we had in this place some thousand weight of pitch, or rather a kind of grey and white gum like unto frankincense, is very brittle of itself. . . .

Six days before we departed hence the Cape merchant of the factory wrote a letter unto our Captain by way of friendship, as he pretended, requesting a jar of wine, and a jar of oil, and two or three pounds of gunpowder, which letter he sent by negro, his man, and a Moor in a canoe: we sent him his demands by the Moor, but took the negro along with us because we understood he had been in the East Indies and knew somewhat of the country. By this negro we were advertised of a small bark of some thirty tons (which the Moors call a *junco*) which was come from Goa thither with pepper for the factory and service of the country.

Thus having trimmed our ship as we lay in this road, in the end we set forward for the coast of the East Indies, the 15 of February aforesaid.

To judge from the foregoing account, the Portuguese factory was at this date on a relatively small scale and may have consisted of temporary mud and lath buildings. The factor's request to the captain of the English ship just before its departure suggests that he had to live rough and to do without many small luxuries, being dependent for supplies upon infrequent and not very reliable communication by ship with Goa and Mozambique. But his position undoubtedly improved considerably when the Portuguese acquired possession of Mombasa very shortly after Lancaster's visit to Zanzibar. The construction of Fort Jesus at Mombasa in 1593 helped to make his position very much more secure. Five years later the Viceroy of India delivered lengthy instructions to the commander of that fort regarding his administration of the East African coast. Amongst other things he gave orders that 'no married Portuguese men, half breed, or Christian, living with his wife' was to dwell in any place, 'where they served neither God nor His Majesty'. Certain places were named by him as being places where such persons might live. One of these was Zanzibar.

We hear very little of the trade carried on by the factory in these early days. In 1606 a Dominican friar, named Gaspar de São Bernardino, saw a vessel arrive at Mombasa with a cargo of slaves from Zanzibar, but it is clear that at that date this traffic had not yet assumed the proportions which later gave the island a most unenviable notoriety.

In 1627 Pedro Alvares Pereira was sent to investigate certain complaints which had been made regarding the conduct of Marçal de Macedo, commander of Fort Jesus at Mombasa. Though his report appears to be no longer extant, we learn something from a summary thereof which was sent by the Viceroy of India to the King of Portugal on December 26, 1627.

The complaints came from a number of local rulers on the East Coast of Africa. Pereira attributed much of the trouble which had given rise thereto to the avarice and exactions of the commanders of Fort Jesus. He described the 'king' of Zanzibar as being a great friend of the Portuguese, but declared that the Portuguese residing in his kingdom were unworthy of that friendship. Many of the Portuguese then dwelling in the island were soldiers, who had deserted from the garrisons at Mozambique and Mombasa and had married and settled in Zanzibar. They were a lawless and violent set of people, who had no regard for justice and had been guilty

D

of many assaults and robberies. Even the local Augustinian priest, who was Vicar of Zanzibar, was far from blameless. In Pereira's opinion the presence in the island of these unofficial settlers was so detrimental to the Portuguese Crown that he recommended that no Christian should be allowed to remain in the island. Even the church, which had been erected there some years previously, ought to be abandoned.

The statement that Portuguese deserters had settled in the island is confirmed by an anonymous description of the East African coast, which is now to be found in the National Library at Lisbon and has been published be Senhor A. Botelho da Costa Veiga, Director of the Library. This description must have been written at about the time that Pereira was making his report. It is very brief. The writer tells us that the island is 'inhabited by Arabian Moors. The king is very friendly to the Portuguese, many of whom live with him and pay him rent'.

At Mvuleni in the northern part of the island of Zanzibar are the ruins of two mysterious buildings which may be of Portuguese origin and may be the work of settlers such as are referred to by this anonymous writer. One is situated at Mvuleni opposite to the island of Tumbatu. The other is situated about a mile to the east in the interior of the island. The seashore where the first mentioned building stands is called *Pwani ya Wadebuli*, that is, 'the beach of the Wadebuli', the mysterious race referred to in Chapter II. The other bears the interesting name of *Panga* or *Pango Mzungu* (the place or cave of the European), there being a well in a cavern within its walled enclosure. The two buildings may bear no relation the one to the other and each of them may have been built by people of entirely different races, but at the present time the local inhabitants attribute them both to Europeans.

The blockhouse stands on the east shore of Mkokotoni harbour, which, as an old Portuguese chart shows, was known to the Portuguese as a good anchorage. A European, whom local tradition alleges was Portuguese, has inscribed some letters and figures on a baobab tree on Tumbatu island on the western shore of the harbour. It is therefore evident that Mkokotoni harbour was used by the Portuguese as an anchorage and it may be that the building on the shore is a fortified farmhouse constructed by them. In view of its name the case for the theory that the house at Panga Mzungu was of Portuguese origin would appear even stronger. As Mr. J. S.

Kirkman, Warden of Coastal Historical Sites in Kenya, has pointed out to me, the long passage running through the building on the seashore and the enclosure of the spring without the boundary wall of Panga Mzungu would appear to be non-Arab features. No other remains, which possibly may be attributed to the Portuguese, are to be found outside the peninsula on which their factory stood, but that does not necessarily mean that there were no Portuguese settlers in other parts of the island. Their buildings may as often as not been made of mud and lath and in some instances a farm may have been abandoned after a very short occupation.

Writing at the beginning of the seventeenth century, the Dominican Friar, João dos Santos, had no good report to give of those of his fellow countrymen who were then residing in Zanzibar. He gives more than one instance in which his compatriots were guilty of high handed conduct, which was not confided to military deserters who were beachcombing on the island but also to responsible officers, such as the official in charge of the Portuguese factory.

On one occasion the factor compulsorily requisitioned a boat belonging to a certain Moor, named Chande. The owner asked the factor to release the boat, as he wanted it for a trading venture of his own. 'But the factor scoffed at this and would not give it up, saying he had need of it for the king's service (which is the cloak with which they cover the many exactions which they make of the Moors on this coast).' In so doing, he overlooked, or else was unaware of the fact Chande had the reputation of being a sorcerer of no mean ability, in whose demonic powers dos Santos himself clearly believed. As soon as the boat was ready, the factor

ordered the anchor to be weighed and the sail unfurled. As soon as this was done, the sail was filled with a fair wind, which blew astern, but the *pangayo* would not shift from the place where it was, so that the vessel remained stationary under full sail for more than an hour. Then the factor, the other Portuguese and the Moors, who were there, went to assist, being all astonished at this thing which they had never seen happen before. Then one of the Moors told the factor, who was abusing him, that the *pangayo* would not shift from that place unless Chande willed it and unless he was given a present. As a result of this the factor went to Chande's house and made many requests to him to release the *pangayo* so that he could send it to Malindi, because the voyage was a very important one and he would not have acted thus by force, save for the necessity he was in; and he would send it back as soon as possible and pay the freight money, and would not make use of it at any other time, unless it was offered to him. The sorcerer was appeased by these explanations and the fair words which the factor had spoken to him, and declared himself to be satisfied. He at once went to the seashore, where the *pangayo* lay with its sail filled and yet without shifting from that place, and said in a loud voice: '*Pangayo*, go and prosper wherever the factor sends you'. The very moment that the Moor ceased from saying these words, the *pangayo* left the place where it was like an arrow, and set forth by the channel, and made its voyage safely.

A Portuguese soldier was rash enough to assault Chande, who, as we are told by dos Santos, in retaliation weaved certain spells with the result that,

whenever the soldier opened his mouth to speak, before he could say a single word, he crowed like a cockerel, his paunch so swelled with his crowing thus clearly in the manner of a cockerel, that the soldier became ashamed and did not dare to leave his house, or to speak with any person, because everybody laughed and jeered at him.

After remaining in this state for about a month, the wretched soldier ate humble pie to the sorcerer and the spell was removed.

There was, however, one other class of Portuguese settler regarding whom we have a good deal more information. One of the principal objects of the Kings of Portugal was the propagation of the Christian Faith in their dominions overseas. Further to the south, places like Mozambique and Sofala became important centres of missionary activity almost from the first day that those places came into the Portuguese possession. In the early days of the fifteenth century the Franciscans had established themselves at Kilwa, but their efforts came to an end when the garrison was evacuated in 1518. Thereafter until Mombasa was occupied by them in 1593 the only footholds possessed by the Portuguese to the north of Cape Delgado were at Malindi and in Pemba and Zanzibar. As each of these places was under the government of a ruler, who was a friend and ally and not a mere vassal of the King of Portugal, and as each of these rulers was a staunch Muslim, reasons of policy deterred the Portuguese from making any organized missionary effort in any of these three places.

Nevertheless individual priests made the best of such few

opportunities at proselytization as came their way. In his *Aethiopia Oriental* the Dominican friar named João dos Santos, who laboured principally at Mozambique and on the banks of the Zambesi between 1586 and 1595, tells us the story of one inhabitant of Zanzibar who by his efforts was persuaded to renounce Islam for Christianity. This was a lad of about seventeen years of age, who was the son of a deceased brother of the King of Zanzibar. How the two first got into communication with each other is not known, but Santos tells us that he sent the youth 'certain messages and admonitions secretly by certain Portuguese, having notice of his good inclination and his desire to become a Christian'. Eventually, the youth decided to take the momentous step. He accordingly embarked secretly at night on a pangayo belonging to a Portuguese and went to Kerimba island, where he found Santos. After giving him further instruction, Santos baptised him, giving him the name of André da Cunha, and sent him to be educated at the Dominican convent at Mozambique. Dos Santos tells us that

the king, his uncle, learning of his flight and that he was in my company and had become a Christian, was very much disgusted and enraged, and said that the time would come when I should pay him for this affront and the theft of his nephew, who had been brought up as his heir, because he had no sons.

The after history of young André da Cunha is not known, but one thing is certain, namely, that his conversion to Christianity had the effect of barring all chance of his succession to his uncle's throne.

As already mentioned, 'a Moor which had been christened' acted as intermediary between the Portuguese factors and Sir John Lancaster's ship and one asks oneself whether he was not also at that very same time acting as an intermediary between Santos and the King of Zanzibar's nephew.

In 1596 an Augustinian Convent was established at Mombasa by Francisco da Gama, a lineal descendent of Vasco da Gama. The objects of this mission were twofold, namely, to minister to the spiritual wants of the Portuguese and converts to Christianity along the East African coast and also to gather others into the fold.

According to the *Livro da Fazenda* in 1606 there were in addition to the Augustinians stationed at Mombasa 'vicars' at Lamu, Pate and Faza on the mainland, but none at Zanzibar. At some date between then and 1612 a hermitage (*ermida*) was established at Zanzibar and a vicar installed there. Until 1612 the East African islands and coast formed part of the diocese of the Archbishop of Goa, but by a Papal Bull of January 21 in that year Paul V created a new diocese having Mozambique as its See and extending from Cape Guardafui to the Cape of Good Hope. Amongst the places mentioned in that Bull is Zanzibar.

From a history of the work of the Augustinians in the East, which was compiled by Manoel de Ave Maria in 1817, we learn that the Church was called Our Lady of Grace (*Nossa Senhora da Graça*). From other sources we learn that it stood upon part of the site of buildings, which is now known as the Old Fort and which was constructed partly out of the materials of the Church. Writing in about 1634 in the *Livro do Estado da India Oriental*, Antonio Bocarro informs us that the 'king' of Zanzibar 'does all possible favours' to the Vicar of the Church. From this statement it may be inferred that there had been no lasting ill feeling in regard to proselytizing of the king's nephew by João dos Santos. It is also not unreasonable to presume that the friar, whose conduct was condemned by Pedro Alvares Pereira in 1627, was an exception to the generality of Vicars of Zanzibar, the majority of whom seem to have earned the good will and respect of their Muslim neighbours. Manoel de Ave Maria tells us that 'our religious converted innumerable souls' in Zanzibar. He mentions in particular Boaventura da Cruz Ozorio, who died in 1632 after having spent twenty-five years as a missionary in India and East Africa. He tells us that he 'was noted for his works of charity at Mombasa and Zanzibar, where he resided for many years, and performed many miraculous works (*obrou milagres*), drawing into the flock of the Church many infidels by his example and teaching'. It would appear to have been largely due to their restraining influence that Zanzibar remained loyal to the Portuguese in 1632 when practically the whole of the rest of East Africa rose in rebellion against them.

At this period the fortunes of the Portuguese factory and the other settlements in Zanzibar were largely influenced by events occurring beyond the island itself. In 1580 Philip II of Spain managed to seize the Crown of Portugal and hold it until his death in 1598. He was followed by a son and grandson of the same name. Philip IV of Spain and III of Portugal held the two crowns until

1640, when John IV of the Portuguese house of Braganza liberated his country. Portuguese historians refer to the sixty years during which their country was under Spanish domination as 'the Spanish Captivity'.

Except for the fact that a number of Spaniards began to enter the Portuguese colonial service, there were at first no serious repercussions in East Africa to the seizure of the Portuguese throne by Philip II of Spain. But it soon came to be realized that one result of the union of the two crowns was that Portugal found herself embroiled in the quarrels of Spain. The Netherlands had rebelled against Philip II. At first they had to act largely on the defensive, but by the beginning of the seventeenth century they had become sufficiently strong to carry the war into the enemy's dominions, including those on the seaboard of the Indian Ocean. In addition, England, which ever since the days of Edward III had been the hereditary ally of Portugal, was in a state of war with Spain and willy-nilly Portugal was dragged into that quarrel on the Spanish side. Like the 'Hollander rebels', the English were ready to strike at their enemy in the Indian Ocean.

As already seen, the first English ship to call at Zanzibar was the *Edward Bonadventure* commanded by Sir James Lancaster. As also seen, no actual hostilities took place on this occasion, but there was a strong mutual suspicion on either side. As subsequent official Portuguese correspondence shows, Lancaster's visit caused great uneasiness both at Lisbon and at Goa and a number of instructions emanated from both places as to the measures to be taken against English interlopers and 'Hollander rebels'.

A number of English ships did in fact follow in Lancaster's wake as far as the Cape of Good Hope, but the great majority of them thereafter struck to the north east from the Comoro Islands. It was not until the early days of 1609 that another English ship called at Zanzibar. At the beginning of the previous year the *Union* and *Ascension* sailed in company from Woolwich, but became separated in the vicinity of the Cape of Good Hope. The *Ascension* eventually made Pemba, but the *Union* sailed for Zanzibar hoping that she would find the *Ascension* there. The fortunes of the *Union* were subsequently narrated by one Henry Moris in a letter to Samuel Bradshaw of March 11, 1609(–10).

They went on shore, and at first were kindly entertained: but at their next going ashore, they lay in ambush, and as soon as they landed, sallied out upon them, and killed the Purser presently, and one mariner, and took one of their merchants prisoner; yet by great chance they got off their boat and came aboard. The names of them that were slain were Richard Kenu, Purser; the mariner's name I have forgotten, but the merchant's name that was taken prisoner was Richard Wickham. They put to sea again about the month of February 1608(–09).

Some time later the French traveller, Francois Pyrard de Laval, met Wickham whilst he was still a prisoner of the Portuguese at Goa. He tells us that Wickham

was long in prison, in company with us, and it was intended to put him on his trial for having been taken in the act of sounding. He said they had slain his cousin in cold blood, as I have already related, and had raised his head on a pike for a trophy. His misfortune was to have been taken with the lead in his hand, that being a dangerous implement on the Portuguese coast. Eventually he departed for Portugal in one of the carracks which started when I did.

After this we hear no more of English visitors to Zanzibar for many years to come, but, according to himself, a certain John Henderson of Fordell in Perthshire came to Zanzibar some years afterwards. Later in life Henderson was knighted by Charles I for his services in the Scots War of 1639, which services he continued to render in the Second Scots War of the following year as well as in the Civil War. According to himself his visit in his younger days to Zanzibar took a most romantic turn. The story of that romance is to be found in an inscription on a portrait in the Scottish National Gallery at Edinburgh, where Henderson's own portrait now hangs. Next to his portrait is one of two women. The woman on the left might pass for a European. She wears a bejewelled coronet and carries an orb surmounted by a bejewelled cross in her hand. The woman on the right is an unmistakable African with the woolly hair and thick lips not infrequently found in members of her race. In the background is a two-masted vessel and a tropical coast-line, in the centre of which is what is evidently intended to represent an oriental town.

An inscription on this last mentioned portrait explains how it now comes to be hanging amongst the worthies of Scotland. It reads as follows:

John Henderson of Fordel, travelling in his youth through several pairts of Asia and Africa from ye year 1618 to ye year 1628 was delivered into slavery by a (?Barbarian) in Zanquebar on the coast of Africa where a Princess of that countrie falling in love with him even to renouncing her religion and country contrived the means of both their escape and getting aboard a ship trading up ye red sea landed at Alexandria where she died, whose picture John Henderson caused take with her black maid after their own country habit.

That is all that we know about this romance. It has certain resemblances to the contemporary story told by Captain John Smith of his rescue by Pocahontas. Though doubts have been cast upon that story, it does not necessarily follow that Henderson's story is untrue. One would have liked to have had some slight corroboration of it from other sources, but lack of such corroboration does not necessarily impeach its veracity. In after years Sir John Henderson married a lady of his own country, who bore him five sons and five daughters. In the circumstances one must ask oneself whether he would have gone to the trouble and expense of having a maidservant painted, if the story had been a figment of his imagination. It is a strange story which may or may not be true.

To judge from the apparent silence of Portuguese chroniclers and of official records, life on the island of Zanzibar would appear to have been uneventful for many years. In the *Livro do Estado* Bocarro tells us that the island

is for the most part inhabited by Arabian Moors, who most of them have a Moorish king, who is a great friend of the Portuguese. . . . The King thereof does everything which is for the common good. He is not a vassal of His Majesty and pays no tribute, but he favours and helps the Portuguese rather than be their vassal.

It is to be noted 'most of' the Arabian Moors accepted this 'Moorish King' as their ruler. As we know from other sources, the people dwelling in the islet of Tumbatu and the parts of the main island adjacent thereto had their own independent ruler. It is to be noted that, unlike the majority of the local rulers on the East African coast, the 'king' of Zanzibar had ceased to be a tributary of the Portuguese, but had come to be recognized as being of the same status as was once accorded to the rulers of Malindi, namely, as a friend and ally of the King of Portugal.

Striking proof of the cordiality of the relations between the people of Zanzibar and the Portuguese was afforded in 1631 when the sultan of Malindi and Mombasa seized Fort Jesus, massacred the Portuguese and preached a Jehad (holy war) throughout East Africa. Many of the local chiefs and rulers, including those of Pemba, flocked to the standard of the Sultan, Yusuf bin Hassan, but the ruler and people of Zanzibar remained loyal to the Portuguese.

At the end of 1631 a fleet arrived from Goa to recapture Mombasa. The Portuguese landed on the island, but were unable to retake Fort Jesus. In March 1632, it was decided to raise the siege and return to Goa. Two vessels were detained to remain behind at Zanzibar under the command of Pero Roiz Botelho, who had instructions to co-operate with certain other vessels left behind at Pate in blockading Mombasa. As he expected that the Portuguese would return in greater strength with the next favourable monsoon to renew the attack upon himself, Yusuf bin Hassan decided to evacuate Fort Jesus and make his way to Mecca in search of reinforcements. He accordingly left Mombasa in May. News of his departure took some little time to reach Botelho at Zanzibar. It was not until the following August that he proceeded to Mombasa and reoccupied Fort Jesus without having to strike a single blow.

After the recovery of Mombasa the Viceroy of India gave orders for the settlers in Zanzibar to be transferred to Mombasa. The *Livro do Estado* tells us that this order was given

in the belief that it was necessary for the revival of the fortress. As it will be seen, it was very necessary that they should not live amongst the Moors because of the great solitude and because it was to the hurt of their consciences and of the reputation in which the Portuguese name is held by the true Moors living in those countries, who do not submit to our jurisdiction.

The factor and the Vicar of Zanzibar were allowed to remain on the island.

Though in the course of the next few years the rebellion was ruthlessly suppressed, the Portuguese never fully recovered from its effects. Thereafter their power in East Africa began steadily to wane. The history of the next sixty years is a history of constant revolts in one coast town or island after another. Only Fort Jesus in Mombasa could the Portuguese really feel that they had a secure foothold. Their monopoly of trade and their supremacy in the

Indian Ocean was gradually slipping out of their hands into those of the English and the Dutch. In the middle of the seventeenth century they found themselves confronted by yet another formidable rival in another quarter. Affonso de Albuquerque had captured Muscat in 1507. The Portuguese subsequently erected a fort there and the place remained in their hands for close on a century and a half. In 1649 Sultan bin Saif became ruler of Oman and he at once set to work to drive the Portuguese out of his country. In the following year he expelled the Portuguese garrison from Muscat. Emboldened by this success, he and his people carried the war into the enemy's country and fought against them in all parts of the Indian Ocean, both by land and sea.

In 1652 a number of vessels from Oman raided Zanzibar. They sacked the Portuguese settlement there and killed a number of Portuguese. Amongst other places they destroyed the Church and made a prisoner of the Vicar, Manoel de Nazareth, whom they put to death, when he refused to renounce his Faith. The 'Queen' of Zanzibar and her 'son', the 'King' of Utondwe on the opposite mainland, transferred their allegiance to the ruler of Oman and paid him tribute.

Francisco de Seixas Cabreira, who had ruthlessly suppressed Yusuf bin Hassan's revolt in 1631, was sent back to Africa to deal with this new uprising. He organized an expedition comprising 120 Portuguese soldiers, 40 Indian sepoys and 120 local auxiliaries from Mombasa. With this force he proceeded to Zanzibar, where he landed and destroyed the Queen's town. His flotilla then engaged ten dhows from Pemba, which were returning from a raid on Kilwa and Mafia. He captured five of the vessels and drove the remainder on shore at Zanzibar, where he engaged the crews in hand-to-hand fighting. After an absence of sixty days he returned to Mombasa, bringing with him 400 Christians, who had been captured by the enemy and forced to become Muslims. One thing, however, Cabreira failed to do. He arrived too late, and he also lacked the military strength to intercept and to destroy the Omani raiders.

After this the Portuguese reoccupied their factory and rebuilt the Church at Zanzibar. In course of time a number of other Portuguese settlers returned to the island. By the end of the century one of their number, a certain João Nunes, had built a substantial stone built house close to the Church. As will be seen hereafter, others managed to muster a force of close on fifty fighting men to reinforce the garrison of Fort Jesus. The rank and file of this contingent were local inhabitants – a fact which suggests that these Portuguese settlers must have been landowners on a fairly considerable scale.

The Queen who broke faith with the Portuguese in 1652 appears to have been the lady whom tradition calls Mwana Mwema. According to one account she was married to an Arab from Yemen. According to another she was the elder sister of two brothers, who eventually persuaded her to abdicate. According to tradition, Mwana Mwema was succeeded by a ruler named Yusuf, of whom we know nothing save that he reigned for many years and thereafter slept with his fathers. After his death it is said that his kingdom was divided into two parts. The southern portion, which had Kizimkazi for its capital, was allotted to his son Bakiri. The northern portion, which extended as far as and included the site of the modern city of Zanzibar, was given to his daughter Fatuma. This lady is said to have married Abdulla, 'king' of Utondwe, to whom she bore a son named Hassan.

According to Manoel de Ave Maria, the historian of the Augustinians, one Manoel de Conceição was Vicar of the Church of Zanzibar, 'where he was cruelly put to death by the Caffres in February, 1694'. No details are given as to the circumstances in which he was murdered. The motive behind it need not necessarily have been religious bigotry. It may have been a repercussion of the rising which took place in Pemba in that year. Later events show that Queen Fatuma most certainly was not accessory thereto.

Fatuma came to the throne towards the close of the seventeenth century and was still Queen of Zanzibar in 1711. Unlike her predecessor Mwana Mwema, she remained consistently loyal to the Portuguese – and this at a time when almost every other East African ruler had gone over to the rising power of Oman.

In March, 1696, seven Arab vessels from Oman, which were said to be carrying 3,000 men, arrived at Mombasa and laid siege to Fort Jesus, which held out until December 1698, when the feeble remnants of the Portuguese were overpowered.

Nine days after the arrival of the enemy the commander of Fort Jesus decided to try to get in touch with Mozambique and beg the commander of that fortress and the captain of any passing ship to bring to Mombasa reinforcements of men, arms and ammunition. One José Barroso volunteered to make the journey. He set out with eight men in a vessel described as a *coche*, which was no more than a large-sized dug-out canoe. On his way south he called at Zanzibar, where he asked the Queen to collect provisions for the beleaguered garrison. On his way back from Mozambique he found that she had collected sufficient provisions to fill three vessels. These vessels were manned by three Portuguese settlers in the island. Of these Miguel de Faria brought thirty men trained in the use of firearms, Feliciano Teixeira brought ten seasoned warriors and Antonio de Brito six followers. On their way from Zanzibar to Mombasa they were met by some enemy vessels, but Barroso and his companions fought them off and they succeeded in reaching Fort Jesus with their much needed men and cargoes.

Thereafter Queen Fatuma continued to make efforts to smuggle food into Mombasa. Not all these attempts were crowned with success. The besiegers managed to intercept and capture eighteen of these blockade runners. Eventually, the Arabs decided to teach her a lesson by raiding her island. As the expedition consisted of only fifteen coches or dug-out canoes, the raiding party cannot have been a very large one. When the raiders reached Zanzibar, the Queen and her followers fled into the bush. By that date the factory and the church had been abandoned, but there were still a few Portuguese on the island. One of these, who had been too ill to make his escape, was killed. Another, named Vas Cavaco, was able to drive off the raiders with the aid of two men armed with firearms. Shortly afterwards Vas Cavaco made his way to Zanzibar. He returned shortly afterwards in a coche with three volunteers to Zanzibar, where he was able to charter a coasting vessel from Malindi, in which he set out for Goa to urge the dire necessities of the defenders of Fort Jesus. This was not the last of his blockade running exploits. In July 1697 he brought a coche loaded with provisions from Zanzibar. After entering Mombasa harbour the coche ran aground, but Cavaco saw to the off-loading of its provisions despite the heavy fire of the Arabs. On this occasion another vessel from Zanzibar also ran aground and fell into the hands of the enemy.

On Christmas Day, 1696, a relieving squadron, commanded by Luis de Mello de Sampaio, arrived from Goa off Mombasa. The commander made no attempt to enter Mombasa harbour or to attack the enemy shipping. After lying off Mombasa for a month he sailed for Mozambique, leaving behind a fifty-gun frigate, *Nossa Senhora de Valle*, to cruise off Mombasa, but the frigate remained there only a few days after the departure of the main flotilla. It then proceeded to Zanzibar, but tarried there only until the south-west monsoon set in in May, when it returned to Goa. It carried with it a letter, dated March 30, 1697, from Queen Fatuma to the Viceroy assuring him of her continued loyalty to the Portuguese Crown. She also continued to try to smuggle provisions into Fort Jesus.

In the last days of 1697 another relieving squadron arrived off Mombasa from Goa. Once again no attempt was made to enter the harbour or to attack enemy shipping. Eventually part of the fleet returned to Goa. On January 28, 1698, the flagship and a galliot arrived at Zanzibar. They stayed there until April, when they set sail for Goa. No further attempt was made by them to succour Zanzibar despite the earnest entreaties of Queen Fatuma.

On March 13, 1700, instructions issued from Lisbon to the Viceroy at Goa bidding him thank the Queen of Zanzibar for the services which she had rendered to the beleaguered garrison in Fort Jesus. In all probability this letter of thanks never reached Queen Fatuma. On December 13, 1698, the Omani Arabs surprised and overpowered the handful of defenders in Fort Jesus. Two days later a relieving squadron arrived from Goa. Seeing the red flag of Oman flying over the fort, the squadron sailed on to Zanzibar. In vain Queen Fatuma urged the commander to try to retake the fort or at least to ascertain how it had fallen and also to destroy the enemy shipping in the harbour. All that the commander would do was to bombard an Arab settlement on the opposite mainland at Utondwe. Thereafter, without making any attempt to ascertain the fate of the defenders of Fort Jesus, the Portuguese fleet returned to Goa.

Queen Fatuma was left behind in Zanzibar, very possibly at her own request. She inevitably had to pay for her loyalty to the Portuguese, She, her son Hassan, a prince called Sagafo and a Sherif called Ahmed were made prisoners by the Arabs and carried off to Oman.

CHAPTER IV

THE PORTUGUESE IN PEMBA, 1506–1695

IN 1505, when on his way to India to take up the post of Viceroy, Francisco de Almeida attacked and gained possession of the island of Kilwa. After having constructed a fort and left a garrison there, he sailed past Zanzibar and Pemba to Mombasa and Malindi and thence to India. In 1506 the commander of the fort of Kilwa sent a caravel to Malindi with a cargo of slaves and merchandise. Either on its outward or homeward voyage, the vessel called at Pemba. The commander, Gonçalo Vaz de Goes, reported that the inhabitants were of a peaceful and quiet disposition and that the island 'abounds in foodstuffs, which all the large ships of Mombasa and Malindi obtain, as do all the other neighbouring places. In it there are four or five rival kings. In it also there is much sugar cane, many fig trees and other fruit trees'.

In 1508 João da Nova, a Spaniard in the service of the King of Portugal, 'wintered' at Pemba. Barros informs us that during his stay 'he had not found the people to be stubborn, but in every respect peaceable and tractable'.

In September 1509, a fleet of fourteen sail under the command of Fernando Coutinho put into Pemba to obtain water. Relying on previous reports as to the peaceable character of the inhabitants, the landing parties took no precautions against attack. It may be that the islanders took alarm at the formidable size of the visiting armada and misdoubted its intentions but, in the words of Barros,

whatever the reason, when our men landed to obtain water, they fell upon them from an ambush where they were lying in wait, and compelled them to retreat hurriedly, some of them receiving wounds from their arrows. As the land was very rugged and far from being sparsely wooded, the commander did not think fit to chastise them for this, and he was also anxious to take advantage of the favourable weather, it being already late in the year.

So he left for India without retaliating.

In the following year Duarte de Lemos was despatched to take punitive measures against the inhabitants of both Zanzibar and

Pemba. After dealing with the people of Zanzibar in the manner described in the preceding chapter, Lemos passed on to Pemba. News of the measures which he had taken in Zanzibar had reached Pemba ahead of him. The people of the latter island showed little stomach for resistance. The Sheikh (*Xeque*) tried to temporize by alleging 'the sterility of the land as an excuse for not paying tribute or providing the Portuguese with provisions'. That excuse was quickly waived aside. The Sheikh then sent a few provisions to the Portuguese so as to keep them temporarily at bay. Thereafter he secretly embarked at night with a number of his people and made his way to Mombasa. On discovering this, the Portuguese landed and made their way to the Sheikh's town (*povoação*). On arrival 'they found everything had been cleared out, so that they could not find even a firebrand to set fire to the buildings of the palace'. They would appear then to have made their way across from the western to the eastern shores of the island to the fortified village of Pujini. Barros tells us that, after leaving the 'king's town', by 'wandering through the island in search of cattle, they found some tracks and came to some dwellings in a deserted village which were fortified in the manner of a fortress, where the Sheikh had collected his treasure, because on account of us he was afraid to keep it near the sea'. The soldiers carried off as much of this treasure as they could and, returning to their ships, set sail for Malindi.

For rather more than a decade after this punitive expedition Portuguese chroniclers have nothing more to say about Pemba. During this period the local rulers made some sort of acknowledgement that they were subjects of the King of Portugal and owed tribute to him. As mentioned in the preceding chapter, in 1522 in common with the ruler of Zanzibar the 'king' of Pemba pleaded inability to pay that tribute on the ground that the inhabitants of the Kerimba Islands refused to pay tribute to him. The silence of historians suggests that the rulers of Pemba were nothing loth to make this acknowledgement so long as the tax collector never called to demand the tribute money. If he did call, a little procrastination accompanied by the payment of a small instalment and a lavish victualling of the visiting ship might induce him to go on his way without waiting for payment of arrears in full.

When on his voyage from Mozambique to Pate in 1571, Francisco Barreto called at Pemba and installed his own nominee as ruler of the island and imposed upon him an obligation to pay an annual tribute of 200 pardaos. It would, however, appear from subsequent correspondence that the sultans of Malindi regarded Pemba as forming part of their dominions. When therefore this puppet died some thirty years later, the King of Portugal gave orders for the island to be restored to Malindi, unless the deceased had left an heir. As the puppet had left a son, the sovereignty of Pemba descended to him.

Either during the reign of the father or else that of the son a Portuguese settlement was established upon the island.

According to a local chronicle, which was written on borassus palm leaves in 1850 by one Shame bin Makame el Shirazi, a large party of Shirazi migrated from Witu on the mainland and settled in different parts of Pemba. Ten years after their arrival a Portuguese arrived and asked for their friendship. The Shirazi agreed to allow him to settle in the land, provided he brought over seven tribes from the mainland. He accordingly did so and was then given a place to settle in for a period of twenty-five years.

The same chronicler tells us that the ways of this European were evil and finally led to his expulsion from the island together with certain of his pagan followers. In his *Aethiopia Oriental* the Dominican João dos Santos has little to say that is good concerning his fellow countrymen in Pemba. One of the chapters in his book is entitled 'The Island of Pemba and its trickeries' (*empofias*). This is what the author has to say regarding those trickeries:

In this island there are always many Portuguese, some being married traders settled there, and some being soldiers. They suffer from the diseases of the land by reason of their rich and gross manner of living, which they adopt because of the island's abundance and fertility. They have such dominion over the Moors of the island that they – and more particularly the wandering and idle soldiers – deprive them even of fire. This they do, not because they are in need of anything, but because they themselves do not cook and they mock the Moors. Besides they collect everything of which they have need, without asking permission from them; nor do they pay anything for these things. So much oppressed are these poor Moors by these perpetual requisitions, which are imposed on their plantations by the Portuguese, including not only those dwelling in the land, but likewise traders, who come from elsewhere, that they can hardly live. If a chicken belonging to a Moor enters the dwelling house of a Christian and he (the Moor) asks for it, the Christian replies that the chicken came to his house because it wanted to become

E

a Christian, and he therefore cannot give it back to him. By this same method of plunder they take goats and pigs, which the Moors have reared to sell to the Portuguese. If a Christian passes by the door of a Moor and he happens to be hurt by a stone, or he in any way stumbles, or some other harm befalls him, the unfortunate Moor – man or woman – whose dwelling it is, has to pay in full for the harm that he has received, either in cloth, or in chickens, or in sacks of rice, in which manner the Christian can reimburse himself at will, and there are many other oppressions and frauds, which they do to them, and which the Moors call trickeries, (*empofias*) so that through out all the coast they are called Pemba tricks.

Being unable to endure the oppressions and the affronts, which they continually received from the Portuguese, they resolved to rebel against their own King, who had allowed and consented to these things, which resolution they put into effect. One night they attacked the Portuguese town and their own King's dwelling, and they were nearly successful, killing many, men, women and children. The king, together with some Portuguese, who managed to escape from this attack, fled, embarking in some pangayos, which were in the sea near the island.

In 1589 Tomé de Sousa Coutinho found the fugitive king at Malindi on the mainland. Coutinho had been sent by his brother, the Viceroy of India, to subjugate Mombasa, the inhabitants of which place had allied themselves to a Turkish corsair named Mir Alibet. After the people of Mombasa had been duly chastised, Mateus Mendes de Vasconcelos, the Captain of the Malindi coast, was despatched to put the King of Pemba back into his own again. Dos Santos tells us that

some ships went in his company, so that, if the islanders did not want to obey their king, they could be punished and the king be put in possession by force of arms. When Mateus Mendes arrived at Pemba, he met with no resistance and no dispute of any sort. He peacefully put the king in possession of his kingdom, because the whole coast was filled with great fear by reason of the coming of the fleet. Consequently they encountered no difficulty and accomplished everything with the greatest of ease.

Nevertheless, some two or three years later the king was once more driven from his kingdom. This time he took refuge at Mombasa, where the Portuguese had recently erected Fort Jesus. Faria y Sousa tells us that his subjects, 'provoked by the villainies of the Portuguese, forced him and them to return to Mombasa, having killed many, and deprived the rest of any hope of returning to that island'.

When in 1596 Francisco da Gama 'wintered' with his fleet at Mombasa, he found there 'a Prince of the island of Pemba' and learnt that 'his kingdom had been seized by a tyrant'. He promised to restore the fugitive to his kingdom, but he himself was anxious to reach his seat of government in Goa, where matters of more importance than the restoration of a princeling in East Africa were awaiting his urgent attention. Therefore he did nothing himself. In fact, certain written instructions which he gave to the Portuguese commander of Mombasa suggest that he may not have been much impressed by the fugitive. Whilst he instructs the commander to show favour to 'Facca Vane Munganate, Chief of Pemba', he somewhat significantly talks of setting up 'a new king' on that Island.

I strictly enjoin upon you, [he wrote] the (affairs of the) Island of Pemba and its pacification, because it is from there that the commotions against the fort come. For this reason I have given you orders that the new king shall be set up and supported and favoured in all things, as I expect of you. . . . I return again to commending the king of Pemba to you, in order that you may bestow all necessary and proper help for taking possession of that island. If he wishes to reside in Mombasa, you should provide him with a dwelling inside the fort, *so that he may be safer*.

The last words may be significant. Do they mean that even on the mainland and under the immediate protection of the newly erected Fort Jesus the exiled King was not considered to be safe from the vengeance of his former subjects? What is certain is that the exile died soon after those words were penned and rumour had it that he had been poisoned.

The Viceroy of India had the dead king's brother conveyed to Goa, where he was offered the kingship provided that he would become a Christian and marry a Portuguese wife. The brother hesitated and the Viceroy decided to bestow Pemba on the Sultan of Malindi. On learning of this, the King of Portugal refused to confirm the appointment and gave orders that the island should be handed over to the dead king's brother. As was only to be expected the Sultan of Malindi thereupon sent a letter of protest to the Viceroy. In the meantime the dead king's brother had agreed to

become a Christian and was baptized in the name of Felipe da
Gama. He was also in due course married to an orphan girl, named
Anna de Sepulveda. She bore her husband a son, who was baptized
in the name of Estevão.

In pursuance of instructions from the Viceroy at Goa the
commander at Mombasa took steps to try to put Dom Felipe on
his dead brother's throne. On arrival of the expedition in Pemba, it
was found that a certain Motabira, who claimed to be acting under
the orders of the Sultan of Malindi, 'had so stirred the natives
of the island to rebellion that they did not wish to obey Dom
Felipe'. The result was that on December 18, 1599, the Viceroy
had to report to the King of Portugal that the attempt to put Dom
Felipe in his kingdom had met with no success. Back in Lisbon
the newly crowned Philip II of Portugal felt that he could only
acquiesce in the existing state of affairs. On January 25, 1601, he
wrote to the Viceroy bidding him give the writer's namesake of
Pemba every possible assistance and commending him in the
meantime to the care of the Augustinian Fathers, who were then
at Mombasa erecting a monastery.

But Dom Felipe was not content to live upon charity. In 1604
he wrote to Lisbon asking that he might be put back in his
brother's kingdom. On March 6, 1605 a letter was sent from
Lisbon to the Viceroy at Goa, complaining that the commander
at Mombasa said nothing in his letters 'as to the state in which he
finds this person; for which reason we recommend to you that you
arrange to effect this and give the said king all the help and favour,
which present circumstance permit'.

As we learn from a subsequent letter which the King of Portugal
addressed to the Viceroy at Goa, the Sultan of Malindi had been
enjoined to assist Dom Felipe in recovering his brother's throne
and had professed himself ready to do so, but, as has already
been seen and as the letter itself shows, the Sultan of Malindi had
an eye on Pemba for himself. Consequently any assistance, which
he may have rendered to Dom Felipe, cannot have been very
whole-hearted. Eventually, in despair of obtaining any real assistance from this or any other quarter, Dom Felipe set out secretly
for Pemba, leaving his wife behind at Mombasa. On arrival in the
island, he declared that he had renounced Christianity and returned
to Islam. But this change of faith produced no change in the
attitude of the islanders towards him. On December 24, 1605, the

Archbishop of Goa wrote to inform the King of Portugal that Dom Felipe had been poisoned.

On receipt of this news the King of Portugal sent a long letter to the Viceroy of India, which is dated January 16, 1607. Its contents show that for a number of reasons the writer was greatly worried as to what arrangements were proper to be made for the future government of Pemba. Not only was he king of Portugal; he was also King of Spain and trouble in his Spanish dominions was also causing him considerable anxiety. During his father's reign the people of the Netherlands had thrown off the Spanish yoke and for the past forty years had been steadfastly fighting a war of liberation. Though at first the revolted provinces had been forced to act largely on the defensive, by the opening of the seventeenth century they were carrying the war well into the enemies' dominions overseas. Not only were they attacking Portuguese and Spanish possessions on the shores of the Atlantic, but they were also engaged in hostilities in the Indian Ocean. In 1601 two Dutch pinnaces had been sighted off Pemba. In 1607 a Dutch fleet attacked and very nearly captured the strongly fortified Portuguese island of Mozambique. In that same year an English ship, commanded by William Keeling, called at Socotra and was informed by certain of the islanders 'that there are eight Hollanders upon Pemba, who have been there three or four years, whereof two are turned Moors'. To judge from certain of the contents of the already mentioned letter of the King of Portugal there is reason to believe that the information given to Keeling had some substance in it. Certainly the possibility that the Dutch might take possession of the island caused the King of Portugal considerable anxiety.

As a devout Christian, Philip II of Portugal would have been very pleased to have seen a co-religionist on the throne of Pemba. But Dom Estevão was a mere infant and in such difficult times his installation as King appeared to be out of the question. Therefore the Viceroy 'should arrange to send the said child to Goa, at my expense, so that he may be brought up in the doctrines of Christianity and in good manners for my service'. As for Pemba, it was necessary

to secure speedily the recovery of the island, which is in the hands of enemies who support the Dutch rebels, and when you have recovered it, I recommend to you first to take counsel regarding the recovery and protection of the said island and to carry out what is decided upon, taking care that in this you make provision that the said island shall be held at my free disposition and in the manner most suitable to my service.

But whatever decision the Viceroy might make with the advice of his council as being best for his master's service must be submitted to his royal master in Lisbon for confirmation. For this reason Philip II desired to have a report

as to the grounds offered by the King of Malindi and the convenience of giving him the ownership of the island, and also the grounds offered on behalf of the child, Dom Estevão, and send me a copy of any agreement which is reached and likewise the opinion of the primate Archbishop (sc. of Goa) as to what is most convenient for this realm.

In another letter which was written eleven days later, the king asks the Viceroy to 'send me your personal views regarding the successor to Dom Felipe, King of Pemba, and as to the danger there may be as to his safety by reason of events which have happened in that island as a result of his death'. Thereafter the instructions contained in the previous letter are repeated more or less word for word. Pemba was in fact causing his Majesty of Portugal no little anxiety. The man on the spot must at once take all measures necessary to preserve the island for the Portuguese Crown, but the man on the spot must also clearly understand that whatever decision he might reach must be subject to confirmation by his royal master in Lisbon.

A letter of the King of Portugal, which is dated February 10, 1612, refers to the possible claims of Dom Estevão to the island of Pemba. Presumably the child was still alive when that letter was written, but that is the last that is heard of him. Doubtless, he was sent to Goa to receive a Christian education, but we do not know whether he reached manhood. All that we do know is that after his father's death the sovereignty of Pemba passed out of his family.

The family, into whose hands the government of Pemba now fell, was that of the 'king' of Malindi 'the ancient ally' of the King of Portugal since Vasco da Gama's day. In 1592 Mombasa had fallen into the hands of the Wasegeju, a tribe which at that date lived in the hinterland behind Malindi. The Wasegeju had handed the place over to Sultan Ahmed of Malindi, who in 1593 entered into an agreement whereby the Portuguese were to be allowed to erect a fort and settle at Mombasa, whilst the Sultan himself was to be allowed to take up his residence on the island and was granted one-third of its revenues. But these concessions failed to satisfy him. He not only claimed that Pemba belonged to him from times past, but also asserted that his past services to the Portuguese entitled him to be rewarded by a grant of the island to himself. His sovereignty on the mainland was limited almost entirely to the island of Mombasa and the town of Malindi. The hinterland immediately behind those places was not very fertile and was peopled by African tribes, whose cultivation of the soil appears to have been limited to the supply of their own immediate needs and whose friendship for the people of the coast was notoriously fickle. On the other hand, Pemba was extremely fertile and had for a long time been regarded as the granary of both Malindi and Mombasa and was clearly a most desirable acquisition.

On the death of Dom Felipe, Sultan Ahmed at once put in a claim to be given the island of Pemba. Correspondence between Lisbon and Goa goes to show that the Portuguese on the spot strongly supported his claim. Something had to be done, and done very quickly, about Pemba. If at the moment there were no Dutch upon the island, they might nevertheless take possession of it at any time. With Pemba as an enemy base, the safety of the newly erected Portuguese fort at Mombasa would be distinctly in jeopardy. The man on the spot had already been told to exercise his own initiative and to exercise it with all speed. On December 14, 1606 the Archbishop of Goa, who was acting temporarily as Viceroy of India, wrote to inform the King of Portugal that Pemba was in a state of rebellion and that Sultan Ahmed had been entrusted with the defence of the island, which had been granted to him in the name of the King of Portugal without payment of tribute. As might be expected, the financial side of this transaction failed to meet with approval in Lisbon. At a later date, acting on instructions from the home government the Viceroy Martin Affonso de Castro gave Sultan Ahmed a charter granting him the island upon condition that he paid the rent and tribute for the same which formerly had been paid by Dom Felipe.

Further correspondence, which passed between Goa and Lisbon, shows that Sultan Ahmed was successful in restoring order in Pemba. Portuguese records give no details as to the means employed by him, but an undated petition of his declares that he was put to considerable expense in bringing about this state of affairs and that he had got into debt.

It is possible that an Arabic chronicle, found at Jambangome in Pemba, is referring to Sultan Ahmed when it states that at the first hour of the morning on 4 Dhul Haj 1014 (April 23, 1606) thirty Frankish ships which were under the command of a Nazarene (Christian) Frank named 'Jojone' and had on board over 1,000 Shirazi and their slaves, arrived at Pemba. Without vouching for the figures given by the chronicler, who is silent as to the object and results of their visit, it seems clear that Portuguese on this occasion had come to assist Sultan Ahmed, who was of Shirazian stock, in getting possession of Pemba.

The chronicler says the newcomers established settlements in various parts of the island. A few Portuguese soldiers were left on the island to give Sultan Ahmed or his representative physical and moral support. In April of 1607 the Dominican friar, Gaspar de Santo Bernardino, spent five days at Chake Chake when on his way to Socotra and Egypt. He and his companions met with a friendly reception at Pemba, but he formed a poor opinion of the Portuguese garrison. 'Would to God', he wrote, 'they were fewer since in these parts they are accustomed to live as much according to their will as against the divine will: often liberty leads to licence. For this reason they are esteemed but little and are despised'.

The Jambangome chronicler tells us that 'John Francisco', or John the Frank, returned to Pemba two years after his visit in 1606 and stayed one week in Pemba. This statement certainly has some foundation in fact. From other sources we learn that a certain 'Frank' did spend twelve days at anchor off Pemba in the middle of December 1608, but he was not the same Frank as had brought the Shirazis and their slaves to the island two years before. He was paying his first and only visit to Pemba. He was in fact the first Englishman to visit the island.

As mentioned in the last chapter when dealing with the misfortunes of the *Union* at Zanzibar, that vessel set out from England in company with the *Ascension* commanded by Alexander Sharpeigh. The two vessels lost sight of each other during the voyage and Sharpeigh decided to sail for Zanzibar, where he hoped to make his rendezvous with the *Union*. The *Ascension* was, however, carried past Zanzibar and on December 10, 1608, sighted

Pemba, 'at which time we stood along the land with a fair gale, sending our boat ahead to sound to find an anchoring place; which going about a point of land there was a great bay with broken islands to the offing about two miles'.[1] There the *Ascension* dropped anchor in fourteen fathoms of water.

Next morning Sharpeigh sent a skiff to try to get in touch with the inhabitants, but the boat party was unable to do so. On December 12, John Jourdain, one of the factors, was sent on the same mission. He tells that he 'went with the pinnace two miles up, where we saw some people which fled from us'. Eventually some eight of them returned to the shore. Jourdain then proceeded on land, wading 'above the knees in ooze'. He learnt from the people on shore that the island was called Pemba and not Zanzibar and 'that that island did belong to the Portuguese; and that if we were Portuguese we should be welcome; if not, they had nothing to say to us. So I told them that we were Portuguese and their friends; and that we only desired to have water and fresh victuals for our money'. The spokesman of the inhabitants then told Jourdain that he would advise 'the king' of their coming. 'Rowing down the river' towards the *Ascension*, the pinnace got in touch with some fishing canoes. After they had been given 'drink, aquavita, and some toys', one of the fishermen took the English on shore and showed them a small spring of fresh water, 'which came out of a clay ground, not all of the best, nor any great quantity'.

Jourdain then returned to the ship and reported to Sharpeigh, who sent a party on shore to get water. Whilst they were engaged in this task, 'came some of the country people down, which seemed of good fashion'. One of them said he was the King's brother and he 'instantly showed us a silver ring, whereon was engraven the number of villages and houses or cottages in the land, and said he was ruler or governor of the place'. The watering party agreed to leave two men ashore as hostages and the soi-disant king's brother then proceeded on board the *Ascension* where he spent the night. He announced that there was a better watering place further within the woods and that the king had instructed him 'to furnish us

---

[1] The latitude of this anchorage is given by Covert as 5° 20′ south and by Revett as 5° 27′ south. These latitudes and the description of the anchorage point to the bay as being either Jambangome Creek or else Chake Chake Bay. The island on which a member of the crew was later buried would appear to be Mesale Island off Chake Chake Bay. In view of the local chronicler's statement that the vessel stayed three nights off Ras Mkumbuu, it seems evident that Chake Chake Bay was the place of anchorage.

with anything that the country did afford'. He also gave the erroneous information that the Dutch had taken Mozambique.[1] Either he or else some of his companions followed this information up by volunteering the further information 'that the Portuguese were their enemies and made slaves of as many as they would take, and therefore had no trade with them; which', as Jourdain observed, 'was contrary to what the poor men I spoke with at first told me'. According to William Revett, a factor on board the English ship, it was clear that the islanders were 'taking us to be Flemings', that is to say, people against whose activities the Portuguese had strictly warned them.

According to Jourdain, Sharpeigh was at first favourably impressed by the king's brother and his companions. But next day a number of incidents occurred which roused the suspicions of the English. In the first place, when they landed, they were taken to 'a little village' in the woods, where the hostages had spent the night, they found they had to pass, 'between a lane of armed men, some fifty persons, with their darts, swords, bows and arrows'. Secondly the guide, who was to have taken them to the new watering place, first showed them 'some hole which the rain had filled' and then told them that the real water supply was still further off in the woods. Fearing that the story of this spring was merely a ruse to draw them into an ambush, Sharpeigh decided to return to the ship, leaving the boatswain with a small party to fill the water casks at the spring which had been shown to them the previous day. When the boatswain returned on board, he brought further disquieting news. He himself had wandered off into the woods to the 'cottage', where the hostages had passed the night and 'where he perceived some men in Portuguese apparel, with rapiers, with many other strangers, which had not yet been seen, which hid themselves from them'.

Sharpeigh decided that the sooner the *Ascension* got away the better and gave orders that the water casks should be filled with as little delay as possible under cover of a screen of armed men. But filling the water casks was slow work as the spring, at which they had to be filled, yielded only two or three tuns a day. On December 19, the water and covering parties had proceeded on shore as usual. Shortly afterwards Sharpeigh and some of the merchants landed with the object of getting in touch with the soi-disant king's

[1] The Dutch unsuccessfully besieged Mozambique in July and August 1608.

brother. One of the crew, who could speak Portuguese, went to the 'cottage' to announce that they wished to speak with the king's brother. On arrival at the cottage this man saw 'six Portuguese or men in Portuguese apparel with their rapiers . . . , in long branched damask coats lined with blue taffeta, and under the same white calico breeches'. He at once hurried back to the watering party with this information. He was closely followed by the king's brother, who said he had brought some cattle for the English and asked them to go up into the wood to fetch them.

Answer was made that if it pleased them to bring the cattle or anything else they had to the water's side, that we were there ready to receive it and pay for it. Now perceiving that we suspected their treachery he, lieu of blushing, turned from the hue of a mulatto to be white, and presently went his way without more words, seeming discontent.

Shortly afterwards 'another of the gentlemen' came and assured the English 'that the party that brought the cattle was sick' and asked that one of the Englishmen should go up and look at the animals and also take back some oranges and lemons as a present for Sharpeigh. One of the party, who spoke Portuguese, volunteered to go, 'but the fellow never came again. The young man that went was born in Greenwich, his name being Edward Churchman'. Less than half-an-hour after his departure a flight of arrows was discharged from the neighbouring bushes and trees into the midst of the watering party. The covering party returned the fire with their muskets and the Englishmen managed to get on board the ship's boats with the exception of Edward Churchman and the boatswain's mate, John Harrington, who was left behind shot through the head with an arrow. The watering party then made for the *Ascension*.

The next day we went again aland with our long boat and skiff well armed, with a flag of truce for a parley with them about a man[1] which they had betrayed the day before; but none would come to speak to us. They made many bravados out of the woods, not within shot, but would come not near us; but we saw many of them issued out of the woods at many places; which perceiving it vain to lose any more time,

---

[1] This was Edward Churchman. Thomas Jones, the *Ascension's* boatswain, informs us that he 'afterwards died in Mombasa of a bloody flux, as I was credibly informed of the Portuguese'. (Purchas, *His Pilgrimes*, I. 228.)

we fired a volley shot into the woods, and went into the watering place and brought away the dead man[1] and the davit, both lying near together. The man we buried as we went aboard, upon one of the islands.

'Having', in Jourdain's words, 'had much discontent for a little stinking water', the *Ascension* weighed anchor and made sail, but her troubles were by no means over. That night the ship ran on a sandbank, in a stiff gale, but by good fortune the wind dropped shortly afterwards and she managed to float off. Next morning they met three sailing-ships heading for Pemba. A boat was lowered from the *Ascension* to board them. The vessels struck sail and certain of the leading men were brought on board the *Ascension*. They proved to be 'mullatoes and negroes', who said they were bound from Mombasa to Pemba and that 'they had some quantity of Indian commodities, wherewith they traded from place to place, which they bought at Mombasa in barter of rice and other provision which they did usually carry from Pemba thither and to other places on the coast'. Sharpeigh proceeded to tell them 'how treacherously their countrymen of Pemba had dealt with us'. This information was followed up by the Master of the *Ascension* and others making 'foolish signs unto them, showing the yard's arm, that they should be there hanged; which put them into a desperate fear, although there was no such matter meant'. After making these signs, the master invited one of their member into his cabin to study a chart, 'understanding that he had some insight in navigation, and understood the sea card'. Whilst the two were closeted in the cabin, word was brought to the master that his visitor had a knife up his sleeve. The master told his visitor to hand over the knife. The Moor at first denied that he had got one and then suddenly drew it and stabbed the master, 'and therewith he gave a loud cry, that his fellows that were without hearing began likewise to stab those that were near unto them'. In actual fact only two other Englishmen besides the master were stabbed and all three recovered of their wounds, but a ship's boy called out 'Kill, kill, my master is killed', whereupon every Englishman seized the nearest weapon handy and set upon the Moors.

In a very short time all were overboard, either dead or alive, for many of them lept overboard, which were slain in the water by those that were in our boats, so that I think not one of them escaped, except a

---

[1] John Harrington, who was found 'in the bushes dead with many wounds, as well by arrows as swords'. (*Journal of John Jourdain*, p. 38.)

little boy and a maid of some eight years old; one was taken up in the chains, and the other out of the pangaya or prow; which was a girl, which when she saw her mother drowned, she lept overboard three times, that we had much ado to save her. . . . There were three of the boats, one of which set sail with some two or three men to carry the news to Pemba.

After this tragedy the *Ascension* continued on its way to Aden. We learn from Bocarro that the three vessels belonged to 'Moors of Malindi'. According to information subsequently given by some Portuguese to Thomas Jones, boatswain of the *Ascension*, 'they were the chief gentlemen of the coast of Malindi and of the blood royal'. Therefore 'great lamentation' was made for them. According to Bocarro, who writes regarding their action with approval, the Moors had concealed their knives on their persons for the express purpose of attacking the English. According to Jourdain, shortly before the incident the master had 'given the order that none should wear his weapon, seeing that these people came un-armed' and according to Thomas Jones, the boatswain, most of the Englishmen were in the boats at the time and only fifteen of their number were actually on board the *Ascension* as against fifty Moors. This serves to explain the subsequent conduct of the Englishmen and to some extent to excuse it, but the excessive form which their retaliation finally took must be attributed to very badly frayed nerves.

The *Ascension's* visit to Pemba was purely fortuitous but apart from the fact that it was the first English ship to call at the island, the story of that visit discloses one or two interesting facts. Firstly, the island is shown to have thrived on the export of foodstuffs to the mainland in exchange for Indian and other commodities. Secondly, if there was any foundation for the information given to Captain Keeling in 1607, the Dutchmen, who were said to have come to Pemba some years before, had evidently disappeared by the time of the *Ascension's* visit. Finally, the hostility which the islanders had shown to the Portuguese in the time of Dom Felipe had, for the time being, disappeared. Sultan Ahmed with Portu-guese assistance had managed to bring the island under effective control and the people were for the time being well disposed to the Portuguese.

At Lisbon, Goa and Mombasa the Portuguese might very well have flattered themselves that the problem of Pemba had been very satisfactorily solved, but this state of affairs was not to last for any length of time. On August 28, 1609, Hassan, the son of Sultan Ahmed, wrote to the King of Portugal to announce his father's death and to express his own desire to remain a friend of the Portuguese Crown. The letter was accompanied by a petition asking that the dead man's son might receive everything which the Portuguese had formerly given to his father, including the island of Pemba. The grant to Sultan Ahmed of Pemba had only been for life and subsequent correspondence between the King of Portugal and Viceroy of India showed that they doubted whether that grant should be renewed in favour of the son. In a letter of February 10, 1612, the King stated that the capability and loyalty of Hassan bin Ahmed were as yet unknown and consequently he should undergo a period of probation before any final decision was reached. The King further added that the rights of Dom Felipe's son must not be overlooked. He also expressed a fear that the Turks from the Red Sea might seize Pemba with the aid and complicity of its Moorish inhabitants. In the circumstances he requested the Viceroy to consider whether Hassan bin Ahmed should not take the island in partnership with a Portuguese subject, paying the same dues as his father had paid. Finally, he recommended that the King of Malindi and his partner should be required to fortify the place in Pemba at which people were in the habit of disembarking.

In the meantime Hassan bin Ahmed had begun to fall foul of the Portuguese commanders at Mombasa upon other grounds. In 1614 he was invited to Goa to state his case to the Viceroy, but Hassan believed that, if he went to Goa, he would be detained as a prisoner. He therefore fled to the mainland where he was murdered at Rabai at the instigation of the Portuguese commander.

Ignorant of all these happenings, the King of Portugal had on February 6, 1615, instructed the Viceroy of India that Pemba should with all possible diligence be handed over to the ruler of Malindi on the same terms as his father had held the island. When the news of the Sultan's murder reached him, the King wrote again on March 6, 1616, insisting that the rights and wrongs of the dispute between the dead man and the Portuguese commander should be strictly inquired into. If diligent inquiries should show that the late Sultan was guilty of treason, then his son should be deprived of the succession to the throne and the kingdom should be given to the late Sultan's brother. The murdered man's child should be sent to Goa, 'where he should be received into a convent and, after being baptized, should be brought up in the Christian Faith'.

On the strength of these instructions Muhammad bin Ahmed, brother of the late Sultan Hassan bin Ahmed, was given the kingdom and Yusuf, the late Sultan's child, was sent to Goa. As the result of the later inquiries it was, however, held that Simão de Mello Pereira, the commander at Mombasa, was responsible for the death of Sultan Hassan bin Ahmed. Accordingly on January 20, 1618, the King of Portugal gave instructions for the murdered man's son to be restored to his kingdom. During his minority the child was to be received into the convent of Our Lady of Grace at Goa and maintained there at the King of Portugal's expense. If at the age of discretion he was found to be unfitted for kingship, it was recommended to the Augustinian Fathers that they should receive him into their order and that, after he had taken the habit and become professed, he should be sent to Portugal.

In the meantime Sultan Muhammad bin Ahmed's reign had come to a sudden end. Like his brother, he perished at the hands of an assassin. Some time before his death he sent to Lisbon an undated petition complaining that Pemba had not been given to him. He explained that he needed the revenues of the island to support him in a war against the Muzungulos, whose 'king has done me great insolences and grievances without being punished, killing seventy or more of the Moors of Malindi'. He further complained that his steadfast loyalty to the Portuguese had not been meeting with its just reward.

The reason why he did not receive the grant appears from other letters which passed between Lisbon and Goa. Dom Jeronimo d'Azevedo, who was Viceroy of India, acting in accordance with instructions contained in a royal letter of 1612 and with advice tendered to him by the Captain and the Judge of the fortress at Mombasa, had granted a lease of the island to one Antony Varella, whom the Viceroy describes as being 'an old Christian' (*Christão velho*) that is to say, not a Jew. A letter, which the King of Portugal sent to the Viceroy on March 15, 1617, inclines to misdoubt the wisdom of the Viceroy's step. The Viceroy replied that he was satisfied with the credentials of Antonio Varella, that the lease had been granted for three generations subject to the same clauses and conditions as appeared in the lease which was formerly granted to Dom Felipe and that the grant was without prejudice to the grant of one-third of the revenue to the Prince of Mombasa.

According to the Jambangome chronicle 'Johon Francisco' came to Pemba in 1612 with three ships bringing presents to the Shirazis. This visitor looks suspiciously like the new lessee, Antonio Varella, seeking to ingratiate himself with the inhabitants on becoming their new landlord. But this is merely conjecture. In so far as Portuguese chronicles are concerned, there is one of many irritating gaps in respect of events in Pemba. We do not know what became of Antonio Varella's lease or how Pemba was administered whilst Hassan's son Yusuf was receiving his education in the Augustinian convent in Goa.

In 1626 Hassan bin Ahmed's son Yusuf arrived back in Mombasa, a baptized Christian calling himself Dom Jeronimo Chingulia and wedded to a Portuguese girl. As some sort of atonement for the treatment meted out to his father, he was accorded all the privileges and perquisites, which had been given or ordered to be given to his father. These included the island of Pemba. But the results were not those which the Portuguese had expected.

The new Sultan's reign was short. Like his father, he soon fell foul of the Portuguese commander at Mombasa, this latter suspected the Sultan's loyalty and in 1631 was meditating sending him under arrest to Goa; but the Sultan got wind of his plans and forestalled them. He gained entry to Fort Jesus under the pretext of wishing to pay the commander a visit. Having entered, he murdered the commander with his own hands and his retinue overpowered the garrison and gained possession of the fort. This was followed by the massacre of all the Portuguese in the town of Mombasa except four men, who managed to escape to Pate.

Thereafter Chingulia publicly declared that he had renounced Christianity and, as Yusuf bin Hassan, preached a Jehad (holy war) against the Portuguese. He called on all Muslims in East Africa to rally to his cause. Many cast in their lot with him, amongst them being the inhabitants of Pemba. As was only to be expected, when news of these events reached Goa, a Portuguese fleet was sent to recapture Mombasa. It arrived off the island in the early days of 1632 and landed on the island, but Yusuf bin Hassan successfully held out against them in Fort Jesus and eventually the Portuguese commander withdrew his men. After their withdrawal Yusuf bin Hassan, realizing that the Portuguese would probably renew the attack the following year and, fearing that this second attempt might be successful, decided to abandon the fort. He accordingly dismantled Fort Jesus and set sail for Aden. For several years thereafter he waged a piratical war against Portuguese shipping, but eventually died, or, according to another account, was assassinated at Jedda in 1638.

On learning that Yusuf bin Hassan had quitted Mombasa, Pedro Rodrigues Botelho, who had been left with two vessels at Zanzibar to keep watch on Yusuf's movements, proceeded to Mombasa and reoccupied the island and fort without encountering any resistance in August, 1632. He subsequently reported that he had subdued a rebellion in Pemba, after having killed the African leader of the revolt, and that he had once more compelled the islanders to pay 600 sacks of rice as yearly tribute. It was even suggested that the Portuguese should at this date abandon their headquarters at Mombasa in favour of Pemba, as the latter place was more fertile and strategically better situated. But nothing came of the proposal. The climate of Pemba had a bad reputation and Botelho's claim to have reduced the islanders into submission proved to be wrong.

When in 1634 Antonio Bocarro was compiling his *Livro do Estado da India Oriental* he had to record that Yusuf bin Hassan was held in high regard by the people of Pemba and that he had 'imbued the Caffres with a certain amount of treachery with the result that they took part in the rebellion against the Portuguese and they are still rebellious'. But that rebelliousness was ruthlessly suppressed a year or two later. In 1635 Francisco de Seixas Cabreira was appointed commander of the fortress at Mombasa. In 1639 he set up an autobiographical inscription over the gateway of Fort Jesus in which he informs us that he punished the rebels on the East African mainland 'with a chastisement never expected in India'. He likewise tells us that he 'chastised Pemba, killing on his own responsibility the revolted rulers and all those of any repute, and made them pay the tribute which they had refused to pay to His Majesty'.

The Jambangome chronicler would appear to fix the date of this subjugation of Pemba having taken place in about 1636. He tells us something about the ruthlessness of this particular 'Frank',

F

who he calls 'Jojone'. He threatened to distrain upon the persons
of the Shirazi and their children and on their property for all
arrears of past tribute. Eventually he seized ten of the children of
the leading inhabitants as hostages for such payment. Thereafter
the Shirazi had perforce to submit and to pay a large sum in order
to redeem their children as well as give a written bond for future
payments of tribute. Two years later Cabreira *alias* Jojone was
back again and received the tribute money which the inhabitants
had agreed to pay. The Jambangome chronicler then proceeds to
tell us that 'after about one year Jojone died, and the people of
Shiraz thanked God for his death'. But this was a piece of wishful
thinking. In 1639 Cabreira left Mombasa on promotion to a higher
post in India. As the islanders were to learn some years later,
'Jojone' was still very much alive.

The Portuguese had agreed to accept a payment of tribute in
kind many years before Yusuf bin Hassan's revolt. Writing in
1634 Bocarro tells us in his *Livro do Estado* that pigs 'were formerly
bred by the Portuguese when they lived here. They caused the
natives such mischief that they were ordered to be taken from
here to the fortress of Mombasa and in place thereof the island
was made to pay a tribute of six hundred bags of rice'. As a letter
which the King of Portugal wrote on January 25, 1614, to the
Viceroy of India shows, this commutation had already taken place
at that date. In actual fact it was very much of a unilateral bargain.
The Portuguese had brought a nuisance to the island and the
people of Pemba were required to pay for its abatement. Moreover,
the nuisance never was abated. Today in Pemba the European
wild pig (*sus scrofa*) still exists in Pemba, having ousted entirely
the red African bush pig (*sus potomachaerus nyassae*) which is still
to be found in Zanzibar.

When Francis de Seixas Cabreira declared on 1639 that he had
'reduced into subjection to His Majesty the coast of Malindi
which he had found in revolt owing to the tyrant king', he was
undoubtedly speaking the truth. His energetic measures had
left the dwellers on that coast, and on the island of Pemba in
particular, thoroughly cowed for the time being.

In 1640 'Kabitan bin Jojone', the Portuguese tax collector,
arrived in Pemba and received the tribute money. In 1644 he
returned with five ships. Once again he collected tribute, but he
also distributed a number of presents amongst the islanders.

Despite this generosity the people of Pemba 'thanked God for his death', which was reported to them a year later. Two years later another tax collector, 'Kison bin Jojone' arrived in the island to demand tribute. We shall return to his visit a little later on.

When the Portuguese reoccupied Mombasa, they found there 'an old man, called Faquevalle, whom the Viceroy made Governor of the kingdom of Malindi and Mombasa in gratitude for his loyalty and fidelity'. This Faquevalle belonged to the family of the 'tyrant king', Yusuf bin Hassan *alias* Chingulia. As members of his family owned land in Pemba as late as 1907, it seems very probable that either he or another member of his family was installed as ruler of Pemba. Whoever the new 'king' may have been, the relations between him and the Portuguese officials were just as unsatisfactory as they had been in the days of the 'tyrant king' and his predecessors. On December 3, 1645, the King of Portugal wrote to the Viceroy at Goa informing him that a number of East African rulers including the 'king' of Pemba, had written to Lisbon complaining of the many vexations and excesses of which the local Portuguese officials had been guilty.

As instructions which were sent to the commander of Mombasa in 1646 show, at that date the people of Pemba were not only in a position to resist attempts by the Portuguese to levy tribute, but were even able to carry the war into the enemy country and to attack the town of Faza in the Bajun islands, the inhabitants of which were loyal to the Portuguese.

The Jambangome chronicle tells us that at about this time Kison bin Jojone, the Nazarene Frank, came and demanded tribute. He demanded more than was agreed upon by his father Jojone and his brother Kabitan. The people of Shirazi refused. . . .

Then Kison in great anger left the place, but soon, after the lapse of two months, he came back. He came with five ships full of Nazarenes. He remained for three days and then landed and Kison bin Jojone demanded the tribute. Once again the islanders refused to pay. Then Kison declared war, but the Shirazi fought with him for thirty-two days and thirty-two nights. Kison could not conquer the Shirazi and left together with his companions. After the lapse of some years Kison bin Jojone came back, accompanied (according to the chronicler) by sixty-five ships full of Nazarenes. He again demanded tribute and the Shirazi refused. Again he waged war, but the Shirazi fought for two months. They killed thirteen hundred and fourteen Nazarenes belonging to the people of Kison, and he did not get anything. In this war the Shirazi lost three hundred and sixty-four people. Then Kison and his people went back.

All the figures given by the chronicler would appear to be grossly exaggerated. At this date the Portuguese lacked both the shipping and the man-power to send such large expeditions to Pemba as the chronicler would have us believe. Nevertheless, the fact remains that the people of Pemba at this date were able more than once successfully to resist by force of arms attempts by the Portuguese to levy tribute.

In his letter of December 3, 1645, the King of Portugal stressed to the Viceroy of India the pressing and urgent necessity for re-dressing the grievances of the local East African rulers. In order that there should be no semblance of excuse for future complaints from those persons, the King directed that 'no greater jurisdiction be exercised than is necessary and the customs of these kingdoms should be observed'. It was a counsel of perfection, in which there can be little doubt that the Viceroy fully concurred. But, as in the days when Portuguese commanders at Mombasa came to logger-heads with the Sultans of Malindi, instructions from headquarters at Goa were slow in reaching their destination and it was quite impossible to keep an effective check upon subordinates who lived over a thousand miles away on the opposite shores of the Indian Ocean. Consequently the relations between local Portuguese officials and the inhabitants of East Africa went from bad to worse. In 1648 Pate was in a state of rebellion and three years later the people of Pemba and other parts of East Africa called in the Arabs of Oman to rid them of the Portuguese yoke.

In 1650 Francisco de Seixas Cabreira was recalled to Africa to deal with a situation similar to that which he had so vigorously handled fifteen years before. On August 30, 1653, he wrote a report regarding his activities. He had been unable to get in touch with the enemy ships from Oman and the forces at his disposal were limited. With 120 Portuguese and 40 Indian soldiers and 120 men from Malindi he had proceeded to Zanzibar, where he had success-fully put down the rebellion. He had then proceeded against ten dhows belonging to the King of Pemba, which were returning from a raid on Kwale (near Mafia), Mafia, and Kilwa and which he encountered off the coast of Zanzibar. He captured five of the dhows and had driven the other five ashore on Zanzibar island, where his men had engaged the fleeing crew in hand to hand fighting. After sixty days he had returned to Mombasa. In other words, he had only been very partially successful. Zanzibar had been suitably dealt with and the people of Pemba had received a heavy blow by reason of the loss of their shipping, but this time he had been unable to visit their island with the same chastisement as he had inflicted some fifteen years before. What was more significant still, the Omani fleet had got away unscathed.

Cabreira was only twenty-seven years old when in 1635 he was appointed to his first command in East Africa. He was over forty when he returned for the second time and evidently the people of Pemba failed to recognize him; in fact they believed, as already said, that he had died more than ten years previously. The Jamban-gome chronicle calls him 'Kison bin Jojone' and tells us that in about 1655 he arrived with seventy ships (which is clearly an exaggeration) and landed on the Mkumbuu peninsula. There was a levy *en masse* of the inhabitants to oppose him. When Cabreira demanded tribute, he was told to depart as they did not believe him to be the son of the former tax collector, Jojone. He was further told that if he was Jojone's son, he must produce evidence of the fact, such as the ring mounted with a red jewel which Jojone had always worn. Cabreira promptly slipped off his finger a ring mounted with a red jewel and showed it to the assembled chiefs. The islanders were completely taken aback. Remembering Cabreira's past reputation and his recent activities, they had little stomach for resistance and decided to agree with their adversary quickly. Cabreira is said by the chronicler to have demanded 16,000 dirhams as tribute, but after some haggling he is alleged to have agreed to accept 1,200 dirhams. Cabreira then sailed away and the islanders solemnly called down the curses of heaven upon him. The chronicler alleged that these curses were fulfilled and that Cabreira was shipwrecked and drowned at sea shortly afterwards But once again it was a case of wishful thinking. Portuguese records show that Cabreira was still alive in 1662.

After 1655 Cabreira disappears from the East African scene. The submission which he had extracted from the people of Pemba was of but short duration. The record of events after his departure is one of the gradual decline of Portuguese authority in East Africa and the slow but steady rise of the fortunes of Oman. By 1680 the only place in East Africa to the north of Cape Delgado in which the Portuguese could claim to have any secure foothold was Mombasa. Other places, such as Pate, might from time to time be temporarily reduced into subjection, but they soon broke out into rebellion again. As the Portuguese relied very largely upon Pemba for the provisioning of Mombasa, they naturally made strenuous efforts to maintain their hold upon the island. But declining man-power made this task increasingly difficult and in the last twenty years of the seventeenth century there were several reports of revolts in Pemba.

In 1679 Pemba was nominally under the government of a queen, who was certainly well disposed towards the Portuguese, but the lady was not living in her kingdom. In that year she was in Goa, where she became a convert to Christianity and eventually, in the absence of direct heirs, donated her kingdom to the Portuguese after her death. She was still in Goa in 1681, but returned to Pemba shortly afterwards, Between 1682 and 1684 she was paying tribute in kind to the Governor of Mombasa. But her conversion to Christianity was hardly likely to have raised her in the estimation of her Muslim subjects and subsequent events showed that her throne was far from secure. In August 1686 the commander at Mombasa wrote to inform the Viceroy at Goa that Pemba was in a state of unrest and that consequently Mombasa's food supplies were being seriously jeopardized. One of the regents had fled from the island and allied himself with a 'King of Bumba', who was planning to make himself master of Pemba. According to another report the 'Prince of Quendoa' had crossed over from the main-land and caused disturbances, whilst the Queen of Pemba had been compelled to take refuge on a Portuguese frigate.

This is the last that we hear of the royal lady. We hear nothing of her reinstatement. Possibly like 'King Felipe' before her, she made her home in Mombasa and was maintained by the Misericordia, but owing to the difficulty of extracting rice from her rebellious subjects in Pemba the Misericordia's bounty may have been somewhat attenuated.

It is possible that this is a case in which established fact lends some measure of corroboration to local tradition. 'Quendoa' appears on Portuguese maps some distance to the north of the modern Dar es Salaam and would appear to equate with Kendwa, a village situated near Fungu Yasin, between Dar es Salaam and

Bagamoyo. 'Bumba' would appear to equate with Kitapumbwe, a village a few miles to the north of Kendwa.

Pemba people have a traditional story of an invasion of their island from the regions of Tanga and allege that the cause of this invasion was the misdeed of a daughter-in-law of the sadistic Mkame Mdume, of whom mention has been made in Chapter II. Mkame Mdume's son, Haruni, lived at Chwaka at the north end of Pemba had a very jealous wife. This lady discovered that, when her husband went each day to the principal mosque of the town to pray, he was in the habit of visiting another lady living nearby. His wife resolved to put a stop to these meetings and accordingly built a smaller mosque, called the *Msikiti ya Shoko* ('the pea mosque') close to the palace, where she could keep an eye on his devotions. The mason, who built the mosque, is said to have come from Tanga on the mainland. He did his task so well that Haruni's wife feared her husband might get him to make another like it. To prevent this she cut off the mason's right arm and drove him away. He went back to Tanga and returned with an army of his tribe – possibly the Wasegeju, who had recently arrived at the coast near Tanga and who settled in various parts of Pemba at about this date. The invaders set fire to the town of Chwaka by night and destroyed it. The inhabitants were rounded up and taken to the nearby Nyamburi creek, where they were massacred To this day the inhabitants point to a wall close to the creek, which they call Ukuta wa Damu (the wall of blood), and to a patch of red sand in the middle of the adjoining white sand.

Such is the tale. The story of the mason bears a strong resemblance to like stories told in many other lands, including that of the builder of the mosque at Kizimkazi in Zanzibar. It is not therefore suggested that the lady, who had taken refuge in Goa in 1679, fled there because she had cut off a man's arm. It has also to be admitted that the Msikiti ya Shoko would appear to belong to the eighteenth century, but the legend may have been current in Pemba long before that mosque was built. What is to be noted is that the 'queen', who fled from Pemba to Goa in about 1679, fled there because of an invasion from the mainland. If, as is sometimes the case, this is an instance in which local tradition bears some kind of relation to some established fact, I know of no instance except this in the history of Pemba in which such a correlation would appear to exist. But it must be left to the reader to say how far – if at all – he or she accepts this particular tradition as containing a substratum of truth.

Apparently the Portuguese managed to recover their hold on the island, but not for long. At the end of 1693 Pascal de Abreu Sarmento called at Pemba on his way to take up his appointment as commander of the fort of Mombasa. He found the inhabitants of the island in a state of rebellion, but managed to bring them into subjection. Nevertheless the inhabitants did not long remain sub-missive and very soon after his departure the Viceroy had to send soldiers to maintain law and order. Details of this new revolt are not forthcoming but one thing is significant. Hitherto all reports of dealings and disputes between the Portuguese and the inhabi-tants of Pemba had referred to the latter as Moors. In 1693 the trouble makers in the island were for the first time called Arabs, that is to say, immigrants from Asia – people whom the Portuguese would gladly have expelled, but they were powerless to carry out their wishes.

The garrison, which the Viceroy sent to Pemba, proved quite unable to hold the inhabitants in curb. On November 16, 1694, the Viceroy informed his royal master in Lisbon that a ship had just reached Goa from Mombasa with the news that Pemba was once more in rebellion. Sarmento was dead and his successor lacked experience. Therefore, as the Viceroy told the King of Portugal, 'this commotion causes me some anxiety. Its causes are variously explained to me, each narrator writing to defend his favourite'. In the circumstances, the Viceroy was sending a more experienced officer, named João Rodriguez Leão, in a galliot to Mombasa. 'I am ordering the said captain to inquire into the causes of this rebellion; and, having verified the facts, I shall proceed against the Moors and shall report to your Majesty'. But, as the Viceroy had to explain, there was one constantly recurring obstacle to speedy action at a time when speedy action was urgently needed. At the time of writing the monsoon was unfavourable and the new commander and the war galley could not possibly sail for at least another month.

On December 6 of the following year the Viceroy reported that Leão had proceeded with several ships to Pemba and had managed to drive out the Arabs, but that they had shortly afterwards returned to the island. In the circumstances the Viceroy had sent instructions to Leão to proceed to the island and deal with this new situation. It is, however, very much to be doubted whether by the time these instructions reached, or should have reached, Mombasa, Leão was in a position to comply with them. In March 1696, the Arabs of Oman laid siege to Fort Jesus at Mombasa. João Rodriguez Leão was in command of the fort and stuck to his post until his death from disease in the following October. The siege continued until mid-December 1698, when the Arabs overpowered the feeble remnants of the Portuguese garrison. After that any hope the Portuguese may have had of recovering Pemba was at an end.

CHAPTER V

ZANZIBAR UNDER THE ARABS OF OMAN, 1698–1815

For rather more than a century after the overthrow of the Portuguese, history has little to say regarding either Zanzibar or Pemba. At occasional intervals some rather unusual event happened, which momentarily drew attention to Zanzibar. Otherwise there is little to record.

One such event happened very shortly after the Arabs got possession of Zanzibar. It related to an English ship which was not of quite so reputable a character as that commanded by Sir James Lancaster. The vessel in question was the *Speaker*, which had been captured off Madagascar by some pirates commanded by one George Booth. After having increased her armament to fifty-four guns and manned her with a crew of 240 men,

the pirates now sailed for the East Indies by way of Zanzibar where they stopped to take in provisions. Some of them went ashore to buy provisions and the Captain, being sent for by the Arab Governor, went with about 14 men in company. They passed through the guard, but when they were well inside the Governor's house, all were cut off, and at the same time others in different houses of the town were set upon which made them fly to the shore. The longboat which lay agrappling off shore (at a kedge) was immediately put in by those aboard her.

Though not above half a dozen of the pirates brought their arms ashore, yet they plied them so well that most of the men got aboard the boat. The quartermaster ran down to the shore sword in hand, and though he was attacked by many, he behaved himself so sturdily that he managed to get into a canoe in which he put off and gained the long-boat. In the interim the Arab fort played on the pirate ship which returned their salutes very warmly. Thus in the end they all got on board with only the loss of Captain Booth and about 20 men and then shaped their course for the Red Sea.

The mention of the fort is interesting. Though in the days of the Portuguese there had been soldiers on the island for the protection of the factory, there had been no fort. The Arabs must herefore have constructed this fort almost immediately after taking possession of the foot-shaped peninsula. Acting on information given to him by a spy, the Portuguese Viceroy at Goa reported on August 10, 1710 to the government at Lisbon that it was 'a ridiculous fort' and that it had been constructed out of the material of the Augustinian Church and the house which formerly belonged to a certain João Nunes. At this date it was probably little more than a stone breastwork. In a chart compiled by Alexander Dalrymple and dated February 5, 1774, it is described as 'the fort or factory, where there is some small guns, which appears like a ruined church'.

According to the information given by the aforesaid spy there were fifty soldiers in Zanzibar commanded by one Said. There were three cannon in the fort. One of these covered the wells and another the fishing village at Shangani Point. The third pointed towards the residence of Queen Fatuma, who together with her three fellow captives had been allowed to return to Zanzibar in 1709. One of her descendants owned the land upon which the Cathedral of the Universities Mission to Central Africa now stands. That may have been where Fatuma resided. At any rate she was given a very clear intimation that she was still under superveillance. The spy also made a brief mention of Pemba. In 1710 there were thirty soldiers, who compelled the inhabitants to fell timber and take it to Mombasa, whence it was sent to Muscat for purposes of shipbuilding.

Queen Fatuma died sometime between 1710 and 1728 and was succeeded by her son Hassan, whose father was Abdulla, 'king' of Utondwe. She was no doubt buried in the family burial ground adjoining the fort on its south side.

Early in 1726 news reached Goa that the civil discord, which had at this date broken out in Oman, had spread to East Africa. The Arabs of Mombasa had taken one side and those of Zanzibar the other. Partisanship had eventually reached such a pitch that Mombasa had sent an armed expedition to Zanzibar. After a five months' siege the garrison at Zanzibar had surrendered on the promise of a free passage to Arabia. They had, however, disembarked at Pate and were once again proving a source of trouble to the Arabs at Mombasa.

This and other information regarding dissensions amongst the Arabs led the Viceroy at Goa to decide to make an attempt to recapture Mombasa. The expedition was despatched in 1728 and

arrived at Mombasa at a very opportune moment. Ahmed bin
Said, the actual governor, had gone on a pilgrimage to Mecca,
leaving as his deputy one Nasser bin Abdulla el-Mazrui, whose
oppressive conduct had led to a revolt. The result was that the
Portuguese recovered Mombasa almost without a shot being fired
or a blow struck. On March 12, 1728, Sheikh Muhammad bin
Said, 'the general of the Arabs', and Sheikh 'Fachani', Governor
of Zanzibar, signed a formal capitulation whereby the island and
fort were handed over to the Portuguese and the Arabs were
granted ships and free passage back to Arabia.

After the surrender of Mombasa the rulers of the neighbouring
islands and coast towns were summoned to make their submission
to the Portuguese Crown. In due course 'Muinha Mocu' (Mwinyi
Musa) appeared at Mombasa to make submission on behalf of his
father 'Aufalume Assane' (Mfalme = Sultan Hassani) of Zanzibar.
'Bin Sultan', ruler of Pemba, likewise made his submission.
Shortly afterwards Joachim da Costa Ribeiro was sent with seven
companions to re-establish the factory at Zanzibar. As the report
of 1710 shows, the principal buildings in the old Portuguese settlement had been demolished and it was obvious that the work of
reconstruction would prove slow and expensive. On January 23,
1729, the Viceroy of India wrote to Lisbon to report that the
Portuguese commander needed 30,000 xerafins (or about £2,000)
for the upkeep of Mombasa, Zanzibar, and Pate and that it was
quite impossible to raise the money locally. On August 31, a reply
was sent from Lisbon bidding the Viceroy to try to obtain a loan
from the Banyan merchants in India or else from the Society of
Jesus. He was at the same time bidden to reinforce the fleet and
garrisons in East Africa.

Before this reply could reach Goa the necessity for the loan had
come to an end. The Portuguese had recovered their lost ground
with unexpected ease. Having done so, they, by their subsequent
conduct, proceeded to forfeit every right to hold what they had
thus gained. Both the Chronicle of Mombasa and official Portuguese records show that they treated the local inhabitants, to whom
in no small measure they owed the recovery of Fort Jesus, in a
most high-handed fashion. The result was that the inhabitants rose
against them. Many of them were taken by surprise and killed.
The remainder took refuge in Fort Jesus where they held out for
six months. Finally on November 26, 1729 they were compelled to

capitulate and the remnant of the garrison set sail on two dhows for Mozambique.

During the siege an ineffectual attempt was made to relieve the garrison by means of a ship from Mozambique. In August 1729 this ship called at Zanzibar expecting to find the factor and his seven companions there and to meet with a friendly reception from the king and his subjects. But, as soon as Joachim da Costa Ribeiro and his companions heard of what was afoot at Mombasa, they decided to take refuge in flight. The relief ship therefore arrived to find the factory abandoned. At first the local inhabitants treated the crew in a friendly manner, but they suddenly fell upon a landing party and killed the captain and another member of the crew. The remainder had to beat a hasty retreat to the ship's boat and owed their lives very largely to the valour of the ship's chaplain, who had come ashore with a sword beneath his cassock and used it to good effect in covering the retreat of his companions.

With the hurried flight of Ribeiro and his companions the Portuguese settlement in Zanzibar came finally to an end. From time to time various projects were set afoot at Mozambique to recover Mombasa by taking advantage of civil discords on that island. In 1766 and 1796 ships actually set out from Mozambique for this purpose. In the former case the expedition was abandoned owing to bad leadership and in the latter case the solitary schooner which was sent relinquished the project after meeting with a hostile reception at Mombasa. In neither case would it appear that any Portuguese ship called at Zanzibar or Pemba on the way to or from Mombasa.

As the Mombasa Chronicle tells us, the final eviction of the Portuguese was achieved by the local inhabitants without external aid. Realizing, however, that the Portuguese might send a strong force to recover the place, they sent to Muscat to ask for the protection of the ruler of Oman. In due course three ships-of-war arrived from Muscat and Muhammad bin Said el-Maamri was installed as Omani governor.

In so far as Pemba was concerned, one gathers that the ruler thereof was swimming with the tide in whichever direction it flowed. 'Bin Sultan' had made what would appear to have been no more than a nominal submission to the Portuguese when they recovered Mombasa. When the Portuguese were thrown out of that place, he found little difficulty in making a like submission to the Arabs of Oman.

Sultan Hassan bin Abdullah of Zanzibar had in the past been friendly to the Portuguese. He was probably not at all sorry to see the Omani garrison quit Zanzibar in 1726 and was ready to welcome the Portuguese factor and his companions two years later but, when these last mentioned persons took to flight, it is not surprising that he and his people made a complete *volte face*. He had once already suffered over ten years of exile for his friendship to the Portuguese and now he was once more faced with the prospect of the same, if not a worse, fate. In the circumstances it was more or less inevitable that he should decide to agree with his adversary quickly. According to the story the negotiations between the leading Omani Arab and Sultan Hassan were conducted with a screen placed between them. Tradition said that the screen was placed between the two negotiators at Zanzibar 'to obviate all attempts at favour, corruption or bribery', but daggers can easily be concealed beneath flowing robes and easily drawn; also capture by force or treachery was not unknown as forming at this date part of the technique of negotiations in the east. A screen was therefore a very wise and necessary precaution.

We have no information as to the terms of the agreement reached by the contracting parties. According to tradition Sultan Hassan had done much to clear the bush on the foot-shaped peninsula where the town of Zanzibar now stands. He agreed to leave the fishing folk in undisturbed possession of their settlement at Shangani Point. Tradition asserts that these fishermen made no objection to other persons coming and settling on the peninsula, provided that they were consulted on all important affairs affecting the place, and that their names were mentioned in *all* public proclamations. Doubtless, they saw to it that these conditions formed part of the terms of the treaty entered into by Sultan Hassan with the representative of Oman.

It is said that the first Arabs to settle on the peninsula were Mafazi from the island of Patta, who would appear to have arrived as the result of one of the many civil wars which are recorded in that island's history. They settled about five hundred yards to the north-east of the Arab fort in the Mwavi quarter (so named from a large Mkunavi (acacia) tree) near the site of the present Ismailia Khoja Jamatkhana. Later the Arab colony was increased by the arrival of a number of Shatri from Mafia, who would appear to have sought refuge from the raids on that island by the Sakalava of Madagascar. In the course of time certain of these immigrants crossed the creek and acquired plantations in the main island, but this form of expansion would appear to have been very slow and gradual. It was not until the nineteenth century that it was carried out on any large scale, According to a report made to the Governor of Ile de France (Mauritius) the number of Omani Arabs in Zanzibar in about 1776 did not exceed 300 and they were hated by all other Arabs and half-Arabs along the coast.

History has nothing to say of any eventful occurrences in Zanzibar or Pemba for a dozen years or so after the final expulsion of the Portuguese from the first mentioned island. After that the apparent calm was disturbed owing to the repercussion of events, which had taken place in Oman. After the death in 1711 of Seif bin Sultan, the ruler of Oman who had captured Fort Jesus, his country drifted into a period of come thirty years of civil strife. In 1741 the Yorubi dynasty was supplanted by that of Busaidi, when Ahmed bin Seif el Busaidi was elected to the throne a year or two later. This change of dynasty met with a mixed reception in East Africa. Many of the local Omani governors, including Muhammad bin Uthman el-Mazrui at Mombasa, refused to acknowledge Ahmed bin Seif and declared themselves to be independent rulers. One of the few places which accepted the change was Zanzibar and even there, according to a Pate chronicler, 'the Busaidi Arabs . . . had got hold of Zanzibar through making friendship with the people, but had not yet taken it entirely'. Ahmed bin Seif had, however, succeeded in installing a kinsman, Abdullah bin Jaad el-Busaidi, as governor of the island together with a garrison for his support. This undoubtedly gave the Busaidi faction a strong foothold on the peninsula on which the fort stood but we are told nothing as to the attitude either of Arab settlers in the interior of the island or, more important still, of the Mwenyi Mkuu, the ruler of the indigenous people.

Ahmed bin Seif tried to obtain possession of Mombasa by assassinating the Mazrui governor, but the people rallied to the side of the murdered man's brother, Ali bin Uthman, with the result that Mombasa reasserted its independence in 1746.

In previous chapters mention has been made more than once of the dependence of Mombasa upon Pemba for its food supply. At some period, which cannot be definitely fixed but which may date back to the days in which Portuguese governors at Mombasa were constantly reporting the island to be in a state of rebellion, Pate managed to obtain the dominant position in the northern part of Pemba. Shortly after his accession to the sovereignty of Mombasa Ali bin Uthman decided to attempt to oust Pate from the position which it then enjoyed in Pemba. At that date the ruler of Pate is said according to one account to have been a woman named Mwana Mimi, whose *Wazir* (chief minister) was one Fumo Bakari. This *Wazir* had made himself unpopular with the people of Pemba, who sent a message to Ali bin Uthman at Mombasa offering to place themselves under his overlordship. Ali thereupon sent an expedition to Pemba, which drove out the agents and soldiers of Fumo Bakari and established Ali's maternal uncle, Khamis bin Ali as governor.[1]

The people of Pate retaliated by sending an expedition to Mombasa itself, relying upon assistance from the malcontent Nine Tribes of the Swahili. Except for the destruction of the village of Kilindini and some skirmishing in the outskirts of the town of Mombasa very little fighting took place. At the end of three days operations abruptly terminated. The invaders re-embarked and returned to their own country. Rumour had it that they had been bribed. This may be true, but later events in Pemba go to show that an agreement had been reached whereby both Mombasa and Pate were each to have their own representatives in Pemba. Some twenty years later one Badi-Suleiman was representing the Sultan of Pate in Pemba. He was murdered at the instigation of the Mazrui ruler of Mombasa in retaliation for the murder of the representative of the Mazrui at Pate.

In 1755 Ali bin Uthman decided to make an attempt to conquer Zanzibar. Part of his force was recruited in Pemba by Masud bin Nasser el-Mazrui, who had succeeded as governor of that island on the death of Khamis bin Ali. The remainder came from Mombasa under the personal leadership of Ali bin Uthman and his nephew, Kheluf bin Qodib. The attackers effected a landing on the

---

[1] This account is taken from Guillain, i. 548. According to the Jambangome Chronicle a large party of Nabhani, led by one Haruni el-Maghlum, migrated from Pate to Pemba in 1608. That same chronicle suggests that, except when acting in combination against the Portuguese, these settlers kept themselves aloof from the other inhabitants. Mwana Mimi would appear to be the same person as Mwana Khadija, who according to some versions of the Pate Chronicle ruled Pate from about 1762 until about 1775.

peninsula where the town of Zanzibar now is and soon made themselves masters of the northern part thereof. The defenders withdrew into the fort and retained possession of the southern portion of the town. They had evidently been taken by surprise and, as the monsoon was unfavourable, they had little hope of relief for many months. It therefore looked as if Zanzibar must inevitably fall into the hands of the invaders, but that was not to be. Treachery upset all calculations. Masud bin Nasser aspired to succeed Ali bin Uthman, who was childless, as ruler of Mombasa and Kheluf bin Qodib had a number of grievances against his uncle. One day Ali bin Uthman was found murdered. Suspicion fell upon his nephew, who was himself killed by a Segeju chief, who had accompanied the expedition and who was a staunch friend of the murdered governor. After these tragedies the command devolved upon Masud bin Nasser, who embarked all the attacking forces and returned to Mombasa.

Masud bin Nasser succeeded as ruler of Mombasa the man whose murder he is alleged to have instigated. He died in about 1775 and was succeeded by Abdullah bin Muhammad el-Mazrui, who died on December 18, 1782 after an uneventful reign. There was a dispute as to his successor, which was eventually decided in favour of the deceased ruler's brother, Ahmed bin Muhammad. One of the other claimants, Abdullah bin Zahor, agreed to accept the governorship of Pemba as a consolation prize. A third claimant was made governor of the Giriama, a tribe dwelling on the mainland to the south of Mombasa. The disappointed claimants, however, combined to attack Mombasa. After effecting a landing and taking possession of Kilindini, the two were driven out of the island of Mombasa and forced to take refuge on the mainland, where they were attacked and killed by the Wa Nyika.

During this same period a number of Dutch vessels from the Cape of Good Hope were paying periodical visits to Zanzibar in search of slaves. The earliest of these would appear to have called at the island in 1742. These visits appear to have continued until about 1777. In 1776 a Dutch vessel arrived at Zanzibar to find a European competitor in the field in the shape of a French trader, named de Clonard. Either owing to the machinations of de Clonard or to the obstruction of the Arab governor, he found it impossible to purchase slaves at the island and so proceeded to Madagascar in search of a cargo. In 1777 the Dutch frigate *Jagtrust* left Table

G

Bay on July 1 and reached Zanzibar on August 2. The commander later reported that the Arab governor was obstructive. He informed the captain of the *Jagtrust* that he would not be allowed to do business until two 'Moorish' ships from Muscat had completed their cargoes, alleging, possibly quite truthfully, that he had instructions to this effect from his royal master in Oman. Nonetheless, with the help of two 'Moorish priests' the Dutchman managed to ship 100 slaves. When the Muscat ships had set sail, the governor continued to be obstructive and asserted that the Europeans could only purchase slaves through himself. Certain 'Swaliers' then advised the captain of the frigate to proceed to Kilwa. The *Jagtrust* accordingly left Zanzibar after a stay of exactly two months and, proceeding to the mainland, managed with the help of the 'Swaliers' to make up their cargo to 328 slaves. After her visit we hear no more of Dutch vessels calling at Zanzibar for slaves. Very possibly the attitude taken up by the Arab governor served as a deterrent.

At about the same time as the Dutch gave up calling at Zanzibar a few English ships began calling there. The hydrographer, Alexander Dalrymple, published in 1774 and 1784 two charts compiled by English seamen who had visited Zanzibar. The earlier of these charts describes itself as a 'Plan of the Road or Harbour of Zinzinbarra or Zanzibar' and contains a statement by the compiler that 'we lay here 6 months', which would appear to show that the crew of this vessel had a friendly reception at the hands of the local inhabitants. The other was compiled by the commander of the *Bonadventure Grab* of Bombay, who visited East Africa on two occasions in search of cowries and on two occasions anchored in Mkokotoni harbour off Tumbatu island. On one of these voyages this anonymous map maker tells us he sailed in company with Captain Simon Matcham of the East India Company, who died in 1770 and whose son George married Nelson's sister. As the writer thought his anchorage off Tumbatu 'a proper place' and as he twice anchored there, it is reasonable to infer that his reception was likewise friendly.

But English shipping in these regions was insignificant as compared with that of the French. The French East India Company had taken possession of the island of Bourbon (Réunion) as early as 1664, but French settlers were relatively few in number until about a century later. In 1715 the same company likewise took possession of Mauritius which had been abandoned by the Dutch five years previously. Their acquisition of these important strategic points in the Indian Ocean more or less coincided with the final expulsion of the Portuguese from Mombasa, Zanzibar, and all their erstwhile possessions to the north of Cape Delgado. The annexation of Mauritius had been merely formal and without the accompaniment of any occupation. In 1721, however, a settlement was established. Even then conditions for more than a decade were so precarious that the Directors of the French East India Company were seriously meditating the abandonment of the island. But all thoughts of this quickly vanished when Bertrand François la Bourdonnais was appointed governor both of the Isle of France (Mauritius) and of Bourbon. When la Bourdonnais landed at Port Louis in 1735, he found there only one good house and a number of miserable huts. In the course of twelve years he completely transformed not only Port Louis but also the whole of the two islands committed to his charge, revived the sugar industry, which had been started by the Dutch, and improved the coffee industry by importing plants from Mocha in Arabia. He also introduced cotton, indigo and manioc and established a prosperous ship-building industry.

The arrival of increased numbers of French colonists and the growth and expansion of all these industries called for an increased labour supply. The easiest obtainable and cheapest form of labour was that of slaves. When la Bourdonnais first arrived in Mauritius in 1735 there were 600 black people on the island, of whom the majority were slaves. In 1767 the number of slaves had risen to 25,154 in 1776, to 37,915 in 1789, and to 49,080 in 1807. Bourbon benefited in a similar manner to Mauritius by the development of economic crops of a like nature and therefore had a similar increased labour supply. In 1777 this island's slave population had risen to 25,047: ten years later it was 28,457. The slaves were obtained at first from Madagascar, Mozambique, and West Africa. As the voyage from the place of supply to the two islands was a long one and as the conditions under which they were shipped were appalling, many of these unfortunate people died before ever reaching their destination. Others were so weakened and debilitated by the effects of the voyage that they died shortly after their arrival or became totally incapacitated for hard manual labour. On arrival men and women were sold separately with the result that families were broken up and taken to different districts. As a race the survivors were not prolific and runaways, who took refuge in the interior of the islands, were not infrequent. Consequently the supply of slave labour never came up to the demand.

As already seen, a visiting Dutch trader found a French competitor in the slave trade at Zanzibar in 1776. It was possibly owing to the representations of that Frenchman, de Clonard, or a compatriot of his named Morice that the Dutchman found himself boycotted and had perforce to leave the island without a cargo. Morice tells us that at about the time of the Dutchmen's visit de Clonard experienced certain 'difficulties and a small war' (*les difficultés et la petite guerre de M. de Clonard*). As he gives no further details, we do not know whether this *petite guerre* had any connection with the Dutchman's visit. Morice says he had foreseen the possibility of such trouble, which rather suggests that he had no high opinion of his compatriot's tact. At any rate, when in the following year the Arab governor sent him a number of letters 'full of courtesy', Morice replied 'I would have gone there, had I not thought that de Clonard's war had made him ill disposed towards the French. In reply he wrote that I always knew that I should be well received and I should come whenever I wanted to come'.

Morice obtained a lot of interesting information regarding the island. It was the sole remaining East African possession of the rulers of Oman and

in truth it would take very little to dislodge them from Zanzibar. I know quite well that there are not three hundred Arabs in the whole of the island, although I suppose it has forty thousand inhabitants.

Zanzibar is an island, which was taken by the Moors and in respect of which they have an incontestable right, which they are prepared to vindicate when they think they can be successful. When they have done so, I say we ought to negotiate with them to have a fort there when the revolution takes place. . . . In Zanzibar there has always been one of the descendants of the former kings of Zanzibar, who bears the title of king and who, when he walks abroad, holds a kind of court. He is publicly called the king of Zanzibar, although he is under the rod of the governor of Zanzibar. The person who was king last year (Sultan bin Hassan el Alawi) died during my stay in Kilwa (in 1777). Undoubtedly they will elect in his place one of his sons who, like his father, will have the title of king without exercising any authority, which resides absolutely in the hands of the governor named by the Imam of Muscat.

They charge three per cent on all merchandise imported and exported and send to him (son of the Imam of Muscat) every year a vessel of four hundred tons with goods which are sold in the colony in exchange for ivory and the teeth of sea cows [sic].

The island of Zanzibar . . . is fertile. Its crops are rice, millet, maize and coconuts and different kinds of fruit. It is not hilly, but is thickly wooded with trees suitable for building purposes. There are about sixty thousand souls [sic], of whom the larger number cultivate the soil. Its port can hold sixty men of war and one hundred merchant ships without taking into consideration all the other places of shelter along the coast, which are considerable.

The great deterrent to any rising on the part of the Moors was the fort in the town of Zanzibar. Morice, therefore advocated a joint Franco-Moorish expedition from Kilwa to wrest Zanzibar from the Arabs of Oman, but this project was stillborn. The French authorities in Mauritius were on good terms with the ruler of Oman and the French settlers in the island were carrying on a profitable trade with Muscat in sugar and other commodities which they did not want to jeopardize.

Shortly after the visit of Morice to Zanzibar civil discord in Oman once again had its repercussions in Zanzibar. Ahmed bin Said, Imam of Muscat, died at the end of 1783 or the beginning of 1784. Said bin Ahmed, the eldest son of the deceased Imam was chosen Imam in his stead, but his younger brother Seif bin Ahmed disputed his claim. Realizing that he had little chance of success in Oman itself, Seif set sail for East Africa, where he hoped to reduce Zanzibar and other places to his submission and to carve out a sultanate for himself.

Seif bin Ahmed reached Zanzibar in the early months of 1784. He summoned the governor, Khalfan bin Ahmed, to make his submission, but the latter refused. Seif than landed and occupied the northern part (the 'toe') of the peninsula, the inhabitants of which took sides with him. No serious fighting followed. Seif had detached part of his forces under his son Ali to recapture Kilwa, whence the Omani Arabs had been expelled in about 1770. It was probably owing to this diversion that he made no attempt to capture the fort, which he was content to invest in a not very rigorous manner. In the course of time the ranks of the defenders were thinned by desertions and it appeared as if Seif were on the verge of success, but he had left matters too late.

In the last months of the year a relieving squadron arrived from Oman under the nominal leadership of the Imam's son Ahmed. The effective command was in the hands of Sultan bin Said, another brother of the Imam. On arrival the Sultan had an interview with his recalcitrant brother Seif. He was able to persuade him that resistance would be useless. Seif was then permitted to retire and to take up his residence at Lamu, where he died shortly afterwards. Sultan bin Ahmed and his nephew then returned to Oman by way of Mombasa, where they arrived on January 20, 1785 and procured a written acknowledgement from the Mazrui governor that Fort Jesus belonged to the Imam of Muscat.

During the next thirty years Zanzibar and Pemba appear to have enjoyed comparative peace. History has nothing to record during that period of internal quarrels or strife or of events arising from repercussions of such quarrels and strife in Oman or elsewhere in Arabia or Africa.

In 1795 the Portuguese Captain-General of Mozambique reported that five or six English ships from Surat were visiting Mombasa, Zanzibar and Kilwa each year to pick up cargoes of ivory gold and cowries. The port of origin of these ships, however suggests that, whilst they may have flown the English flag, they were Indian owned and manned. At this date some six Portuguese slave ships were sent each year from Mozambique to the same ports, but this was only half the number of slave ships sent each year to those places by the French in the Isle of France (Mauritius).

A certain M. Dallons, who made his first voyage to Zanzibar in 1799, delivered on August 24, 1804 to the French Governor of Mauritius his 'Reflections' on French commercial relations with East Africa. It contains much interesting information.

The government of Zanzibar is in the hands of the Prince of Muscat. He is continually changing the governor owing to his fear that too well established a governor will take away his dominion. As in Pemba, Mombasa and Patta the choice of commanders has become day by day more difficult, he puts eunuchs in charge of this place (sc. Zanzibar) and splits up their powers. The military command is entrusted to a man of this king, (and) civil command and customs are entrusted to a Banyan or an Arab whose rich estates at Muscat guarantee that he will be faithful to the prince; and the mainland is entrusted to a third person on giving him the same security.

. . . All the fees and customs duties appear . . . to amount to forty thousand dollars yearly. These are paid in at the end of each north-west monsoon in the months of March and April, at which time the new governor arrives and as a rule is guilty of atrocious and revolting vexations, which are always concealed under the veil of being in the Prince's interest. He is often supported by the Arabs and the inhabitants of the upper class called Kertty (Harthi). They are nearly always intervening in the official acts of the government.

When we go to trade in this island, we at first sight promise ourselves that business will be good, but we are quickly deprived of our hopes. On our arrival the government gives us an interpreter, who is undoubtedly under its orders, and under the appearance of enjoying the greatest possible liberty we depend entirely on this man. If we bring such merchandise as cloves, sugar, iron etc., the government demands that it shall have preference at the same price and offers us on the spot and, unknown to us, has prohibited the natives of the country from having any competition with it; and by various methods, which they employ, the French are always compelled to submit to a price fixed by the government and to payment to the governor by an atrocious breach of good faith and are thus caused a loss of 30 per cent.

Before entering into any business transactions the French are obliged to make very costly presents to the Government and to the interpreter, who is a pliant and sociable person on whom they depend for success; and if his intense greed is not satisfied he impedes them in every way so as to foil them.

The black captives are sold by auction and the bawling of the public vendors. It is with these last mentioned persons that the interpreter carries on business which ruins the French. They increase the price of the blacks at will and finish by making us afraid that they will be unable to obtain them at any price whatever, because, as they say, their religion forbids them in such a case to sell to whites. If in such case one makes a complaint to the Arab governor, he makes an appearance of expediting your labours, but matters remain in the same state as before until, after having been involved in one difficulty after another, we come to the end of our business. Then the Governor comes on board the vessel to count the blacks and levies a duty of eleven dollars a head. Having obtained the duty, the governor loads the French with offers of his services, which come to nothing more than not exacting further presents.

The natives of the country also trade in blacks. They transport them to various settlements – to Muscat, the Red Sea, and the Persian Gulf –

and although in this respect they have nothing to fear from our competition, they pay no more than one dollar as duty. They do everything
they can to keep us away from the island. The interests and the policy of
the Prince of Muscat bids us go there, but it is certain that his governors
have no regard for either of these things.

Though he is a formidable person in his own country, the Sultan of
Muscat exercises only a feeble control at a distance. During my last
stay at Zanzibar I saw some French people arrive with an order from
the Sultan to the government of the island to allow them to trade
freely. The result was unfortunate owing to the opposition, which was
instigated against them, and this proves that orders from the Prince
regarding ourselves will not be executed in Zanzibar unless our government protects our trade in these parts in a striking manner.

. . . This island is governed at present by Baouder as military
commander and a eunuch named Yakut as chief of the customs. . . .
It is this Yakut who has always prevented the French from having
communication with the continent. I am the only person who has
obtained this favour. Nevertheless I was surrounded by a numerous
escort, which was given me ostensibly for securing my safety, but
really in order not to allow me to have dealings with any except those
whom he did not wish to conceal from me.

Dallons advocated the posting of a French Resident at Zanzibar
and the despatch of a strongly worded letter from the Governor of
Mauritius to Yakut and another to Muscat asking for better treatment to be accorded to French traders visiting the island. But his
proposal was made in the middle of the Napoleonic wars, when
neither the French home government nor the Governor of
Mauritius could spare the shipping or the officer to put Dallons'
'Reflections' into effect.

It has of course to be borne in mind that Dallons was a man with
a grievance and that certain of his allegations may have been over-
stated, but there seems little doubt that the officers of the Imam of
Muscat in Zanzibar were out to feather their own nests at the
expense of their royal master and that many of their exactions
would certainly not have met with the latter's approval had they
been brought to his notice.

It is also interesting to note that Dallons mentions cloves and
sugar as being amongst the commodities brought by the French
from Mauritius to Zanzibar. Pierre Poivre had managed to obtain
clove plants from the Moluccas and to introduce them in Mauritius
in 1775, but from the use of the word 'Gerofles (Girofles)' in the

'Reflections' one gathers that it was the dried fruit and not the plant itself which was imported at this time into Zanzibar. Similar remarks apply to Dallons' reference to sugar, which had been a staple crop almost from the earliest days of the French occupation of Mauritius. Mills for crushing the cane had been established in that island during the governorship of la Bourdonnais (1735-47).

Dallons is clearly wrong in suggesting that the Imams of Muscat were constantly changing the governors of Zanzibar. As will be seen, Yakut, who was an Abyssinian eunuch, was left in charge of Zanzibar for at least ten years and eventually died there.

It must have been only very shortly before Dallons made his first call at Zanzibar that two British men-of-war, the *Leopard* and *Orestes*, made a fortnight's stay at the island. These two vessels were under the command of Commodore John Blankett, who had orders to proceed to the Red Sea to frustrate any plans made by Napoleon to invade India by way of Egypt. A north-east monsoon and an adverse current prevented them from getting much further north than the Juba River, where shortage of provisions had compelled them to put about. On February 1799 they reached Zanzibar, having in six days covered the same distance southwards as it had taken then more than two months to cover when proceeding in the opposite direction. Lieutenant Bissell of H.M.S. *Leopard* gives the following account of what subsequently transpired.

At 2 p.m. I was sent by the Commodore with two boats, well armed (having an interpreter), to endeavour to form an intercourse with the inhabitants, (at) half-past 3 landed the interpreter close to the town, among the immense crowd on the beach, keeping the boats at (anchor). The interpreter soon returned to the boat with the chief of the island, and informed us we could obtain all kinds of refreshments at this place. I went to look at the watering place, and then returned on board: when I found that some country boats had been alongside, with presents for the Commodore, and inviting him to come on shore. We got a pilot next morning and ran close into the inner harbour at low water, through a very narrow channel, scarce three-quarters of a mile wide and (anchored about three-quarters or one mile from the town. The fort saluted us with three guns, as did a ship lying there under Moorish colours and bound to Muscat. Several of the natives came on board with refreshments for the people. The Commodore went on shore two days after to return the visit of the chief of this place, whom we saluted at his coming on board and going on shore. Here we got wood, water, bullocks and every kind of refreshment.

Apparently the water question presented some difficulty. There were several wells in and about the town, but the inhabitants would not allow the water to be taken from some of the wells from religious motives. So the ships' companies had to go to the Mpopopo Stream to the north-east of the town, 'where you roll your casks some distance from the beach, and bale out of the stream; but at high water it is rather brackish; it is therefore advisable to fill with the falling tide, and take them off on the flood'.

Though provisions were plentiful, 'as the governor or chief made a monopoly of the sale of all kinds of articles, we paid exorbitantly dear for them'. On the day before the ship's final departure, 'the chief came on board and received payment for our supplies at this place, being about 2,500 dollars'.

On the other hand, it was discovered that

the inhabitants sell their things much cheaper. . . . In their modes of traffic, they are singular. A guinea is of no value; but an anchor button, or a button of any kind is a gem in the eyes of the lower class of people. An instance occurred on board the *Leopard* where they refused a guinea, which was offered in change for some fowls; and a marine's button put an end to the bargain.

Bissell noted that 'the small trading vessels from Muscat and the Red Sea, after discharging their cargoes, which is chiefly dates, always dismantle and move into the inner harbour at the back of the town, and wait the return of the monsoon'.

'The town is composed of some few houses, and the rest are huts of straw mat, which are very neat.'

One significant piece of information was given to Bissell. 'There had not been an English ship in Zanzibar within the memory of the oldest inhabitant.' On the other hand, the inhabitants 'have a great deal of trade with the French for slaves and coffee; and many of them talk that language in consequence'.

There was one brief reminder of that fact that France and Great Britain were at war when

the *Orestes* captured a small French lugger off the NW. point of the island; but (on) the account he gave of himself, of his having come from the Isle of Mahé, one of the Seychelles, in search of some of his country-men who were supposed to be wrecked off the coast of Mozambique, the Commodore suffered him to depart.

Though the war might be called a global war, it still retained some of the characteristics of a 'gentlemen's war'.

The relations between the visitors and the inhabitants were most cordial. We are told that

some of the higher order of the inhabitants chose their favourites amongst the officers, to whom they were very kind, taking them near their houses (for they never admit them inside), and seating them in a little recess, entertained them with fruits, and every nicety possible, while some of their slaves were employed in loading a boat with coconuts, poultry, eggs and everything that was to be had. This was repeated by many of them, and (they) would not receive any remuneration for it. The natives are very timid in themselves, but when they are in throngs they appear not so; most of them, when one friend visits another, he leaves down his arms outside the door, and then goes in; otherwise it is considered a signal of hostility.

The *Orestes* and the *Leopard* left Zanzibar on March 5, 1799 and eventually reached Mocha nearly six weeks later.

Until the capture of Mauritius and Bourbon at the end of 1810 British shipping in the Indian Ocean was liable to capture by French vessels operating from those islands as well as from the Seychelles. In 1809 two British men-of-war were sent up the East African coast to reconnoitre and report as to French activities and influence at Zanzibar and its vicinity.

The first of these vessels was H.M.S. *Caledon* commanded by Captain J. Tomkinson. This vessel made Zanzibar on July 2, 1809, but had to stand off again and did not finally drop anchor off the town until twelve days later. He went on shore to interview the governor, whom he calls 'Al Conty', but who would appear to have been Dallon's *bête noire* Yakut. He presented a letter of introduction to him from the Bishop of Mozambique. He was informed by him that the French usually had a good deal of trade with the island, but that during the past year very few French vessels had called. He attributed the last mentioned fact to the activities of British cruisers. French activities were mainly confined to vessels carrying eight to ten guns, which had been fitted out in Mauritius and Bourbon and were manned by European officers and Lascar crews. These vessels used to come to Kilwa and Zanzibar to purchase slaves, corn and rice in exchange for money, corns, gunpowder or clothing. From Zanzibar they would run across to the Seychelles, where they stayed until the north-east monsoon set in.

They then took advantage of the favourable wind and the fact that at that season the British usually had lifted the blockade off Mauritius to return to that island.

Whilst at Mozambique Tomkinson had met an English merchant named Vincent who had been captured by the French in 1808 and had been landed at Zanzibar, where he had stayed until March of the following year. He informed Tomkinson that there were two French vessels trading at Zanzibar at the time of his departure and 'that during his stay on the island the port was never without a French vessel, sometimes two or three, they always went to Mahé (in the Seychelles archipelago), (and) the Isle of France (Mauritius)'. The captain of a small Arab vessel which had left Zanzibar in about May of the same year said there were two French vessels there at the time of his departure, which 'he conceived would remain a month or two, as their cargoes were being procured from different ports of the coast to the north and south of that place by boat'.

H.M.S. *Caledon* left Zanzibar on July 19, 1809, after a stay of only five days. Captain (afterwards Rear-Admiral) William Fisher of H.M.S. *Racehorse* made Zanzibar on October 15 following. He at once sent an officer on shore to wait on the Governor and to ask permission to purchase refreshments. The officer received the answer 'that the island and everything on shore were at my command'. Next day there were the same professions of friendship, but the actual disposition to be helpful fell very short of those professions. Fisher was lent the services of an interpreter named Saleh, who proved to be 'a perfect Frenchman'. The visitors were in fact very soon given to understand that the inhabitants resented their interference with French trade with the island.

The revenue paid to Muscat each year was said to be 40,000 dollars or its equivalent in ivory. An extensive trade was being carried on with Madagascar and the Persian Gulf and had been carried on till recently with Mauritius. The exports consisted of slaves, gum, ivory, antimony, blue vitriol and senna. In return the French had supplied Zanzibar with arms, gunpowder, cutlery, coarse Indian cloths and Spanish dollars. There was also a ship-building industry on the island, dhows of 200 tons burden being constructed.

The governor had about one hundred troops, who were employed on police duties. The island itself was more or less defenceless. The principal agricultural products were corn and rice, which were mainly grown for local consumption. Cattle, sheep and poultry were also plentiful.

One of Captain Fisher's complaints against the governor was the difficulties he made about supplying a pilot to take the *Racehorse* to Pemba. Eventually on October 21 the vessel had to proceed without one and in consequence went aground when trying to pass between two of the outlying islets. Fortunately it floated off at high tide without any serious damage.

On arrival at Pemba Captain Fisher received a message from 'the Prince of Mombasa' *alias* Rizike bin Mbarak el-Mazrui, who had succeeded as governor in the death of his father Mbarak bin Rashid bin Athman in 1806. Rizike was 'short, stout, hard favoured much pock-marked, and one eye a little defective; about thirty-five years of age'. There was an exchange of presents. Evidently, Rizike was already beginning to feel that his position in Pemba was not very secure, for he explained that he had 'long been desirous of placing himself under the protection of the English and the offer was actually made to the Bombay Government'. Fisher was very much in favour of accepting the offer.

Pemba exceeds any place I ever saw in fertility. . . . The inhabitants are a timid inoffensive race, the island bounds in wood and water; cotton grows wild, paddy, maize, a species of calavance and tobacco ground in extreme abundance; they export great quantities to Zanzibar. Perhaps there is no part of the world where an establishment may be secured at so trivial an expense; the returns for our manufactures would be ivory, gold dust and dollars, as well as local produce.

Unfortunately fever and dysentery began to appear amongst the crew of the *Racehorse*, despite plentiful supplies of fresh meat and vegetables. So on October 31, Fisher set sail on his return voyage without having examined the island as thoroughly as he could have wished. Unlike a brother officer a few years later, he decided not to accept the Rizike's offer without reference to the British Government. He reported the offer to the commander-in-chief at the Cape of Good Hope, Rear-Admiral Bertie, who in due course passed his report on to the Secretary to the Admiralty, but the matter proceeded no further after that.

On January 2, 1811, the East India Company's cruiser *Ternate* (Captain Thomas Smee) and schooner *Sylph* (Lieutenant Hardy) sailed from Bombay on 'a voyage of research on the East Coast of Africa'. They made their first landfall in Africa at Socotra and then proceeded down the coast to Zanzibar. On the way he called at Pate, where they were told that there was a small French vessel trading at Zanzibar. On February 23 they dropped anchor off Zanzibar and sent the interpreter on shore to acquaint the *Hakim* (Governor) of their arrival. Next day the two commanders paid the Governor a ceremonial visit. 'He received us,' they reported, 'with great civility, and made many professions of friendship and assistance, which, however, in the sequel we did not find him disposed to act up to. We were saluted on landing and on coming off by the fort and a ketch in the harbour'.

The visitors soon discovered that the Governor, Yakut, was far from popular. 'Yakut's ruling passion is love of power, to attain which he himself lives like a beggar and tyrannically extorts from the inhabitants large sums, which, with his own savings, he faithfully transmits as the price of his continuance in power. The people, however, who live under his sway, detest and despise him.'

As already said, despite all his professions of friendship, he was disobliging to the visitors.

The general conduct of this personage has since proved very unaccommodating. I was desirous during my stay here of procuring a house for the purpose of receiving the visits of the well disposed, and unsuccessfully applied to the *Hakim* for one, or the use of a French factory for a few days. I am told he forbade anyone to furnish me, and has used every endeavour to keep visitors away from the ship. He is a person warmly attached to the French interest, and derives great pecuniary advantages from the trade to this port. The welcome news of the capture of the Isle of France (Mauritius, on December 3, 1810) was brought here by the Surat vessels which arrived in the middle of March. The *Hakim* would not credit the account until it was confirmed by a ship from Muscat a few days ago.

Regarding the town of Zanzibar Smee tells us that

it is large and populous, and is composed chiefly of . . . huts, all neatly constructed with sloping roofs. There are, however, a good number of stone buildings in it belonging to the Arabs and merchants; and in the centre, close to the bank stands a fort; it is square with a tower at each corner, and a battery or outwork towards the sea, in which I saw four or five guns of French (? Portuguese) manufacture remarkable for their length. . . Zanzibar. . . is the only assemblage of habitations on the island that deserves the name of town or even village; for the principal part of the inhabitants without the town being slaves of landholders, are scattered over their respective owners' estates.

The Hakim had 'an assistant or councillor' and three Arab officers to command the garrison, which comprised four to five hundred armed slaves. The revenue was said to amount to 60,000 crowns or dollars, 'though', wrote Smee, 'I have reason to believe it to be much more'. It was derived

from land tenures and customs; and though there is no regular land tax levied, yet it is sometimes resorted to raise a supply, an instance of which happened while we were there. One of the Imam's ships arrived from Muscat with a demand for 25,000 crowns to assist him in opposing the Wahabi, though I sincerely believe it was to defray the repairs of this very ship which brought the demand and which was going to Bengal for that purpose. As this sum was not in the Hakim's possession, he immediately imposed a kind of land tax, so much to be raised in each district, the chief man of which was ordered to collect it and be answerable for its payment at a stated time, in default of which he was to be imprisoned. The other source from which the revenue proceeds is a custom of five per cent allowed by the Imam to be gathered on all imports. This, however, is often very injustly collected and few, I believe, except Arabs ever pay so little on their goods as the lawful sum. . . . We were told the French pay voluntarily a premium of ten dollars each for the slaves they take, to secure the good will of the governor; they are in consequence great favourites, and from this circumstance we may easily account for his colossal coolness to us, which was not lessened by his hearing of the surrender of the Isle of France while we were there, on which occasion both vessels fired a royal salute. . . .

It would appear the Surat traders are subject to much imposition and extortion at Zanzibar, as the Hakim, over and above the usual duties of five per cent, seizes such part of their cargoes as he fancies; and the *nahodas* (captains) of the three vessels now here have declared to me that, in collecting the duties on Surat goods imported, he is not guided by any invoice prices, but fixes a valuation on them far below the prime cost from the hands of the manufacturer; and as he (the Hakim) pays himself in kind, (he) takes good care to detain for his own use such articles are as most saleable at the time, by which means the merchant pays on an average fifteen per cent, and sometimes more, beyond the established rates fixed by the Imam.

The *Ternate* and *Sylph* had reached Zanzibar just at the end of the period of the north-east monsoon, when vessels were beginning to assemble for the purpose of making the return journey to Arabia, the Persian Gulf, and India. At the end of March just under sixty vessels of all descriptions were mustered, 'besides a variety of country boats constantly arriving and departing, and two large boats building. Some seasons upwards of one hundred large dhows, etc., have been known to arrive at this port from Arabia and India'. Nevertheless, Smee was given to understand that its trade appeared to be on the decline and yielding place to Mombasa and Lamu; one is disposed, however, to think that this particular piece of information was not very accurate.

The trade of the coast is chiefly in the hands of the Arabs from Muscat, Mukalla, etc., and a few adventurers from Cutch and the coast of Scinde. The principal imports at Zanzibar are Surat cloths, to the amount of about twelve lakhs of rupees (Rs. 1,200,000) annually, besides beads, cotton, sugar, ghee, fish, dates and grain, and about two hundred candils of iron bar, which is partly distributed for use along the coast. English woollens are in no demand, consequently not imported.[1]

The exports are slaves, elephants' teeth, raw dammar (? copal), rhinoceros' hides and horns, cowries, wax, turtle shells, corn, coconuts, etc.[2]

The duties collected here on merchandise are said to amount to about one and a half lakhs of dollars annually (150,000 dollars), but as imposition and extortion are occasionally resorted to, they may be considerably more. The Imam of Muscat receives from hence a clear sum of 60,000 dollars.

With regard to the principal article of export, namely, slaves, Smee had a good deal to say:

The number of slaves annually sent to Muscat, India the Isle of France (Mauritius) are [sic] estimated at not less than 6,000 to 10,000. . . .

The inhabitants of Zanzibar consist of Arabs (and) descendants of Arabs from Swahili mothers. The Arabs are not very numerous; but the principal part of the slaves and the island property belong to them. . . . The Swahilis form by far the major part of the population, and are almost all slaves to Arabs – 800 or 900 of them sometimes belonging to one individual. They are in general purchased in their native country on the opposite shores, when young, and are brought here by the slave

---

[1] In another part of his report Smee states that china-ware earthen jars, toys and ornaments were also imported from Surat, rice was imported from Bombay and Pemba. The dates came from the Persian Gulf and the salt fish and ghee from Socotra.

[2] In another part of his report Smee adds beeswax to this list. He also says the ivory was principally sent to Surat.

merchants, who dispose of them either to the Arabs, or the merchants, etc., for exportation. Those are fortunate who fall into the hands of Arabs, who are justly famed for their mild treatment of their slaves. They are allowed a small habitation on their master's estate and not being overworked, and the fertile soil furnishing with little trouble the means for their subsistence, they seem to enjoy a considerable portion of contentment and happiness – a strong proof of which is that they propagate freely.

All, however, are not equally well situated; and the advocates for the slave trade ought to witness the market of Zanzibar, after which, if they possess the slightest spark of feeling, I will answer for an alteration in their present opinion. The show commences about four o'clock in the afternoon. The slaves, set off to the best advantage by having their skins cleaned and burnished with coconut oil, their faces painted with red and white stripes, which is here esteemed elegance, and the hands, noses, ears, and feet, ornamented with a profusion of bracelets of gold and silver jewels, are arranged in a line commencing with the youngest, and increasing in the rear accordingly to their size and age. At the head of this file, which is composed of all sexes and ages from six to sixty, walks the person who owns them; behind and at each side two or three of his domestic slaves, armed with swords or spears, serve as a guard. Thus ordered, the procession begins, and as it passes through the market place and principal streets, the owner holding forth in a kind of song the good qualities of his slaves and the high prices that have been offered for them. When any of them strikes a spectator's fancy, the procession stops and a process of examination ensues, which for minuteness is unequalled in any cattle market in Europe. The intending purchaser, having ascertained that there is no defect in the facilities of speech, and hearing, that there is no disease present, and that the slave does not snore in sleeping, which is counted a very great fault, next proceeds to examine the person: the mouth and teeth are first inspected, and afterwards every part of the body in succession, not even excepting the breasts, etc., of the girls, many of whom I have seen examined in the most indecent manner in the public market by their purchasers; indeed there is every reason to believe that the slave dealers almost universally force the young females to submit to their lust previous to their being disposed of. The slave is then made to walk or run a little way to show that there is no defect about the feet; after which, if the price is agreed to, they are stripped of their finery and delivered over to their future master. I have frequently counted between twenty and thirty of these files in the market at one time, some of which contained about thirty (slaves). Women with children newly born hanging at their breasts and others so old they can scarcely walk, are sometimes

H

seen dragged about in this manner. I observed they had in general a very dejected look; some groups appeared so ill fed that their bones seemed as if ready to penetrate the skin.

In addition to Arabs and Africans Smee found a number of Banyans in Zanzibar. They appeared to have the most part of the trade in their hands. Apparently few of them were in any sense permanent residents and for many years to come none of them brought their wives and their families to Zanzibar. Like many of the Arabs, they were seasonal visitors, who arrived with one monsoon and departed with the other. Like the French, they had to submit to the extortions of the Arab officials. In fact, but for the presence of the two British ships they would have been victimized at the close of the trading season of 1811.

The Surat merchants, who had often complained of the Hakim's treatment, represented that he had demanded 3,500 crowns from them as their proportion of the tribute exacted by the Imam of Muscat, and in failure of payment had threatened them with imprisonment. As these people were trading under the English flag, and were, in fact, British subjects, Captain Smee did not conceive that a foreign prince had any right to tax them, especially as they had already paid the customary port dues. Impressed with these sentiments, he made a representation to the Hakim, who consequently withdrew his claims, but privately threatened the merchants with a double imposition after our departure. To prevent this, it was determined to leave the *Sylph* to countenance them during their stay, and convey them across to India at the breaking of the rainy season.

On April 9, 1811 the *Ternate* weighed and made sail for Mocha. Two days before her departure Yakut, 'who had been extremely inimical to us during our stay, and always anxious for us to be gone', paid a long deferred ceremonial call on Captain Smee. 'When both ships dressed and saluted him, and he was notwithstanding his ill behaviour, treated with the greatest attention.' On the day of the *Ternate*'s departure, Henry Golding, a member of the crew, was found dead between decks and was buried on Chapani, which was then known as Frenchmen's Island and was later called Grave Island and was to become the last resting place of many of Golding's compatriots.

As Smee says, almost all the slaves exported from Zanzibar originally came from the mainland. Ivory, which formed the next most important article of export, came entirely from the continent of Africa. Towards the close of the eighteenth century there would appear to have been a marked increase in this trade at the expense of the Portuguese at Mozambique. Tanga, Mombasa and other ports further to the north not unnaturally attracted to their harbours ivory and other commodities from their own immediate hinterland, but to the south of those parts there was, with the exception of Kilwa, no place which could be described as an entrepôt for trade with the interior of Africa. At one time Mozambique had been to a fairly large extent the clearing house for exports from Kilwa and the ports to the south thereof, but these commercial relations had been mainly due to Kilwa's historical connection with the Portuguese. When in 1784 Kilwa submitted to an Omani governor and garrison, its inhabitants began to use the much nearer clearing house at Zanzibar, which was steadily growing more and more popular with Arabs, Indians and Frenchmen alike.

On August 22, 1795 the Governor of Mozambique wrote to Lisbon to say that the Africans from the hinterland of the Portuguese ports on the mainland often chose to make long journeys to Zanzibar, where they received not only superior cloth but also better exchange value than in Mozambique. As he further explained in another letter written a year later, by going there native craft were able to avoid the currents and variable winds which during certain months of the year made navigation difficult in the Mozambique Channel.

In 1797 Francisco José Maria de Lacerda Almeida was appointed governor of the Portuguese territory on the Zambezi. In the following year he set out on expedition which was planned to cross Africa to Angola on the west coast. He himself died on October 18, 1798 in the district of Cazembe on the borders of what are now Northern Rhodesia and the Congo. In his diary he more than once referred to the diversion of trade from Mozambique to Zanzibar. 'Thence these people receive all the ivory exported from the possessions of the Cazembe; whereas formerly it passed in great quantities through our port of Mozambique.' In an entry bearing date September 13, 1798 he explained that this change had come about 'not only because they get more for their ivory, but also because Zanzibar is nearer than our possessions'.

About the same date cups, plates, dark blue cotton cloth, copper wire and cowrie shells were finding their way up from the east coast by way of Karagwe into the kingdom of Buganda, where they were being exchanged for ivory by Kyabagu (*c*.1780) and Sema-kokiro (fl. *c*.1797–1814), two of the rulers of that land.

In 1856 James Erhardt compiled his famous 'Slug Map' showing the trade routes from the East African coast into the interior. One such route led from Kilwa to Lake Nyasa and others from Bagamoyo and other mainland ports in the vicinity of Zanzibar up to what is now Tabora in Tanganyika, whence a well-known trade route struck north to Lake Victoria. It was down such routes as these that the ivory of Cazembe and Buganda must have travelled to the coast and thence by a short sea voyage to Zanzibar.

By the beginning of the nineteenth century Zanzibar had become a very important entrepôt, which was each year making very considerable contributions to the treasury of Oman. An Italian, named Vicenzo Maurizi, who acted as royal physician at Muscat between 1809 and 1814, said the capitation tax on slaves alone was yielding 75,000 dollars a year. Clearly Zanzibar had grown sufficiently in importance to receive more attention from its overlord in Oman than had hitherto been devoted to it.

CHAPTER VI

THE COMING OF SAID BIN SULTAN TO EAST AFRICA, 1814–28

THE Napoleonic Wars were global wars, though not upon the same scale as the world wars of the twentieth century. Between 1793 and 1812 the navies of Great Britain and France had been constantly fighting in the Indian Ocean. Napoleon himself had conceived plans for destroying British rule in India and for that purpose had tried unsuccessfully to make an alliance with the rulers of Oman. French subjects had also tried to assert a commercial and political influence in East Africa. The result was that at the conclusion of peace in 1814 it was quite impossible for the countries dwelling on the shores of the Indian Ocean to revert to the same condition of affairs as had existed at the beginning of the Napoleonic Wars.

In 1793, in so far as Great Britain was concerned, the Indian Ocean had been very much the preserve of the East India Company. Private British traders had from time to time ventured into those seas, but they were frowned upon and not encouraged. Even after the end of the Napoleonic Wars the Indian Board of Control had tried to assert that the Indian Ocean was its private domain, but circumstances had changed after twenty-two years of warfare. During those wars intercourse between Great Britain and India had been from time to time seriously interfered with by French commerce raiders, which had been based not only on French possessions in India but also on the French islands of the Seychelles, Isle of France (Mauritius) and Bourbon (Réunion).

By the treaty of Vienna the Seychelles and Isle of France, which had been captured during the wars, were ceded by France to Great Britain and placed under the administrative charge of the Colonial Office, and not of the Board of Control. The route from the Cape to India had been cleared of commerce raiders by the British Navy and it was obvious that the East India Company would in future have to depend upon assistance from that source for the policing of the sea route to India. 'John Company' had perforce to recognize that the Indian Ocean was no longer its private preserve.

The interests of the Board of Control and the East India Company had been almost entirely centred on India and the lands further to the east. From time to time the Company's ships had called at several of the ports and islands along the East Coast of Africa, but the Company's knowledge of the countries and people dwelling along that coast was very slight and their interest in them was even more slender. On the other hand, the British Government's interest in those countries had been roused from the very date when they first acquired a territorial foothold in the Indian Ocean. As the result of the humanitarian movement in England the first Slave Trade Abolition Act was passed in 1807 and in the following year British cruisers were specially detailed to enforce its provisions in the Atlantic Ocean. Attention was first of all drawn to the traffic off the West African coast and in the Atlantic Ocean, but the capture of the Isle of France and its satellite islands drew attention to the fact that there was likewise a considerable traffic in slaves in East Africa and that amongst the persons deriving large profits therefrom were the ruler of Oman and many of his subjects. For close on a century after the Treaty of Vienna British efforts in East Africa were largely devoted to effecting, firstly, the abolition of the slave trade and, secondly, the abolition of the status of slavery.

The rulers of Oman had been more than once approached by the French during the Napoleonic Wars, but both Sultan bin Ahmed and his son, Said bin Sultan, had eventually decided to throw in their lot with the British. One undoubted reason for their so doing was because the British Government at Bombay was close at hand and was in a position from time to time to render them aid and support in their troubles with their neighbours in the Persian Gulf and in the eradication of piracy in those seas, whereas the French could only give vague promises of such help without being able to implement them. It was likewise to the British interest to have an ally in the Persian Gulf. Whilst abolitionists in England might indignantly exclaim against the tolerance of slavery and the slave trade in East Africa by an Arab ruler in Asia, men nearer to the spot, namely, at Bombay and later at Mauritius, realized, firstly, that these two institutions were centuries old and could not be destroyed by a mere stroke of the pen and, secondly, that their ally at Muscat might well risk his throne, supposing he was ready to offer his whole-hearted support to the cause of abolition and, finally, that they ran a grave risk of forfeiting his friendship by pressing him too hard on this very thorny subject. Consequently, the policy of the British Government was to adopt a gradual approach to the question of abolition and to begin by obtaining minor concessions from Said bin Sultan, which would neither antagonize him nor seriously impair his popularity with his somewhat turbulent subjects. In exchange for such concessions the British Government was ready to adopt a policy of nonintervention in regard to his claims to sovereignty in East Africa.

At the time of his father's death in 1804, Said bin Sultan was only fourteen years of age. He and his elder brother Salim were supplanted as rulers of Oman by their cousin Bedr, the son of that Seif bin Ahmed, who had unsuccessfully attempted to wrest Zanzibar from Said bin Ahmed in 1784. This usurpation did not last long. Bedr bin Seif was assassinated on July 31, 1806, either by Said bin Sultan personally or else with his full knowledge and consent. Thereafter Said bin Sultan remained undisputed ruler of Oman until his death in 1856. At first he had for a nominal colleague his elder brother Salim, who lived until 1821 but was content to leave the reins of government in his younger brother's more capable hands. During the first decade of his rule Said bin Sultan was fully occupied in consolidating his position in Oman and in dealing with affairs in the Persian Gulf. It was not until after the close of the Napoleonic Wars that he began to devote his attention to his East African dominions.

His attention was partly drawn to East Africa by the requests made to him by the British Government to take measures to curtail the slave trade, but it was also drawn in that direction by the territorial claims which had continually been asserted not only by his Busaidi ancestors, but also by the members of the Yorubi dynasty whom his grandfather, Ahmed bin Said, had supplanted. The territory thus claimed included the whole of the coast line from Cape Guardafui to Tungwe Bay, just to the south of Cape Delgado. It also embraced certain islands off the coast of Madagascar and the Comoro Islands as well as Mafia, Zanzibar and Pemba. As Portuguese records show, there were undoubtedly Arabs and 'Moors' trading in all these places in Portuguese times and the Yorubi claim had originally been based upon the fact that

Seif bin Sultan had freed them from Portuguese domination in 1698. But many of the claims had little or no foundation in fact. Doubtless, many of these traders and settlers looked to Oman for protection from the Portuguese and other European and African races, but the Yorubi were never in a position to guarantee such protection. The result was that many of these settlements shook off any allegiance they might have once accorded to Oman and regarded themselves as independent states. Along the Somaliland coast many of the Arab settlements were only too ready to ask for Omani aid in times of stress, but were rarely willing to admit that this placed them under any obligation of allegiance. Further to the south, the involved history of such places as Lamu and Pate is one of constant disputes as to succession; each claimant sought for external aid: one party would almost inevitably appeal to Oman and the other to Mombasa. At Mombasa the Yorubi dynasty had installed members of the Mazrui clan as local governors and these had disavowed their allegiance to Oman when the Busaidi supplanted the Yorubi dynasty in 1744. It is true that in 1784 a written acknowledgement had been obtained from the Mazrui Governor that he held Fort Jesus of the Sultans of Oman, but no attempt had been made to enforce the terms of that document. Pemba, which from Portuguese times, if not earlier, had always been more or less an appanage of Mombasa followed the example of the Mazrui. Any allegiance which the Comoro Sultans had ever owed to Oman was repudiated at the time of the expulsion of the Yorubi dynasty in 1744. Arab and Swahili settlements in the islands off Madagascar and the coast to the south of Cape Delgado apparently followed suit.

The only places along the East African coast, to which at the beginning of the nineteenth century the rulers of Oman could make any substantial claim, were Kilwa Kisiwani, Mafia and Zanzibar. Kilwa had been compelled to accept an Omani governor in about 1784 and Mafia, which was regarded as an appanage of Kilwa, had shared the same fate at the same time. As seen in an earlier chapter, any dispute as to the sovereignty of Zanzibar was definitely decided in 1753 in favour of the Busaidi dynasty after an unsuccessful expedition of the Mazrui from Mombasa. From both Kilwa and Zanzibar a fairly large revenue was arriving at Muscat, mainly derived from a capitation tax imposed on slaves imported into those territories.

Seyyid Said bin Sultan had many ambitious plans in mind. Not the least of these was an extensive shipbuilding programme so as to provide himself in times of war with a strong navy, which would be easily converted into a useful merchant fleet in times of peace. All these designs, however, cost money, which was not easily obtainable from his none too docile subjects in an arid land like Oman. The revenue derived from East Africa was therefore a useful supplement to that obtained from local sources. But, as Atkins Hamerton once wrote, this supplement yielded 'but a small revenue' and Seyyid Said had a strong, and by no means unfounded, suspicion, that his governors and other officers in East Africa were feathering their nests at his expense. He was therefore anxious to set his East African house in better order and to give his own personal superintendence to that task.

Seyyid Said's expansionist plans were mainly due to the Mazrui of Mombasa. If the members of that clan had not definitely thrown down the gauntlet at his feet, military operations in East Africa might have been postponed for quite a considerable time, but their aggressive acts courted hostilities. In 1807 they had installed their own candidate as Sultan of Pate in opposition to the Busaidi candidate. Six years later they had decided to attack Lamu, but met with a disastrous defeat. The people of Lamu then appealed to Oman for aid. Seyyid replied by sending a small garrison and a governor with instructions to build a fort.

In 1814 the Mazrui Sultan of Mombasa died and was succeeded by his son, Abdullah bin Ahmed el-Mazrui. Soon after his accession Abdullah received a message from Oman, directing him to send the customary present to his overlord. Abdullah replied by sending a *deraja* (coat of mail), a *kibaba* (measure of capacity), a small quantity of gunpowder and some bullets. It was intended as an act of defiance and was accepted as such. Affairs in the Persian Gulf still prevented Seyyid Said from taking immediate steps to avenge the insult, but he was resolved that in due course of time Abdullah should learn that

> His jest will savour but of shallow wit,
> When thousands weep more than did laugh at it.

Confident that distance gave them immunity from any attack from Oman, the Mazrui continued their expansionist policy after the death of yet another Sultan of Pate in 1819 by sending troops there to place their nominee on the throne. A message from Seyyid Said directing Abdullah bin Ahmed el-Mazrui to withdraw his men was ignored. In 1822 Seyyid Said decided to send a fleet under his cousin, Hamed bin Ahmed el-Busaidi, to put matters to rights. The ships called first of all at Barawa on the Somali coast and at Lamu. At both these places the inhabitants agreed to recognize the sovereignty of Oman. On arrival at Pate, they found a Mazrui garrison commanded by Mbarak bin Ahmed, brother of the Mazrui Sultan of Mombasa, who at first successfully warded off the assaults of the Omani fleet, but later ran short of munitions and supplies and agreed to withdraw his troops to Mombasa.

This set back was followed by an even more serious one for the Mazrui in Pemba. At the beginning of the nineteenth century the governor representing the Mazrui in Pemba had been Mbarak bin Rashid el-Mazrui, who had built a fort, a house and a mosque at Chwaka at the north-east end of the island. Mbarak bin Rashid had died in 1806 and had been succeeded by his son, Rizike, who, as mentioned in the last chapter, had felt his position to be so insecure that he had three years later offered to place the island under British protection. Nothing, however, had come of the offer. Thereafter Rizike became increasingly more unpopular with the people of Pemba. This unpopularity was due in part to the rivalry of the members of the Ismaili and Miskiri clans who were resident in the island. There also appears to be little doubt that it was fomented by propaganda emanating from the Omani Governor of Zanzibar, Muhammad bin Nasser el-Mauli, doubtless at the instigation of Seyyid Said in Muscat. The discontent also spread to the African inhabitants of Pemba and about a year before the Mazrui lost Pate, two Diwanis (local rulers), named Ngwachani and Athmani, proceeded to Muscat to seek the aid of Seyyid Said bin Sultan.

According to a local chronicle a written compact was drawn up between Seyyid Said bin Sultan and the deputation and was sealed by the typically African ceremony of making blood brotherhood. The local chronicle (written in 1850) gives the text of the pact as follows:

Diwani Ngwachani and Diwani Athmani came to Muscat and made an agreement with the Seyyid (to the effect) that, if the Seyyid should expel the Mazrui, they will be his allies and will be of one accord (*shauri*) with him; and that they will make their people pay dues (*ushuru*) to the

Seyyid; that such payment shall be ghee and mats; and that he (the Seyyid) will be allowed to build wherever he likes. Then the Seyyid agreed and blood brotherhood was made in connection with the agreement. And for whosoever sees this it is a binding agreement and he must comply with it. Written by Mwinyi Shame wa Mwinyi Shame and Shah Ali Athmani and Ngwachani Makame Diwani.

Naturally, the embassage did not escape the notice of the Mazrui. Tradition says Diwan Ngwachani was seized on his return to Pemba and thrown into prison with the threat that he would be killed if Omani troops landed in the island. As no Omanis appeared within the next twelve months, Ngwachani was released. Two months later the unexpected happened. Having learnt of the arrival of the Omani fleet at Pate and that the Mazrui governor had left Pemba on a visit to Mombasa, Muhammad bin Nasser el-Mauli, Governor of Zanzibar, landed in Pemba and captured the Mazrui stronghold at Chwaka.

Mbarak bin Ahmed el-Mazrui was sent with a force from Mombasa to recover the island. He disembarked on the Mkumbuu peninsula and advanced on the fort at Chake Chake, which Muhammad bin Nasser el-Mauli had made his headquarters. Mbarak was unsuccessful in his attack and, falling back on his ships, found that a man-of-war from Zanzibar had captured all of them. In the circumstances, Mbarak had no alternative but to surrender. He was promised free transport for himself and his men to the mainland, provided he renounced on behalf of the Mazrui all claims to the island of Pemba. To these terms Mbarak had perforce to agree.

On his return to Mombasa, Mbarak was bitterly reproached for his want of success. He therefore resolved to make another attempt to regain Pemba. As the Mazrui had lost almost all their shipping in the previous fighting, he had to march his troops overland to Mtangata opposite to Pemba. Thence his troops crossed over to the island by night. In the interval between the two expeditions the garrison on the island had been reinforced from Pate by troops under the command of Hamed bin Ahmed el-Busaidi. A certain amount of fighting followed, but Mbarak made little or no progress. As further reinforcements were believed to be on their way from Oman, he eventually decided in about April 1823, to abandon his attempt, re-embark his men and return to Mombasa. Ever since then Pemba has formed part of the dominions of Zanzibar.

The Mazrui of Mombasa had always regarded Pemba as their granary. Its loss was therefore a serious one. It weakened considerably their power of resistance to further attacks from Oman. Seyyid Said bin Sultan evidently appreciated this fact and decided that the time had come to press home his claims on Mombasa itself. The squadron, which he sent, consisted of no more than three vessels and would appear to have been far too weak to tackle the Mazrui in their stronghold of Fort Jesus, but owing to intervention from a quite unexpected quarter the attempt was never made.

Realizing their complete inability to make any prolonged resistance to any attack by Mombasa, the Mazrui had sent a deputation to Bombay to ask that British protection might be accorded to them. The Bombay Government had declined to grant their request, but it so happened that Captain William Owen of H.M.S. *Leven* was in Bombay at the time. His vessel was engaged on a hydrographical survey of the East African coast and had called at Bombay to revictual and to refit, after which it was due to return to the scene of its labours after calling at Muscat on the way. The deputation from Mombasa got into touch with Owen, who gave them a sympathetic ear and promised to try to help them.

Before leaving Bombay, he had informed the Governor, Mountstuart Elphinstone, that 'the surest, if not the only, means of putting an end to the diabolical traffic in slaves' would be by granting the Mazrui British protection, but Elphinstone had declined to reconsider his decision. Owen, however, was firmly of opinion that the acquisition of Mombasa 'would be a desirable object' and accordingly 'he had made up his mind to take the possession of it until the pleasure of His Majesty should be known'. It was with this resolve that he reached Muscat on Christmas Day, 1823.

Shortly after his arrival Owen had an interview with Seyyid Said bin Sultan. In the course of that interview Owen managed to turn the conversation to the question of the slave trade. He bluntly informed Seyyid Said that his officers in East Africa were making no attempt to put down this traffic. Said replied by informing Owen that he would give Owen full authority to punish slave traders without reference to himself at Muscat. He then proceeded to enlarge upon his claims to British friendship. Owen interrupted him by declaring that the only key to such friendship and the one 'sure way to the Empire of East Africa at which he was aiming' would be 'the total abolition of the slave trade throughout his dominions in the course of the next three years'. He then went on to inform Said that he was shortly proceeding to Mombasa and that he fully expected to be asked to grant its inhabitants British protection. In such circumstances, 'I should feel it my duty to my King to grant it to them, in which my principal motive would be the suppression of that hellish traffic'. Realizing that he had possibly gone a bit too far, Owen hastened to add that he did not wish Seyyid Said to think that he 'intended to operate against his just interests in any way'. If only Said would agree to suppress the slave trade throughout his dominions, then Owen would refuse to grant protection to the Mazrui and would use all his influence to persuade them to submit to Said's authority. Said replied that he would be happy if the British dominions would extend from the rising to the setting of the sun and that it would give him sincere pleasure if they would take Mombasa. Owen thought he detected a note of insincerity in these last words: perhaps a less single-track minded person might have substituted the word 'irony'. 'But', continued Said, 'to put down the slave trade with Muslims, that was a stone too heavy for him to lift without some strong hand to help him.'

Owen left Seyyid Said's presence convinced that, as 'his power and his purse are upheld by this infamous commerce', no good thing would ever come out of Muscat. He weighed and made sail on New Year's Day, 1824, and reached Mombasa on February 8, 1824. Outside the harbour were three blockading vessels. On the island of Mombasa the British flag could be seen flying over Fort Jesus. The *Leven* fired a gun for a pilot, which was answered by the largest of the blockading ships. The commander of that vessel came on board the *Leven* and piloted her into the harbour. As the result of negotiations with the Mazrui, Owen agreed, subject to the confirmation of His Britannic Majesty's Government, to place Mombasa under British protection. The 'Chief of the Mazrui tribe' was to continue to exercise sovereignty over Mombasa and its dependencies and was to have an agent of the protecting power residing on the island. The most important term in the treaty concluded between Owen and the Mazrui was, in the eyes of the first named, that of abolishing the slave trade at Mombasa. In the eyes of the latter, who accepted that term with considerable mental reservations, the most important term was that declaring that Great Britain should reinstate the Chief of Mombasa in his former dominions, which of course included the *terra irredenta* of Pemba. After these negotiations an armistice was arranged. The commander of the blockading squadron was instructed by Owen to proceed in company with the *Leven* to Pemba. Lieutenant Reitz of H.M.S. *Leven* was landed to assume duty as British Resident and the British flag was formally hoisted over Fort Jesus. That flag remained flying over Fort Jesus for over two years.

From Mombasa the *Leven* sailed to Pemba, arriving at Chake Chake on February 15, 1826. Mbarak bin Ahmed el-Mazrui with fifty of his followers sailed on board the *Leven*. It would appear evident that the Mazrui were so insistent on their demands for the immediate restoration of Pemba to Mombasa that Owen decided that he must use his utmost endeavours to bring about that island's early restoration by persuading the Omani governor to yield it up peacefully. Nasser bin Suleiman, the Governor of Pemba, had received instructions from Muscat, to render every assistance to the ships of Owen's surveying squadron. In compliance therewith he supplied the *Leven* with cattle and other provisions, but he was adamant in his refusal to hand over the island to the Mazrui. As he very properly said, it would be a betrayal of his trust for him to do so. This Owen had tacitly to admit. All that he could do in the circumstances was to patch up a *modus vivendi* between the Mazrui and the Omani governor of Pemba. The latter was told that he must respect and give security to the persons and property of the people of Mombasa, so long as they conducted themselves peaceably and paid such dues as Seyyid Said bin Sultan was entitled to claim from them. He also directed Nasser bin Suleiman to hand back a Mazrui owned dhow to its owner. Mbarak bin Ahmed el-Mazrui was allowed to land with his followers, presumably so that they might make suitable arrangements for the management of their property in Pemba. They later rejoined the *Leven* at Zanzibar.

The above is Owen's version of his transactions whilst in Pemba. Somewhat later Nasser bin Suleiman gave his version to Seyyid Said. According to him Owen had demanded the surrender of Pemba 'in threatening and unbecoming language'. He asserted that Owen had used further expressions, which Seyyid Said afterwards declared 'it is not becoming to repeat'. Other evidence shows that Nasser bin Suleiman was prone to exaggeration. Furthermore, as the conversation between him and Owen had to be conducted through an interpreter, there was ample room for misinterpretation. But Owen was a naval officer of the old school, who ill brooked non-compliance with his wishes. An Arab Governor who gainsayed him may well have received the same sort of dressing down as was meted out to errant midshipmen on the quarter-deck of H.M.S. *Leven*.

From Pemba Owen proceeded to Zanzibar. That island had been visited a few weeks earlier by another survey ship, H.M.S. *Barracouta*. One of the officers had placed a few flags as survey marks on some trees on the islands lying off the town of Zanzibar. This had been followed by Owen's proceedings at Mombasa. Clearly flag planting by British naval officers was the order of the day. Consequently, Owen's reception at Zanzibar was not very cordial, if, as the Governor, Muhammad bin Nasser el-Mauli, subsequently alleged, Owen told him that 'he had found friends in the men of Mombasa, but Seyyid Said had not behaved to him as a friend'. Relations were not improved by closer personal contact. Owen was given to understand that the governor 'possessed the entire monopoly of the slave traffic at Zanzibar' and attributed his unfriendliness to this cause. He managed to 'direct' the governor, who in this matter was alleged to have acted 'from either respect or fear', to release two prisoners, whom the Omani blockading squadron had kidnapped at Mogadishu whilst on its way to Mombasa. But he failed to induce the governor to agree to the retrocession of Pemba to the Mazrui.

From Zanzibar Owen sailed to Mauritius. On January 19, 1825, he returned to Mombasa. He was once again urged by the Mazrui to obtain the restoration to them of Pemba. At a meeting held on January 24 he told the leading chief

that he intended going there in a few days and on his arrival he will request the governor to withdraw his people from the lands of Pemba to the fortifications and to restore to them (the people of Mombasa) their grain and cattle, which had been treacherously taken away by the Imam's people. He would, moreover, write to the Imam of Muscat to give up the island of Pemba to them, which request he had no doubt would be granted.

Mbarak bin Ahmed el-Mazrui was again to accompany him, this time in a vessel of his own. The day before the *Leven* was due to sail for Pemba, Owen was informed that Mbarak intended to embark 400 men on his vessel. Owen thereupon summoned a meeting of the chiefs for the following day.

When they had all assembled, Captain Owen informed them that he was surprised to hear that four or five hundred men were going with Mbarak to Pemba, which would look more like war than peace. Therefore he would only take three chiefs with two servants for each to go to Pemba and Zanzibar with them, to hear what is arranged and to tell the same to Suleiman bin Ali (the Sultan of Mombasa) and the people of Mombasa, and they will bring back the orders of Captain Owen to govern the people of Mombasa with regard to Pemba.

According to Nassor bin Suleiman he proceeded on board the *Leven* on its arrival at Pemba, where

he found. . . Mbarak and two hundred men. After some conversation Captain Owen proposed that I should deliver into Mbarak's charge the whole of the subordinate *bandars* (ports) of this island. I refused to comply, stating that I had no authority for such action, but that the Imam's chief Liwali (governor), Ahmed bin Seif, at Zanzibar could probably give a more satisfactory reply to his demand.

Before leaving Pemba, Owen wrote to Lieutenant Emery, who was then the British Resident of Mombasa to inform him that 'the regulations he made last year for the restitution of the private property of the Mombassians have been strictly fulfilled'. In a further letter he informed Emery that

He has written to His Highness Said bin Sultan, wishing him to deliver the island of Pemba to the English as soon as a sufficient force can be sent to occupy the fort, until His Majesty's pleasure be signified. He likewise says he has made the same arrangement for the Island of Pemba as he did last year, viz., that the people of Mombasa should be permitted free ingress and egress to and from Pemba, to enjoy their property and commerce in place, but to pay the duties in the same manner as at Zanzibar to the governor of Pemba. Captain Owen directed that no vessel be permitted into Mombasa from Pemba without a pass from the governor of Chake Chake, in order to secure the payment of duties, and, if any of the inhabitants of Mombasa should err in any manner against His Highness's authority so that the officer at Pemba should think it necessary to arrest them, they are to be sent to Mombasa to the English Commandant with the statement of their crime in writing and he is to keep him on parole to answer, when a ship arrives at Mombasa to try the case.

On February 8, 1825, the *Leven* dropped anchor off Zanzibar. The *Narrative* of Owen's voyage tells us that

he made the necessary arrangements with Seyyid Muhammad (bin Nasser el-Mauli) of Muscat for preserving the peace of North East Africa until the British Government should have come to a determination respecting the acceptance of the territory, and until then Captain Owen desired that no force or illegal interference should be attempted by the Imam's officers.

Once again, we have another version of the transactions from the opposite party. According to Ahmed bin Seif, the actual Governor of Zanzibar, Owen announced

that, unless His Highness agreed to abolish the Slave Trade at every port under his authority on the coast of Africa, he would be deprived of the whole of his dominions in that quarter, but that, if he agreed to this measure, the settlements of the Portuguese should be taken from them and added to his dominions.

As previously said, we have to bear in mind the possibilities of misinterpretation, distortion and exaggeration of what Owen actually said. But, in reporting this conversation, Ahmed bin Seif, suggested to Seyyid Said bin Sultan that the latter offer might be well worth accepting, 'as the territory (of the Portuguese) was of considerable extent and value'. It is therefore quite possible that, whatever Owen might by his actual language have intended to convey, he was interpreted as having uttered something partly in the nature of a threat and partly of an inducement to persuade Seyyid Said to give his consent to the total abolition of the slave trade throughout his African dominions.

On February 10, 1825, Owen weighed anchor and made sail for the Seychelles. This was his last appearance in East African waters. The Protectorate which he had established over Mombasa lasted until July 26, 1826, when the British flag was hauled down by Captain Charles Acland of H.M.S. *Helicon*, because the Mazrui announced that they were not prepared to abide by the terms of the agreement which they had made with Owen. Before this the British Government had refused to ratify Owen's proceedings, because, firstly, reports which had been received from Captain C. R. Moorsom of H.M.S. *Ariadne* indicated 'that there did not appear on his proceeding to Mombasa any general disposition on the part of the inhabitants to belong to Great Britain', and secondly,

I

'because no ratification of the Protectorate could take place without compromising the good faith of the British nation with other powers, with whom it has long been united in the most cordial amity'.

During the existence of that protectorate there was a general cessation of hostilities in East Africa. The rank and file of the inhabitants were not interested in the dynastic and territorial claims of the Busaidi and Mazrui. They were only too anxious to follow their peaceful callings. When Owen proclaimed the British Protectorate of Mombasa, the inhabitants of Mombasa and the crews of the blockading squadron had proceeded to fraternize. As Owen admitted, Nasser bin Suleiman, the Governor of Pemba, had faithfully carried out his promise to Owen to arrange for the restitution to the Mazrui of their private property in that island. Captain Moorsom later informed the naval officer commanding at the Cape, that 'many complaints have been preferred to Commodore Nourse and myself, that the stipulations had not been attended to; but on investigation it did not appear that blame attached to the governor'. Nasser bin Suleiman in fact carried on a friendly correspondence with the British Resident at Mombasa, to whom he showed innumerable acts of courtesy. He also at the Resident's request supplied the British establishment with provisions and other things, such as materials for the building of a boat. As long as the British flag flew over Fort Jesus there was a free and uninterrupted commerce between Mombasa and the islands of Pemba and Zanzibar.

When their conduct is compared with that of Seyyid Said's officers, Owen's protégés at Mombasa do not stand in nearly so favourable a light. They detained the wife of Nasser bin Suleiman, Governor of Pemba, as a prisoner despite the armistice. Even after Owen had directed that they should send her back to her husband, they delayed to do so for a further two months. When a Pemba dhow was wrecked on the coast to the south of Mombasa and plundered by the local inhabitants, the Mazrui absolutely declined to do anything to assist the British Resident in securing restitution of the stolen property and punishment of the offenders and even actively obstructed his attempts to see that justice was done. The observations of the hydrographer, James Horsburgh, in his *Indian Directory* seem therefore very much in to the point, when he tells us that at this date 'Zanzibar is preferable to the other ports on this coast; and there is less chance of treachery, it being under the government of Oman and more civilized'. As Commodore Christian wrote of the Mazrui after Captain Acland had hauled down the flag of the protecting power over Fort Jesus, 'they have no great claim to protection from me, nor any right to expect that I should interfere in any dispute or difference they may have with the Imam of Muscat. Humanity alone would justify any representation to His Highness in regard to them'.

The Governor of Mauritius (Sir Lowry Cole) wrote to Seyyid Said on September 16, 1826, to inform him that the British Protectorate over Mombasa had been withdrawn and to commend the inhabitants to his 'benevolent consideration'. To this letter Seyyid Said replied that he was 'pleased beyond measure that the English Government has abandoned the settlement of Mombasa and removed its flag thence. I consider this measure had been dictated by a feeling of delicacy towards myself, and am grateful to the King of England and to Your Excellency on that account'. He made no reference in the letter to the attitude which he proposed to adopt towards the Mazrui.

That attitude was revealed in a letter which he sent to Mombasa towards the end of 1826. Seyyid Said demanded the immediate surrender of Fort Jesus to the bearer of the letter and intimated that failure to comply with this demand would be the signal for the renewal of hostilities. Seyyid Said's messenger was told in reply that the Mazrui were prepared to recognize the overlordship of Oman, but would never surrender the fort unless compelled by force of arms. As proof of his desire to remain at peace with Seyyid Said, the Sultan of Mombasa offered to send certain of his relatives to Muscat to negotiate a friendly settlement with Seyyid Said.

These envoys set out at the end of the south-west monsoon of 1827. When half-way on their mission they met the Omani fleet under the personal command of Seyyid Said bin Sultan. Its numbers and armament were so formidable that, on paper at any rate, it appeared to be beyond the power and means of the Mazrui to offer any effective resistance.

The fleet reached Mombasa on January 4, 1828. An abortive attempt was made to procure the surrender of Mombasa without bloodshed. It was followed by a corvette entering Mombasa and bombarding the town. Negotiations were then reopened and eventually a convention was drawn up which both parties swore

on the Koran to observe. Fort Jesus was to be handed over to
Seyyid Said, who was to be allowed to garrison it with fifty men of
the Hinawi clan, who were friendly to the Mazrui. Salim bin
Ahmed, the Mazrui Sultan of Mombasa, was to be allowed to
reside in the fort with members of his family, but was to acknowledge the sovereignty of Oman. He was also to be allowed to collect
customs duties and to retain half thereof. On January 7, 1828 the
red flag of Oman was hoisted over Fort Jesus. Subsequently,
soldiers from the Omani fleet arrived daily at the fort on ostensible
visits to their comrades in the garrison. None of them, however,
was ever seen to leave. The result was that in the course of a few
days there were 200 Omani soldiers in Fort Jesus.

By this date the north-west monsoon was well set in and an
immediate return to Muscat was therefore out of the question.
Seyyid Said was anxious to inspect his East African dominions and
to give the necessary instructions for their better administration.
He accordingly proceeded with the majority of his fleet and troops
to Zanzibar. He arrived to find there an American merchant,
named Edmund Roberts, who on January 27, 1828, addressed a
memorial to him setting out at length his many complaints against
Seyyid Said's officials in Zanzibar. Later, when Roberts had
returned to the United States, he wrote a number of letters to
Senator Levi Woodbury of New Hampshire urging the appointment of an American Consul at Zanzibar. In that correspondence
he describes Seyyid Said's first arrival at the place which he
eventually made his home.

In the month of January last the Sultan of Muscat arrived at the
island of Zanzibar from a successful expedition against two of his
revolted places, Mombasa and Pate, bringing with him a force consisting of a 64 gun ship, three frigates of 36 guns, and two brigs of 14 guns
and about one hundred armed transport dhows, with about six thousand
soldiers. Immediately after his arrival he sent for me and inquired into
my situation, treated me in the most friendly manner, and ordered me
to be paid forthwith. I had a number of interviews with him during my
stay there. He showed an almost entire ignorance of the country, its
resources &c &c, and I should not at all exaggerate if I should even say
its situation. He frequently expressed a strong desire to be on a friendly
footing with the United States and to enter into a commercial treaty
with them. . . .

You ask if he has any 'navigation' of consequence. If you can form
any estimate from the number of vessels at Zanzibar, it would appear

to be very extensive. There were at Zanzibar, exclusive of transport dhows, upwards of two hundred and fifty sail of dhows, bagalas and other craft with pilgrims, drugs, coffee, fish, water &c &c from Suez, Mocka, Jedda, the seaport of Mecca and the island [sic] of Berbera in the Red Sea, and from Bombay, the ports of the Persian Gulf, the coast of Africa as far south as Mozambique, and I saw but a small part of their commerce. I endeavoured to ascertain the value and extent of their commerce, and the number of their vessels &c, but I could not obtain any satisfactory information. . . .

. . . I believe I told you the object the Sultan had in view in sending me to obtain bombs, shells &c. He declares the Portuguese shall not own an inch of territory on the East Coast of Africa. 'Have I forgotten', said he, 'the treatment my ancestors received from the vile Portuguese three hundred years ago – from these vile hogs (you know they detest pork having a mixture of Judaism in their religion) from those accursed worshippers of wooden images &c &c?' – 'By the beard of Mahomet,' said he, at the same time stroking down the noble beard which reached to his girdle, and the fire flashing from his eyes, as though he would annihilate the whole race with a look, 'I will overwhelm them like the sand of the desert.' Mozambique he cannot take without bombarding it, and he is anxious the English Government should not know of his designs and therefore he wants his battering train from this country. The bomb vessels he can easily construct.

It is unfortunate that this description of Seyyid Said comes from a man with a personal axe to grind and who – to put it somewhat mildly – was evidently exceedingly prone to exaggeration. Having apparently reduced Mombasa into his possession, it is quite probable that Roberts found Seyyid Said in an exultant mood. It may be that he somewhat incautiously spoke of the possibility of expelling the Portuguese from Mozambique but, whatever he may have said, we can be certain that he did not do it 'stroking down the noble beard which reached to his girdle', because we know for a fact from a portrait of him made a few years later by a compatriot of Roberts that Seyyid Said's well trimmed beard reached nowhere near his girdle. As so recently as February, 1826, Seyyid Said had entered into a treaty of friendship and commerce with the Governor of Mozambique, one may perhaps crave leave to doubt whether Roberts' version of Seyyid Said's words has a scintilla of foundation in fact.

Said bin Sultan had, however, not come to Zanzibar merely to listen to the complaints of disgruntled American traders. He had come to look at a land regarding which he had heard much whilst in Muscat. Having looked on that land, he saw that it was good. It was no Pisgah view. Almost from the very first moment that he set foot on the island's shore, he made up his mind to make it his permanent residence. Thereafter, as Captain Brucks of the Indian Navy reported a year or two later, Seyyid Said's 'very respectable naval force. . . is, with Zanzibar his principal care and study'. On the occasion of this, his first, visit and on other later occasions, affairs on the Persian Gulf called him back from time to time to Oman, but he always went there with great reluctance. In later years the Bombay Government more than once instructed the British Consul in Zanzibar to represent to Seyyid Said that his Asiatic dominions needed more care and attention than could be given to them by a ruler residing in Zanzibar.

One of the first measures taken by him was to make better arrangements for the administration of his African dominions. The past history of Oman had shown that the tie between that country and its overseas dependencies was always very slight and there was a tendency to disregard orders from headquarters and at times even to declare their independence of the rulers at Oman. The case of the Mazrui at Mombasa is one in point. Even members of the reigning family exhibited this tendency. Seyyid Said's father, Sultan bin Ahmed, had tried to solve the problem by appointing a non-Arab, namely, one Yakut bin Ambar el-Habshi, an Abyssinian eunuch, as Governor of Zanzibar. Neither Dallons nor Smee who visited Zanzibar in 1803 and 1812 respectively, had a high opinion of him. Both had much to say about his exactions from foreign visitors and residents, which were made in the name of his royal master, but which were as often as not made without the Sultan's knowledge or consent and went to line the Governor's own pocket. Dallons further reported that he was very much under the thumbs of the members of the Harthi clan, who had long been settled in Zanzibar and regarded the Busaidi as *parvenus*. According to him, they were frequently intervening in matters relating to the administration of government.

Yakut died some time before 1820 and was succeeded by another Abyssinian slave, Ambar bin Sultan el-Habshi, who died two years after his appointment. Seyyid Said then entrusted the reins of government of the whole of East Africa to an Arab, Abdulla bin Juma el-Barwani, but he was soon dismissed on suspicion of treachery. His successor Ali bin Nasser el-Jabri, died after three years and was followed by Khalfan bin Suleiman el-Abri, who made himself intensely unpopular in Zanzibar and was eventually by Seyyid Said's orders thrown into prison where he died. He was followed by Muhammad bin Nasser el-Mauli, who appears to have been sent out from Oman especially to deal with Captain Owen after the declaration of the British Protectorate of Mombasa. Thereafter Seyyid Said entrusted the Government of Zanzibar to a near kinsman, Nasser bin Hamed el-Busaidi, who appears to have been in administrative charge of the island at the time of Seyyid Said's arrival in 1828.

After his arrival Seyyid Said decided to leave his favourite son, Khalid, as governor of his East African dominions. Khalid, the son of a Circassian concubine, was then only thirteen years of age – two years younger than his father had been when he recovered the throne of Oman. The appointment was of course made as an intimation to the world at large, which included Arab residents in Zanzibar, that Seyyid Said intended to take the governance of the island into his own hands as part of his domain. At the same time a thirteen year-old boy could not be expected to hold his own without the assistance of an older person. For this purpose Seyyid Said selected a kinsman, Suleiman bin Hamed el-Busaidi, brother of the most recent governor of Zanzibar, to act as Khalid's *wazir* (adviser). As Said himself was shortly returning to Oman and as even in later years there were long spells in which urgent affairs on that region called him back from Zanzibar to that country, a great deal depended in those early days on the capability and loyalty of the wazir. After events were to show that the Seyyid Said's selection was a wise one.

Suleiman bin Hamed was later described by a British Consul as being 'not a clever man, but a kind, good sort of a person. . . . This man has much influence with the pagan chiefs on the coast of Africa'. The following is a description of him given by Captain Guillain who met him in 1846.

Seyyid Suleiman was at this date fifty-seven years of age. He was a man of middle height, but sturdily built, of a bronze tint, with large black eyes and a thin aquiline nose, a thick and hanging upper lip, indicating a satisfied luxuriousness and cruelty (which was not true of his character, because, although he is voluptuous, he is by no means bloodthirsty). He has a long, greyish beard. His face is noble and his appearance inspiring. He is in fact a remarkable specimen of the Arab type. He is endowed with plenty of common sense, and is liberal minded and tolerant in apparent contradiction to the religious dogmas which he professes. At the time of my first visit to Zanzibar (in 1838) he gave me proof of this tolerance which was as flattering as it was convincing, by presenting his wife and daughter to me unveiled.

Suleiman is preoccupied with the cares of government and his own private affairs, which include commercial speculation and agricultural developments, which are each of them equally extensive. He is always thereby increasing his wealth and has become the biggest landed proprietor in the country after the Sultan.

Notwithstanding his many preoccupations, he spares the time to make himself very obliging to the French. . . .

He outlived Seyyid Said and acted as wazir to two of the latter's sons and successors, Majid and Barghash, dying on December 10, 1873, when not far short of ninety. He maintained his ordinary health to the very end and was able to appear in public and sit in *baraza*. One day after ascending the palace steps, he suddenly lost his power of speech and the end came quickly. As was perhaps natural, in his old age the liberal minded tendencies of his younger days gave way to a more reactionary spirit. Hence Dr. Kirk's obituary is not nearly so complimentary as the character given to him by Guillain.

The late Seyyid Suleiman, as representative of the Beit el Wakil (the house of the administrator), and holding an influence on the court above that of the Sultan himself, took an active part in everything that passed in Zanzibar within the memory of the oldest inhabitant. A confirmed slave dealer, when the traffic was largely carried on with Bourbon and the Brasils, and partisan throughout with the French, he has always opposed English influence. Obstructive to every advance, and mostly selfishly corrupt, while the most influential of those about the Sultan, in his loss little is to be regretted. His death, however, weakens the House of al-Busaidi in Zanzibar; for although no friend of the present Sultan (Barghash), who, however, unable to set him aside, found it politic to give him a position in public above himself; he was a great support to the late Seyyid Said, and all looked to him, especially since the death of Muhammad bin Salim, as to the father of this house. . . . There is no one to take the old man's place, or command the services of the people of the coast as he did.

This indictment is in many ways a scathing one, but it has to be remembered that it comes from the pen of a man with directly opposite views to those of Seyyid Suleiman, especially in regard to such matters as slavery and the slave trade. The last two sentences thereof do, however, contain a somewhat grudging tribute to the old man's constant fidelity to the ruling family in Zanzibar. Like Bismarck, his faults were neither few nor small but he might well have had written upon his tomb words like unto those which the Iron Chancellor caused to be inscribed upon his grave; 'A true Arab servant of Seyyid Said bin Sultan'.

The youthful Khalid and his wazir were given a large house at Mtoni as their residence. The much mutilated ruins of this building still stand some three miles to the north of the town of Zanzibar. In Seyyid Said's day there was no road between it and the town and the Sultan himself, as a rule, made the journey between the two places by boat. It would appear to have been selected by Seyyid Said precisely because it was rather difficult of access. Many of the Arab settlers in the island – and in particular the members of the el-Harthi clan – did not relish the idea of the island coming under more direct rule from Oman and might well have tried by a *coup d'état* to get rid of or make a prisoner of Seyyid Said's youthful delegate. The risk of such a *contretemps* was not quite so great in the country as in the town. The palace at Mtoni was, moreover, ready for immediate entry into possession. It had been built by an enterprising Arab named Saleh bin Haramili el-Abri, who is reputed to have imported cloves from Bourbon in about 1818 and to have planted the two earliest clove plantations in the island at Mtoni and Kizimbani. During the governorship of his kinsman, Khalfan bin Suleiman el-Abri, he appears to have thrived considerably, but later he fell upon evil times. Cloves were not his only line of business. His visit to Bourbon had shown him that another extremely profitable line would be the supply of slave labour to that island. In 1822 Seyyid Said had prohibited the traffic in slaves with Christian races, but Saleh bin Haramili had disregarded that injunction. Seyyid Said taught him the errors of his ways by depriving him of his house and plantations with the result that Saleh died a beggar.

In addition to the acquisition of these properties Seyyid Said at about this date acquired other properties in the island. He obtained a town house by purchase from a leading Arab. He took possession, as former master, of a plantation at Kichwele belonging to his Abyssinian ex-slave, the former Governor Yakut. By similar means he acquired another plantation at Bumbwini, belonging to a deceased *akida* (military commander) named Tangwizi. Finally, he acquired by purchase a plantation at Mukangageni from Saleh bin Haramili's son.

Seyyid Said left Zanzibar for Oman in about April 1828, soon after the south-west monsoon began to blow. Most of his troops and all his fleet returned with him. A brig-of-war and a few soldiers were left behind to garrison the fort in Zanzibar and to lend support to Seyyid Suleiman bin Hamed and the youthful governor. In all probability Seyyid Said hoped to return before the end of the north-west monsoon, but affairs in Oman detained him longer than he could have wished. It was not until November 1833, that he was able to set out again for Zanzibar.

There is very little record of what transpired in Zanzibar during his five years' absence, but during that time Seyyids Suleiman and Khalid managed to hold their own. In September 1829 H.M.S. *Jaseur* called at the island. The usual visits of courtesy were exchanged between ship and shore. On September 10 some of the British officers were invited to a banquet at Mtoni, where they were received by a military guard of honour. After the repast the senior officers returned to their ship by boat, but certain of the junior officers decided to proceed by land, but 'they found it a much more serious and disagreeable undertaking than they had imagined, on account of the track being intercepted by streams and marshy ground'.

On the whole the visitors were not greatly impressed by what they saw.

The town is large, but not populous. The streets are narrow, badly paved and dirty; and most of the best houses have been allowed to fall into decay. The shops are few and badly stocked. . . . We went to the slave market every day, but found only a few of those poor creatures exposed for sale in consequence, we presumed, of our presence. We always observed amongst them some pretty girls, gaily dressed, decorated with flowers in their hair, and painting upon their persons, in order to set them off to the best advantage, after the same fashion as practised in the Brazils. The Imam of Muscat, being bound by his treaty with England, to prohibit the slave trade in all places within his government, we had reason to believe that the enquiries of Captain Lyons respecting the slave trade had put a temporary restraint upon their traffic. . . .

They told us that the slave trade was at an end, the market was only used for the purposes of the domestic trade; however, we had every reason to feel assured that it was still covertly practised.

The British officers appear, however, to have been favourably impressed by the fourteen year-old Khalid, who 'had a great taste for manly exercises, and was particularly distinguished for skill in horsemanship. He had brought some fine Arabians with him, which was the more necessary as horses were very scarce in Zanzibar, there being not more than five in the island'.

In 1835, when Seyyid Said was once more back in Oman and the reins of government were again in the hands of Seyyids Suleiman and Khalid, the American warship *Peacock* visited Zanzibar. By that date Khalid had attained the age of twenty and was beginning to take a more active part in the administration of the island. Every afternoon after the hour of prayer he used to preside over a court of justice held in the open air outside the gate of the fort. He was assisted in this task by three judges. There were a number of outward and visible signs of peaceful progress. An aqueduct was under construction from some springs at Chem Chem which was eventually to bring water to Mtoni palace and also down to the seashore so that ocean going vessels could avail themselves thereof. A new palace was being built in the town of Zanzibar.

CHAPTER VII

SEYYID SAID BIN SULTAN IN ZANZIBAR, 1833–56

THE principal reason which brought Seyyid Said back to East Africa, was fresh trouble with the Mazrui at Mombasa. In 1829 they had managed to recover Fort Jesus and to make a prisoner of Said's governor, Nasser bin Suleiman. For various reasons only a very half-hearted attempt was made to recover the fort. Eventually Said re-embarked his troops and sailed to Zanzibar, leaving only a frigate to blockade Mombasa.

When Captain Hart of H.M.S. *Imogene* arrived at Zanzibar on January 30, 1834, he found the Sultan installed in his palace at Mtoni. Said was still mortified by his want of success against the Mazrui and asked Hart if the English would object to him obtaining military aid from Madagascar, but, as Hart's testimony shows, however disappointing the failure before Mombasa may have been, Seyyid Said had at least the satisfaction of knowing that in Zanzibar his kinsman, Seyyid Suleiman, could render him a faithful and just account of his stewardship.

His Highness the Imam's whole revenue is stated to be about 250,000 dollars a year; that is about 150,000 from Zanzibar and 100,000 from Muscat. . . . Previous to His Highness' visit last year, he only received about 30,000 to 40,000 dollars (from Zanzibar). . . . This revenue appears very small when compared to his fleet and establishment. However, he is said to be very rich, arising from trade, and by property coming to him at the death of his servants, who are expected to leave him their riches.

He has a squadron of one line of battle ship, three frigates, corvettes and a brig, which appears to constitute his great pleasure and amusement; and he has now given an order to the English brig (then lying off Zanzibar) to bring out naval stores to the amount of 30,000 dollars. When on board he conducts everything himself, gets under weigh, shifts her berth, or brings her to anchor by giving every word of command.

He is said to have twenty merchant ships of different kinds, but I could not learn where or how they were employed. There was only one of that description at Zanzibar, and she was going to the Mauritius, to endeavour to get an engineer for the steam-engine (for a sugar cane crushing plant) she brought thence last year. . . .

His Highness the Imam possesses absolute power. He has lately built a palace at Zanzibar, and is giving every encouragement to trade and improving the island by planting clove trees and sugar cane, which thrive in a remarkable manner. It has been supposed that His Highness will on some future day make this his chief residence in preference to Muscat. . . .

The Imam has only about two or three hundred troops, which he brought from Muscat, but there appear to be a great number of police armed with spears.

Hart was given to understand that, 'if things remain quiet at Muscat, he will remain here (sc. at Zanzibar) for a year or two'. In fact he remained only until July or August 1834, when he took advantage of the south-west monsoon to return to Oman. One of the chief objects of his return was to prepare another expedition against Mombasa. That expedition sailed from Muscat with the north-east monsoon at the end of 1834. Once again the expedition failed to recover Mombasa and Said proceeded down the coast to Zanzibar. On this occasion he made only a short stay at Zanzibar and returned to Muscat as soon as the south-west monsoon set in. Before leaving he gave instructions that an attempt should be made to undermine Mazrui influence in Mombasa by bribery of certain of the leading inhabitants.

When he set out on his fourth voyage to East Africa, he found that the seeds of corruption had yielded a good harvest of discontent. He reached Mombasa in the last days of 1836. He managed to gain a foothold on the island at Kilindini after encountering little or no resistance. Thereafter he was in no hurry to force the issue. The Mazrui were suffering almost daily from desertions and in February 1837, Rashid bin Salim the last Mazrui ruler of Mombasa, sued for peace. The terms of the new treaty were in almost every respect the same as those of 1828. Rashid was allowed to remain Governor of Mombasa, but was to acknowledge the suzerainty of Seyyid Said. He was no longer to reside in Fort Jesus, but was to hand the place over to Said's troops. After having taken possession of Fort Jesus and having placed a garrison of 500 Baluchi and Arab soldiers inside, Seyyid Said sailed for Zanzibar. Some months later Rashid bin Salim el-Mazrui proceeded to

Zanzibar to do formal homage to Seyyid Said. The latter gave him a gracious reception. Nevertheless, he was determined that there could be no peace at Mombasa until the governorship of that place was taken out of the hands of the Mazrui. On his instructions Seyyid Suleiman bin Hamed tried to bribe Rashid bin Salim into relinquishing the post. Rashid was offered a lump sum down of 10,000 dollars and an annual pension of 300 dollars together with a residence in Zanzibar. Alternatively, he was offered the governorship of either Pemba or Mafia. He rejected all three offers and returned to Mombasa.

Less than two months after Rashid bin Salim's return to Mombasa a corvette arrived there. It brought Seyyid Khalid bin Said, who was by then a youth of nineteen, and Seyyid Suleiman bin Hamed. The leading Mazrui hastened on board the vessel to pay their respects to the Sultan's son. After exchange of the usual courtesies Khalid invited his visitor to enter the fort and see Suleiman bin Hamed, who wished to speak to him about some matter of business.

Rashid entered the fort and was at once seized and thrown into prison. Similarly some twenty-five to thirty other Mazrui, in groups of two or three, were enticed into the fort only to meet with the same fate.

When it was realized that none of the Mazrui were coming out of the fort, suspicion was roused. During the night all the rest of the clan fled to the mainland. Those who had fallen into their enemies' hands were taken on board the corvette and conveyed to Zanzibar. After remaining there about a month, the prisoners were despatched to Bandar Abbas in the Persian Gulf. Some of them were thrown overboard. On arrival the survivors were placed in irons and thrown into prison, where they all died of starvation.

'Said's war at Mombasa', wrote Colonel Miles, 'had been marked throughout by a series of perfidies and this cruel murder of the gallant Rashid and his companions fittingly completed his conquest.' It is impossible to say that this verdict is wrong. The story leaves an indelible stain on Seyyid Said's character.

The elimination of the leading Mazrui removed the most formidable of the disputants of Seyyid Said's authority on the East African mainland and made his possession of Pemba doubly sure. But it by no means left him in undisputed possession of the East African coast, as was evidenced in 1843 by the crushing defeat
E

which the people of Siu on the island of Patta inflicted upon a strong punitive expedition sent to reduce them to submission. In other places there was a tendency for the local Arab governors to flout those of Seyyid Said's orders which did not please them and it was not always possible to deal adequately with them, when they showed themselves to be recalcitrant. Even more slender were Seyyid Said's claims to sovereignty of places to the south of Cape Delgado, which, on the score that Arabs were settled there, included various islands off the coast of Madagascar. When the French proceeded to occupy certain of these places, Seyyid Said could do no more than raise an ineffectual protest.

In Zanzibar itself Seyyid Said found that he had plenty to do before his East African house could really be set in order. In the first place, he discovered that there was at least one other ruler on the island, namely, the person who is commonly known as the Mwenyi Mkuu and who was recognized by the Hadimu as their hereditary ruler. More will have to be said about Said's dealings with the African races of Zanzibar and Pemba in a later chapter. Here it will suffice to say that he agreed to recognize the Mwenyi Mkuu's authority over the free African population of Zanzibar and to grant him a subsidy.

The more immediately pressing problem confronting him was how to deal with those of his own compatriots whom he found settled in Zanzibar. Hitherto in Oman the Sultan – Yorubi and Busaidi alike – had only been recognized by other Arab clans as being *primus inter pares*. The state had need of a titular head, but the extent to which the Sultan could assert his sovereignty over his very turbulent peers entirely depended upon the individual for the time being holding the post and there was always the possibility that, as happened with the Yorubi in 1744, the reigning family might be ousted by some rival clan. Ahmed bin Said, the founder of the Busaidi dynasty, had strengthened his position by combining with his temporal office the spiritual one of Imam and of Muscat. Ahmed's son and successor, Said, had likewise combined the two posts. He retained that of Imam after his deposition in 1791 by his brother, Sultan bin Ahmed. After Said bin Ahmed's death in 1803 the Imamate, which in principle had always been elective, passed out of the Busaidi family. Seyyid Said bin Sultan, though often so styled by Europeans, made no claim to be, and was never recognized by his compatriots as being, Imam of Muscat and was entirely dependent on the secular arm for the assertion of his sovereignty.

As his early experiences had taught Seyyid Said, rival clans were not the only persons who might unseat the ruling Sultan. Members of his own family were just as likely to make the same attempt. As one of Said's sons told a British Consul many years later, there was only one rule governing the royal succession and that was the longest sword. It speaks much for the strength of Seyyid Said's personal character that he, who had been deposed at the age of thirteen and had come back into his own again only two years later, should thereafter have been able to hold his own in Oman and Zanzibar for half a century. There were plenty of intrigues and even rebellions in Oman, but he experienced no such troubles at the hands of his compatriots in Zanzibar. As a mere youth he evidently inspired the confidence of his elders and in his old age he had earned his subjects' affection and respect.

Several things largely helped to make Seyyid Said's path smooth in Zanzibar. First and foremost, he was fortunate in the choice of a number of very loyal servants as governors in his East African dominions especially in the long and faithful service rendered at all times to him and his sons and successors by his kinsman, Suleiman bin Hamed el-Busaidi. Secondly, the formidable armada which accompanied Seyyid Said on his first visit to Zanzibar in 1828, followed as it was by frequent visits of his men-of-war, was a strong deterrent against native rebellion. Thirdly, the number of immigrants from Oman and other ports of Arabia, who followed in Seyyid Said's wake and were largely dependent upon him for support and protection, soon outnumbered the earlier Arab settlers in Zanzibar and Pemba, who might otherwise have been a constant source of trouble.

The most prominent of the earlier Arab colonists belonged to the el-Harthi clan. It was reported in 1859 that 'the members of this tribe possess very large landed estates and numerous slaves; they are the oldest Arab settlers in the island and appear always to have an idea of some day obtaining the sovereignty of it'. At that date it was alleged that the adult male members of the clan numbered about eight hundred and that Abdulla bin Salim, the head of the clan, possessed 1,500 slaves, all armed and ready to hand to take part in any quarrel which he might have. Fortunately, they had made themselves unpopular and had little or no influence with the other leading Arab clans of Shaksi, Miskiri, and Shatri. All the same, their armed slave retinues were obviously a potential source of danger to order and good government. There was reason to believe that they were out to foment trouble and discontent wherever they could in the hope that they could thereby obtain power for themselves. When Seyyid Said was resident in Zanzibar, he was well able to nip any such conspiracies in the bud. When affairs in the East called him back to Oman, he always made Abdulla bin Salim, the leading member of the Harthi clan, accompany him as a hostage for the good behaviour of his kinsmen in Zanzibar.

Earlier Arab settlers in Zanzibar were not the only compatriots of his who caused Seyyid Said a great deal of worry and trouble. There were also the persons, who are referred to in the correspondence of early British Consuls as 'the Northern Arabs', who for many years had been a regular feature of the life of Zanzibar. In 1799 Lieutenant Bissell described how 'the small trading vessels from Muscat and the Red Sea, after discharging their cargoes, which are chiefly dates, always dismantle and move into an inner harbour at the back of the town and wait till the return of the monsoon'. But the crews were not just ordinary seafaring men, guilty of no more than the occasional outburst in which sailors of all nations sometimes indulge at the end of a long and tedious voyage. Though he was writing after Seyyid Said's death at a time when the reins of government were in the hands of a weaker ruler, Colonel Rigby's description of the Northern Arabs shows the character of the people whom Said had to control.

These pirate boats leave their own coasts just after the commencement of the north-east monsoon and arrive at Zanzibar during December, January and February, and they leave the coast of Africa to return north with the commencement of the south-west monsoon about the middle of March; each boat is crowded with armed men; they bring nothing for sale; and they take no cargo back; in fact their boats are so filled with men that they could not possibly take any cargo. Their sole object in coming to the coast is to procure slaves either by kidnapping or by clandestine sale.

During the time the Northern Arabs are here, Zanzibar resembles a city with a hostile army encamped in its neighbourhood; every person who is able to do so sends his children and young slaves into the interior of the island for security; people are afraid to stir out of their houses,

K

and reports are daily made of children and slaves kidnapped in the outskirts of the town; they even enter houses and take children by force. . . . Suri Arabs have been found carrying kidnapped children through the public street in large baskets during the day, their mouths being gagged to prevent them from crying out.

Rigby's description of these people as pirates was strictly accurate. They did not confine their depredations to the land. They preyed at sea on others who were carrying on a more legitimate commerce. In 1827 an American merchant brig was pursued by a number of pirate dhows off the coast near Lamu, but the captain of the brig was able to report that he had 'outdistanced all but one, which was frightened off by getting guns out'. Other vessels proved a more easy prey. In 1833 an act of piracy, 'attended with cruel and aggravated circumstances', was committed on a Cutch vessel off the coast of Zanzibar by inhabitants of Sur. In 1837 Seyyid Said wrote from Zanzibar complaining of the aggressions committed by the compatriots of Sheikh Sultan bin Saggar (of Ras el Kheimah) upon the inhabitants of the coast. In 1852 a ship from Ras el-Kheimah, when on her return voyage to the Persian Gulf from the African coast, and while still in the neighbourhood of Zanzibar, committed piracy on a vessel belonging to that port. There is reason to believe that these were far from being isolated acts of piracy. Every year more than one dhow disappeared without trace on its homeward voyage from East Africa. Some may have foundered at sea, but dead men tell no tales. If they could, the indictment against the Northern Arabs might well have contained many more counts. In this connection it is significant that the governments of the United States (in 1833), France (in 1844) and the Hanseatic Republics of Lubeck, Bremen and Hamburg (in 1859) deemed it necessary to have inserted in treaties which they concluded with Seyyid Said and his successor a clause providing that, if any vessel belonging to their nationals was taken by pirates and such persons or their property brought into the Sultan's dominions, such persons should be set at liberty and the property handed over to the owners, or a Consul or other authorized agent.

In the days of sail it was well nigh impossible to police the Indian Ocean in such a manner that solitary undefended vessels should not fall an easy prey to sea robbers and Seyyid Said was able to do little to prevent such crimes. But, whenever he himself was in Zanzibar, he took strong measures in his attempts to put a stop to the depredations of the Northern Arabs on land. Writing on April 29, 1847, at the close of the dhow season, the British Consul, Colonel Hamerton reported that, in the past

the maritime inhabitants of the Arabian Coast used to procure a great number of slaves from Zanzibar, and even violence and murder has been resorted to by the Northern Arabs to procure slaves, but of late years these practices have greatly declined since the residence of His Highness the Imam at Zanzibar. I have frequently in the course of conversation urged his Highness to take measures to prevent this outrageous conduct on the part of the Northern Arabs; and certainly His Highness has taken measures at various times to prevent it, but I have great satisfaction in being able to state for the information of the Honourable the Governor (of Bombay) in Council that, since the commencement of the present year 1847, His Highness has adopted the most strict and vigorous measures to put a final stop to this practice. The Arabs from Sur and the Persian Gulf have been prevented (from) living ashore and in December last the Imam cited to his presence every slave broker in Zanzibar and before the whole *durbar* ordered them not to sell slaves to the Northern Arabs; and told them that in the event of its being discovered that they had disobeyed these orders, he most positively would punish them with death.

This last threat was doubtless never intended to be carried out, but it came from an autocratic ruler who could punish disobedience of his order in a number of other deterrent ways and doubtless it had its effect, though one can well imagine that there were a number of clandestine infringements of Seyyid Said's orders. In fact, as a later letter of Hamerton's shows, the British Consul was well aware that such orders as these were unpopular and that attempts were not infrequently made to evade them, whenever it appeared probable that such evasion could be made with absolute immunity from punishment. Therefore, when in 1850 Lord Palmerston wrote from England to Hamerton suggesting that Seyyid Said should take more energetic measures in dealing with these lawless visitors from Arabia, Hamerton took up the cudgels on the Sultan's behalf. He informed Palmerston that, whenever he made representations on the subject to the Seyyid Said,

the Imam always replies that the Almighty God well knows that he has done all in his power – of which I am well aware – to stop the export of slaves from his African dominions; that he had issued orders (and) made proclamations to forbid it; and had done all he could to prevent

his subjects from selling slaves to the Northern Arabs. Now the Imam
has certainly done all this but, as I have on former occasions informed
your Lordship, the Imam's orders to his people are or are not obeyed
by them just as it suits their interests to do so. Nevertheless, I assure
your Lordship that comparatively few slaves were exported northwards
from the Imam's dominions during the year 1849.

Moreover, despite the unpopularity of such measures with
certain of his subjects and despite all allegations from England that
he was not doing as much as he ought to do, Seyyid Said did not
weary of well-doing. In 1851 he took additional measures to try
to suppress the activities of the Northern Arabs. On March 13,
1851, Hamerton informed Commodore Wyvill that

the slave market always held here has been closed by order of His
Highness the Imam since the 3rd of last month and it is not again to be
held in Zanzibar until the northern boats have left this [sic] which will
be by the end of this month. No slaves have been imported from the
coast of Africa to this island for the last four months – since December –
and the slave brokers have been forbidden to sell any slaves to the
Northern Arabs; and they have not done so as yet this season; and this
is the first time I have ever known the Imam's orders strictly obeyed by
any of his people.

It is difficult to say how far Seyyid Said, who was in many
respects a remarkably enlightened person, realized the moral and
economic necessity for the abolition of the centuries old institution,
to which he had been accustomed and upon which he himself had
largely depended from the days of his childhood. But he may at the
very least be credited with the realization that on their annual
visit to Zanzibar the Northern Arabs were as big a curse to his
subjects as an invading army and that the best way of discouraging
them was by placing a ban on their most lucrative form of business.
The vested interests of the slave broker and the slave owner led to
more than one outcry on their part, but Seyyid Said realized that
the general good of the whole community required that such
interests should be disregarded. Though he was aware that his
measures would raise outcries in certain quarters, he believed – and
rightly believed – that in this matter he would have the support
not only of the British Government but also – and more important
still – the material aid of British warships patrolling the Indian
Ocean. But, as Hamerton wrote in his letter to Commodore
Wyvill, he had his misgivings. He was only too well aware that,

'when I am gone from this, and the Imam (is) away', mischievous attempts would be made in certain quarters to 'undo many things done for the suppression of the slave trade'. As after events were to show, those misgivings were unfortunately to prove well founded.

There was yet another element in the population which was a potential source of very grave danger, namely, the slaves themselves. Generally speaking, the members of this class lacked the sense of unity which might have enabled them to rise with any chance of success against their masters. They were of many mixed races and languages. Many of them were on the whole humanely treated and had no desire for liberty or to do violence to their masters. There undoubtedly were other slave owners, who treated their servants with callous cruelty, but they would appear to have been in a very small minority. In such cases, if the victim was not prepared meekly to endure his lot, he might resort to violence against his master, and even to assassination, or else he might abscond either to the mainland or else into the interior of the island, but public opinion was rarely so deeply roused that a large body of slaves was ready to rise *en masse* to avenge the wrong done to any of their number. Nevertheless, in Zanzibar, as in other lands where the social system was founded on slavery, there did arise from time to time a Spartacus, who had a true sense of leadership and could lead his fellow captives in an armed rebellion which came very near indeed to complete success.

One such rising took place in Zanzibar in about 1840 during one of Seyyid Said's absences in Oman. It appears to have been mainly confined to members of the Zigua tribe, whose home lay in the interior of Africa a short distance from the mainland coast directly opposite to Zanzibar. According to Burton many of them 'had been cheaply bought during a famine for a few measures of grain'. The immediate cause of their rebellion is not known. The outbreak took two forms. According to a well-concerted plan a large party of the conspirators assembled one moonlight night on one of the plantations. They made their way thence to the seashore to the north of Zanzibar roadstead. Arriving there in the early hours of the morning, they boarded a number of Arab dhows, surprised and killed or overpowered the members of the crew, raised anchor, made sail and crossed over to the mainland. The whole plan was so rapidly executed that there was no time to organize any effective resistance. Those of the revolted slaves who were not able to obtain passages in the dhows took refuge in the interior of the island, where they were joined by a number of malefactors and other malcontents. Such few troops as were in the island proved quite incapable of dealing with the situation. The outbreak appears to have begun in the middle of the year, when the possibility of reinforcements arriving from Arabia or the Persian Gulf was completely out of the question. The rebellion therefore lasted for six months. It was finally suppressed by Seyyid Said's maternal uncle, Ahmed bin Seif, who arrived with a body of mercenaries from Hadhramaut.

There was never again a rising of so formidable a character as this, but as the history of the Abassid Caliphs in Mesopotamia shows, slave risings were not always just isolated incidents. They could often assume alarming dimensions. There was always the lurking fear that history might repeat itself in Zanzibar and that the slave owners might find themselves overpowered by sheer weight of numbers. The masters were in fact living on the crater of a dormant volcano, which might at any time erupt. Fortunately for them, there was thereafter no violent eruption. If there had been, it would have found the masters wholly unprepared to meet it.

In addition to the control of a very unruly population Seyyid Said had a number of administrative problems to tackle. One of the most important of these was the collection of revenue. Not without good reason, he strongly suspected that until his first visit to Zanzibar not a single one of his local governors had rendered a really just account of his stewardship. There was every reason to believe that, after making generous allowances for legitimate expenses and generally recognized perquisites, each one of them had been pocketing far more than he was really entitled to retain. The two Abyssinian eunuchs, Yakut and Ambar, had apparently been great offenders in this respect, though after their deaths some of their ill-gotten gains came under Muslim law into Seyyid Said's hands as being the property of his slaves. The next Liwali, Abdulla bin Juma el-Barwani, was dismissed because Seyyid Said lost confidence in him and Khalfan bin Suleiman el-Abri was thrown into prison for precisely the same reason. Obviously, under the existing system the amount of revenue which flowed into the Sultan's exchequer depended upon the individual energy, honesty and efficiency of his local governors and their subordinates.

Moreover, there could be no audit check upon them, unless proper books of account were kept. At this date book-keeping was not the forte of many (if any) Arabs and least of all of administrative officers who had other duties to perform besides the collection of revenue. If Arab officials in Zanzibar followed the same practice as the Mazrui had followed in the 1820's at Mombasa, they employed a Banyan clerk to collect the customs revenue and to keep the necessary books of account.

Seyyid Said badly needed a steady assured revenue to finance the building of his fleet and for many other projects. He could not afford to be dependent on the only too often doubtful honesty and fidelity of a number of individuals. He therefore had recourse to a measure, which had been adopted in many European countries during the fifteenth and sixteenth centuries. He decided to farm out the collection of the customs revenue to Banyan traders.

According to information given to Sir John Kirk at a much later date, in the time of Said's father, Seyyid Sultan bin Ahmed, the coast of Zanzibar had yielded an annual revenue of 50,000 dollars. If information given to Captain Hart in 1833 was at all accurate, that revenue had dropped at the time of Seyyid Said's first visit to Zanzibar to 30,000 or 40,000 dollars, but had risen by 1833 to 150,000 dollars. This last mentioned figure may have been exaggerated. At any rate when the revenue was first farmed out to the firm of Wat Bania the annual rental was fixed at 70,000 dollars, but doubtless the farmer declared that he was taking a risk and insisted on a large margin of profit. Two years later the rental was raised to 84,000 dollars and the contract passed into the hands of a Banyan of Cutch named Siwji Topan. After the death of Siwji it passed to his son Jairam Siwji who died in 1866.

The annual rental was paid latterly in two half-yearly instalments, but the Sultans not infrequently found themselves short of ready cash long before the next instalment was due. They then used to take an advance from the farmer – a practice which not only led to interminable disputes when settlement day arrived, but often left the Sultan so heavily indebted to the farmer that he had perforce to renew the contract owing to his inability to find the ready money wherewith to pay off his creditor. The result was that it became notorious that the Sultan was receiving barely half the amount of customs revenue actually collected.

Yet another defect in the system was that the farmer of the

customs was not debarred from trading on his own account. Jairam Siwji had for instance extensive business interests in Bombay and Cutch as well as in Zanzibar and East Africa. When such personal interests clashed with his duties as an agent of the Sultan, it is not surprising to learn that the latter had to yield place to the former and that the correspondence of the British Consulate at Zanzibar was full of complaints of the venality, favouritism and extreme partiality displayed by each successive farmer of the customs. To sum up therefore, by his well intentioned introduction of the practice of farming out the customs Seyyid Said not only made a bad bargain for himself but also left behind a *damnosa hereditas* for his successors.

At the time of Seyyid Said's arrival the standard coinage was the Maria Theresa dollar and Spanish crown, which were valued at from $4\frac{1}{2}$ to $4\frac{3}{4}$ to the English sovereign. The smallest coin in circulation was the quarter dollar, that is to say, the dollar cut into four parts. Transactions involving amounts of less than a quarter dollar were usually carried out by payments in kind. Broken sums of money were commonly paid by the kibaba of *mtama* (millet), a measure more or less equivalent to the English quart. The number of *vibaba* which constituted the dollar was subject to considerable fluctuations, but the value of a single kibaba averaged about a half-penny of English money. In order to put an end to these constant fluctuations Seyyid Said ordered small copper coins to be minted in the United States of America. In 1839 a large quantity of these coins were brought to Zanzibar by Captain Andrew Ward in the Salem brig *Waverly*. Their original value appears to have been about 132 to the Spanish crown, but owing to the manipulations of Indian *shroffs* (money dealers) their value soon began to fluctuate as much as that of the kibaba. The monetary system was further complicated by the introduction of pice from India and the acceptance of the dollar, and not the rupee, as the standard coin. It was not until the reign of Seyyid Said's son and successor, Majid that this state of affairs was ended by a decree declaring the dollar to be the equivalent of two rupees, each of which was the equivalent of 64 pice.

Seyyid Said also tried his hand at judicial reform. There is literally no information regarding the judicial system in Zanzibar before his arrival. Muslim law was the fundamental law of the land and, if the same pattern was followed in Zanzibar as existed in

Mombasa in the 1820s, there was a Kathi, or possibly more than one Kathi, to administer both civil and criminal justice. The supreme judicial authority was recognized as being vested in the Sultan, to whom lay an appeal from the decision of a Kathi. In the absence of the Sultan, that appeal lay to the *Liwali* (or governor), who as the duly authorized representative of his royal master sat with a number of Kathis or other persons learned in the law as assessors. The majority of the Arab settlers from Oman belonged to the Ibadi sect, whilst the remainder of the Muslim Asian and African population belonged to the Sunni Shafei sect. It was therefore necessary to have Kathi belonging to each of the two schools.

Seyyid Said realized how essential to the maintenance of peace, order and good government was an efficient and impartial judiciary. He appears to have gone out of his way to find men of real ability to fill the office of Kathi. His principal Ibadi Kathi was a certain Sheikh Muhammed bin Ali el-Mendhri, who wrote at least one treatise on *Tawhid*. His principal Sunni Kathi, Sheikh Muhuiddin bin Sheikh Al-Khatani, was a voluminous writer on the law and tenets of his school. He was also mainly responsible for the building of the Juma (congregational) mosque in the Malindi quarter of Zanzibar. But the conditions under which they and other Kathis had to work hardly tended to a fair administration of justice. There were no official court houses. The Kathis therefore had to sit in their private houses, or else in the public street. As late as 1891 it was reported in Pemba that some Kathis were holding court in the streets of Chake Chake. The result was that the courts were either not open or else too open. Either cases were not heard *coram populo* or else they were heard amid the innumerable interruptions and disturbances which inevitably occurred when the Kathi sat in a public highway. In addition the Kathis were most inadequately paid. It was therefore not surprising that they enjoyed an unenviable reputation for venality and lack of impartiality.

Writing in 1844 Atkins Hamerton, the first British Consul to reside at Zanzibar, reported that 'there are few principal persons who administer justice but, as in most native courts, the best evidence a man can adduce in support of his innocence is found in his pocket from which, if he cannot produce evidence, he will surely be found guilty'. It was a very sweeping indictment of Kathis as a class, but there is evidence to show that it was to a large extent true. Eighteen years later Rigby, Hamerton's successor reported that 'the Kathis are persons of no character, are not at all respected by the people, and bribery is said to be very common. I have myself detected the Kathi in conniving at a most impudent case of forgery, and the exposure and denunciation of it excited no surprise'. Bishop Steere, who was in Zanzibar at the same date as Rigby, declared that 'the character of the Kathis in the *Arabian Nights* might very well stand for a picture of what people say of them now'. This state of affairs has now been changed for the better, but even as late as 1891 Sir Gerald Portal informed Lord Salisbury that the Kathis were living on extortion, bribery and oppression.

As Hamerton wrote in 1844, there was one bright spot about the judicial system of Zanzibar. There was always a right of appeal to the Sultan or, in his absence, to the Governor and 'from His Highness the Imam alone a poor man can obtain justice – who is truly every man's friend; he wishes to do good to all'. Therein lay one of the secrets of Seyyid Said's successful rule in East Africa. Few oriental rulers of his time approached so near to that high standard which requires of a judge that he shall do right to all manner of men, without affection, hatred or ill will.

In addition to being the final court of appeal, the Sultan was the sole and supreme law-making authority in Zanzibar. Here, he was treading on very delicate ground. The fundamental law of the land was the Sharia, that is, the law of Islam, which had never been codified and which had to be ascertained from a large number of sources. Whereas in England it has long been recognized that Parliament can by legislation modify, alter, and even revoke the unwritten provisions of the common law of the land and that such legislation is binding upon and to be enforced by all courts of law, that was not the case in Zanzibar or Pemba. Kathis regarded man-made law with a jealous eye and were ready to ignore it, if in their opinion its provisions offended against the fundamental principles of the Sharia. However great a reformer he might be at heart, a wise ruler would therefore not enact a law which was likely to be a dead letter from its very commencement.

There was no uniform method by which Seyyid Said pro-mulgated such laws as he made. Fiscal laws were confined to the levying of customs dues on imports and exports and were made known to all concerned by the simple method of hanging up notices of the tariffs in the customs houses. Social legislation was apparently confined entirely to anti-slavery measures agreed upon by treaties between the Sultan and the British Government. The terms of those treaties were communicated by letter to Seyyid Said's local governors and other officials with instructions to enforce them and to punish breaches thereof. In modern times the Sultan has legislated by decrees, made latterly with the advice and consent of his Legislative Council. Only one document purporting to be decree made by Seyyid Said has survived. This was promulgated in 1845 and directed that in the trial of cases each Kathi was to follow the law of the School to which he belonged. The decree then proceeds to say that 'this has been the practice from old times'. In other words it made no innovation, but merely declared what the existing law was and thus resembled the rescript which a Roman Emperor sent to a magistrate seeking his guidance on a point of law.

Seyyid Said is also said to have declared orally that Kathis should not entertain any suit in which the cause of action was more than fifteen years old. This might at first sight look like an attempt at innovation, but it again appears to have been in the nature of rescript indicating the period at which a claim should be deemed so stale that no Kathis ought to consider it. Like the so-called 'decree' it is evidence that Seyyid Said had greatly at heart the fair administration of justice to his subjects.

In 1844 Hamerton reported that serious crimes, such as robbery or murder, were rare, though petty thefts were fairly frequent. As Captain Guillain reported two years later, there was no such thing as a police force in the island. The soldiers of the garrison were expected to effect arrests and otherwise enforce the orders of those in authority. At the time of Captain Guillain's visit there were only forty-eight soldiers in Zanzibar and only about four hundred all told throughout the Sultan's East African possessions, of whom 250 were stationed at Mombasa. In the island of Zanzibar the enforcement of law and order beyond the limits of the town itself was left mainly to the Mwenyi Mkuu, the hereditary ruler of the Hadimu, and his subordinates or to Arab settlers and their bands of armed retainers. As most of these persons were not prepared to enforce any measure or process, of which they did not approve, it cannot be said that Seyyid Said's writ consistently ran throughout the island.

Guillain tells us that the garrison was mainly composed of Baluchis and Arabs from Hadhramaut, who were paid either three dollars a month without rations or two-and-a-half dollars with a ration of rice. They were reinforced in times of emergency by the armed retainers of local Arab Sheikhs. The regular soldiers were 'grotesquely decked out in the uniform of the Indian sepoy'. It was difficult to estimate the number of irregular troops whom the chiefs could place at the Sultan's service, as this depended upon the goodwill of the Sheikhs. Experience further showed that, when employed by the Sultan in punitive expeditions on the mainland, they were found wanting in courage and every other soldierly virtue. Even as policemen the regular troops were of very little value. In 1860 Colonel Rigby reported that

they patrol the streets of Zanzibar by night, and guard the prisoners in the fort. They are, however, accused, and I believe justly, of committing most of the robberies which occur; and when employed to prevent the Northern Arabs from stealing slaves and kidnapping children, they are known to be the most active agents in supplying these people with stolen slaves and children. They are all arrant cowards and greatly fear the northern pirate tribes.

On paper Seyyid Said possessed one of the most formidable navies in the Indian Ocean. He had always been interested in nautical affairs and there is no doubt that as Lieutenant Wellsted says, he had been encouraged, by the Government of India to build a large fleet for the suppression of piracy in the Persian Gulf. That fleet later proved useful when Seyyid Said led his expeditionary forces against Mombasa and other places which disputed his authority in East Africa. It also contributed to the security of his foothold in those regions when affairs of state took him back to Oman. The presence of one of his ships-of-war off Mtoni or off the town of Zanzibar was a useful deterrent showing to the el-Harthi and the members of other turbulent Arab clans that the Sultan's arm was a strong one. It also served to keep in check the Northern Arabs during their visits to Zanzibar.

Most of the men-of-war were constructed or acquired in India. One – the eight-gun brig *Vestal*–was purchased from an American in Zanzibar. Two others, the four-gun corvette *Faza Allum* and the ten-gun brig *Nasr*, were constructed by Parsi shipwrights at Zanzibar in the creek which virtually separated the main island

from the peninsula, on which the town of Zanzibar stood. Most of
the timber for the framework came from the island itself, but the
masts were obtained in Madagascar. Captain Guillain tells us that
at the time of his visit in 1846 Seyyid Said was seriously contemplating the construction of a graving dock in part of the creek, but
for a number of reasons the idea was eventually dropped.

Latterly, when the necessity for keeping the entire fleet in commission no longer existed, the men-of-war began to deteriorate.

At Mtoni, [wrote Guillain after his visit in 1846] the ships are dis-
armed, without awnings or other coverings, and are exposed to the
intemperate climate. When one of them is about to sail and requires a
sail, some rigging, or a mast, it is obtained by removing it from the
equipment of the other ships, in such a manner that when the day
arrives for sending them to sea, the necessary things for their equipment
are no longer to be found.

As regards personnel, the Sultan is obliged to have recourse to
foreigners. If one of his ships is to undertake a long voyage, for example,
to double the Cape of Good Hope, an officer borrowed from some
European or American marine is always on board for the purposes of
navigation. With regard to seamen, apparently they can be easily
obtained with such a vast extent of coastline and in latitudes which are
frequented by an infinite number of Arab vessels. But the prodigious
amount of money required to equip these useless men-of-war is wanting
when it comes to manning them and paying adequate crews. Also, when
it comes to manning vessels-of-war with men who are accustomed to
the irregular modes of navigation of native vessels, to mould them into
discipline, to undertake manoeuvering in line and the control of arma-
ments, this is a thing, which cannot be improvised and particularly
calls for an efficient corps of officers and instructors, which the Sultan's
navy lacks. Consequently, but for the assistance given by men specially
obtained from India, the Red Sea, and Baluchistan, the Sultan's navy
would consist of vessels in which nobody knew how to fire a cannon
or a rifle.

To a man, who was described by Captain Hart, as taking
absolute control of every vessel he boarded from the time of getting her under weigh to bringing her once more to anchor and by
Captain Brucks as making his navy 'his principal care and study',
this gradual deterioration of his fleet must have been distressing,
but Seyyid Said lacked the funds to keep it in a full and proper
state of efficiency. He tried to stay the rot by dismantling the
armament of some of the ships and sending them as merchant

vessels to Bombay, the Gulf of Bengal, Batavia and other islands in the East Indies as well as to Europe and America. In 1838 he sent his seventy-four-gun line of battleship *Liverpool* to England as a present to Queen Victoria. In 1840 the twenty-gun corvette *Sultani* went to New York and was towed thence sixty miles up the Hudson River to Newburgh. The *Sultani*'s next voyage was in 1842 to England. In 1849 the frigate *Caroline* proceeded to Marseille.

One result of all these voyages was that the *nahodas* commanding the Sultan's ships came to occupy a somewhat unusual position in the Sultan's service. They were often entrusted by Seyyid Said with special commissions for the purchase of articles required not only for the Sultan's personal use but also for the purchase of what may be termed public stores, such as, arms and naval and military equipment. Some of them also managed to acquire some knowledge of the languages of the countries which they visited. In 1855 Hamerton recorded that 'His Highness employs his *Nahodas* (who all speak English) when transacting business with Europeans, and these men are supposed to be the ministers by strangers. Some of the nahodas speak French'.

Apart from the officers of his naval and military forces and his local governors and Kathis, Seyyid Said had no officers of state. His affairs were sufficiently multitudinous to necessitate employment of a clerical staff. In Hamerton's words, 'the Imam has not any regular ministers, or secretaries for different departments; he has two men who write his letters and convey messages to Europeans. These men are ill paid and not trustworthy'.

Certain prominent Arabs – of whom the most important was his kinsman, Suleiman bin Hamed, were described as *Wazirs* of Seyyid Said. This word has often been translated as meaning 'ministers', but this is misleading. The Sultan might from time to time call one or more of them to him for purposes of consultation, but they were in no sense permanent ministers of state. To quote Hamerton yet once more:

The Imam's government is of a purely patriarchal character, there are no establishments of any kind similar to those existing in the states of Native Princes in India. . . .

All the respectable men at Muscat and Zanzibar generally attend daily at the *durbar*, or when the Imam holds his assembly three times a day. They do not interfere in the government, but if called on by the Imam they would do as desired.

From all the foregoing it will be gathered that Hamerton's epithet 'purely patriarchal' was perhaps the most appropriate which could be given to Seyyid Said's rule in East Africa. If one examines it, one is at a loss to find anything outlining some definite line of policy. He ruled East Africa in the same manner as he and his predecessors had ruled Oman, namely, by reliance in his own personal ability to perform the task. In so doing, he was not mistaken. Occasions might arise when he felt he must have recourse to the sword or to underhand methods such as bribery or even rank treachery and breach of good faith, but he was wise enough to know that such weapons are dangerous and apt to be turned against him who uses them. He was therefore sparing in his use of them and relied more upon ruling with the goodwill of his fellow Arabs as well as of his African subjects.

As both Roberts and Hamerton said, Seyyid Said does not seem to have realized the economic potentialities of his African dominions until he paid his first visit to the island. During that brief visit in 1828 he had, however, been quick to realize quite a lot of things.

Edmund Roberts tells us that at the time of Said's first visit

there were at Zanzibar, exclusive of (military) transport dhows, upwards to two hundred fifty sail of dhows, *bagalas* and other craft with pilgrims, drugs, coffee, fish, water &c from Suez, Mocha, Jedda, the seaport of Mecca, and the island of Berbera in the Red Sea, the ports in the Persian Gulf, the coast of Africa as far south as Mozambique, and I saw but a small part of their commerce.

One is aware that, to suit his own purposes, Roberts was given to inflating his statistics but, even after making a generous discount for exaggeration, it is clear that Zanzibar was an important port of call and an important entrepôt for the exchange of the wares of Asia for those of Africa.

In addition to this vast assemblage of merchant shipping Roberts reported that he had 'frequently seen the elephant hunters from thirty days' journey into the interior and the Governor of Zanzibar occasionally sent presents to the negro kings a long distance inland and he said they considered themselves as slaves of the Imam'. In all probability these visitors were Wanyamwezi dwelling in the region of what is now Tabora in Tanganyika. After he acquired Mombasa, Said also discovered that the Wakamba used to bring ivory down to an annual fair, which was held at Kwa Jomvu a few miles inland from Mombasa. Even before reaching Zanzibar the revenue derived by him from the capitation tax on slaves had made him aware that other chattels besides ivory were brought to the coast from the interior of the African continent. Finally, Seyyid Said's confiscation of Saleh bin Harameli el-Abri's plantations at Mtoni and Kizimbani showed him that, in addition to its indigenous products, the soil of Zanzibar was capable of producing certain other valuable economic crops.

Seyyid Said was quick to realize that all these things could be used not only to his own personal advantage but also for the better establishment of peace and good order in his East African dominions, Oman was an infertile land with an almost negligible annual rainfall and a tropical climate. The inhabitants, of whom many were nomads, were an unruly lot, who ill-brooked interference from any central government. However strong their Sultan might be, he was constantly beset by hostile intrigue and there were periodical rebellions. Seyyid Said had started his early career with most of the handicaps and disadvantages which had confronted the son of Robert, Duke of Normandy. Like William, when he crossed the English Channel to establish a new kingdom, he saw in his expeditions across the Indian Ocean a means of diverting the subjects' energies into other spheres than those of plot and counterplot.

The Arabs were therefore encouraged to leave their own country and acquire lands in Zanzibar and Pemba, which could be turned to far more profitable advantage than those of Oman. On their arrival they were encouraged by the Sultan to grow not only the indigenous fruits of the soil, but also a number of potential economic crops which were imported from other lands. Seyyid Said, moreover, practised what he preached.

He eventually had some forty-five plantations in the island. On every one of these experiments were made in the growing of new crops.

It has not infrequently been asserted that Seyyid Said was responsible for the introduction of cloves, but this is not strictly accurate and, if true, would hardly redound to his credit. He did not take a leap in the dark and plant his own estates with a crop of unknown adaptability to the local soil and of equally unascertained economic value. From certain 'Reflections' which he addressed in 1801 to the French Governor of the Isle of France (Mauritius) we learn that a certain Monsieur Dallons had already at that date imported cloves into Zanzibar. From the fact that we hear no more of cloves for seventeen years we may perhaps conclude that, if these imports were clove seedlings, this early experimental planting was unsuccessful. According to Guillain a certain Monsieur Sausse, a Creole of Bourbon or Isle of France or the Seychelles, brought the next batch of cloves to Zanzibar. Without naming Sausse, Ruschenberger, a surgeon in the United States Navy, gives the date of this experiment as 1818 and the first place of planting as Saleh bin Harameli el-Abri's plantation at Kizimbani. Ruschenberger's description of this plantation as containing in 1835 trees varying in height from eight to twenty feet and yielding on an average six pounds of cloves a year suggests that this date must be approximately correct. It would appear that Sausse was allowed, on lease or otherwise, to make use of Saleh's land for experimental planting and that he spent a lot of time and labour on the task. Burton tells us that Sausse 'succeeded in extracting an excellent oil, the clove oil of commerce being generally made by distilling cinammon leaves. This novelty became a universal favourite with the Zanzibar public, who held it to be highly medicinal, and used it especially for inflammations'. When therefore Seyyid Said confiscated the plantation at Kizimbani, some of the trees there must have been at least ten years old and Sausse's experiment had proved to be a success. It is therefore no denigration, but rather a commendation, of Seyyid Said to say that he profited by the experience of others to encourage an industry which has brought lasting wealth to Zanzibar and Pemba.

Not all of Seyyid Said's agricultural experiments were successful, but it was only by an extensive process of trial and error that discovery could eventually be made as to what were the economic crops best suited to the soils of Zanzibar and Pemba. Clove cultivation proved a lasting success which far outweighed many other unsuccessful experiments with other crops.

Seyyid Said's measures for the increase of the trade and wealth of his East African dominions – and incidentally to find employment for the more restless spirits amongst his countrymen – were not limited solely to the expansion of the agriculture of the two islands of Zanzibar and Pemba. The presence at the time of his first arrival in Zanzibar of elephant hunters from the interior of the

L

main continent had made him realize that continent was capable of yielding a number of profitable exports.

Some time before 1839 Seyyid Said himself was sending his own caravans into the interior. The American Consul, Richard Waters, recorded in his diary that on June 21 in that year 'two hundred men started for the interior of Africa. They go to trade for His Highness and will be gone about a year'. This, however, was not the first of such caravans. Eleven days after these two hundred men set out a party of American missionaries arrived at Zanzibar in the Salem brig *Waverly* on their way to India. Through the instrumentality of Waters one of their number, Ebenezer Burgess, got in touch with a 'very respectable man who had been five times far into the interior', and certain other Arabs and Nyamwezi who had been members of previous caravans. One of these caravans had returned eighteen months previously after an absence of just under six months and another more recently. From them Burgess obtained a good deal of information about the trade between Zanzibar and the interior of the continent. The second of these caravans had been led or accompanied by a man, who 'the Sultan sent. . . for the purpose of exploring'. It had returned with an emissary from the paramount chief of Unyamwezi, 'who had come at the request of the Sultan to make some form of treaty for the safety and success of his subjects, when on their trading expeditions'. From him Burgess learnt of the existence of Lake Tanganyika. Within a year or so of this embassy caravans from Zanzibar had reached the shores of that lake and shortly afterwards a fairly large Arab colony was established at Ujiji. In 1843 the first Arab caravan reached the court of Suna, ruler of Buganda on the shores of Lake Victoria. Not all the Sultan's ventures prospered. When in 1844 he arrived in Zanzibar as supercargo of the Salem bark *Star*, Michael William Shepard recorded in his journal that 'His Highness sends every year one hundred men into the interior to explore and obtain what ivory and produce of the country as they can and seldom more then twenty to thirty return, the rest dying on the road'. The figures he gives are in all probability somewhat exaggerated, but there can be little doubt that from time to time the climate and unfriendly African tribes exacted a heavy toll in lives from these caravans.

At the end of Seyyid Said's reign a new trade route had been opened up across Lake Tanganyika between the east and west coasts of Africa and was being used by Arabs and Swahili traders alike. On April 3, 1852, one such caravan, which had been led by three 'Moors' from Zanzibar and comprised forty porters, arrived at Benguela with ivory and slaves to exchange for merchandise. The barometer which best indicated the rapidly increasing prosperity of Zanzibar in 1844 was the annual rental paid by the farmer of the customs, 125,000 dollars. Thereafter the lease was renewed once in every five years at a minimum increased rent of 30,000 dollars. Yet, despite his oft reiterated protests, the farmer continued to make a handsome profit out of the lease.

CHAPTER VIII

SEYYID SAID AND THE AFRICAN INHABITANTS OF ZANZIBAR AND PEMBA

WHEN Seyyid Said bin Sultan of Oman first visited Zanzibar in January 28, 1828, he found that apart from Arab settlements and the slave population appendant thereto, the main population of the island consisted of two tribes – the Hadimu and the Tumbatu. As their name denotes, the cradle of this latter tribe was the islet off the north-west coast of Zanzibar. The dividing line between them and the Hadimu was ill-defined, but was very roughly speaking at about the sixth parallel of south latitude, the Tumbatu occupying the area to the north thereof and the Hadimu the rest of the island. In proximity to the sixth parallel one finds to this day interspersed villages of Tumbatu and Hadimu, each village nonetheless insisting upon its tribal individuality.

Like so many African tribal names, Hadimu is a nickname, meaning 'slave', which was given to the local African inhabitants by Arab immigrants. Undoubtedly the name was given to them in contempt, but it was none the less untrue. The Hadimu were neither conquered nor enslaved by the Arabs. Rather understandably, the name has of recent years become unpopular amongst certain members of the tribe, who now prefer to call themselves 'Shirazi' to indicate their supposedly Persian origin, though the number who can really claim to have Persian blood in their veins is possibly relatively small.

In default of a better appellation it is somewhat difficult to find a more suitable name for the tribe than Hadimu. The members thereof are of very mixed origin, consisting of immigrants from different parts of the mainland, who have arrived in the island at very different dates. Many of them are relatively newcomers, who entered Zanzibar little more than six generations ago and either absorbed or supplanted earlier arrivals. It is interesting to note that over a course of many years there would appear to have been a more or less continuous arrival of newcomers from the mainland by way of Unguja Ukuu, which might almost be described as having been used by them as a kind of base transit camp for immigrants. Thus, it is generally acknowledged by the people of the east coast villages of Chwaka, Mapopwe, Charawi Ukongoroni, and Michamvi that their forbears entered the island from the mainland by way of Unguja Ukuu. Those of Mapopwe say an ancestor came from Ras Kimbiji, on the coast to the south-east of Dar-es-Salaam, married a woman of Unguja Ukuu and then went to Mapopwe to cultivate and finally settled there. Another interesting migration was that of a Swahili family about six generations ago from Lindi, some 250 miles to the south of Zanzibar, who purchased a *kiambo* (family property) from a Hadimu at Maungani and installed themselves there. It is quite possible that these and other similar migrations were due to piratical raids by the Sakalava, who made themselves masters of most of the island of Madagascar in about the middle of the seventeenth century and retained that supremacy until the close of the following century. As late as 1822 they raided the island of Mafia. This would certainly explain the arrival in Zanzibar of the Matemwe, who claim to have come from Mayotte in the Comoro archipelago.

It is also interesting to note that these colonists appear to have found the land lying to the north of Unguja Ukuu more or less unoccupied and that there were next to no human habitations close to the seashore. The explanation of this first fact would appear to be that the southern and eastern portions of the island were less fertile and that the bulk of the African population was settled in the more fertile belt on the western side of the island. The second fact must be attributed to the fear not so much of pirates as of 'black birders', who arrived in dhows and kidnapped women and children. Thus the people of Makunduchi at the southern end of the island, have a story of three women, who went down to the seashore to catch *dagaa* (whitebait) and were driven mad on beholding a devil coming towards them in a canoe, holding a trident in his hand and speaking an incomprehensible language. Children were not infrequently enticed on board slave dhows by promises of dates and sweetmeats. This kidnapping, however, does not appear to have been upon any extensive scale and it may be said that the Hadimu as a whole were never enslaved. On the contrary, they employed slave labour. The supply was obtained from the mainland and was brought over in African dhows which landed their cargoes at Chwaka, Pongwe, and Kiwengwa on the east coast.

By no means all the immigrants, who now make up the Hadimu tribe, came from the regions to the south of Zanzibar. As might be expected, other families claim to have come from the mainland opposite to Zanzibar. Some of them claim to have come from the mainland near Windi, which lies between Bagamoyo and Saadani and little more than twenty-five miles from the town of Zanzibar.

They were fishers by trade, and one day they were driven by storms to the west coast of Zanzibar island. Finding it fruitful, they settled along this bit of the coast, calling it Shangani (sc. Shangani Point at the 'heel' of the former peninsula on which Zanzibar town now stands). . . . They went back to the mainland to get themselves wives.

Some three miles to the north of Windi and only twenty-three miles from Shangani point lies the village of Utondwe whence the former rulers of the Hadimu claim to have come.

Other immigrants came from even further north. At Manga-pwani certain of the inhabitants claim to be an offshoot of the Segeju tribe, who now occupy a strip of the mainland coast on the borders of Tanganyika and Kenya. Furthermore, a number of words in the Hadimu vocabulary bear resemblances to those found in the language of the Giriama, Pokomo and other Nyika tribes in the hinterland behind Mombasa.

In view of these many different and diverse origins of the tribe it is not surprising to hear that there are also different forms of the Hadimu dialect. The speech generally of Zanzibar is known as Kiunguja. According to Ingrams the most archaic form of the Hadimu dialect is that spoken in Jambiani and Makunduchi, two villages in the south-east of the island. He describes their dialect as 'totally incomprehensible to a person knowing only Kiunguja, owing not only to the number of different words and the peculiar conjugations of the verbs, but to its unusual pronunciation which is very nasal'. Travelling only a few miles up the east coast one comes to Bwejuu and Paje, where the dialect varies a little from the dialect of Makunduchi and has forms peculiar to itself. Proceeding even further northwards, nearly every village has a different form of speech. Similarly, the south-west coast of Kizimkazi, which is barely seven miles from Makunduchi, has a number of forms of speech peculiar to itself. All these dialects are known today as

Kikale or Kikae, a word meaning 'archaic'. Naturally, improved communications have led to an increased use of Kiunguja amongst the Hadimu, but the old dialects are still spoken in the villages themselves; especially amongst the women folk, who are still the depositories of Kikae.

Briefly, therefore, it may be said the Hadimu are offshoots from mainland tribes of many different origins, who have arrived in Zanzibar at very different dates. Their one common link, giving them a sense of unity, was the fact that they acknowledged the sovereignty of a single ruler, who was known as the Jumbe or Mwenyi Mkuu ('the great lord').

This dynasty was of Shirazi, as distinct from Hadimu, origin, that is to say, the members of mixed Asiatic and African blood into which other Asiatic blood had been introduced as it would appear as the result of fairly frequent intermarriage in a number of generations with full blooded Arabs. Portuguese records show that they had a close connection with Utondwe on the mainland nearly opposite to the modern town of Zanzibar. Tradition says that their regalia, which included a drum and wooden horn, came from that place.

The relations between the family of the Mwenyi Mkuu and the Portuguese have been described in previous Chapters. Hassan bin Abdulla, the Mwenyi Mkuu who had made his submission to the Portuguese at the time of their temporary recovery of Mombasa in 1728 appears to have made a complete *volte face* when the Portuguese were expelled once and for all in the following year and to have made his peace very quickly with the Omani Arabs. The precise terms of the agreement are unknown, but it is evident that the Omani Arabs were allowed to reoccupy the fort, which they had built some thirty years previously. It is also said that some fishermen, who were then settled in the Shangani quarter of what is now the town of Zanzibar claimed a right to be heard at these negotiations. They are said to have raised no objection to the Omani Arabs reoccupying the fort and settling in what now comprises the northern part of the Stone Town of Zanzibar, provided that they themselves were consulted in all important affairs affecting the place and that their names were mentioned in all public proclamations.

Hassan bin Abdulla was the son of a member of the Alawi clan from Hadhramaut, who had married his mother Fatuma, the 'queen' of Zanzibar who had been so steadfastly loyal to the Portuguese even in the days of their adversity. Having made his peace with the Omani Arabs, Hassan bin Abdulla was allowed to end his days as Mwenyi Mkuu. He was succeeded by his son Sultan, who died in 1771. It was during the reign of this last named that the Busaidi clan overthrew the Yorubi dynasty in Oman and Ahmed bin Said, the grandfather of Seyyid Said bin Sultan, became ruler of Oman (1744–83). Writing in 1828, at the time of the grandson's first visit to Zanzibar, Edmund Roberts tells us that, fearing another invasion by the Portuguese, the people of Zanzibar placed their island 'under the protection of the grandfather of the present Imam; or rather they yielded sovereignty to him on condition that their king and his descendants should be paid eight thousand dollars per annum'. Writing at the time of his special mission to Zanzibar in 1873, Sir Bartle Frere tells that

> Seyyid Said . . . did not obtain possession of Zanzibar itself till he had purchased the surrender of the sovereignty of the Swahili chief by the promise of a large pension and the continuance of certain forms of sovereignty. The pension was never regularly paid, but the forms of sovereignty were continued and are, I believe, still maintained on ceremonial occasions and in grants of land &c.

It would appear that Said bin Sultan promised to fulfil his grandfather's engagement more regularly in future, but, as Sir Bartle Frere wrote, the pension was never thereafter punctually paid.

The Mwenyi Mkuu, to whom Said bin Sultan renewed this promise of a pension, would appear to have been a grandson of the original promissee, named Ahmed bin Hassan el-Alawi. According to Lyne, he came from the mainland, probably from Pangani, during Said bin Sultan's reign and settled in the centre of the island at Bweni, near Dunga and some twelve miles from the town of Zanzibar. He built a stone house at Bweni, the ruins of which can still be seen.

The Mwenyi Mkuu would appear to have come to the town of Zanzibar at the time of Said bin Sultan's first visit in January 1828. He may have been summoned by Said for the purpose of establishing a working arrangement between themselves. Edmund Roberts, who was also in Zanzibar at that date, tells us that 'the king and princes of the Swahili I have the honour to be personally acquainted with and have frequently visited them'. We know for a fact that the Mwenyi Mkuu's successors in title owned land at Mkunazini in the town of Zanzibar and that their burial ground was adjacent to the fort. In all probability therefore Roberts was received by the Mwenyi Mkuu at his town house. This Mwenyi Mkuu also enlarged the Jami (principal) mosque in the town in about 1839.

We have no details of any meeting between Said bin Sultan and the Mwenyi Mkuu in 1828. There can have been very little bargaining on this occasion for Said's entire fleet was anchored off Zanzibar together with transport dhows carrying several thousand soldiers. In the circumstances the Mwenyi Mkuu could not choose but hear. The *modus vivendi* reached must have been a dictated one.

Part of the arrangement reached would appear to have been that the Mwenyi Mkuu should be responsible for the collection of a yearly *kodi*, or tax, of two dollars from each Hadimu as a contribution to Said bin Sultan's revenue. This was a personal tax and not, as might appear from its name, a hut tax. It was collected in two equal instalments, the first being payable at the time of the gathering of the crop after the *vuli* rains, which end in about December, and the second at the season of the *mwaka* rains, which fall in about August. It was the duty of the *masheha* (or headmen) to collect this and bring it to the Mwenyi Mkuu, who remitted it to the Sultan at Zanzibar. In a letter of A.H. 1249 (or A.D. 1833) Said bin Sultan informed the Sultan 'that five hundred dollars of kodi has arrived, that he wants the remainder sent on, and that, if the *Jumbe* has any wants, he is to let him, the Seyyid, know'. This rather suggests that the Jumbe or Mwenyi Mkuu was holding back part of the tax collection, presumably because he claimed a lien for his unpaid pension. At a later date the matter was compromised by permitting the Mwenyi Mkuu to retain half the amount of the kodi in lieu of any claim to pension and to remit the other half to the Sultan.

Another stipulation made by Seyyid Said bin Sultan was that the Mwenyi Mkuu should be responsible to him for the supply of necessary labour from amongst the Hadimu to meet the Sultan's wants. Doubtless this system of *corvée* had been exacted by the Mwenyi Mkuu himself before Seyyid Said's arrival and the effect of these instructions was that he now had to share this labour supply with the Sultan. At first the principal form of this labour appears to have been cutting timber for building purposes and carrying it to wherever it might be required. Later, with the spread of cultivation of cloves, the Hadimu were expected to turn out to pick the cloves of the Sultan and Mwenyi Mkuu and to cut and carry the long poles required for making the ladders which were required for picking purposes. The duty of collecting the necessary labour quota fell on the *sheha* (or headman) of each district. The workers were not given any wages, but they were each given a supply of mtama after each day's work, which they had to cook for themselves. Each contingent worked for one month. If at the end of that month the work had not been completed, they were relieved by a fresh contingent of Hadimu and allowed to return home.

The Mwenyi Mkuu, Hassan bin Ahmed, married Mwana wa Mwana, the hereditary sheha or ruler of the Tumbatu, an event which, as will be seen, was to prove of considerable political importance. Apart from this, we know very little about him. The fact that he was neither born nor bred in the island tends rather to suggest that the Hadimu regarded him as an alien, who may have been imposed upon them by the ruler of Oman, and for that reason he was unpopular with his subjects. He died in 1845.

His successor was Muhammad bin Ahmed el-Alawi. At the time of Hassan's death the new ruler was living with the principal sheha of Dunga, one Kimameta bin Mgwa Mchanga, of the Mchangani tribe. He is said to have been wazir (chief adviser) to his predecessor who was also his brother, but doubt has been cast upon this statement. What seems evident is that, in whatever degree (if at all) Muhammad bin Ahmed was related to his predecessor, he succeeded him, not by hereditary right, but as nominee of Seyyid Said bin Sultan. Albeit, Seyyid Said was still content to leave the maintenance of order and good government of the Hadimu in the hands of the Mwenyi Mkuu so long as the latter remitted to him a reasonably sufficient sum as representing his share of the poll tax collection and also supplied the proper quota of corvée labour for public works and work on Seyyid Said's plantations. As in the course of time more and more land came under cultivation for cloves, and other economic crops, the labour demands of Seyyid Said and his successors appeared to have increased, especially at the time of harvest. Though an increased supply of slave labour could fulfil the demands for ordinary maintenance work on the plantations, it could not always suffice at the time of harvest, more especially in years of abundance. The result was that in the course of years the indent for *corvée* labour from the Hadimu would appear to have increased in frequency and in size.

It may have been that it was these increased labour demands which ultimately led to friction between the Omani Sultans of Zanzibar and the Mwenyi Mkuu. Though there is no written record of any differences between them, tradition tells us that in the time of Seyyid Said the Mwenyi Mkuu was thrown into prison at Zanzibar. The same night, however, the prisoner miraculously disappeared and was next heard of on the mainland, where he stayed for two or three years. During that time no rain fell in the island of Zanzibar. So Arabs and Hadimu alike petitioned the Sultan to pardon the Mwenyi Mkuu and allow him to return. Their request was granted and immediately after the exile's return rain fell abundantly. Reading between the lines of this legend, it seems safe to infer that for some reason or other the Mwenyi Mkuu was arrested and deported and that he remained in exile for two or three years. Those years may or may not have been years of drought. If they were, the Hadimu doubtless spread the story that this was the manner in which their ruler avenged his ill-treatment. What would appear more certain still is that the Sultan found great difficulty in obtaining either tax or labour without the co-operation of the Mwenyi Mkuu and so the latter was eventually recalled and reinstated.

Either before or after this incident the Mwenyi Mkuu appears to have more or less abandoned his town residence and to have taken up his permanent abode at Dunga, where he built himself a fortified stone house. After he went into residence the building was guarded by armed sentries. Both these two facts would appear to indicate that in his latter years his relations with the Omani Sultan living some eleven miles away in the town of Zanzibar were far from cordial. The house took many years to build and was only occupied by the Mwenyi Mkuu during the last days of his life.

The withdrawal of the Mwenyi Mkuu from the town of Zanzibar tended to put him out of touch with most members of the European community, but he was always ready to extend hospitality and assistance to any European who came his way. In June 1862, he was visited by Colonel Pelly, the British Consul, who stayed at his house for two days and reported that 'I found the Sultan to be a man of about seventy years of age, much self reposed and with much native dignity of manner'. A year later the French explorer, Alfred Grandidier, visited him and received from him letters addressed to his chiefs bidding them give Grandidier every assistance as he wandered through the interior of the island. As a result Grandidier was able to journey free of all cost to himself, and to arrive back in Zanzibar with a whole herd of goats as well as poultry and sacks of millet and rice.

Burton who visited Zanzibar in 1857, tells us that at that date the Mwenyi Mkuu's name was mentioned in the Khutbah or Friday Sermon, but 'he was never, however, admitted to any equality with the Arab ruler'. In a consular report written in 1860 Colonel Rigby said 'the Mwenyi Mkuu has now but little authority' but added that 'in time of war his influence is of great weight, as it entirely depends upon him whether the Hadimu responds to the call of arms of their Arab leader'. Only a year before these words had been penned the truth of that statement had been proved when, at the direction of the Mwenyi Mkuu the Hadimu rallied to the side of the Sultan of Zanzibar at the time of a threat of an invasion by Seyyid Thuwein bin Said, Sultan of Oman. Though Seyyid Said would appear to have intended that Muhammad bin Ahmed (who was commonly known as Sultan Hamadi) should be more or less a puppet ruler, it seems clear that this Mwenyi Mkuu had greater influence amongst the Hadimu than had his predecessor. Strange tales are still told as to his supernatural powers. There are also somewhat sinister stories as to the unlimited exercise by him of the powers of life and death, but such stories are current regarding other rulers in Zanzibar and Pemba. They are not intended to be in disparagement of them but rather as proof of the power and dignity of the person, to whom they are attributed. Doubtless, as some of these stories assert, an intense desire to prevent any dimunition of his *heshima* (dignity) made him insist upon somewhat extravagant acts of homage and obeisance from his subjects during his walks abroad and led him to punish their omission with great severity. When in his latter days old age confined him within the walls of his castellated mansion at Dunga, which had armed sentries posted outside, the dignity which hedged him and the tales already told about him inspired fear rather more than reverence. Nevertheless, his rule was clearly not detested. The story of his deportation fully proves this.

The Mwenyi Mkuu's government of his dominions was not inefficient. As certain traditions show, there was apparently a time when the Hadimu country was divided up into two or more petty 'kingdoms'. By the time that Sultan Hamadi became Mwenyi Mkuu, all these had become united under a single overlord. As will also be seen later, in Sultan Hamadi's day the sovereignty of the Mwenyi Mkuu was also extended beyond the limits of the Hadimu country into the northern part of the island occupied by the Tumbatu. For administrative purposes, his dominions were divided into districts, which corresponded in size, and in some cases more or less in extent, to the *Mudirias* into which Zanzibar is divided at the present time. Each of these districts was under the control of a sheha (plural, masheha).

Originally the appointment of the Sheha was in all probability, entirely in the hands of the people of the district. When the Mwenyi Mkuu began to make his influence felt throughout the island, this method of appointment appears to have been outwardly maintained, but the appointment became subject to confirmation by the Mwenyi Mkuu, who in some instances intimated his desire as to which of several candidates was to be elected. This led to candidates applying personally to the Mwenyi Mkuu for appointment and accompanying their application with a present. The Mwenyi Mkuu would then communicate his wishes to the people of the district. In due course the favoured candidate would arrive at Dunga with a number of the people. The Mwenyi Mkuu would then ask whether the candidate was the man they wanted as sheha and the people would dutifully reply in the affirmative. The party would then return to the district, accompanied by a messenger who proclaimed to the inhabitants that the Mwenyi Mkuu had approved the appointment. The new sheha then had a turban of *bafta* (thin bleached calico) placed on his head as the outward and visible sign of his appointment. The successful candidate thereafter held his post during the pleasure of the Mwenyi Mkuu. He could be arbitrarily dismissed, either for incompetence or misconduct or because a rival approached the Mwenyi Mkuu with a suitable present.

In the days when the popular election of the sheha had been unfettered, the tendency had been to choose a man from one of the leading families, as on appointment the holder of the post was expected to entertain upon a lavish scale. In consequence there was also a tendency in some cases for the post to become hereditary in the sense that the sheha was always elected from amongst the members of one particular family. In such cases the person, who was the popular choice, became a power behind the throne and continued to rule the district despite the installation of the Mwenyi Mkuu's nominee. This clandestine influence tended, however, very much to diminish when the Mwenyi Mkuu issued orders that the masheha were to report in person to him periodically so that he might keep in touch with the affairs of every village.

Sometimes the sheha was assisted in his duties by a person called the *mkubwa* (elder). Apparently, there was never more than one such officer in any district. He was selected for the post by the sheha and the appointment was approved by the Mwenyi Mkuu. When the poll tax and the corvée were introduced, the Mwenyi Mkuu appointed local officers called *shakua* to collect the tax and to see that the necessary labour was forthcoming.

In each *shehia*, or district administered by a sheha, were a number of villages varying in extent and population. Each village was an administrative unit in itself, upon which largely depended the maintenance of order and good government throughout the whole of the territory of the Mwenyi Mkuu. Each village had its own constitution and its own administrative hierarchy. There were minor differences, but the tendency was for each village to conform in this respect more or less to the same pattern. The affairs of each village were as a rule controlled by a council comprising four members, generally known as the *Watu Wanne* (or four persons), though in some places they were known merely as the *wazee* or elders. The membership of each village council would appear almost invariably to have been four. In practice, the four men generally came from the four principal *milango* (families) of the village. The senior member was known as the *mkubwa wa mji* or *sheha wa mji* (village headman or chief), who acted as treasurer and collector of dues and fines leviable on behalf of the village community.

Though towards the end of his reign Seyyid Said bin Sultan issued letters of appointment to some of the masheha, it is clear that both he and his immediate successors very rarely (if ever) came in personal contact with Hadimu. Everything concerning them was left entirely in the hands of the Mwenyi Mkuu and his subordinates, who sternly vetoed any appeal by aggrieved parties from Dunga to the Arab Sultan in Zanzibar. According to a statement made by a very old man to Mr. J. T. Last in 1901, 'in the old days the Jumbe did as he liked; he could kill, imprison, seize persons or goods as he wanted them; and if at any time he did exceed his power and was called to account, the matter was quietened down by a present to the Sultan'.

Such then was the system of government prevailing in the greater part of the island of Zanzibar when Seyyid Said bin Sultan first arrived in 1828. It had its obvious imperfections but on the whole it worked. As said, Seyyid Said was perfectly content to tolerate this form of indirect rule, which might in certain circumstances have endured almost to the present day. Its breakdown was in a large measure due to economic rather than to political reasons.

When Seyyid Said reached Zanzibar, Arabs had already begun to acquire land outside the peninsula on which stood the town of Zanzibar. It is somewhat difficult to say what was the extent of this early Arab settlement, but to judge from the situation of the plantations which Said acquired in 1828 it would appear that, although it did not extend very far to the south of the town, it extended in the opposite direction along the coast to the north thereof as far as Bumbwini about twelve miles from Zanzibar. Its maximum penetration into the island would appear to have been about six miles, to Kichwele and Kizimbani, but by no means all the land comprised within those limits had as yet come into Arab hands.

The position, however, began to change very quickly after Seyyid Said decided to make Zanzibar his capital. He was followed from Oman by a large number of his compatriots, who were eager to settle in more productive lands than the arid country which they had left behind them. Furthermore, Seyyid Said's active encouragement of the planting of cloves, sugar cane, and other economic crops led to an increased demand for land. Though some of this development was effected by disafforestation, a great deal of it was brought about by expropriation of the original landowners.

Whilst there may have been cases in which a Hadimu landowner was evicted by an Arab with a strong hand and a multitude of people, and that in other cases expropriation was procured by means of fraud, the general impression is that many of these changes of ownership were brought about by means which would have borne scrutiny by a court of law. Upon occasion no doubt the head of a family or a sheha, with his mind more set upon lining his own pocket than of the fiduciary responsibilities which he owed to others, sold to an Arab land which native custom deemed to be inalienable. In other cases a Hadimu might be induced to relinquish or abandon his land by a species of cold war waged by Arab neighbours in such manner that continued occupation of the land, to which the Hadimu was entitled, became intolerable. There appear also to have been quite a number of other cases in which, as has happened in instances of colonization by alien races in other parts of Africa, the contracting parties were in reality not consenting *ad idem*. The grantors believed that they were offering one thing and the grantee believed that he was receiving something entirely different. Local custom regarded all land as being communal, incapable of permanent alienation and merely conferring upon its occupants a limited usufructuary right, whereas the Arab immigrant conceived of the land as being something akin to individual and alienable freehold such as was recognized by the law of his country of origin. In such cases the land may as often as not have changed hands at a fair market price, but the vendors did not realize that they were being asked to change the whole nature of their existing system of land tenure.

Whatever the methods employed, during the next half-century the general trend of events was for the Hadimu to remove out of the more fertile area in the western portion of the island into the less fertile areas in the eastern and southern portions of the island. When the Mwenyi Mkuu removed from the town of Zanzibar to Dunga, this exodus tended to increase. The result was to create what in other territories has been called a native reserve, where the inhabitants were left very much to conduct their own affairs in their own way, provided they paid their poll tax and supplied the necessary demands for corvée.

The dual monarchy came virtually to an end on the death of Sultan Hamadi on June 25, 1865. He left an only son surviving him, a boy named Ahmed, who was only twelve to fourteen years old at the time of his father's death. This boy was duly recognized by Seyyid Said's successor, Majid, as ruler of the Hadimu. A contemporary picture of Ahmed and his father shows that, whereas the last named had all the appearance and dignity of a high born Arab, none of his imposing features had descended to his son. After his succession the son left Dunga and went to reside in Zanzibar.

In all probability his removal to the town was encouraged by
Seyyid Said's son and successor, Seyyid Majid, who wanted to
have the boy under his eye. Sir Bartle Frere found the youth
living in Zanzibar in 1873 'in considerable style', but considered
him to be 'apparently destitute of any qualities which could make
him of much political importance', though he was 'regarded as one
of the magnates of the place'. The young man died very shortly
afterwards in March 1873, of smallpox.

The only remaining members of the Mwenyi Mkuu's family
were the five sisters of Ahmed bin Muhammad. At the time of
their brother's death all of them were minors and three died before
attaining majority. The other two married into prominent Arab
families. One succeeded to her father's *shamba* (plantation) at
Bweni and the other to her father's shamba at Dunga, but neither
of them was allowed to assume the title of Mwenyi Mkuu.

The early history of Tumbatu Island has been given in Chapter
II. As there said, the present inhabitants assert that they belong
to a mixed race sprung from African and Asiatic immigrants who
arrived in the island about the end of the twelfth century of the
Christian era. Anthropological evidence would appear to suggest
that this tradition may have some foundation in fact.

After this there is a gap in Tumbatu history extending over
more than five centuries. We next hear of the island as being ruled
by a sheha, a post which could be held by a woman as well
as by a man. The first recorded sheha was in fact a woman named
Mwana wa Mwana, who is said to have married Hassan, the
Mwenyi Mkuu of the Hadimu, who died in 1845. The marriage
of these two did not, however, at once lead to the union of the two
tribes. Legend has it that for the sake of his wife the Mwenyi Mkuu
excused the Tumbatu from payment of all taxes, but the more
probable explanation is that the Tumbatu displayed their traditional spirit of independence, by declining to pay any such
impositions.

Confirmation of this view is forthcoming from the fact that
Mwana wa Mwana was succeeded as Sheha by her son Ali, who,
however, did not succeed her husband as Mwenyi Mkuu. Ali's
rule does not appear to have lasted any great length of time. He
was followed in rapid succession by four children and grandchildren – male and female. The last of the grandchildren – a
namesake called Ali – was succeeded by a certain Msellem, who

M

was appointed to the post either by Said bin Sultan or else by his son and successor, Majid. Msellem was not a member of the hereditary family, from which the Sheha had hitherto been chosen and was placed under the orders of Sultan Hamadi, the Mwenyi Mkuu who died in 1865. After Sultan Hamadi's death a letter went forth from Zanzibar confirming Msellem as Sheha under Sultan Hamadi's son, Ahmed, 'to hold the same position as he used to do in the time of Sultan Muhammad'. The letter then proceeded to say that 'no person amongst the Hadimu [sic] of Tumbatu shall disobey his orders, for he is their overseer as much as, and perhaps even more than he was before'.

The rapidity with which Mwana wa Mwana's descendants succeeded each other and the ultimate appointment of a Sheha from outside her family suggests that Said bin Sultan was deliberately trying to compel the Sheha of Tumbatu to become subordinate to the Mwenyi Mkuu and that the members of the hereditary family were not proving at all amenable to this plan. The final injunction contained in Seyyid Majid's letter would appear to indicate that in 1865 the islanders of Tumbatu were not accepting with the best of grace either Msellem as their Sheha or their subordination to the Mwenyi Mkuu.

After this compulsory union of the Tumbatu with the Hadimu the subsequent history of the former tribe followed the same pattern as that of the latter. They still, however, retain their old dialect and preserve much of their old *mila* (customary law), each of which is in many respects different from that of the Hadimu. Whilst those now settled on the main island of Zanzibar have in the course of close association with people of other races and languages dropped much of their former spirit of xenophobia, those still living on the island of Tumbatu still maintain their aloofness and do their best to discourage alien immigration, even when the would-be immigrant is a member of some other African tribe.

Like the people of Zanzibar, the indigenous population of Pemba is of many very mixed races and origins. Those races have reached the island at very different dates. The Kilwa Chronicle tells us that immigrants from Shiraz in Persia arrived there at the end of the tenth century of the Christian era. There are also records and traditions of other immigrants from Arabia and the Persian Gulf who arrived in the island at later dates. Many of the archaeological remains in Pemba show cultural influences from Asia, which in the course of centuries have tended to become africanized. There appears to be little doubt that over a long period of years – and more particularly during the two centuries of Portuguese domination in East Africa – the flow of immigration from the east became gradually reduced and that the earlier immigrants began to intermarry with the local African tribes and thus to produce the people of mixed origins, who now call themselves Shirazi. As local chronicles show, these descendants of Asiatic settlers were also reinforced by other persons of mixed blood from the mainland. Thus, a large party of Shirazi is said to have arrived from Witu on the mainland and to have settled 'in all four corners of the island' some ten years before the advent of the Portuguese. Another party of Shirazi, who are said to have been over one thousand strong, were brought by the Portuguese to Pemba in 1606. They too settled in different parts of the island. Shortly before their arrival a party of Nabhani from the island of Patta had installed themselves in the northern part of Pemba. Tradition also asserts that at the end of the seventeenth century there was a large scale invasion of the island by the Segeju, a Bantu tribe then dwelling in the region of Tanga.

As Portuguese records and local chronicles and traditions show, at the beginning of the sixteenth century the island was divided between five chiefs, who were mutually independent of each other. It is impossible to say how long this state of affairs lasted.

At the beginning of the nineteenth century the generally recognized title for the local chief would appear to have been Sheha wa Mji or Mkubwa. Slightly higher in rank was a chief called the Diwani, who might exercise authority over a number of these inferior chiefs, but it was not necessarily a *sine qua non* that a Sheha or Mkubwa was the subordinate of a Diwani. The authority of a Sheha was almost invariably limited to a single village or cluster of hamlets, whereas a Diwani had several villages under his rule. The Sheha had a council of elders to advise and assist him. This body was known as the *Watu Wazima* and varied in composition from about four to six members.

Throughout the centuries the people of Pemba always exhibited a spirit of sturdy independence. *Force majeure* compelled them upon occasion to agree to pay tribute to the Portuguese, but they frequently evaded or even successfully resisted demands for such payment. They were ready to accept aid from Oman to shake off the Portuguese yoke, but they were no more ready to acknowledge Mazrui sovereignty than they had been to acknowledge Portuguese. When they eventually invoked the aid of Seyyid Said bin Sultan to shake off the Mazrui yoke, a deputation comprising two diwanis from the southern part of the island and other representatives of the islanders proceeded to Muscat. According to a local chronicle something in the nature of a treaty was drawn up and sealed by the ceremony of blood brotherhood. No mention of was made in that pact of any cession of sovereignty of territory. The inhabitants agreed to pay *ushuru* (duty) in consideration of the Sultan affording them assistance and protection, such payment to be made in kind by delivery of ghee and mats. The Sultan was to be allowed to build on the island wherever he liked but, as the ceremony of blood brotherhood and the wording of the accompanying agreement showed, the people of Pemba were to become his allies and to be of one *shauri* (accord) with him.

After the expulsion of the Mazrui the Sultan kept a fairly considerable garrison in the island comprising some of his compatriots, natives of other parts of Arabia, Baluchis and others. Some of these intermarried with the local inhabitants and became absorbed into the communities to which their wives belonged. Others brought or sent for their womenfolk in Asia and proceeded to acquire land. Other Arab colonists soon followed in the wake of the garrison, and set themselves up in commerce and agriculture. As in Zanzibar many of these devoted their attention to clove planting, which had already passed well beyond the experimental stage at the time of Seyyid Said's death. Planting vastly increased after the disastrous hurricane of 1872, which wrought havoc in the clove plantations in Zanzibar but only reached the southern end of

The result of all these migrations and of the expansion of the clove industry, was that the newcomers gradually acquired more and more of the land in the fertile belt on the western side of Pemba, while the original inhabitants began to withdraw into the less fertile regions on the east coast. But the pattern was not quite the same as occurred in similar circumstances in Zanzibar. Pemba is only fourteen miles wide at its widest point and does not possess the same backbone in the shape of a central ridge, which sharply divides the fertile from the less fertile belt in Zanzibar. In many places – more particularly in the south of the island – the fertile belt extends very nearly to the east coast. The result has been that the withdrawal of the original inhabitants to the eastern side of the island did not enable them to keep themselves as much aloof from newcomers as the Hadimu had been able to do in Zanzibar. Consequently indirect rule of the Sultan through their recognized tribal authorities was supplanted by more direct rule of the local Arab Liwali (governor).

It is difficult to form any estimate as to the extent of the authority of any diwani in Pemba at the beginning of the nineteenth century. Diwani Ngwachani and Diwani Athmani claimed to be descended from a certain Shame wa Makame, who is said to have ruled over the whole island at the beginning of the sixteenth century, but it is evident that, though Ngwachani and Athmani may have been momentarily recognized as the islanders' leaders in a general uprising against the Mazrui, their actual administrative authority was limited to the southern part of the island.

Diwani Ngwachani died very shortly after the expulsion of the Mazrui and his death was soon afterwards followed by that of his brother Diwani Athmani. The way was then left clear for a change over from indirect to direct rule. Ibrahim, the successor of Athmani, would appear not to have been a member of the ruling family. He was evidently the nominee of the Sultan of Zanzibar and was likely to be more docile than any relative of his predecessor.

In Zanzibar the hereditary post of Mwenyi Mkuu came to an end through default of male heirs. In Pemba the hereditary post was abolished because local circumstances proved that the services of the holder of that post could be more easily dispensed with.

CHAPTER IX

RELATIONS OF SEYYID SAID WITH PORTUGAL, FRANCE AND GERMANY

ALTHOUGH, as previous chapters have shown, English, French and Dutch ships had from time to time visited the East African coast, until the latter part of the eighteenth century the Europeans best known to the dwellers on that coast were the Portuguese. The same was true of the inhabitants of Oman. Their country had been subjugated by the Portuguese, who had not been expelled until 1650. As already mentioned, the Portuguese were finally expelled from Mombasa and all their East African possessions to the north of Cape Delgado in 1729.

As conquerors belonging to a different race and religion from the conquered, it is not surprising to learn that the Portuguese left no good report behind them. Amongst the coast natives of East Africa they earned the uncomplimentary name of 'afriti' (devils). Though they were finally turned out of all East Africa to the north of Cape Delgado, bag and baggage, the war between them and the Arabs of Oman was never officially concluded by a treaty of peace. The Portuguese were living in the constant hope that their opponents would one day make themselves so unpopular in East Africa that they would be invited to send a small armed force to expel them and would thus be able to regain their lost foothold. 'Shadow' establishments were from time to time formed to take charge at Mombasa as soon as that place was recovered. Thus, on March 22, 1745, we learn from instructions which went out from Lisbon that a certain officer had been granted the reversion of the post of Sotto-Major (second-in-command) of the fort of Mombasa and that it had been decided that, if the fort had not been recovered at the time when that reversion fell in, he must be given another post in India. As Fort Jesus was never retaken, the officer in question, like many others, had to look for employment elsewhere.

In 1798 emissaries reached Mozambique from Mombasa and assured the Portuguese Captain-General that the people of Mombasa would be very glad to see the return of the Portuguese because (amongst other things) 'the Arabs of Muscat, who were established at Zanzibar, threatened to take possession of their island, and the people of Mombasa knew how harsh would be their rule compared with ours'. There was a delay of three years before any action was taken on this report. At this date Mozambique was suffering from lack of man-power and also from the necessity of having to refer to Lisbon before any action of major importance could be undertaken. In 1801 a schooner, which was not inappropriately named *Embuscada* ('the ambush'), was sent to Mombasa to recover that place. It was accompanied by another vessel carrying some soldiers, but nothing came of this – the last – effort of the Portuguese to recover Mombasa. On November 25, 1801, Isidoro de Sa, who commanded the expedition, reported that he had not been well received in Mombasa and had therefore decided to return to Mozambique.

Although the Captain-General of Mozambique was constantly trying to promote fifth column activities within the African dominions of the rulers of Oman and although the state of war had never terminated by any treaty of peace, in course of time there arose on either side a state of non-belligerence. By 1792 vessels from Zanzibar were visiting Mozambique for purposes of trade and three years later the Captain-General of Mozambique reported that some half-dozen Portuguese ships were visiting Mombasa, Kilwa and Zanzibar in order to pick up slaves, who were ultimately shipped to Brazil. But the lack of a treaty of peace meant that the boundary between the territories of the King of Portugal and the ruler of Oman was never properly defined. As will be seen, this omission led to a long dispute between the two states.

Cape Delgado happens to be a prominent cape on the coast of East Africa, which at once suggests itself as a suitable natural feature to be adopted as a boundary mark separating the coast lying to the north and south thereof. In fact an Anglo-Portuguese Convention of 1817 declared the cape to be the northern boundary of the Portuguese territories in East Africa. But that convention could not bind Seyyid Said, who asserted that his dominions extended to the village of Tungwe on the shores of a bay lying just to the south of Cape Delgado.

An attempt was made in 1826 by Sebastião Xavier Botelho to get this boundary question settled. It was afterwards alleged that Seyyid Said had received the proposal favourably, but he appears to have evaded giving a binding answer to it. In February 1826, a commercial treaty was concluded between Portugal and Oman. That treaty permitted the Sultan's vessels visiting Mozambique to pay the same import duty, namely, ten per cent. *ad valorem* as did vessels from the Portuguese Indian possessions of Diu and Daman, provided they carried ship's papers authenticated by the Sultan's seal, but it made no mention whatever of any international boundary. In 1877 Dr. Kirk, then British Consul at Zanzibar, was shown a document purporting to be a treaty which was dated 12 Ramadan, A.H. 1242 (May 27, 1829) which definitely declared Tungwe to be that boundary, but it was clear that this so-called treaty was never ratified. On March 28, 1828, an ambassador of Seyyid Said was induced to assent to a treaty which declared 'that the limits of the territory of His Highness the Imam of Muscat on the east coast of Africa, to the north of the Portuguese possessions shall not extend beyond Mingoya and those of his Most Faithful Majesty, shall extend to Tungwe inclusively', but, as Colonel Playfair, then British Consul at Zanzibar, pointed out in 1861, this treaty, which incidentally left the promontory of Cape Delgado in no man's land, was never ratified by Seyyid Said himself.

A month or so before this unratified treaty was concluded a young Portuguese naval officer, named Ferdinando da Costa, arrived in Zanzibar. He came ostensibly to congratulate Seyyid Said on his having obtained possession of Fort Jesus at Mombasa, but in reality to spy out the land. He was granted an interview by Seyyid Said, who informed him that he 'had the same esteem for both the English and the Portuguese nations'. If, as Edmund Roberts alleged, Said had at about the same time styled the Portuguese as 'those vile hogs' and 'those accursed worshippers of wooden images', the indirect compliment paid to the English was most distinctly not a flattering one.

One does not imagine that Seyyid Said was in the least taken in by da Costa. His dislike of the Portuguese was a hereditary one and he was doubtless well aware that the Portuguese still aspired to recover Mombasa. His profound mistrust of persons of that race was exhibited in October 1838, when he accorded an interview to a certain Torres Texugo, who subsequently wrote a long letter to Thomas Fowell Buxton on the subject of the East African slave trade. Apparently Texugo had come to Zanzibar in the hope of persuading Said to abolish that traffic.

Knowing me [he afterwards wrote] to be a Portuguese and just arrived from Mozambique, (he) made several minute inquiries regarding the state of the colony, particularly as regards the fortress, the number of troops, their discipline, how many ships of war were stationed there, and their size; and he asked me finally how the Portuguese Government, after having signed, as he himself had done, a solemn treaty for the abolition of the slave trade, allowed it still to be carried on in its settlements. My answers were dictated by prudence and I endeavoured to destroy in the best way I could any ulterior object which the Imam had in view. I mentioned to him that it was reported at Mozambique that the Lisbon Government wished to enter into negotiations with him. His answer was conveyed in a significant laugh, accompanied by an assurance that he only desired that the Lisbon authorities would make his vessels, visiting Portuguese settlements, pay the same duties (sc. instead of the ten per cent. fixed by the treaty of 1826) as he imposed on theirs in his ports, viz., five per cent on all goods imported or exported.

In 1843 the Captain-General of Mozambique paid a personal visit to Seyyid Said at Zanzibar. It was somewhat significant that this officer lacked the necessary means of transport and had to take advantage of an offer of a passage on board H.M.S. *Cleopatra*. As he was careful to explain in reporting to Lisbon the result of his visit, 'this voyage cost the state nothing'. History is silent as to whether Tungwe was discussed when the Captain-General met Seyyid Said. If it was, Seyyid Said managed once again to evade committing himself in any way. A new treaty was drawn up, but it was confined to tightening up the regulations regarding the ship's papers of Arab and Swahili vessels visiting Mozambique.

Colonel Playfair, who visited Tungwe in 1863, reported that 'the district is governed by a quasi-independent chief or Sultan of Arab descent'. It was this quasi-independence which made Tungwe a bone of contention between Zanzibar and Portugal for rather more than half a century. The chief was ready to play one state off against the other, whenever it suited his convenience, and in so doing to arm each disputant with plausible arguments in support of its claim.

The Portuguese alleged – apparently with justice – that from 1765 onwards the chief of Tungwe had been formally appointed by themselves, but it is clear that by 1826 the chief had a foot in both camps and was careful to obtain recognition by King and Sultan alike. It was not until the succession as chief in 1837 of one Ahmed

Sultan that the dispute really came to a head. On appointment Ahmed Sultan wrote to inform the Captain-General at Mozambique that he had received a Portuguese flag from his predecessor. In 1844 he allowed a Banyan trader to settle at Tungwe and to carry on business with India and Zanzibar. As this was contrary to the Portuguese revenue laws, he was ordered to expel the newcomer. Ahmed Sultan refused to comply with the order and later offered resistance to an armed party, which was sent to see that the order was carried out. Later a gunboat was sent to enforce the order. By that time the Banyan had left, but – in the words of a subsequent Portuguese memorandum – 'the people on board did not disembark because of the hostile attitude displayed by the Sheikh'. By 1845, however, Ahmed Sultan had decided to change his attitude and gave a friendly reception to a commission sent from Mozambique.

Ahmed Sultan's encouragement of Banyan immigrants was because they attracted trade to his territory. The most important article of commerce was the traffic in human beings, which gave him substantial middleman's profits. In the course of the next few years this trade had grown to such dimensions that Banyan traders had erected a number of barracoons in Tungwe Bay for the reception of slaves pending transhipment elsewhere. In 1850 the British Consul at Zanzibar remonstrated with Seyyid Said for allowing this state of affairs and on May 6 in that year the Sultan authorized British men-of-war to land in this and other bays and destroy all barracoons found there. Acting under this authority, Captain Bunce of H.M.S. *Dee* proceeded to Tungwe Bay and destroyed the barracoons. Three Banyans, who had been left in charge there by a compatriot, were taken as prisoners to Zanzibar and deported thence to India. Not a word of protest emanated from Mozambique alleging violation of Portuguese territory. The reason was obvious. Even if he had the will, the Governor-General had tacitly to acknowledge that he lacked the power to enforce law and order in Tungwe Bay.

This drastic action may have led Ahmed Sultan's next *volte face*. In 1853 he allowed the Sultan of Zanzibar to establish a customs post and a small military garrison at Tungwe. As the already cited Portuguese memorandum tells us, 'immediately after the Zanzibar occupation in 1853 a small military expedition was directed against Tungwe and having been received in a hostile fashion, was obliged to retire, after having left one of the Sultan's officers dead on shore'. In the following year the Captain-General of Mozambique sent a formal protest to Seyyid Said's son Khalid, who was in charge at Zanzibar during his father's absence at Muscat. Khalid, however, appears to have ignored the protest.

Such was the posture of affairs at the time of Seyyid Said's death. Matters remained unchanged for another thirty years after his death. From time to time the Portuguese Government lodged protests against the continued occupation of Tungwe Bay by Zanzibar, but the Sultan's customs post and soldiers remained there until 1887, when Seyyid Said's son, Barghash, was compelled to relinquish his claims to Tungwe Bay after two Portuguese men-of-war had bombarded and set fire to the undefended villages of Tungwe and Meningani.

After the final expulsion of the Portuguese from Mombasa the European nation which had for many years had the closest and strongest connection with Zanzibar was France. As early as 1722 the commander of a French man-of-war visiting Muscat concluded an agreement with the Yorubi ruler of Oman fixing at five dollars the capitation tax on slaves exported from the Sultan's African dominions in French vessels. Though this agreement soon afterwards became a dead letter, vessels began to arrive in increasing numbers at Zanzibar and Kilwa for the purpose of shipping slaves to the Isle of France (Mauritius) and Bourbon (Réunion). Though at the beginning of the Napoleonic Wars, relations were temporarily strained by the capture by a privateer from Mauritius of a ship from Oman, intercourse began to increase between the two French islands and Zanzibar and Oman. In 1798 Sultan bin Ahmed, the father of Seyyid Said, was employing a Frenchman as captain of one of his vessels and other Frenchmen were seeking to establish a factory either at Muscat or else at Bandar Abbas, which was then in the possession of Oman. As the Napoleonic War was then raging, this friendliness somewhat perturbed the British Government at Bombay, who eventually induced Sultan bin Ahmed not only to dismiss and expel his French captain and to refuse any trading concession to that captain's compatriots, but also to come to the assistance of the British, if they were attacked in Sultan bin Ahmed's dominions or in his territorial waters. In the Sultan's outlying dominions, however, the friendly feeling for the French still continued. In 1799 Lieutenant Bissell reported that the people of Zanzibar 'have a great deal of trade with the French for slaves and coffee, and many of them talk that language in consequence'.

Shortly after Seyyid Said regained the throne of Oman, the *Vigilant* a French privateer put in to Muscat for shelter and repairs. The captain of a British frigate demanded that the vessel should be ordered to leave that port. In pursuance of the treaty obligations concluded by his father with the East India Company Said ordered the vessel to depart. The result was that the *Vigilant* was promptly captured by the British frigate. Reprisals came some months later when another French privateer seized the cargoes of eight Muscat vessels near Ceylon. Seyyid Said then made an appeal for protection to the Bombay Government, but failed to obtain a satisfactory reply. He accordingly decided to make his peace with the French. On June 16, 1807, he entered into a treaty with General Charles Decaen, Governor of the Isle of France (Mauritius) wherein he agreed to allow the French to seize contraband of war on Muscat ships proceeding to enemy ports as well as the property of his subjects found on enemy ships. He also agreed to allow French commercial agents to reside at Muscat. Decaen, however, was hard put to it to protect the French islands in the Indian Ocean and was therefore unable to take much advantage of the treaty. Twelve months later Seyyid Said sent an envoy to the Isle of France requesting that Muscat vessels might be allowed to trade between ports in British India and, despite the injunctions contained in Napoleon's blockade decrees, Decaen felt it politic to sign a subsidiary agreement to that effect. As Captain Smee learnt in 1811, the French were 'great favourites' in Zanzibar and the capture a few months previously by the British of Mauritius was far from popular.

The loss of Mauritius and the Seychelles more or less put an end for the time being to French trade with Zanzibar. At the close of the Napoleonic Wars Bourbon remained in French hands and was used by them in an attempt to recover the political and commercial advantages, which they had previously enjoyed on the coasts of the Indian Ocean. Replying in 1817 to a letter introducing a French merchant who was visiting Muscat, Seyyid Said informed the Governor of Bourbon of his strong desire to renew the bonds of friendship which had formerly existed between his country and the French colonies. The result was that in 1817 and again in 1822

commercial treaties were drawn up fixing the customs tariffs
payable by the French to the Sultan and *vice versa*.

Some seventeen years later relations between Seyyid Said and
the French Government became distinctly strained. The trouble
arose from the fact that both he and the French monarchy had
their eyes on Madagascar. Arab and Swahili ships had been trading
with the island in the days of the Portuguese supremacy and had
from time to time established settlements on its northern shores.
Later Seyyid Said received an appeal for help from a certain Queen
Seneekoo (or Tsihometa), who ruled over the island of Nossi Bé,
an island lying off the north-west coast of Madagascar. The
inhabitants of that island were Sakalavas and were in constant fear
of being conquered by the Hovas of the main island. For this
reason Seneekoo's ministers concluded a treaty with Seyyid Said,
whereby the Queen agreed to surrender 'all her dominions on the
island of Nossi Bé to Said and further agreed to pay him thirty
thousand dollars and a duty of five per cent. on all imports from
the island'. In return Seyyid Said undertook to 'take charge of the
fort and to protect us on the sea side and generally protect us as he
does his other subjects'. It appears that in compliance with the
terms of this treaty Seneekoo sent a quantity of beeswax to
Zanzibar as 'tribute money', or rather, as consideration for the
protection which Seyyid Said had undertaken to afford to her and
her subjects. Either before or after the conclusion of the treaty a
certain number of Zanzibaris settled in Nossi Bé, but there is no
record of any garrison having been established there.

Prior to the outbreak of the Napoleonic Wars the French had
had a number of establishments on the coast of Madagascar, which
were handed back by the British to the French in 1816. In 1840 the
French Government decided to extend its possessions in and near
that island as well as on the main continent. In the summer of 1840
the French corvette *Dordogne* (commanded by Captain Guillain)
arrived at Zanzibar. It so chanced that Seyyid Said was at the time
in Muscat, having left his favourite son, Khalid, in charge of
Zanzibar. Under the tutelage of his kinsman, Suleiman bin Hamed,
the son had become an intense admirer of the French and their
ways, as was shown by his calling one of his principal clove plantations Marseilles. At this date he was only twenty or twenty-one
years of age. When therefore the commander of the French vessel
landed and requested permission from Khalid to establish 'a

French agent' at Zanzibär and 'to erect a fort and buildings at Mogadishu and Barawa, where they said they wished to form a settlement', he may have been very surprised at the rebuff which he received. Although Khalid may have been young in years, he was already in sage counsel old. Acting doubtless on the advice of his kinsman and mentor, Suleiman, he appears to have referred the French officer to his father, declaring that he himself had no authority to grant the request. Whereupon the French corvette weighed anchor and made sail, not for Muscat, but for Nossi Bé, where Queen Seneekoo was invited to accept a French protectorate. According to first reports reaching Zanzibar the invitation was declined.

After his visit to Nossi Bé Captain Guillain proceeded to Muscat to get permission for the French Consul to take up his residence at Zanzibar and to obtain Seyyid Said's consent to a new commercial treaty. The Sultan had been forewarned that the Governor of Bourbon was proposing to make overtures of this description. As long before as October 31, 1839, he had written to the Bombay Government asking for their advice as to whether he ought to enter into any such treaty. He was told in reply that 'he was recommended not to enter into any engagements of the kind addressed to him, nor even any new convention with the French'. The result was that Captain Guillain left Muscat on August 25, 1840, without having obtained Said's assent to the treaty of 'effecting the chief object for which he was deputed to this place, namely, the installation of Mr. Noel as Consul at Zanzibar'.

Doubtless, Guillain's departure after his fruitless errand gave Seyyid Said intense satisfaction, but on November 11, 1840, he 'received authentic intelligence of two towers being built by the French at Nossi Bé'. Later reports said two French frigates had arrived at that island, had landed a large number of people, and begun to build a fort and storerooms without the slightest reference being made to the Governor of Zanzibar.

On March 5, 1841, Seneekoo formally ceded her island to Admiral Hell of the French Navy in consideration of a yearly pension of twelve hundred francs. Writing to report this cession to Seyyid Said, the lady discreetly omitted all reference to the pension and apologized for her conduct by explaining that 'we do not want them, and I am sorry I have been obliged to allow them because your people were not with us'. As Hamerton reported, Seyyid

Said had done 'nothing but send them a red flag'. Said appealed to the British Government to intervene but, after making due inquiry Palmerston had to inform Seyyid Said 'that there is a material difference between territories which have for a length of time belonged to a Sovereign and districts which have only recently tendered their submission to such sovereign, and over which he has exercised no practical authority'. Therein lay the rub. As Queen Seneekoo had said, 'your people were not with us'. By itself the red flag of the Sultan could not be deemed to be satisfactory evidence of an effective physical possession. In the absence of any proper entry into such possession, Seyyid Said's claim had to yield place to that of the French.

Immediately upon receipt of the news about Nossi Bé Seyyid Said set sail for Zanzibar. He was followed later by the British Consul, Atkins Hamerton, who arrived on May 4, 1841, to find Said 'dejected and broken spirited' in consequence of the confirmation of all the information which had previously received regarding the French at Nossi Bé. The refusal of Palmerston to take up the cudgels on his behalf further depressed him. He told Hamerton that the French 'intend to take the Mrima (mainland) from me, and yet, my friends, the English do nothing to prevent them. My people at Kilwa are in great fear that the French intend coming there'. Hamerton replied that 'the reports in circulation regarding the coming of the French to the Mrima are circulated by Your Highness's people, who are in the interests of the French'. He nevertheless promised to proceed personally to investigate at Kilwa by the first available British man-of-war. He went to Kilwa in H.M.S. *Grecian* in December 1841, and on the 27th of that month announced that there was no foundation for the reports regarding French activities. Later in 1842, however, the French brig-of-war *Messager* visited Kilwa and approached certain 'chiefs' there regarding the purchase of their island. The chiefs had hastened with the news to Zanzibar and were reported by Hamerton to be 'terribly frightened'. Seyyid Said was equally alarmed. Fearing that the Shirazi Sultan of Kilwa might succumb to the temptation of French gold, he caused him to be deported to Muscat.

In 1843 Seyyid Said's alarm was further increased by the annexation by the French of the island of Mayotte in the Comoro archipelago. Many of the inhabitants of the island had Arab blood in their veins. The rulers of Oman had always claimed to be their overlords, though none of the Busaidi dynasty had done anything affording an outward and visible sign of their overlordship. Seyyid Said's claim to the sovereignty of Mayotte was therefore even weaker than his claim to Nossi Bé. Accordingly he could do nothing except bow to the *fait accompli*.

On November 9, 1844, Captain Romain Desfosses arrived off Zanzibar with three French men-of-war. He had full powers to conclude a commercial treaty with Seyyid Said and also to place a French Consul at Zanzibar. Doubtless, it was felt that the three vessels would have a greater chance of counteracting British influence behind the scenes than the single corvette which had visited Muscat four years previously under Captain Guillain's command. But there was no need of any such counter argument. Back in Europe there had been a change of ministry both in Great Britain and in France. Lord Palmerston was no longer British Foreign Secretary, his place having been taken by Lord Aberdeen. In France M. Guizot had been summoned from the French Embassy in London to take up the post of Minister of Foreign Affairs at Paris. As his letters show, Palmerston believed that war between England and France was sooner or later more or less inevitable, a belief which had been confirmed by the chauvinism of Guizot's predecessor in office in Paris. On the other hand, Aberdeen and Guizot both held that the common interest of the two countries was peace and friendship and, when differences arose – as they did from time to time arise not only in East Africa, but also in other parts of the globe – they could be reduced by this principle to comparative insignificance. Accordingly, the advice tendered by the Government at Bombay to Seyyid Said in 1840 no longer held good. Hamerton, the British Consul, makes no reference in his correspondence to having been consulted at all by Seyyid Said in regard to the treaty. If he was, his instructions were certainly not to oppose it and his advice must have been limited to questions of detail. The treaty was duly signed, sealed and delivered on November 17. Four days later the French flag was duly hoisted on the newly arrived Consul's house and a salute of twenty-one guns was fired by the French corvette *Berçeau* and the Sultan's frigate *Shah Allum*.

As the text of the treaty shows, with the exception of few details it was worded almost the same as one which Seyyid Said had con-

cluded with Great Britain in 1839. It differed in many respects
from that tendered to the Sultan by Captain Guillain in 1840. In
the new treaty it was mutually agreed that the subjects of each of
the contracting parties could reside, trade, and acquire land in the
dominions of the other. The eleventh article, however, prohibited –
as did the corresponding article in the British treaty – the French
from trading on the main continent in ivory and gum between
Mtangata and Kilwa 'until England, or the United States of
America, or any other Christian nation shall have authority to
take part therein'. Certain of the articles in the treaty were, however, destined to sow the seeds of future trouble. The French
Consul was given certain rights of extra-territorial jurisdiction in
disputes between his compatriots and the Sultan's subjects and
also in the administration of the estates of deceased or bankrupt
Frenchmen – rights to which at a later date the French Government clung with a most tenacious persistence. Article IV of the
treaty provided that

the subjects of His Highness the Sultan, who are in the service of the
French, shall enjoy the same protection as the French themselves;
but, if the subjects of His Highness are convicted of any crime or
offence punishable by the law, they shall be discharged by the French
from the service in which they are, and handed over to the local
authorities.

One day it was to be found that not a few of the Sultan's subjects
were to seek refuge behind this Article from the efforts of the Sultan
and the British Government to eradicate the slave trade.

The French squadron departed from Zanzibar leaving behind
a certain M. Broquant as French Consul and also a young naval
officer named Maizan, who was to cause Seyyid Said a lot of worry
and trouble. Maizan had sailed with Guillain to Muscat in 1840
and had thereafter conceived a grandiose plan of traversing the
continent of Africa from east to west. The French Government
had given its approval to the project and the *Berçeau* had conveyed
Maizan to Zanzibar for the purpose of carrying it out. There is
no need to go into details of his subsequent career. As his former
commanding officer Guillain said, he was the author of his own
tragedy. Having declined Seyyid Said's offer of a military escort,
he crossed over after eight months' delay to the mainland. Accompanied by only a few followers, he penetrated inland about sixty
miles to the south-west of the modern town of Dar es Salaam.

N

He reached a village belonging to a Zaramo chief, whose nickname
was Ndege la Mhulo (the bird in the bush), where he was
murdered. When news of this tragedy reached Bourbon, Captain
Romain Desfosses proceeded to Zanzibar to insist on the arrest and
punishment of the murderer. There is no written contemporary
record of the interview between Seyyid Said and the Captain,
but the latter reported to the French Consul that he had 'obtained
from the Sultan a promise that active search would be made for
the murderers'. In the light of what transpired a year or so later
in a subsequent interview between Said and Captain Guillain it
may perhaps be gathered that the Sultan pointed out that, with
every desire to see that justice was done, there were difficulties in
complying with the French officers' demands and that all he had
then promised was to do what he could. When Captain Guillain
arrived a year later at Zanzibar, the French Consul informed him
'that he had no knowledge of any step having been taken to arrest
the *phazi* (chief), and that he was nevertheless convinced that, if
the Sultan seriously desired it, the arrest would be quite easy'.
As the Consul had never set foot on the mainland, this expression
of opinion was of very little value but Guillain, who was a former
commanding officer and personal friend of Maizan, decided he
must force Seyyid Said into taking action of some sort.

The only account of the subsequent interview with Seyyid Said
is that given by Guillain, who decided to ride the high horse. The
Sultan pointed out that Maizan had refused an offer of an escort.
Guillain replied that, 'as the crime had been committed in his
territory and by one of his subjects', he expected him to obtain
full reparation. In the light of what was often alleged in Seyyid
Said's lifetime and after his death, the Sultan's reply is interesting.

The Sultan formally declared to me that (the village of) Ndege la
Mhulo, the scene of the murder, was completely outside his jurisdiction;
that not only was the *phazi* (chief) not one of his subjects, but that he
had no influence over him nor any other chief established in the
interior, except at a short distance from the coast.

He further denied that he had made any promise to Captain
Romain Desfosses. Not being in a position to reply to this denial,
Guillain

expressed the firm conviction that the officer commanding the French
naval forces would not allow the crime to remain unpunished, and in
such case the Sultan should not be in the least astonished at the

methods we should employ, as he denied any possibility of being himself successful and also that he had any authority either over the
murderer or in the country where the murder was committed.

It was a piece of sheer bluff and Said called it. 'His face betrayed
not the slightest emotion and with the utmost calm he gave me to
understand that he would be very much relieved if we acted thus
and made a prisoner of this phazi, regarding whom he had many
complaints but was nevertheless compelled to leave him unpunished.' Finding that he could make no further headway in the
matter, Guillain turned the conversation to another subject.
Later on, Seyyid Said, believing that Guillain's demands had
official backing from his Government, wrote to the Captain assuring him that he had already attempted without success to make a
prisoner of the murderer and that he would continue those efforts
regardless of trouble and expense.

In fulfilment of this promise Seyyid Said directed the Diwan of
the coast town of Sadaani to lead an expedition into the Zaramo
country to exact reparation. According to Burton, the party was
ambushed by the Zaramo and the murderer subsequently made
his getaway. 'A luckless clansman who had beaten the war drum
during the murder' was captured and passed off by the leaders of
the expedition as the actual murderer. For nearly two years he was
chained in front of the French Consulate; after that he was placed
in the fort 'heavily ironed to a gun under a cadjan shed, where he
could hardly stand or lie down'. He managed, however, to keep
alive for nearly a dozen years, dying in about 1858. In such
manner French susceptibilities were satisfied, but the Sultan of
Zanzibar had been put to no little trouble, worry and expense on
account of a young man, who had brought his troubles on himself
and for whose murder the Sultan had not even a vicarious
responsibility.

Doubtless, Seyyid Said watched Guillain's departure in the brig
Ducouedic with considerable relief, but he had not yet heard the
last of him. In August, 1847, news reached Zanzibar that the brig
had put into Barawa and Lamu and the Captain 'had been tamper-
ing with the chiefs and trying to induce them to sell certain ports
to the Government of France. . . (But) the chiefs did not consent
as they said the place belonged to His Highness the Imam'. It was
doubtless gratifying to Said to learn that he could rely on the
loyalty of his officers in these outlying places, but there was always

the risk that their loyalty might be undermined. Many of his Arab subjects had in the past made their living by trade with the French islands in the Indian Ocean and more particularly by the Slave Trade. The Sultan had in 1822 agreed with the British Government to ban any dealings in that trade with the subjects of Christian nations and had thereby made himself extremely unpopular with many of his compatriots. There had consequently grown up a party in his dominions which was either openly or covertly pro-French. On January 1, 1842, Hamerton had reported that 'there is a strong party here in favour of the French. It is in constant communication with them and will no doubt seek their assistance on the death of the Imam'. Writing on the last day of August 1843, to Lord Aberdeen he said this pro-French party 'look upon their coming amongst them as the re-establishment of the Foreign Slave Trade'.

Whilst he was extremely anxious to remain on friendly terms with the French Government and to give every encouragement to reputable and legitimate forms of French commerce, Seyyid Said never shook off his mistrust of France and its political aims in the Indian Ocean. The revolution of 1848 caused a temporary lull in French activities in those regions. In the following year Seyyid Said sent his frigate *Caroline* on a special voyage to Marseille, partly to deliver special presents to the President of the new Republic and partly to advertise and find a fresh market for the products of Zanzibar. He was so far successful in this venture that two French firms were induced to establish themselves in business in Zanzibar. Burton reported that in 1856

These firms choose their employees amongst their captains, who act as supercargoes as well as commanders; they are estimable men, sober and skilful, but painfully lax in dealing with 'les nègres'. Their Consul publicly declared that it was his duty to curb the merchants, as well as to protect the commerce of France.

In the circumstances it is perhaps not surprising to learn that to the end of his life Seyyid Said never shook off his profound mistrust of the French and their methods of diplomacy and commerce.

In 1843 a small German schooner called the *Alph* commanded by a Captain Rodetz and having a crew of only eight, all told, left Bremerhaven on a trading voyage to the Indian Ocean. In the course of its voyage the vessel called at Zanzibar, where it picked up a cargo of miscellaneous produce. It arrived back in Hamburg in August 1843. Thereafter a number of ships from the Hanseatic ports of Hamburg, Bremen and Lübeck began to call at Zanzibar and a German firm, Messrs. A. J. Herz and Sons established itself on the island.

When reporting on the trade of Zanzibar on December 15, 1848, Hamerton stated that

the Hamburg and other Hanseatic vessels have as yet done but little in the way of trade in the Imam's dominions. Their principal traffic has as yet been done in the Red Sea, chiefly in gums. The produce they have taken from Zanzibar heretofore has been coconut oil and copal for cash.

At the same time he had to report that except for cloth from America, most of the other manufactured goods were brought to Zanzibar by the American and Hanseatic vessels, such as muskets, hardware, brass and iron work, cutlery and earthenware were of British manufacture. He omitted to mention, however, one article of export from which Herz and Sons were beginning to derive a very handsome profit. This firm had also been trading on the West Coast of Africa where the currency was cowrie shells, which had hitherto been imported from the Maldive Islands *via* Liverpool. The firm, however, discovered that these shells could be obtained at Zanzibar in almost any quantity, of a good size, and above all at a low price. They promptly sent a ship to Zanzibar, which, after taking a cargo of cowries to West Africa, arrived back in Hamburg in 1846 with a big profit to its credit.

Other Germans, who were not traders, also reached Zanzibar during Seyyid Said's reign, and, having regard to their avowed intentions, it would not have been at all surprising if strict a Muslim, such as Said was, had displayed a marked unfriendliness towards them. It speaks highly for him that this was not so.

After an unsuccessful attempt to start a Protestant mission in Abyssinia a Würtemburger named John Lewis Krapf arrived with his wife Rosine at Zanzibar on January 7, 1844. He and his wife, however, took up their abode with the American Consul, Richard Palmer Waters, who endeavoured to persuade Krapf to stay in Zanzibar and work amongst the local population. Krapf, however, was intent upon establishing himself on the mainland and starting missionary work amongst the Gallas.

Although he was by nationality a German, Krapf had come to East Africa under the aegis of the English Church Missionary

Society and it was the British Consul who introduced him to Seyyid Said at Mtoni two days after his arrival. Krapf subsequently reported to his Society that

I told him in Arabic, which he speaks beautifully, that I had been in Abyssinia and was engaged in instructing people. He expressed his pleasure at my talking with him in Arabic, and asked some questions about the Gallas. I did not think it judicious to speak with him more respecting my object at this first interview. On leaving him he followed as far as the gate of the palace. On the whole I was pleased with him and do not think he will object to my going to the Gallas, although some Europeans think he will be averse to missionaries on the coast.

On February 2, Seyyid Said was at his palace in Zanzibar town and Mr and Mrs Krapf proceeded there to pay their respects.

He met us [says the husband] at the door and conducted us to his audience room. Then he requested Mrs Krapf to see his family, which I was not allowed. He conveyed her to a large room upstairs, which, she says, was splendidly furnished with European articles. His daughters were richly dressed according to Arab fashion and behaved very respectfully in the presence of their father. When he stood, they stood, and when he sat down, they sat down. They were masked from the forehead to the mouth.

He tenderly soothed two little sons, whom he placed at his side and who spoke very confidingly with their illustrious father. Mrs. Krapf states His Highness displayed much of the cordial feelings which unite the members of a family. At last she was regaled with a dinner of numerous dishes, which she had not expected in this remote quarter of the world. The room was furnished with large mirrors, couches and chairs of all kinds: and tables covered with various articles of luxury of European extraction.

When we left him, he presented Mrs Krapf with a Persian Shawl and accompanied us to the gate. I do not say too much and shall not be contradicted by any who know him personally, when I call him the *non plus ultra* of an oriental prince.

When Krapf eventually set out in March for the mainland, he was provided with a letter from the Sultan which read as follows:

This comes from Said bin Sultan: greeting to all our subjects, friends and governors. This letter is written on behalf of Dr Krapf, the German, a good man who wishes to convert the world to God. Behave well to him and be everywhere serviceable to him.

Shortly after their arrival in Mombasa, Rosine Krapf died in child-birth. Six days later her infant daughter followed her to the grave. Krapf himself had been seriously ill at the time of these two tragedies. On his recovery he made several journeys into the interior of the continent to see whether there were any suitable openings for missionary work. As a result of those journeys he once more fell ill and decided to convalesce by making a sea trip to Zanzibar, where he arrived on December 12, 1845. Shortly after his arrival he fell seriously ill again, but was nursed back to health by Hamerton, the British Consul. On February 25, 1846, on his return to Mombasa he wrote to C.M.S. headquarters in London saying:

I cannot omit to notice the kind attention shown toward me by the Imam, not only during my stay in Zanzibar, but especially before my departure. He called on me at the British Residency during my sickness, offered all the assistance I might require, and at last, when I was unable to find a suitable boat for my voyage to Mombasa, he hired a vessel at his own expense. He presented me, beside, with a fine ass, when he was apprised of my inability to procure the animal at Zanzibar.

As was only to be expected, not all Seyyid Said's co-religionists had the same tolerant spirit as he had and it had become known that Krapf had been treated with marked hostility by a number of Muslims at Mombasa. On his departure the Sultan had written to the authorities there instructing them to treat Krapf with kindness. Shortly afterwards Krapf informed Hamerton that in consequence thereof a marked change had taken place in the attitude of the people of Mombasa.

On June 10, 1843, Krapf was joined at Mombasa by a compatriot in the person of John Rebmann. Like Krapf, he had first of all called at Zanzibar. He was introduced by the British Consul to Seyyid Said who eventually paid for his passage to Mombasa as well as assisting him in several other ways. Shortly after Rebmann's arrival, he and Krapf moved from Mombasa a few miles inland to Rabai.

With his very recent recollection of Maizan's murder and the trouble which had consequently arisen with the French, Seyyid Said was not unnaturally somewhat disturbed when he heard of this move. Accordingly when Krapf visited Zanzibar in March, 1847, the Sultan told him 'that the Nyika were bad people and that we ought therefore to reside in Zanzibar rather than in the Nyika land'. Krapf replied 'that the inhabitants of the South Sea islands had been still worse than the Nyika, who were not cannibals, like them. European teachers had gone to those cannibals, had taught them out of the word of God, and now they were quite different men'. The Sultan rejoined: 'If that be so, it is all right; you may stay among the Nyika as long as you choose, and do whatever you please'.

On June 3, 1853, however, Hamerton had to report that there was a complete change in Seyyid Said's attitude towards the missionaries.

I observed [he wrote] after my return to Zanzibar that the Imam's mind appeared to be ill at ease, that something was troubling him; and which I now find to be a communication which the Consul of France sometime since made to the Imam's son, the Prince Khalid, relative to His Highness' title to certain places on the coast of Africa, saying that the Imam had no right or authority to claim places on the coast, which the Government of France was led to suppose (but erroneously) were the territories of His Highness the Imam; that the Consul had been so informed by Dr Krapf, the missionary. Now it appears that while we were at Muscat (the Imam and myself), Dr. Krapf came to Zanzibar and had much conversation with the French Consul relative to the state of the Imam's affairs on the African coast. Dr Krapf answered in writing certain questions proposed to him by the French Consul. The answers went to prove that the Imam had no right to exercise authority at several places on the coast, but particularly at the Pangani River and at Lamu. . . . His fellow missionaries, the Reverend Messrs Rebmann and Erhardt told the Doctor he had better not answer the questions or interfere in such matters with which he ought not to have anything to do. All this has caused the Imam to doubt the intentions of the missionaries. . . . I do not suppose that Dr Krapf was aware of the mischief he was about to do to the Imam's affairs.

As Krapf explained in a letter to Henry Venn, Secretary of the Church Missionary Society, the French Consul had invited him to dinner and that after the meal the Consul 'took up a map and said that he had heard a portion of the coast between Vanga and Pangani did not belong to the Imam'. As Krapf had very recently come from those parts, he asked him whether this was true. A less guileless person than Krapf would have realized that there was an ulterior motive behind the question. But Krapf failed to realize the danger. In journeyings oft into the interior and along the coast of the continent he had acquired a peculiar knowledge of the political situation in those parts and was only too willing to impart his information to others. He accordingly told the French Consul that a chief of Usumbara, known as Kimweri, appointed governors and also levied taxes on the coast near the mouth of the Pangani. That information was undoubtedly true. Hamerton himself had reported on July 13, 1841, to the Bombay Government that the local chiefs on the mainland were levying taxes and that he therefore much questioned 'His Highness' right to many places considered to be his'. All the same it was unwise for Krapf to have imparted this information and still more unwise to have put it into writing – more especially in view of the advice given to him by his colleagues. Seyyid Said's feelings on hearing of the incident are quite understandable. To him Krapf's conduct savoured of ingratitude. Krapf had supplied Said's enemies with ammunition to use against his benefactor.

According to Hamerton, Krapf's indiscretion took a long time to be lived down. Writing again to the Bombay Government on February 16, 1854, he declared that 'there has unfortunately a most unfavourable change taken place in the minds of the peoples of these countries as to the missionaries; and which I regret to say has been caused by the Reverend Doctor Krapf'. But perhaps he was exaggerating. Writing to Lord Clarendon two days previously, he had declared that 'this conduct of Dr Krapf has greatly lessened and injured my influence with the Arabs and shaken the implicit reliance they were accustomed to place in my word'.

Seyyid Said appears to have recovered much more quickly from his first transports of indignation. After Krapf's departure for Europe, his colleague James Erhardt, who was contemplating a journey into Kimweri's country, had an interview with Seyyid Said. Not only did the Sultan make no reference to Krapf's indiscretion, but also offered Erhardt a letter of introduction to Kimweri. As for the unfortunate author of all the trouble, Henry Venn told the Foreign Office that, 'if Dr Krapf has done any harm, he was most anxious to undo it'.

CHAPTER X

SEYYID SAID AND THE
UNITED STATES OF AMERICA

So long as they formed part of the British dominions overseas, the people of the thirteen British colonies on the North American seaboard were prevented from trading in the Indian Ocean by reason of the quasi-monopoly of the East India Company as well as by certain Navigation Acts. When in 1776 the representatives of those colonies signed the Declaration of Independence, they published to the world that 'as free and independent states, they shall have full power to levy war, conclude peace, contract alliances, establish commerce and do all other acts and things which independent states may of right do'. By thus severing the bond with Great Britain the thirteen independent and United States ceased to be bound by any restrictive monopolies or legislation which prevented them from trading in the Indian Ocean.

During the War of Independence there was little or no opportunity for those States to exercise their rights, but after peace was concluded in 1782 the Stars and Stripes began to show themselves in the Indian Ocean. In 1799 a Marine Society was founded at Salem. Its membership was limited to 'persons who have actually navigated the seas beyond the Cape of Good Hope or Cape Horn as masters or supercargoes of vessels belonging to Salem'. In 1804 twelve American vessels are said to have visited East African ports. During the next decade, however, the repercussions of the Napoleonic Wars and – in particular the embargo preceding the Anglo-American War of 1812 and that war itself – resulted in a serious set back to American commerce in the Indian Ocean.

There was a gradual revival after the conclusion of peace in 1815. On July 20, 1825, the Salem brig *Laurel*, Jonathan Lovett, master, dropped anchor in Zanzibar roadstead. On his return to America, Lovett reported that he was the first to display the Stars and Stripes in that harbour.

As he later informed Seyyid Said in a very lengthy memorial, Edmund Roberts, of the state of New Hampshire, 'having by a series of misfortunes lost a large amount of property, was induced to believe that some part of his loss might be repaired by undertaking a voyage to Zanzibar and other ports' belonging to Seyyid Said. After borrowing money from friends, he chartered the brig *Mary Anne* and set sail from New York on June 10, 1827, arriving at Zanzibar on the following October 8. When Seyyid Said reached Zanzibar three months later, Roberts was loud in his complaints of the treatment meted out to him by the Sultan's officers. He had been allowed to sell only to the Sultan's agents, whereas (according to him) English vessels had been allowed to sell to all and sundry, and were not subjected to the heavy duties and harbour dues which had been exacted from him.

Seyyid Said gave Roberts a friendly reception. He told him that he was only too anxious to make a commercial treaty with the United States and was surprised that he had not previously been approached on the subject. He attempted to defend the preferential treatment meted out to British traders by saying, quite untruthfully, that he had already concluded such a treaty with Great Britain. When Roberts suggested to him that he should make a treaty with U.S.A. which incorporated the provisions of that made with Great Britain, he said he could not do so because Great Britain was paying him a subsidy, which was yet another untrue statement. Roberts then declared that, if similar concessions were not given to him and his compatriots, they would be compelled to stop calling at Zanzibar. In the four years preceding Roberts' visit to Zanzibar no less than twenty-five American vessels had called there or else at other ports in Seyyid Said's African dominions. Roberts' threat therefore gave Said cause to think. He eventually decided to ask Roberts on his return to America to urge the United States Government to send a mission to Zanzibar to negotiate a commercial treaty.

On his arrival back in the United States at the end of 1828 Roberts addressed a long memorial to Senator Levi Woodbury of New Hampshire in which he enlarged upon the great potentialities of commerce between the United States and Zanzibar and at the same time stressed the handicaps under which American merchants laboured in the Sultan's territories. In conclusion, he urged the appointment of a Consul to reside at Zanzibar so as to protect American commercial interests.

It was to take some little time before the powers that were at

Washington could be persuaded to take action on Roberts' recommendations. In the meantime trade between Salem and Zanzibar began slowly but surely to increase. In these early days of communication between the United States and East Africa, no European mercantile houses were established either at Zanzibar or at any other port on the mainland. In 1834 Captain Hart of H.M.S. *Imogene* reported 'ships have great difficulty in collecting a cargo, and their plan is to touch upon different parts of the coast, and leave one or two of their crew behind with an interpreter, whilst they visit some other parts or come to Zanzibar which is the great mart and rendezvous'. Ivory, tortoise shell, gum copal and hides were at this date the principal articles which they purchased. The first cargo of gum copal was shipped from Zanzibar to Salem in 1828 and for more than a quarter of a century afterwards became the mainstay of a factory for cleaning gum, which was set up in Salem close to Nathaniel Hawthorne's 'House of the Seven Gables'. That business flourished until 1861 when a ten per cent. duty was imposed upon uncleaned gum. Thereafter gum was cleaned on the East African coast before shipment and much of the business fell into German hands. The Salem factory ceased to thrive and eventually had to close down.

The principal articles given in exchange for these imports were dollars and cotton goods. These latter were for the most part the products of the mills of Salem, Lawrence and Lowell in Massachusetts and of Manchester in the neighbouring State of New Hampshire. Previously almost the only cloth imported into Zanzibar and the adjacent mainland had been a coarse calico from India which was usually called 'kaniki'. Within little more than a decade the unbleached cotton sheeting from the mills of Massachusetts and New Hampshire, which soon came to be called 'amerikani', began to take kaniki's pride of place. In 1848 the British Consul, Hamerton, reported that amerikani had 'come into universal use in Arabia and on the coast of Africa and is fast driving out the British and India manufactured article of this kind which now supplies the markets from Abyssinia to Mozambique'.

In addition to ordinary merchant vessels carrying general cargoes, a number of American whalers used to call at Zanzibar. Their whaling operations were usually carried out in the southern waters of the Indian Ocean and their visits to Zanzibar were almost entirely for purposes of revictualling or refitting.

Occasionally, however, a vessel made catches in Zanzibar waters. When on January 30, 1834, H.M.S. *Imogene* reached Zanzibar, Captain Hart reported that 'it is very common for the South-Sea whalers to come for refreshments' and that one was actually in the roadstead at the time of his arrival. From the commander of the vessel he learnt 'that he had actually caught between two and three hundred barrels of oil, almost between Zanzibar and the next island of Pemba, and this the day after he had been on the ground for some time, and after speaking bore away to the Seychelles for refreshments'. Writing of Zanzibar in 1857 Richard Burton said that at that date 'in July and at the beginning of the north-east monsoon, schools (of whales) migrate up the coast in search of food in the Red Sea. From 30 to 60 lbs of ambergris have been brought up in one year to the island (of Zanzibar) and a little of it is exported to Europe'. Conditions have changed considerably since Burton penned these words. Though at considerable intervals of time schools of whales have been seen in Zanzibar waters and have been stranded on the island's beaches, Zanzibar ceased many years ago to be an operational base for the whaling industry. In those early days the ports of New Bedford and Nantucket were the main contributors to the industry, Salem having a mere tithe of the share of her neighbouring rivals. More will be said about these whale-ships and their officers and crews on a later page.

In 1832 Said bin Sultan set out personally in command of a naval expedition against the Mazrui at Mombasa. On February 9, in that year Captain Burnham, commanding the Salem vessel *Complex*, dropped anchor in Mombasa harbour to find the Sultan engaged in bombarding the town. He expressed to Burnham his great anxiety to conclude the proposed treaty with America and handed to Burnham a letter on the subject for delivery to the President of the United States. Shortly afterwards, having come to terms with the Mazrui, Seyyid Said proceeded to Zanzibar. Whilst he was there, another Salem vessel, the *Tigris*, commanded by Captain John G. Waters, called there. Said took a great liking to Waters. A few years later he sent a present of an Arab horse to him in America. On this occasion he handed Waters a letter which he asked to have published in the United States inviting all citizens of that country to come and trade at Zanzibar. But, according to Captain Hart, when Waters presented the letter to the owners of his vessel, he was told 'No, Mr. Waters, if we allow this to be published, everybody will know of the place and we shall lose our trade'.

Before either of these two letters reached their destination, on January 27, 1832, Edward Livingston, Secretary of State, on the recommendation of Senator Levi Woodbury, at that date Secretary to the Navy, had issued to Edmund Roberts a commission appointing him as 'agent for the purpose of examining in the Indian Ocean the means of extending the commerce of the United States by commercial arrangement with the powers whose dominions border on those seas'. These powers were specifically named as being Siam and Cochin China as well as Muscat. When he was submitting his proposals to Woodbury, Roberts had declared that it was essential that 'the English Government should not know of his designs'. His commission accordingly directed Roberts to keep his mission secret 'from powers whose interest it might be to thwart the objects the President has in view'. Roberts was to be conveyed to his destinations on board U.S.S. *Peacock*, Captain David Geisinger. In order to reduce the possibility of leakage of any information regarding his mission, he was shipped on board as captain's clerk, and his real status was known only to Geisinger and a few of the senior officers. Sailing by way of Cape Horn, the ship proceeded in the first place to Cochin China and Siam, where commercial treaties were concluded with the United States. On September 18, 1833, the *Peacock* arrived off Muscat. Roberts afterwards reported that 'the Sultan at once acceded to my wishes'.

Three days later Seyyid Said gave his assent to a formal treaty. This, the first of a series of similar treaties between the rulers of Zanzibar and European powers, contained nine articles. The second of these articles allowed American citizens full liberty to buy and sell within the Sultan's dominions on such terms as they might think fit.

No price shall be fixed by the Sultan, or his officers, on the articles to be sold by the merchants of the United States, or on the merchandise they may wish to buy; but the trade shall be free on both sides to sell, buy or exchange on the terms and for the prices which the owners think fit.

As at the date of signing the treaty Seyyid Said was still at war with the Mazrui of Mombasa, it was agreed that the munitions of war should only be sold to the government in the island of Zanzibar, 'but in all other ports of the Sultan the said munitions of war may be freely sold without any restrictions whatever to the highest bidder'. The third, fourth and eighth articles fixed the duties to be paid by American citizens in respect of exports, imports, trade licences, harbour dues and other charges. A five per cent. *ad valorem* duty was to be paid on all landed goods and in all other respects American citizens were to pay no more than those of the most favoured nation. The sixth article allowed Americans to reside at the Sultan's ports without paying taxes other than those payable by the citizens of the most favoured nation. The ninth article empowered the President of the United States to appoint Consuls to reside at any port in the Sultan's dominions. Such Consuls were to be 'exclusive judges of all disputes or suits wherein American citizens shall be engaged with each other'. Ratifications of the treaty were exchanged at Muscat on September 30, 1835.

Next arose the question of the appointment of suitable person as Consul at Zanzibar. Reading between the lines of his correspondence with Woodbury, it is clear that Edmund Roberts was after the post. He had even gone so far as to describe himself as 'a Consul of the United States Government' in the memorial which he addressed to Seyyid Said on January 27, 1828, although he had in his correspondence with Woodbury said that 'in consequence of heavy losses sustained in the course of my mercantile pursuits, more particularly by a most barefaced robbery committed under the Berlin and Milan Decrees, I found myself under the necessity of adventuring once more upon the Ocean' on borrowed capital. Apart from any question of his merits or demerits, a number of commercial firms in Salem were anxious that the national representative at Zanzibar should be chosen from amongst themselves. As Captain Waters had been told by his employers, the result of appointing an outsider as Consul would be that 'everybody will hear of the place and we shall lose our trade'. Eventually, the choice fell upon the youngest brother of Captain Waters, Richard Palmer Waters, who owed his appointment to the Rev. J. T. Woodbury, brother of the Secretary of State for the Navy. The Secretary's brother and Richard Waters had become close acquaintances as the result of their membership of the Essex County Anti-Slavery Society.

The first American Consul at Zanzibar was the son of

Robert H. Waters, one of Salem's early nineteenth century sea captains. His two elder brothers, John and William, had followed their father's profession. Their father had died when Richard was still quite young. He had stayed at home and entered a commercial firm in order to support his mother and two sisters. During his voyage out to his new post and during his residence in Zanzibar he kept a journal for his mother's information. Three volumes of this journal still survive as do a book of notes for the years 1842–4 and a large number of his letters. All these throw interesting light on the state of Zanzibar during the early years following Seyyid Said's transference of his capital to the island.

At this date U.S.A. had no specially trained consular service. Waters, like many others, was paid only a nominal salary and was expected to supplement it by working as agent of some commercial firm carrying on business at his place of residence. Instructions were issued to him on April 7, 1836. They were exceedingly brief. They stressed the fact that the Treaty with Seyyid Said gave him 'unusual privileges', but no attempt must be made by him to take advantage of them.

Waters set sail from Salem to take up his appointment on board the brig *Generous* on October 29, 1836. On March 18, 1837, the *Generous* dropped anchor off Zanzibar. The brig *Leader* of Salem fired a salute of thirteen guns as did the Sultan's officers who came on board to welcome the first American Consul to Zanzibar. Waters tells us that he 'invited them to take a glass of wine with me, but they declined by saying it was against their religion to drink wine: they drank a tumbler of lemonade, however, of which they are very fond'. Two days later he proceeded to Mtoni to present his credentials to the Sultan.

We arrived there at half-past eight. Captain Hassan, his secretary, received us at the door and took us into the audience room, where we were introduced to Seyyid Said, Sultan of Muscat and his dependencies. He received me with apparent great good feeling, and invited me to take the seat which he always occupied. We had considerable conversation in regard to the United States and His Highness' dominions. I delivered my credentials from the President to His Highness, expressing his thanks for the service rendered to the American sloop-of-war *Peacock* at the time she got on shore near Muscat. I spent an hour in conversation, assuring His Highness that it was the wish of the President to promote the interest of trade between the two countries.

His Highness expressed the same wish. He offered me any assistance I might wish and said that he was highly pleased that I had come to Zanzibar to reside. I left the Sultan quite pleased with my first interview.

The Sultan offered to pay the rent of any house which Waters might wish to occupy as his Consulate. It took a week to find a suitable place. Another fortnight was occupied in putting the premises into a reasonable state of repair. It was not until April 13, that he moved into these temporarily furnished quarters. On April 23 Seyyid Said paid him a brief visit during which 'he said again, if I wished for anything, call on him'. It was not until May 9 that Waters' furniture arrived from America by the brig *Cherokee*. As he found the neighbourhood undesirable, Waters moved to another house in 1842 in another part of the town. He continued, however, to use his original residence as a none too satisfactory warehouse. In 1842 the thatched roof of this building caught fire and in 1843 its contents suffered serious damage from an invasion of white ants.

One of Waters' earliest duties as Consul was to try to bring about a satisfactory settlement of disputes, which were outstanding between American citizens and subjects of the Sultan. Though the Treaty of 1833 conferred upon him the right to adjudicate in cases in which all the parties were subjects of the United States, it was silent upon the subject of disputes in which one of the parties was not an American citizen. Such cases had accordingly to be adjudicated upon by the Sultan's courts. Unfortunately, the bias of the local Kathis was usually strongly against the foreigner, with the result that visiting American sea captains and supercargoes resorted to extra forensic remedies, which roused the indignation of those against whom such remedies were employed.

Waters' correspondence discloses a long succession of disputes of this character, which had to be brought to the Sultan's notice. As a result relations from time to time inevitably became somewhat strained, but differences were soon settled. Waters began with the undoubted advantage that his elder brother, John, was already known to, and a *persona grata* with Seyyid Said. The two also had one bond of sympathy in their interests in horse flesh. During his residence at Zanzibar Seyyid Said sent the Consul a horse for his personal use and after his departure sent another horse to him in America. Waters' journal records frequent presents of fruit from the Sultan as well as of a boat for his use in visiting ships in the

o

harbour. In addition, Waters was often the Sultan's guest either at his palace or on one of his plantations.

Conversation between the two was not always connected with official business. At times it turned to matters of religion. Waters hailed from the Pilgrim Father settlement of Salem. On January 1, 1837, whilst on his way to his new post, he wrote in his journal:

I have desired to be made useful for the souls of these pagans among whom I am called to reside, that my going to dwell with them for a season may be the means of introducing the Gospel of Christ to them, (and) that the way may soon be opened for missionaries to reside there.

With this resolve in mind, he endeavoured to convert Seyyid Said to his way of belief. Seyyid Said had been on the pilgrimage to Mecca and was a member of the Ibadi sect, which may be described as the Islamic counterpart of the Puritanism of that 'pious, sober and prudent gentleman', Roger Conant, who had founded the settlement of Salem. It is difficult to say how strong were his religious views. Captain R. Mignan, an officer of the Bombay Army who visited Muscat in 1825, described him as 'a rigid observer of the forms of the Mohammedan religion'. He none the less was far from being a fanatic. As Edmund Roberts said, 'all religions within the Sultan's dominions are not merely tolerated, but they are protected by His Highness, and there is no obstacle whatever to prevent the Christians, the Jews, or the Gentiles from preaching their doctrines'. As these pages will show, he treated visiting missionaries with the utmost friendliness and did much to assist them. An even more striking example of his tolerance was shown in the consideration shown by him for his Hindu customs master, Jairam Siwji. When he learnt that the practice of killing cows outside this man's house at the Muslim festival of Id el Fitr, at the close of the month of Ramadan, offended the customs master's religious susceptibilities, he at once gave orders forbidding the practice in that vicinity. A love of dialectic doubtless led the Sultan to welcome discussions with the American Consul regarding the tenets of Christianity. He showed his respect for Waters' staunch Sabbatarianism on the occasion when he refused to accept on a Sunday an invitation to his plantation at Kizimbani, but the Sultan never wavered in his adherence to Islam.

In the meantime Waters was distributing Bibles and tracts amongst the people of Zanzibar and endeavouring to propagate Christianity in discussions with the inhabitants, but much of the

seed fell upon stony ground. He was full of denunciations of Islam
and of the practices of many of those who professed that creed, but
entirely lacked any charitable understanding of the reasons for
their belief. Needless to say, his own aggressive Christianity did
not conduce to the making of converts. It may indeed have
accounted for the assault, which was made upon him by one Amir
bin Said and three of his slaves and which became the subject of a
letter of protest to the Sultan on July 15, 1837. In the same year
his house was constantly assailed with stones and on the recommendation of Seyyid Said he removed to a house in another
quarter of the town.

In 1839 the American Board of Commissioners for Foreign
Missions, a society which had been founded nine years previously
in Massachusetts, sent its first party of missionaries to India. The
journey had to be undertaken by way of the Cape of Good Hope
and from time to time the vessels carrying the missionaries called at
Zanzibar. Whenever they did so, Waters always gave a warm
welcome to the missionaries and at the same time tried to assist
them in every way. When in July 1839, one such party reached
Zanzibar, the Consul introduced them to the Sultan, who gave them
a very friendly reception and took the ladies of the party to visit
the members of his harem, where he presented each of them with a
large red Cashmere shawl. Waters told this party that he was very
anxious indeed to see a mission established in Zanzibar. 'It was his
opinion that a discreet man would be tolerated and have the
prospect of exerting a good influence upon the Arabs and doing
much for Africa'. But the missionaries had a prior assignment in
the Mahratta country whither they continued their journey. After
his brief stay at Zanzibar one of their number, Ebenezer Burgess,
sent a report to the Commissioners in which he stated that, as the
result of inquiries which he had made at the time of his visit, the
island would be a suitable base for working on the adjacent mainland, where 'from what I could learn the tribes I have just mentioned present in prospect a more promising field of labour than
did the Zulus', where the Board had established a mission in 1834.
The commitments of the Board in other fields did not, however,
permit of the Commissioners adopting this recommendation. In
1844 Waters tried unsuccessfully to induce the C.M.S. missionary
Krapf to begin work in Zanzibar. Krapf subsequently wrote that
'I would not abandon my original intention of founding a mission

in Galla land' and with that object in view he crossed over to Mombasa.

There was, however, another facet to Waters besides extreme pietism. He was able to combine a strong business acumen with his puritanical beliefs. He owed his appointment to his post largely to the backing of a number of leading Salem merchants. Richard Waters was therefore expected by them to do all that he could to keep the quasi-monopoly of the Zanzibar trade in the hands of their firms. Waters was allowed to trade and acted as agent for David Pingree, who was a few years later to become mayor of Salem. The 'Notes', which cover the period 1842 to 1844, is full of Waters' business activities, cleaning and weighing gum copal, weighing ivory and selling cotton goods to Banyan traders as well as of his efforts to get the better of trade competitors in the purchase of copal, ivory and other raw materials.

Competitors from Boston and other American ports were bad enough, but British traders were even more unpopular. When in 1833 Captain Hart of H.M.S. *Imogene* visited Zanzibar, he found there an English brig, which was proving 'a great annoyance' to the two American ships in the harbour. The English captain was a certain Robert Brown Norsworthy, whom Hart described as 'a clever, industrious, active, close-handed fellow, and understands perfectly what he is about'. He was 'certainly a great favourite with the Imam', who had placed orders with him for the purchase in England of goods to the value of thirty thousand dollars, and invited him to bring out his family and live in Zanzibar. As he had managed to forestall the Americans in the purchase of gum copal, ivory and other commodities, it is not surprising to learn that the Americans were 'very jealous of him and it is only his good humour prevents their quarrelling'.

Norsworthy was employed by the London firm of Newman Hunt and Christopher of 12 New Bond Street, who sent him back the following year with instructions to take up his residence on shore and to send their ships to pick up cargoes at other East African ports, but, not without reason, his employers soon began to doubt his integrity. Accordingly in 1837 the senior partner came out in his yacht, the *Sandwich*, accompanied by his doctor and private secretary. The result of his inquiries was that Norsworthy ceased to be employed by the firm and the secretary, Mr. Thorn, took his place. Though he once rebuked him for coming to talk business with him on a Sunday, Waters appears to have liked Mr. Robert Newman Hunt. They used frequently to go out shooting and fishing together and to dine with each other. Nevertheless, though Hunt appears to have been lavish in his entertainment, Waters did not allow such hospitality to influence his business relations.

In his efforts to keep Hunt's firm out of business, he entered into an agreement with Jairam Siwji, the customs master, whereby he was to have priority over all other merchants in the disposal of all cargoes belonging to American ships. In May, 1840, Hunt's agent received instructions from two American captains to dispose of their cargoes, but was promptly informed by Jairam Siwji that the business had been transferred to Waters' firm. Five months later the same English agent received similar instructions from another American captain. This time 'Jairam said I must pay half the commission to Waters, with which I was forced to comply'. A year later some tortoise-shell was consigned to Newman Hunt & Co. in settlement of a debt. The letter containing the particulars of the consignment got into Waters' hands, through, it was alleged, the instrumentality of Jairam Siwji. When the consignee asked for the tortoise-shell, he was greeted with the reply 'I have got it, and I guess I shall keep it'.

On May 4, 1841, Captain Atkins Hamerton of the 15th Bombay Native Infantry landed in Zanzibar as first British Consul. Almost immediately after his arrival he was presented not only with the foregoing complaints but also with the grievances of the whole body of Indian traders. He was told that,

whenever they (sc. Waters and Jairam Siwji) thought fit to do so, the goods of native merchants, Banyans and (Indian) Muslims, were detained at the customs house and they were not allowed to sell to whom they pleased, but to whom the monopolists thought fit to allow them (to sell), and if an American vessel was in want of a cargo she must be supplied in preference.

At his first interview with Seyyid Said Hamerton realized which way the wind was blowing.

I observed [he reported] two pictures hung up on either side of Imam's chair in the room where he holds his *durbar*; the subjects were naval engagements between American and English ships; the ship of England is represented as just being taken by the Americans, and the English ensign is being hauled down and the American hoisted at the masthead.

Moreover, at the *durbar* a number of Arabs began 'talking loudly
of the power and wealth of America and the superiority of their
sailors over the English'.

On May 31, 1839, Seyyid Said had entered into a treaty with
the British Government by which he had not only guaranteed to
British subjects (subject to payment of an *ad valorem* duty of five
per cent. on imports) the right freely to trade in his dominions and
had further expressly engaged 'not to permit the establishment of
any monopoly or exclusive privilege of sale within his dominions'
except with respect to ivory and gum copal on the mainland
between Mtangata and Kilwa. It therefore became the duty of the
newly arrived British Consul to insist that this article of the treaty
was observed. He accordingly approached the Sultan on the
subject and quickly found himself up against a party of Arabs, who
'extend all their influence with the Imam to allow' the American
monopoly to continue.

The natives were made for a time to believe that this treaty between
Muscat and England was not yet in force because it had been certified
by Captain Hennell, who was an East India Company's officer; and
positively the Imam appeared for a time to think such was the case –
but I have succeeded in inducing him to think otherwise.

But it was only 'after much trouble' that he 'persuaded the Sultan
to allow British traders to participate in the trade and to enjoy the
same advantages with the French and the Americans'.

But 'the American party' was not yet worsted in the fight.
On September 23, 1841,

the Imam cited to his presence all the principal native merchants of the
place who were British subjects, inhabitants of Bombay, Surat and
other places in India, and required them to sign a declaration to the
effect that they no longer considered themselves as British subjects, but
of their own free will had become citizens of the city of Zanzibar, and
would in no case ever after claim British protection under any
circumstances. This, with the exception of three men, they all refused to
sign, saying they all had wives and children in the British possessions
in India and that no force could compel them to make such a
declaration, and that they would tell all to me, which many of them
immediately did.

Hamerton heard 'that all this was got up by the American
party'. At the time of this incident Consul Waters was away in
Bombay, but

the way in which all communications take place between the American Consul and the American party is through the interpretation of a writer of the Imam's called Ahmed bin Naaman, a fellow who went to America in the Imam's ship *Sultani* and who has led all hands to believe we are very inferior people to the Americans.

So Hamerton decided that he must see Seyyid Said and make it perfectly clear what the position was. The interview took place two days after the Sultan's unsuccessful attempt to persuade the members of the Indian community to renounce British citizenship. It is evident from certain of his observations during that interview that Said was acting for the time being under the influence of 'the American party'. Hamerton tells us he

waited on the Sultan and told him that he had been ill-advised on the subject – and that I should report the circumstances to the Governor (of Bombay), which I did – and I also told His Highness that the people, who signed the declaration, did so through fear and that in case of need the Government would most constantly protect them, as though they had never signed the paper. The Imam said that, if any one being an English subject resided in a country for a certain time he became a subject or citizen of the state in which he resided. I told him it was not the case. He said such was the law of America. I told him the laws of America did not affect us. His Highness then said the people of India were the subjects of the East India Company and not the subjects of the Queen of England.

Hamerton then told him he was

sorry to observe the alteration of His Highness' conduct towards me, and that I was quite aware of the cause of it, and that I strongly advised him not to place too much reliance in what he was told by those, who were not his real friends and who represented matters to him only to answer their private views, and the believing which would to a certainty tend to His Highness' disadvantage. The Imam replied that he himself and his own family had the most profound respect for the British Government and the Governor-General (of India), but what everyone told him he could not but believe to be true, and that certainly he did not experience the same kindness from the British Government of late years that he had formerly done. I replied that His Highness only thought so because he listened too much to the tales told by those, who were unfriendly towards us and who were jealous of the good understanding existing, and which had existed, so long between the British Government and His Highness, but that, please God, our enemies would fail in their object, which was to disturb the friendship between His Highness and the British Government.

The Sultan then hinted that Hamerton was merely the emissary of the Company and not of the British Government, to which Hamerton replied, 'I now tell you what I have told you before – that the interests of the Malaika (Queen) and the Company are not two but one, and in no way different, but one and indivisible'. His Highness said 'So you have always told me. God is great and whatever he pleases will happen'.

There the interview ended. Evidently Seyyid Said was not yet convinced that the allegations of the American party were untrue. When Waters arrived back from Bombay on December 7, he began to spread

all sorts of reports – that the East India Company were ruined, that the charter was never again to be granted. . . , that the Imam had been imposed upon by the Bombay Government, that I have been acting without due authority, that I was only the servant of the East India Company and that there was a Consul on his way from England, and all sorts of reports of this nature, (and) that we had entirely failed in Afghanistan and China.

It so happened, however, that Waters' return more or less coincided with the arrival of H.M.S. *Grecian*. Not only did this ship of the Malaika bring nobody to supersede Hamerton but its commander accorded to him all the honours accorded to Her Majesty's consular representatives abroad by officers of her navy. This largely counteracted all American propaganda. On December 21, 1841, Hamerton presented to Seyyid Said a letter from the Governor of Bombay regarding the suppression of the slave trade. It was a thorny subject and the communication was 'ill received'. Seyyid Said began by harping back to the old theme.

He at first said that he supposed that the letter was from the Company, from the Governor-General or Governor of Bombay – and asked me how it came that the Company had to do with these matters. I told him I was sorry to observe that he was yet under the influence of bad advice – that all he heard about the Company was not true, and that perhaps he might find that the Governor-General possessed power which his advisers did not wish him to understand. He then said he had not said anything in any way disrespectful of the Company – that I have often told him that the government of the Crown (the Royal Government) and that of the Company were not the one opposed to the other – but that it was one and the same and indivisible – and that he believed it. . . .
He muttered about one thing and another and behaved in a way I had never seen him do before. . . . Then he asked me to explain to him how

the letter came to me if written by the Royal Government. I did so and told him I would give him an Arab translation of it the following day and I did so. He then said, 'Ah! Balozi (Consul), see how many and what his people tell me – but, by the soul of the Prophet, you have never deceived me. I will place myself under the protection of the English'.

Seyyid Said then announced his wish to send the *El-Sultani* to England. As he had no officer of his own capable of navigating the vessel to that country, he explained that he must obtain the services of a European and asked whether Hamerton had any objection to Waters' brother-in-law navigating her. The Consul replied that he had none. Hamerton reported that he 'assumed a high tone' at this interview. Whether he was right or wrong or wise or unwise in so doing, his attitude had the necessary effect. Waters evidently had a plausible tongue and may at one time have persuaded Seyyid Said as to the truth of his anti-British propaganda, but Hamerton had for some time past been beginning to shake that belief. After this interview he was finally disillusioned. Hamerton gave him the credit for having been genuinely misled. Writing to Commander William Smyth of H.M.S. *Grecian*, he said, 'Imam's influence has been for some time past on the wane, but the presence of an English ship-of-war always gives him confidence and enables him to treat British subjects with that consideration which, in justice to His Highness, I do believe he wishes to do'.

Thereafter there was no more talk of an American party or an American monopoly. Waters realized that the game was lost. He could not possibly expect to be backed by the United States Government in support of his claim to a monopoly, which was not even a national one but one claimed purely for the personal ends of his own firm. Other American firms had suffered as much as British subjects from his intrigues with Jairam Siwji and the breakdown of his alliance with the customs master afforded as much pleasure to his compatriots as it did to nationals of other states.

One important duty, which Waters was called upon to perform in his capacity of Consul, was that of dealing with cases of insubordination on board visiting American ships and disputes between their commanders and other members of the crew. The conduct of many of these people fell far below the high standards, which

Waters set for himself. On May 24, 1837, he wrote in his diary that he had told certain visitors that 'they must not think that all people in America are like those captains and seamen who come here' and concluded his entry with a prayer for a change of heart in such persons, 'when instead of a curse they may prove a blessing to many heathen souls' by setting them a better example.

The crews of whaling vessels were in particular a frequent source of trouble to the American Consul. At this date life on board American whalers was certainly not a bed of roses. Discipline was stern and many of the commanders were extremely brutal. In 1835 the Federal Government had passed a law which was designed to improve conditions under which seamen served by enacting punishments for officers, 'who from malice, hatred or revenge shall beat, wound or imprison members of his crew or inflict any cruel or unusual punishment'. But the writs of Federal Courts rarely ran as far as the Indian Ocean and the coastal waters of East Africa. More than one American sea captain honoured the well intentioned legislation of Congress far more in the breach than in the observance. When ships arrived at any port, shore leave was as often as not refused to the crew for fear of desertions. Only the captain, his officers, and possibly a few old hands, who were known to be trustworthy, used to row ashore to transact business, obtain provisions, or for purposes of recreation. Nonetheless, seamen found ways and means of deserting.

On May 20, 1843, J. Ross Browne arrived at Zanzibar as one of the hands on board a New Bedford whaler, the name of which he has concealed under the alias of *Styx*. He had shipped as 'a green hand' and later described his experiences in *Etchings of a Whaling Cruise* (first published in 1846). After making due allowance for possible exaggeration, his book remains in many respects one of the best personal descriptions of contemporary life on board an American whaler.

Ross Browne himself was fortunate enough to get the American Consul at Zanzibar interested in his case and through his mediation to procure his discharge and a passage back to the United States. But the stories he tells of his shipmates and members of the crews of other whalers make appalling reading. Thus, in December 1837 the whaler *London Packet* put in to Zanzibar. On arrival nine of the crew refused duty and complained of the brutal manner in which they had been treated by their captain, who, rightly or

wrongly, was alleged to have been a drunkard. The men's allegations may have been true or they may have been grossly exaggerated, but the fact remains that they had refused duty. Waters
asked the Sultan for troops to assist in apprehending the mutineers.
Twenty-two soldiers were sent and the men were hauled off to the
Sultan's fort, which not only Ross Browne but also other writers
describe as an appalling place, quite unfit for the reception and
detention of prisoners of any race. In the meantime their ship
proceeded on a short cruise. According to Ross Browne, when she
returned a few weeks later, several of the prisoners were dead and
the rest were prostrated with fever; to avoid sharing the fate of
their companions, they agreed to return to duty.

In the case of certain members of the crew of the whale-ship
Emma of New Bedford the American Consul took more drastic
steps. Five of the crew refused to obey orders and complained of
the food. They refused to appear at the Consulate when ordered
to do so and had finally to be arrested and brought there in irons.
After personally inspecting the food supplies, the Consul found
them to be fresh and sufficient, but the men refused to obey the
Consul's order to return to duty. Thereupon Consul decreed 'for
the purpose of bringing them to return on board and to duty, and
they each receive two dozen lashes, with a piece of twelve-thread
ratline rope, after which, if they still refuse, to confine them in the
fort and to receive the flogging every day as often as they can bear
it until they submit'. A note is appended to the order stating that
after one flogging 'every man requested to be allowed to go to duty'.

This was not the only occasion on which an American Consul
revealed his belief in the efficacy of the twelve-thread ratline rope
for dealing with recalcitrant seamen. On January 8, 1848, two
members of the crew of the Boston barque *Iosce* received the like
punishment for striking the second mate.

In 1843 an American whaler hauled into Zanzibar to repair her
keel. Three men deserted from her and hid themselves in the town.
A few days later two of them decided to return to duty. The third,
a Scotchman, remained hidden until his ship had sailed. He then
emerged from his hiding place.

Day after day [Ross Browne writes] I saw him wandering about the
streets sick and destitute, without power to relieve him. Far from feeling any sympathy for him, the white traders turned him from their
doors with threats of imprisonment in the fort. The natives, fearing the

displeasure of the Sultan if they did not follow the humane example of the whites, kicked him out of their houses; and for more than two weeks he had neither shelter nor any medical aid, nor, as far as I could learn, any food, except what he could beg from the female slaves when their masters were absent, or occasionally a scrap of bread from Captain F – – 's men, who had been wrecked, and were themselves in great distress. My own situation was so precarious that it was only by stealth I dared speak to him; for I know the penalty of being caught aiding or befriending a deserter; nor was it in my power to relieve his distress, even if this were not the case. Early one morning I heard that a man was found dead on the beach, and that he still lay there. I went down, and was shocked to see the body of the poor Scotchman stretched upon the sand, with his face down, and his eyes and nostrils covered with sand.

With very few exceptions, such as Ross Browne, who was an educated man and who had joined the *Styx* out of a spirit of adventure, the deck hand of a whaler was not as a rule the choicest of his kind. Their officers were very frequently brutes, but their men were a truculent lot who needed an iron discipline. Once on shore after a lengthy cruise under the most trying conditions, it is not surprising to learn that such men should sometimes take the opportunity to desert or, if they did not desert, to behave in a most outrageous manner, which in a place like Zanzibar brought not only themselves but also their more reputable countrymen into discredit. In the circumstances it is understandable, though not entirely excusable, that self respecting American merchants in Zanzibar should close their doors on the crews of whaling ships and treat them as untouchables. Their attitude in this respect moreover, was not confined to deserters. In 1843 the whaler *Bogota* of New Bedford had struck a reef in the Mozambique Channel. The Captain with a few of the crew had managed to get the vessel off and to sail her to Zanzibar, where she had to be beached and became a total loss. No attempt was made by their compatriots to provide for the shipwrecked mariners. They had to live in a temporary cane hut and on very short commons. Within a very few weeks all of the crew, except three, had succumbed to fever.

The humanitarian movement, which looks for the roots of all disorders and seeks to find a remedy for them, had not yet penetrated to the American colony in Zanzibar, except possibly to Richard Palmer Waters, whom Ross Browne gives the credit of being a thoroughly humane man endeavouring to tackle a difficult problem in a just and equitable manner. It was possibly at his suggestion that Seyyid Said conceived the plan of building a house for use as a sailors' home and hospital. It was to be furnished in European style and an American doctor was to be engaged at the Sultan's expense to look after the sick and disabled. Unfortunately the plan never reached fruition. The house was duly built, but at the time of completion there was bitter discord in Seyyid Said's large family. The result of this quarrel was that it became no longer possible for the Sultan's son Hilal and his family to live under the same roof as his half-brother Khalid. New quarters had to be speedily found for Hilal. The sailors' home was ready to hand and Hilal and his family moved in. Nothing further was ever heard of a sailors' home.

At the end of 1839 Seyyid Said sent his ship *El-Sultani* to America with an assorted cargo comprising the products of Zanzibar, East Africa, Arabia and the Persian Gulf. She arrived at New York on May 2, 1840. Thence she was towed sixty miles up the Hudson River to Newburgh. Returning under tow to New York on July 20, she set sail for Zanzibar on September 28, with a cargo comprising (amongst other things) firearms and ammunition, china, beads and bales of *amerikani* cloth. Whilst at New York, the crew underwent a somewhat disagreeable experience. Later Hamerton informed Lord Palmerston that 'they were tormented continually by the mob crowding to see the Arabs, looking on them as a curiosity. Their privacy was intruded on; they were pulled by the beards and otherwise insulted'.

The ill behaviour of the New York populace was in fact such that police had to be posted to prevent people from coming on board the ship and this protection, as the supercargo's accounts show, involved payment of fifty-three dollars to 'Mr. Lax, a police officer'. After he learnt of this 'ill-usage of his people' Seyyid Said frequently complained thereof to Hamerton.

Waters continued to hold the post of United States Consul until 1845. Although he had lost his one time ascendancy over the Sultan, he remained on very good terms with him until he departed from Zanzibar. He left on grounds of ill-health, but appears to have expected to be able to return after a short spell of absence. He in fact never returned, but died at Salem at the age of eighty in 1887. Seyyid Said was absent from Zanzibar at the time of his departure and was genuinely grieved to hear of the Consul's illness.

'This news has upset my mind', he wrote, 'and I hope you are now better. Please inform me about your health by each mail coming towards us.' For some years thereafter there appears to have been an exchange of letters between the two. Said sent a number of presents to Waters and his kinsfolk. Once it was 'a trifling present – it is two packets of Mocha coffee'. On another occasion it was an Arab horse for the former Consul's brother John. In 1846 Richard Waters sent for the horse which Seyyid Said had given to him two years previously and it was despatched to Salem in charge of an Arab groom. By 1848, however, letters had ceased to arrive in Zanzibar from Salem. On June 10 of that year Seyyid Said sent the following letter to Waters:

I have had no letter from you for a long time. You have bought a garden and are quite happy and you have forgotten the friendship which existed between us. I never expected this from you. We still bear the same affection for you. Convey our salaams to your brothers John and William, and all their children, and to your niece Jane.

When he learnt that Waters had decided not to return to Zanzibar Seyyid Said informed him that 'as regards the appointment of a Consul, we cannot interfere with them. Whomsoever they shall appoint shall receive the honour and respect due from us'. Eventually, the post was given to Charles Ward, who arrived in Zanzibar on January 20, 1846. Next day he presented his credentials to the Sultan. Seyyid Said thereafter wrote to President Polk to inform him that 'the Consul, Mr. Ward, is a very sensible man and I feel very happy by his arrival. By the pleasing of God the friendship of the American nation with the Arab is always and constantly increasing'. But relations between the two men were soon to become strained for a number of reasons.

Six months after Ward's arrival the crew of the whale-ship *Ann Parry* of Portsmouth came on shore after sunset. Evidence taken later shows that they got very drunk and that there was a fight between them and certain of the local inhabitants. In the course thereof the headman of the customs house was killed, whereupon the Americans hurried on board their ship. Seyyid Said reported the matter to Ward, who replied as follows:

The undersigned U.S. Consul is deeply grieved in the report of a murder committed by an American seaman and would inform Your Majesty that he gave immediate orders to have the sailors put in irons without delay.

The officer of the *Ann* whale-ship reported to me this morning that my orders were respected and three men were put in irons and one man confessed the horrid deed. The undersigned most respectfully awaits Your Majesty's commands. Whilst it is a painful duty, the undersigned cannot protect a murderer.

The undersigned would suggest to Your Majesty the propriety of having an examination by one of your judges in the presence of the U.S. Consul.

This letter clearly indicates that the writer was conscientiously trying to do his duty and to assist the course of justice, but a more experienced officer would have abstained from stating therein that 'one man confessed the horrid deed'. The only person, who could give evidence of any such confession, was the person to whom such confession was alleged to have been made. The ship's officer, to whom according to Ward's belief the confession had been made, subsequently said that all that the man had admitted was that he had struck somebody in the course of the fight. Consequently, the next day Ward wrote to inform the Sultan that

I beg now to state that it was not reported as certain that the man had said so and, having made further inquiry, I am unable to find any man who had made such a declaration. I did not intend to state it as a fact, but only as a report. On inquiry I find I did not exactly understand the officer of the whale-ship.

Here again, Ward would have saved himself a great deal of worry if only he had actually given the Sultan an amended version of what the officer intended to say. The case in due course came up for investigation in front of a Kathi in the presence of the Consul. Some Portuguese sailors were called and gave evidence that they had been eye-witnesses of the fight, but they were unable to identify the actual assailant of the deceased. The Consul then offered to produce the members of the crew as witnesses, but the Kathi refused to call them and also refused to allow Ward to question the witnesses who had been already called. Great stress was laid in the fact that Ward had told the Sultan that one sailor had admitted the offence. This in the eyes of both the Sultan and the Kathi sufficed and there was no need of further evidence. Seyyid Said told Ward that 'an American killed my subject and you ought to have found out who the murderer was'. It is of course possible that his compatriots were trying to shield the actual offender by concealing what they knew. But a man cannot be convicted of murder or any other offence, because his witnesses have not told the truth; he can only be convicted on reliable evidence showing that he was actually the offender. There was no such evidence in this case and Ward was in no way responsible for its non-production. The Sultan told Ward that the case was 'returned' to him to decide. In the circumstances Ward could not do otherwise than hold that the offence had not been proved as against anybody. It is, however, not surprising that he thereby incurred the suspicion that he was shielding a compatriot from the consequences of his crime. He had been unwise in the first statement that he had made to Seyyid Said, but the correspondence goes clearly to show that he had done his best to assist the Sultan's authorities. Seyyid Said wrote an indignant letter to the President of the United States and Ward sent in his report. No reply appears ever to have been sent from Washington. In 1851 it was reported that the case was 'never alluded to now and the better course would be to let it remain dormant'.

A further bone of contention between Seyyid Said and Ward arose over the interpretation of the second article in the American Treaty of Commerce. That article placed no restrictions on the right of American citizens to trade on the mainland of Africa, whereas the corresponding article in the British and French treaties restricted that right on the mainland between Mtangata and Kilwa. In 1841, when Waters was still Consul, American traders in Zanzibar expressed a wish to trade in the regions from which French and British traders were thus debarred. Waters, who, as already mentioned, was agent of a Salem business house strongly supported the proposal. Seyyid Said announced that he would forbid Americans from exercising this right. As he knew full well that Waters was personally interested in this proposed extension of the field of commercial operations, he decided to send a personal message to Washington by Captain Andrew Ward instead of through the regular diplomatic channels. The result was that on January 12, 1843, Daniel Webster, Secretary of State, wrote to Waters saying that, as he was given to understand that hitherto no American merchants had undertaken any trading activities on that part of the coast, and that as an attempt to do so might unduly damage good relations between U.S.A. and Zanzibar, Waters should not press the matter.

The question of American trade on the mainland having been thus raised, Seyyid Said decided that he must press for the amendment of the second article of the American Treaty so as to conform with the corresponding article in the British Treaty of 1839. For this purpose he wrote no less than four letters to Washington, but none of them elicited any reply. After his final return to U.S.A., Waters wrote to Seyyid Said suggesting that he should give him a power of attorney constituting him a plenipotentiary with full powers to negotiate an amendment of the treaty. To this the Sultan replied:

You said you mentioned to the Government about the affairs of the coast, but you wish me to send you a power of attorney to give you authority in this matter. But, my dear friend, you know it is now over thirty years since the Americans came to trade in these regions, but none of them has proceeded to the coast. Is it the intention to commit mischief in our dominions? But we do not think the Americans intend any mischief or that they would cause injury to us.

. . . With reference to the power of attorney, I have no doubt of your fidelity, but it will be necessary to address a letter to the Government and I have already written four letters to them, but have received no reply from them. This reason hindered me from writing any more. I inform you of this to let you know what has exactly happened.

Though Seyyid Said was reluctant to entrust Waters with a written authority to negotiate an amendment to the Treaty, he appears nonetheless to have hoped that Waters would approach the President of the United States and personally explain the reasons for asking for that amendment. In a letter of January 15, 1846, he wrote to Waters as follows:

I hope you have arrived safely and have interviewed the American President about the matter of the coast. I think your presence there will avert from me the trouble of addressing a letter to the Government and I hope you will attend to the matter and send me a reply soon. You know that nobody can carry on trade with the people of the coast, but we intend this only as a precautionary measure.

A little more than a month after he arrived as Waters' successor, the Sultan's secretary came to Ward with a message from Seyyid Said requesting him to write to the Government of U.S.A. about the amendment of the treaty. Ward decided to interview the Sultan personally. On February 26, 1846, he reported to Washington that he had learnt that,

P

as yet, no American vessels do, or have trade there, but he (sc. the Sultan) is apprehensive that at some future time some individuals may be disposed to do so; . . . and His Highness insisted that, if foreign vessels were permitted to trade in that part of the coast, his revenues at Zanzibar would be very much lessened.

Once again no reply was issued from Washington. On March 13, 1847, Ward reported to the Secretary of State that 'for the last six months the Sultan had been impatient for an answer'. On March 9 he himself had proceeded to the Sultan's palace at Mtoni and that he had informed him that

I had received a letter from the American merchants in Zanzibar on the state and prospects of trade and that they had represented that His Highness had entered so largely into the trade and was preparing to send one or more ships to America, which, should he do so, would ruin their commercial operations and would oblige them to seek a market on the coast, and in view of what they had expressed, I said that, if they wished to take advantages of the privileges of the treaty, I could not prevent it. . . . The Sultan said 'The treaty permitted the Americans to trade in all the ports. I do not call small villages ports, but, if any places have forts and customs houses, they are ports, but not otherwise. Therefore if the Americans attempt to go there for trade, I will prevent them. This is my answer. Now you can write to your government and see what answer they will make'.

Charles Ward accordingly wrote to the Secretary of State at Washington. Seyyid Said once more decided that he would not entrust his letter to the American Consul for despatch through the usual channels. Once again he handed it to Captain Andrew Ward for delivery at Washington. In that letter he insisted that upon a proper interpretation of Article II of the American treaty the word 'ports' meant 'places where there are forts and customs houses'.

Seyyid Said also gave the following account of his interview with Ward to the British Consul Atkins Hamerton:

Mr. Charles Ward told me that the British and American subjects wish to complain to their rulers that 'you have taken part in their trade'. I have answered him what I tell you now, namely, that I, Said bin Sultan, Sultan of Muscat and other countries in Africa, do not agree that the American Government, or the Government of the Great Queen of England, or any other government in the world, can prohibit either me or my subjects from trading in what God has made lawful for me and my subjects, either in my ships or the ships of my subjects, with my countries and the countries which have entered into treaties with us,

provided that no infraction of the rules of the treaties be committed by
us or our subjects, which thing, if God wills, shall never happen. This
is what I have replied to him. Let it be known unto you.

I wish to ask you about the boundary on the mainland between Tanga
and Kilwa, of which Your Highness has knowledge. On that boundary
are there any fortresses or strongholds with soldiers, who are able to
protect foreign ships and foreigners going to and from there for the
purpose of trading within those limits?

In this connection Seyyid Said must have recalled the trouble
which he had experienced with the French Government over his
failure to arrest the person or persons responsible for the murder
of the French explorer Maizan on the mainland.

Finally, in his letter to Hamerton, Seyyid Said enclosed a copy
of the protest which he had addressed to Charles Ward, telling
him that 'my desire is that you will read the same and send a copy
thereof to the Honourable the Prime Minister of the Great Queen
that he may see and know in what circumstances we are in
connection with these affairs'.

It will be noted that the United States Consul claimed to be
addressing the Sultan on behalf of the English merchants in
Zanzibar as well as of his own countrymen. As he did not represent
British interests in Zanzibar, he had of course no right to say so.
None the less his statement was in fact true. The two English
merchants in Zanzibar, without the intervention of their Consul,
had addressed a formal protest to Seyyid Said in language similar
to that employed by the American Consul. They had further
written to the Foreign Office to complain that their own Consul
had 'not evinced the slightest sympathy or consideration for the
situation in which we are placed'.

Hamerton was the member of a very distinguished service with
the best and highest of traditions. His attitude had been perfectly
correct. He had stood up for the treaty rights of British traders in
1841, and had insisted on Seyyid Said observing them and thereby
incurring considerable unpopularity with an influential section of
his own subjects. But he was equally insistent that his own compatriots should likewise conform to the letter and the spirit of that
treaty. The British Government had recognized the right to
reserve the monopoly in certain trades on the main continent to
himself and his subjects. Hamerton could not go behind that
agreement. Similarly, Seyyid Said had as much right as any of his

subjects to take part in commerce and foreign competitors could not complain if he did so. Obviously as representative of Her Majesty's Government, Hamerton could only take up one attitude, however unpopular it might be with his compatriots. Having been asked by Seyyid Said to invoke the aid of the British Government, Hamerton equally properly laid Said's case before the Foreign Office in the following terms:

The fiscal arrangements of His Highness the Imam are of a very primitive nature on the Mrima (the mainland between Mtangata and Kilwa) and his authority is imperfectly established; he has no customs house at the different ports, where Europeans could conduct their usual business; and His Highness has considerable fear as regards their intercourse with the natives who come from the interior to barter their gum copal and ivory, which are the principal articles of value to be obtained there, for beads, muskets, powder, earthenware, cotton, and woollen cloths, and other European produce.

. . . The natives of the Mrima are a peaceable and inoffensive set of people, but the tribes who come there from the interior are different, and His Highness fears that, were European merchants to proceed for commercial purposes to the Mrima, things could not stay long as at present, and besides, His Highness will have to encounter no small difficulty from his own people should he consent to Europeans going to the Mrima, as the Arabs consider and look upon the territory as peculiarly their own place for trade. Should Europeans and Americans proceed (there), then the influence of the Imam, such even as it is, would soon entirely cease to exist. His Highness could not afford to keep garrisons or to build forts in the different places necessary to support his influence and protect foreigners; and as no export duty is levied by the Imam, the Mrima territory would be more or less useless to him; and he also well knows that he could not afford the protection for life and property which the European and American Governments expect in the event of their subjects meeting with ill treatment from the natives. This is the thing which causes more distress of mind to the Imam than the loss of revenue which he expects will accrue from foreigners trading on the Mrima. . . .

The East Coast of Africa is attracting the notice of commercial men of all nations lately, and particularly that part called the Mrima, in consequence of which the Imam entertains the greatest possible fear that, without assistance and kindness from the Governments of the Western World, unfavourable changes may take place.

Europeans have never traded in the Mrima between the ports of Mtangata and Kilwa.

Lord Palmerston approached the Government of the United States on behalf of Seyyid Said. Whilst the American Government was not prepared to surrender the privileges of its citizens under the Treaty, they were at the same time not desirous of pressing their claims unduly. Accordingly, a conciliatory reply was sent. On June 15, 1848, Ward reported that he had presented the President's letter personally to the Sultan and that His Highness' reply was – 'Let your Government do what they please. I don't believe the Americans will make me any trouble on the Mrima'. Thirty years later the fact that once upon a time an American Consul had tried to assert these treaty rights had been completely forgotten. In a memorandum written in 1877 on the subject of this trade monopoly in the Mrima, John Kirk (then British Consul) wrote that 'without question the American traders invariably follow the rule that binds the others'.

When giving his instructions to Captain Andrew Ward in regard to the amendment of the treaty, Seyyid Said had written that 'the American merchants and the American Consul, Mr. Ward, are joined together for this purpose. I conceive this of Mr. Ward, for he is too goodhearted a gentleman and he wishes to please every one of his nationals'. But as the years began to pass, he found himself more and more at loggerheads with the American Consul as regards matters affecting the commercial interests of American firms. Matters came finally to a breaking point in 1850. The whole trouble arose over a very petty affair. On May 24 in that year the Sultan caused a salute to be fired in honour of Queen Victoria's birthday. Ward, egged on by his compatriots, took offence because the same salute was not repeated on July 4. The fact that Ward at this date was a very sick man largely explains the embittered quarrel which followed. On July 5 he called on Seyyid Said personally and demanded immediate satisfaction. Reading between the lines of his subsequent report of that interview, it is clear that the American Consul's approach was the reverse of tactful and lacking in both dignity and courtesy. This was unfortunately followed by the departure of Seyyid Said from his usual suavity by replying in language which cannot be described as even attempting to be conciliatory. The upshot was that Ward informed the Sultan that, if he did not deem fit to comply with his demands, 'my official function will be suspended until the Government of the United States shall take action in the matter. I shall then place

American affairs in the hands of some Consul friendly to the U.S. Government'. To this Seyyid Said replied that,

as to your present answer, it is by way of force (and) not in a friendly way, and surely the American Government will not be acquiescing in your conversation about this, as they are people of sensibility and perfection. . . . If you wish to acquaint the American Government, forward to them this letter and, whatever their answer, we will effectuate it.

Ward thereafter agreed to refer the whole matter to Washington and added that in the circumstances 'I will continue my official relations as Consul as before, but I cannot again hoist the flag of the Consulate until the answer of the United States Government is received'.

Eventually the United States Government had to send Commodore James Aulick, who had been appointed to command the East India squadron, 'to aid the United States Consul at Zanzibar and to carry out the instructions of the Government, and adopt such measures as may seem to maintain the dignity of the American Nation, and the honor of its flag'. Aulick arrived at Zanzibar on board U.S.S. *Susquehannah* on December 2, 1851. It so happened that neither disputant was then present in the island. Ill health had compelled Ward to return to America and the Sultan had proceeded to Muscat eight months previously, leaving his favourite son Khalid in charge of affairs at Zanzibar.

At the time when the dispute first arose, all the Americans in Zanzibar had backed Ward to the utmost, but after the lapse of more than eighteen months they had had time to reflect. On December 5, 1851, three of them wrote to inform Aulick that

We think that the first cause of the difficulty between His Highness and Mr. Ward arose from a misunderstanding of the message sent by His Highness to Mr. Ward. His Highness protests that no intentional insult was offered and that the message he sent to Mr. Ward could not have been correctly interpreted. We have understood from His Highness' people, since this affair happened, that he very much regretted that anything should have occurred to interrupt the friendly feelings which had existed so long between himself and the Americans, and from long personal acquaintance with His Highness, we believe him incapable of offering an intentional insult to our country's flag.

Aulick himself, whilst anxious to do all that was expected of him to maintain the dignity of his national flag, was anxious to bring about a settlement of the dispute which would not unduly humiliate the Sultan or his representative at Zanzibar. In reply to a letter which Aulick had addressed to him, Khalid wrote

You mentioned that you have authority from His Excellency the President to settle the past trouble between us and His Excellency Mr. Ward. I like that very much. I assure you we never treated him badly, but Mr. Ward, by his hot feeling, he did this. Now whatever we see best for both parties, then we will agree together to do it. . . . The friendship between the American and the Arab nations is an old friendship not beginning now.

After this rapprochement, the dispute was speedily settled. Khalid agreed to salute the Stars and Stripes and it was agreed that the guns of the *Susquehannah* should return that salute, gun for gun.

After this ceremony John Francis Webb was formally installed as Consul of the United States and the friendly relations between the two countries were resumed.

CHAPTER XI

SEYYID SAID AND THE SLAVE TRADE

IN previous chapters more than one reference has been made to the slave trade and the approaches made from time to time by the British Government to Seyyid Said for its suppression. It was one of the most thorny problems with which Seyyid Said, and also Atkins Hamerton, as representative of the British Government in Zanzibar, had to deal. Both in Oman and in East Africa slavery was a recognized institution which had existed for countless centuries. It was already old in the days of Muhammad. The Koran accepted it as part of the social order, but insisted that slaves should be treated kindly and allowed to marry. They should also be encouraged to purchase their liberty. It was even better still that a master should free a Muslim slave without payment. A master could make one of his female slaves a *suria*, a status which had resemblances to that of a secondary wife rather than to that of a concubine. She was entitled to her liberty on her master's death and the offspring of the union were treated as legitimate children of the father. But the Koran sternly forbad a master to make money out of his female slaves by pandering. If he did not want them for himself, it was his duty to arrange for their marriage. The Koran, like the Bible, was of course preaching a counsel of perfection. There were masters who disregarded its injunctions, but it is only fair to put on record that a succession of British Consuls reported that domestic slaves in Zanzibar were generally speaking not unkindly treated. There were from time to time instances of shocking brutality, but the offenders would appear to have been very much in the minority.

The worst evils of slavery were connected with the traffic in slaves. These human chattels were obtained from the continent of Africa by divers means. Sometimes children were sold by their parents in time of famine; sometimes captives taken in intertribal wars were thus disposed of by the victors; and sometimes the slave traders acquired their human merchandise by kidnapping or by forcible capture. The worst incidents in the traffic occurred during the journeys of the slave gangs down to the coast, in the barracoons where the captives were detained at the coast until they could be shipped overseas, and in the slave dhows which carried these wretched people to their final destination. There is no need to go into the many harrowing details about slave caravans and slave ships. They can be found in many books.

It is difficult to know what in his heart of hearts was Seyyid Said's attitude to the trade and to slavery as an institution. With regard to the traffic he was indirectly responsible for its increase during the first half of the nineteenth century. His encouragement of the planting of cloves and other economic crops led to an increased demand for labour in the island of Zanzibar and Pemba and the opening up of the main continent to trade meant that increased porterage was required both for carrying up trade goods into the interior and for bringing down the commodities, particularly ivory, which were obtained in exchange for those goods. Voluntary labour was more or less unheard of and the only method of meeting these increased demands was by slave labour. In addition the capitation tax on exported slaves brought in a considerable revenue to the Sultan. Its entire loss would have meant that Seyyid Said had to raise money by other forms of taxation. Anything in the form of direct taxation of his subjects would have been distinctly unpopular and in all probability well nigh impossible to levy. Innovations in indirect taxation would have been just as unpopular with those who had to pay it in the first instance and might have been frequently evaded, if not actively resisted. In this connection it has to be remembered that the revenue derived from taxation of whatever description was regarded as the personal property of Seyyid Said and not as the revenue of the state. It is true that he had to defray the cost of all public services out of it, but the fact remains that in Arab eyes it was the personal property of the Sultan for the time being. New taxation is never popular in any country. Where it apparently goes to fill the purse of a single individual, it is more unpopular still.

Perhaps Seyyid Said's personal attitude to all the problems raised by the institution and the traffic are best indicated by his last will which he made in 1850. He declared

to be free all the male and female slaves who shall remain in his possession after his death, excepting those who are at his plantations, for the sake of Almighty God, and in the hope of His mercy; and he bequeathes to each one of them whatever each may possess; it is to be theirs; and bequeaths to every Abyssinian male or female slave fifty dollars out of his property after his death, and to each of his *surias* one hundred dollars out of his property after his death, and whatever she may possess it is to be hers.

In other words, as a wealthy and devout Muslim, he performed the meritorious act of liberating his domestic slaves and granting them their property and of making special bequests to certain slaves who were especially entitled to his consideration. As the number of slaves thus enfranchised is said to have numbered a thousand and even more, the act was particularly meritorious in Muslim eyes. But his generosity ended when it came to the plantation slaves, who were more or less entirely obtained from the mainland. His own keen interest in the promotion of the cultivation of economic crops had led to large scale purchases on his part of this class of labour. On October 18, 1842, Richard Waters, the American Consul, was informed by Jairam Siwji, the customs master that at that date 100 slaves were being sold in the market every day and that 'His Highness had bought seven hundred slaves within a few weeks past to put on a sugar plantation which he is preparing'. For the sake of his heirs he could not let his plantations go to wrack and ruin for want of labour. He undoubtedly must have seen the dead and dying slaves freshly landed on the seashore at Zanzibar as well as many other glaring evils connected with the traffic. He may have deplored those sights, but for him they were attendant evils, which might or might not be capable of remedy. In his eyes the slave trade was a social and economic necessity which had to be tolerated. Even with the best will in the world he was not in the position to put an entire stop to it. As he told that out-and-out abolitionist Captain Owen in 1823, 'to put down the slave trade with Muslims that is a stone too heavy for me to lift without some strong hand to help me'. As will be seen in this chapter, he from time to time made slight concessions to British public opinion which led to some small diminution of the traffic, but he did not yield ground readily. As more than one British official pointed out, on each occasion his surrender involved some loss of revenue to himself and he never once received any compensation, pecuniary or otherwise, for his sacrifice.

In 1807 the British Parliament passed the Slave Trade Abolition Act. Immediately upon its coming into operation its provisions were promptly enforced by British cruisers in the Atlantic. For a time the navy's operations were concentrated upon the slave trade in West Africa, but towards the close of the Napoleonic Wars attention began to be drawn towards the very considerable traffic on the other side of Africa, and in particular to that stretch of the coast which the Sultan of Muscat claimed to be part of his dominions. In 1810 the Earl of Caledon, Governor of the Cape of Good Hope, wrote home urging that, if at the close of the war 'the French should retain the sovereignty of Mauritius', the East India Company should be asked to use their influence with Seyyid Said to procure the prohibition of the slave trade at Zanzibar. In 1811 the Bombay Government passed an ordinance prohibiting the slave trade. On March 4, 1812, a letter went from Bombay to Seyyid Said, asking him to give publicity to the provisions of this law so that any of the Sultan's subjects visiting Bombay 'may not by its infringement incur the penalties of that ordinance'. Three years later news reached Bombay that 'a vessel with a vast number of slaves on board, bound from Zanzibar to Muscat', had been taken by Jawasmi pirates in the Gulf of Oman and that 'every soul on board had been barbarously put to death'. Sir Evan Nepean, Governor of Bombay, seized the opportunity to write a personal letter to Seyyid Said, urging him to ban the slave trade in his dominions and thus to 'be exempt from the imputation of tolerating it'. As the only thing that was promised to him if he took this step, was 'an assurance that your acquiescence in this proposition will be extremely gratifying to the British Government', it is perhaps not surprising to learn that no reply was sent.

When in 1814 Mauritius was ceded to Great Britain, the provisions of the Slave Trade Abolition Act became applicable to that island. Soon afterwards the British Governor, Sir Robert Farquhar, became greatly perturbed by the discovery that certain of the inhabitants were indulging in the traffic and were even surreptitiously importing slaves into that island. Many others were also more or less openly conveying slaves from Seyyid Said's East African Dominions to the French island of Bourbon (Réunion). Early in 1821 Farquhar requested the senior naval officer, Captain Fairfax Moresby, commanding H.M.S. *Menai*, to make an extended cruise in the Indian Ocean in an endeavour to intercept these slave traders.

In the course of his cruise Moresby called at Zanzibar. Whilst there he learnt that eight vessels had recently sailed thence with an average of from two to four hundred slaves on board. All eight were flying the French flag and were nominally bound for Bourbon, but, as that island was known to be overstocked with slaves, there was reason to believe that their destination was the West Indies. There were still nearly twenty thousand slaves remaining on the island of Zanzibar awaiting transhipment. A boat's party from one small vessel, called the *Coureur* which was flying British colours and was commanded by one Dorval, an inhabitant of Mauritius, had landed on the island and kidnapped some children. When the parents either resisted or attempted to rescue them, they were killed by the boat's crew.

Moresby gave chase to more than one suspected slaver, but most of them outsailed the *Menai* and got away. One vessel was eventually overhauled and brought to after a chase lasting over twenty-four hours. She proved to be the *Succès*, a French vessel from Nantes. When hailed, she admitted that she was carrying a cargo of slaves. There were in fact 342 on board. Correspondence found on board showed that she had been equipped in France for the express purpose of carrying slaves from East Africa to Havannah. She had very recently taken a cargo of 248 slaves from Zanzibar to Bourbon and had then returned to Zanzibar to pick up a further cargo for Havannah, when she was intercepted.

In reporting these matters to Farquhar, Moresby wrote that:

> The Imam. . . holds, if I am rightly informed, little esteem for the island of Zanzibar – an island fertile in the extreme and possessing an excellent harbour. This has not escaped the observation of the French who are busy in that quarter. Thus it must appear that there is an utter impossibility of preventing the illegal traffic in slaves while Zanzibar remains open to the traffic, or whilst French vessels are permitted to navigate amid the dependencies of the Mauritius with impunity.

Acting on this information Farquhar addressed a letter to the 'Sultan of Muscat' and another to the Governor of Zanzibar. That addressed to the Sultan (dated May 10, 1821) began by congratulating him on the suppression of piracy in the seas adjoining his coast. At the same time he was reminded that this success had been in no small measure due to the assistance given to him by the Government of India. After this preface Farquhar proceeded as follows:

I am now writing to his Lordship and shall express to Lord Hastings (Governor-General of India) my confident expectation that, now that tranquillity has been restored in your own dominions, Your Highness will zealously co-operate with the British Government in extirpating the piratical trade that has lately begun to be carried on on a most extensive scale between Zanzibar, Kilwa and other parts of Your Highness' dependencies and the European settlements in these seas – especially the island of Bourbon.

Your Highness must be aware that this trade has been solemnly denounced by all the powers of Europe as contrary to the principles of justice and humanity and that it is only those powers who will not hesitate to commit any crime for the sake of gain that now carry it on.

The letter to the Governor of Zanzibar was written one day later. It reads as follows:

I have the honour to inform Your Excellency that the importation of slaves from Africa into any of the European possession is totally illegal and prohibited by all European powers as being contrary to the principles of justice and humanity; and that all Europeans therefore proceeding to your Government for the purpose of buying and exporting slaves from thence break the laws of their own country and are liable to be treated as felons and considered unworthy of the protection of the country they belong to.

Should therefore any vessel attempt to export slaves from Zanzibar or any other port on the coast or islands of Africa, for any of the islands in these seas, I trust that you will not allow such criminal acts, but that you will seize the persons and property of such wretches and give me immediate notice thereof, that measures may be taken for punishing them according to their deserts.

At the same time I beg that your Excellency will encourage to the utmost every other species of commerce between your Government and this. Your merchants will receive every encouragement and protection here to enable them to carry on their lawful trade; and I trust they will find it a very beneficial intercourse to establish and productive of much increased revenue to Your Excellency's treasury.

One of the slave ships which had eluded capture by the *Menai* was a vessel called the *Industrie*. Information had reached Farquhar that she was making a practice of carrying slaves from Mozambique and Zanzibar to Providence Island, to the north of Madagascar, and landing them there. After they had remained there a sufficient time to become 'frenchified' (*francisé*), they were conveyed to Mauritius under the colour of being the domestic servants of French inhabitants of that island. The captain of one was Mongin, a naturalized British subject and 'a man notorious for his crimes, and for whose apprehension a reward of two thousand dollars had been offered by this government, in order that he might be brought to justice for acts of piracy and murder committed by him on the Malay coast in pursuit of the same nefarious commerce'. Moresby was therefore requested to make a special effort to seize this vessel on his next cruise.

Moresby made his way northwards. On August 4, 1821, when he was approaching Zanzibar, the *Industrie* was sighted from the *Menai's* masthead anchored in Zanzibar roadstead and engaged in loading a cargo of slaves. As the wind had failed, the *Menai* dropped anchor and two boats were despatched to take possession of the *Industrie*. The boats were under the command of the First Lieutenant, George James Hay. Some of the *Industrie's* crew escaped to the shore. The vessel had no flag flying. Her commander asserted that she was a French vessel, but the search disclosed that she was carrying both English and French flags. The ship's papers showed that 'one Bataille of Mauritius is the person who has directed her movements and is no doubt the true owner'. There were 140 slaves on board. The commander and all the ship's officers were British subjects as were a number of the crew.

The Governor of Zanzibar sent a message to Lieutenant Hay claiming that the *Industrie* was under his protection. He demanded her immediate release; otherwise the shore battery would blow both vessel and captors to bits. Hay sent back a message to the effect that 'the governor might blow away and be d – d'. He then made Mongin, the commander of the *Industrie*, pilot his vessel out of the harbour with a pistol at his head. The shore battery did not open fire. As it was discovered later that there was only one gun fit for service, this was hardly a matter to cause surprise. Subsequently the Governor sent his 'regrets and apologies that he should have mistaken the *Menai's* boats for those of some disreputable pirates lurking in the neighbourhood'.

The *Industrie* was of course in Zanzibar territorial waters and her seizure in the circumstances amounted to a breach of international comity. Moresby fully realized this and in reporting the affair to Farquhar, stated that he had fully explained to the Governor the motives which induced him to make the seizure and 'Your Excellency will no doubt communicate with the Imam of Muscat on the subject'.

Farquhar fully realized that the situation required delicate handling. Seyyid Said might easily take offence and refuse to give any further consideration to any proposals for abolishing the slave trade. He was a firm friend and ally of the Bombay Government, who were glad of his support in the Persian Gulf and the Arabian Sea. If he lodged a protest with that Government, the East India Company might for reasons of policy decline to lend their support to Farquhar's proposals. Accordingly on October 1, 1821, Farquhar wrote once more to Seyyid Said to report and explain the incident 'in order to prevent any misconception of its nature, which might give rise to misunderstandings between our respective governments'.

After explaining that the seizure was of a British owned vessel, commanded by a naturalized British subject and manned for the most part by British subjects, he proceeded to say that:

With this information, therefore, it became the duty of Captain Moresby by all the means in his power to seize and detain the vessel *Industrie*, her crew and cargo, and bring them before the courts of this Island. . . .

Had Captain Moresby hesitated to act as he had done in this case, there can be no doubt that the captain of the *Industrie* (had time been allowed to him to get under weigh) must have escaped from the pursuit, as this vessel had invariably done for the last ten years, and would have landed her cargo of slaves on these islands. The occasion therefore was too fortunate to be lost. The persons and property detained are exclusively subject to this jurisdiction and the vessel was not under any colours.

Captain Moresby lost no time in landing and explaining to the Governor of Zanzibar every part of this transaction, which did not in the slightest degree interrupt the harmony between them.

Having thus explained, I trust to Your Highness's satisfaction the only incident requiring observation, I avail myself of the occasion of renewing to Your Highness the expression of my earnest wishes that a commerce, mutually advantageous to both our respective states, sanctioned and protected by our laws, may be established in the place of the odious traffic that has been abolished. Assuring Your Highness that every encouragement and protection shall be granted to vessels of your dominions and that they shall be received here with the same friendship and indulgence as the vessels of our own nation, I have etc.

Farquhar was not the only person who was trying to move Seyyid Said to put a stop to the slave trade. The attention of the African Institution (the precursor of the British and Foreign Anti-Slavery Society) had been drawn to the extent of the traffic in the Indian Ocean. The Committee were given to understand that

the Imam of Muscat is an old and steady ally of the East India Company. . . . Indeed, the intimacy between the Imam and the Bombay Governor has been such and the confidence of the Mohammedan in Christian benevolence so great that he has (contrary to all usage) been in the practice of sending his sister, to whom he was much attached, annually to Bombay with a large suite there to pass some months for the benefit of her health.

They were accordingly of the opinion that 'the British Government therefore have only to express the desire to the Imam that the slave trade at Zanzibar should cease' and that thereupon 'he would readily enter into a treaty for that purpose and as readily agree that the East India Company's vessels of war should enforce its execution'.

On March 21, 1821, the Duke of Gloucester, as President, and the Directors of the Institution addressed a memorial to the Chairman of the Court of Directors of the East India Company urging the Company 'to interpose their powerful mediation with the Imam of Muscat for the entire abolition of the slave trade at Zanzibar'. The Chairman replied, assuring the Duke of 'the Court's most cordial concurrence in the benevolent views entertained by the members of the Institution'.

He then mentioned the previous correspondence on the subject which had passed between the Bombay Government and Seyyid Said in 1812 and 1815, but informed the Duke that they were not aware of any reply having been sent to the second of these letters. Instructions, were, however, being sent to the Bombay Government to renew their appeal to Seyyid Said to abolish the traffic. In their letter, to the Governor of Bombay, the Court of Directors stated that they had 'been both disappointed and mortified by not being able to find upon your records any reply from the Imam' to the letter of 1815. The matter was one of deep interest to the

Court and the Governor should 'leave no prudent means untried to obtain from the Imam the desired concession'.

It was realized in Bombay that Seyyid Said was being asked not only to forego a considerable amount of his personal income in the shape of the capitation tax on slaves, but also to do something which would make him extremely unpopular with his subjects. Any attempt on his part to prohibit the entire traffic would be difficult to enforce and might seriously jeopardize his position on the throne, if not his life. Correspondence therefore passed between the Governors of Bombay and Mauritius discussing what concessions might reasonably be demanded from Seyyid Said. Whilst, as already said, slavery and the buying and selling of slaves had been recognized by Islam as being valid and lawful, there was warrant in the Sharia for the statement that Muslims should not make such sales to non-believers. Seyyid Said was therefore in a position to prohibit his co-religionists from dealing in the traffic with the subjects of Christian nations without arousing their indignation. Accordingly, he was ready to make this concession. Either at the latter end of 1821 or else in the early days of 1822 he sent letters to all his officers in Africa 'positively prohibiting the sale of slaves to any Christian nation'.

Farquhar, however, was anxious to obtain in black and white a treaty whereby Seyyid Said not only bound himself and also his heirs and successor to prohibit for all time traffic in slaves with the subjects of European states, but furthermore to authorize British cruisers to seize Arab vessels which infringed this order. As the cutting-out exploit of the *Menai* had been in respect of a Christian owned vessel, Seyyid Said had not taken serious umbrage at this violation of his territorial waters. The same incident had also shown him that he was not in a position to prevent its repetition in the like circumstances. He also realized that units of his own navy would be most reluctant to enforce his orders on this subject. In February 1822, an Arab vessel arrived at Port Louis, Mauritius, bringing to Farquhar 'a very civil letter' in which Seyyid Said professed his anxiety to meet as far as possible the views of the British Government in regard to the slave trade. At the same time he asked to have his vessels put upon the same footing in Mauritius as they enjoyed in the ports of British India. In the circumstances Farquhar reported that he had 'deemed it politic to accede to his request'.

Q

In June 1822, Farquhar requested Moresby to proceed to Muscat in order to obtain his signature to a treaty abolishing the European slave trade in his dominions. Moresby was furnished with six 'requisitions' and instructed to endeavour to obtain Seyyid Said's assent to each of them. On arrival at Muscat, Moresby was told by 'the chief man or prime minister' that shortly before the French had endeavoured to purchase the island of Zanzibar – information which may or may not have been true. The negotiations proceeded quite smoothly. Said insisted that he could not ban the export of slaves to Muslim states, but that he was perfectly ready to prohibit their sale to subjects of all Christian states. He was further ready to permit British cruisers to seize Arab vessels contravening this prohibition and to order the offenders, who were thereby breaking a precept of Islamic law, to be punished. Eventually, he delivered under his hand and seal answers to each of the six requisitions delivered to him by Moresby. These amounted in effect to an unqualified acceptance of Farquhar's demands and the two documents, taken together, embodied and constituted the terms of the Treaty.

Seyyid Said signed and sealed the Treaty on September 22, 1822. He undertook thereby to repeat the orders already issued to his officers prohibiting the sale of slaves to any Christian nation and at the same time to direct such officers to seize all vessels contravening this order and to punish their commanders. He also consented to allow the settlement of an agent of the British Government 'in Zanzibar and the neighbouring parts for the purpose of having intelligence and watching the traffic in slaves with Christian nations'. He likewise consented to allow British warships to seize all vessels laden with slaves bound for Christian countries. This concession was not to come into force until four months after the date of the Treaty, and, in order 'that it may be understood in the most comprehensive manner' it was agreed that after the expiration of that period British cruisers might seize all Arab vessels laden with slaves for foreign markets found to the eastward of a line drawn from Cape Delgado, passing sixty miles to the eastward of the island of Socotra and thence to Diu Head, being the western extremity of the Gulf of Cambay, unless driven across that line by stress of weather. Finally, it was agreed that, as from four months after the conclusion of the Treaty, all ships were to carry passes certifying the port of their departure and the port of their destination. If any vessel was found beyond Madagascar or in the sea of Mauritius without such a pass, it could be seized by a British cruiser and handed over to the Sultan's authorities for disposal.

In implementation of his bond Seyyid Said at once despatched the following circular letter to all his local governors in Africa:

Whosoever receives this letter at Zanzibar, at Kilwa, or any ports within my dominions, this is to let you know that I have permitted my friends, the English, to keep an agent in any part of my country they may choose; and you are to give a house to the English Agent, and wherever he may stay, you are to pay him great respect, and nobody must refuse to receive the Agent.

Owing to ill health Fairfax Moresby left Mauritius on June 1823. Sometime after his departure the following letter reached that island with the sole superscription 'Captain Murzeeby'. It eventually reached Moresby in England. Its contents were as follows:

Captain Murzeeby – Dear Sir, Since you left Muscat you did not write me untill these date.

I have the pleasure to inform you that I have received a letter from my men from Zanzabare, who informs me a French Marchent Ship arrived there. The Captn of the Ship he publiced saying they required Firewood and water. The Captn of the Ship he slyely wanted to make Bargin with some of the inhabitant of that place for Slaves. However he striked Bargin with Six of those men on the subject. These 6 men who desired the Captn to go behinde of the Island (so) that they would give him Slaves. Afterwards the head man of the Island he founded that the Captn has made Bargin with those people. As soon as the head man had this information, he immediately send a boat with a few Sepoys after the Ship. Soon after the Ship saw the boat following them they made all possible sail and got off from it, but some people says the Ship got Slaves and others says none. Among of those Six men, three of them the head man of the Island he gotted and Put them in Iron and had sent to Muscat. The other three had desarted in the Jungle. The French Ship went to Kelvah (sc. Kilwa). As soon as I have receved the letter about this subject, I immediately Dispatched my Ship Sulley to Kelvah and Zanzabare to bring those people who had made the Bargin about Slaves with the French Captn. As soon as I get them under my possesion I will severely punnishing them and will properly Corrected as an example for the Rest. As the headman of the Island does not mention these Ships name, therefore I could not mentions in my letter to you.

I have to inform you about these Particular. You dont belive that I have made an Agreement between me and the Breetish. If you require any thing to bee dun in these place I am ready to do at any tim.

I remain,
Dear Sir,
Yours truly
(L. S.)

Muscat,
  17th June 182
    1823
  P.S. – After I wrote you this letter I have inquired from the people arriving from the Islend of Zanzebar on account of the Captn Name and the Ship Name. Ships Name they could not make it out. As to the Captns Name (it) is Dubois and the supercargo's name is Dinna.

Further evidence that Seyyid Said and certain of his officers were trying to do their best to observe the terms of the Treaty was forthcoming when Commodore Nourse called in H.M.S. *Andromache* at Zanzibar on December 1, 1823. He learnt that about fifteen days before his arrival a vessel, under French colours and carrying twenty-four guns put in to Zanzibar. It was reported, to Nourse that she had come direct from France for the express purpose of purchasing slaves. Permission was refused and she then set sail professedly for Muscat.

Nourse was informed that Seyyid Said 'had issued the most positive orders prohibiting the traffic in slaves with any Christians whatsoever'. He was satisfied from all the information that he was able to obtain that 'these orders had been most strictly attended to by the Governor of Zanzibar'. At the same time, 'with a view to promoting and enforcing strict fulfilment of the Treaty', Nourse 'provisionally appointed a Consul, with the consent of the Governor of Zanzibar, and in conformity to the tenor of the Treaty to reside at Zanzibar'.

The 'Consul' in question was a local Arab, named Saleh. When Farquhar reported this appointment to Lord Bathurst, he was informed that the noble lord could not recommend an irregular appointment of this nature for His Majesty's confirmation. Nevertheless he was fully aware of the utility of establishing some communication with Zanzibar in order that the Governor of Mauritius and naval officers could obtain authentic information regarding the traffic in slaves. For that reason he was prepared to allow Saleh to consider himself as being the Agent of the Government of Mauritius at a salary of 100 dollars.

Saleh died in about 1826. There appears to be no record indicating how far he performed his duty of looking out for infractions of the Treaty. The only known task that was given to him to perform occurred in 1824, when Captain Owen of H.M.S. *Leven* visited the island. Owen found certain members of a Mauritian vessel marooned on the island and 'directed the English resident to give each of them one month's pay, and the same allowance of provisions usually supplied to Indians in India'.

On October 29, 1826, Sir Lowry Cole, then Governor of Mauritius, appointed Khamisi bin Athmani as Saleh's successor. If Guillain is to be believed, this was a case of the poacher turned gamekeeper, for it was alleged that Khamis had once been the captain of a slave dhow. His last previous post had been that of interpreter to the British establishment, which Captain Owen had set up in Mombasa in 1824. When that protectorate was hastily withdrawn in 1826, a number of the liberated slaves, who had been rescued by the British authorities from slave dhows, ran away in a panic. In the following year Khamis bin Athman managed to get in touch with most of them. Through his instrumentality some of them were embarked upon a British warship and conveyed to a new home at Simonstown, South Africa. Others were too sick to be moved and Khamis was provided with money for their care and maintenance. Apart from this we know nothing as to the manner in which he performed his 'consular' duties. We know that, whilst he was at Mombasa, he indulged in private trade. Very probably he continued to do so when he took up his residence in Zanzibar. In 1832 he was sent as an envoy by Seyyid Said to Ranavolana, Queen of Madagascar. Two years later he paid a visit to England. After the abolition of his post in 1841 he was employed by Seyyid Said in the combined posts of secretary, major-domo and general factotum. He was a remarkable linguist, speaking in addition to his native Swahili, English, French, Portuguese, Hindustani and Malagasi as well as Arabic. He was consequently in great demand as an intermediary in transactions between European merchants and the local inhabitants.

Shortly after he had upon his own responsibility placed Mombasa under British protection, Captain Owen called at Zanzibar and thereafter expressed the opinion that the Governor of the island 'possessed the entire monopoly of the (slave) traffic at Zanzibar' and accordingly was making no attempt to enforce the Moresby Treaty. But Owen was an out and out abolitionist, whose highly prejudiced opinions must be accepted with some measure of caution. On May 24, 1825, Captain C. R. Moorsom, who had visited Zanzibar and Pemba more than once during the preceding fifteen months, reported that 'I have no reason to believe that the present Governor (of Zanzibar) permits any infraction of the Treaty, though he can hardly be expected to oppose with energy any attempt by French vessels to procure slaves in the vicinity'. In all probability this was a fair summing up of the situation. In his attempts to enforce the provisions of the Treaty, the Governor had to work single handed and to make himself intensely unpopular with his fellow countrymen. Not only were many of his compatriots unco-operative and most obstructive, but there were times when he was on extremely delicate ground. If he tried to interfere with vessels flying the French flag, he ran the risk of involving both himself and his royal master in considerable trouble. In the circumstances he could hardly be expected to enforce the provisions of the Treaty with any great energy.

CHAPTER XII

THE BRITISH CONSULATE
AT ZANZIBAR

THOUGH by the Moresby Treaty Seyyid Said undertook to prohibit the trade in slaves with British subjects, he did not specifically agree to take measures to enforce that prohibition. It is clear from the terms of the Treaty that he looked to British cruisers to enforce its provisions. As he had told Owen, he himself could do nothing in regard thereto 'without a strong hand to help me'. During the two years in which the British flag flew over Fort Jesus at Mombasa, British warships were frequently to be seen in the waters adjacent to Zanzibar and doubtless their mere presence acted as a strong deterrent to slave traders. But after the flag was hauled down in 1826, there was a considerable diminution in the number of such visits and the slave traders were able to carry on their business with comparative impunity.

On his return from a trading voyage to Zanzibar in 1838 a certain Captain Cook informed the abolitionist, Thomas Fowell Buxton, that he had visited the island on several occasions and that he had always seen the slave market, which was held daily, fully supplied. He could not ascertain the number sold annually, but the slaves were constantly arriving in droves of from fifty to one hundred each and found a ready sale. He understood that they were chiefly 'purchased by Arab merchants for the supply of Egypt Abyssinia, Arabia and the ports along the Persian Gulf, to the markets of which countries hundreds were carried off and sold daily. Many, however, are kept in Zanzibar where there are sugar and spice plantations'. It should be noted that the traffic described by him was not being carried on with Christian countries and accordingly did not contravene the Moresby Treaty. Nevertheless it roused the indignation of the British public. Parliament had only very recently abolished the status of slavery in all British possessions overseas and there was a growing demand that the slave trade should be ended once and for all in every part of the globe.

It so happened that at about the same date the British Government was contemplating the concluding of a commercial treaty with Seyyid Said. After the withdrawal of the protectorate from Mombasa the number of British ships visiting Zanzibar and the water adjacent thereto fell off considerably. In 1833 only three British ships called at Zanzibar. When Captain Hart visited the island in the following year he found there three ships flying the Stars and Stripes and an English brig. He learnt that Robert Brown Norsworthy, who commanded this last mentioned ship, had been invited by Seyyid Said to bring out his family and to settle in the island. Norsworthy, who was in the employment of Messrs. Newman Hunt and Christopher, a London firm established in New Bond Street, accepted this invitation. In May 1835, Norsworthy arrived back with his wife and family and took up his abode as agent of his employers in the town of Zanzibar. In 1837 he was in Bombay. On November 23, of that year he addressed a long memorial to the Governor in Council at Bombay. In it he announced that he had resided for three years in Zanzibar 'where he had traded as well as devoting attention to agricultural pursuits'. He declared that the ruler of the country wished to encourage British subjects to settle in his dominions and that the opportunities for profitable trading, were many, but such persons were handicapped by the fact that there was no British Consul in Zanzibar who could afford them the same protection as was then being given to American traders by the United States Consul. Early in 1838 Captain Robert Cogan, formerly of the Indian Navy, arrived in London with a letter from Seyyid Said appointing him as his agent to the British Government. In a letter addressed to the Foreign Office Cogan pointed out that 'America has lately concluded a Treaty by which it gained advantages superior to those of Great Britain and any other State; and Russia, through native agency, is endeavouring to establish an understanding with His Highness.' He therefore urged that a commercial treaty similar in character to the American treaty should be concluded with Seyyid Said and offered his services in bringing this about. His offer was eventually accepted and on September 28, 1838, he was appointed plenipotentiary of the British Government to negotiate such a treaty. Cogan accordingly proceeded to Zanzibar, where on May 31, 1839, a formal treaty was drawn up.

It had been suggested that in addition to procuring a commercial treaty Cogan should endeavour to induce Seyyid Said to tighten up measures to be taken against the slave trade. But Cogan informed Sir James Carnac, the Chairman of the East India Company, that he did not deem such a proposal politic.

The abolition of slavery is a question repugnant to the interests and feelings of His Highness' subjects, and without remuneration would seriously affect the revenues of a Government which from various causes are far from being in a state of financial prosperity. This . . . presents to me difficulties in obtaining any further amicable concession from the Government of Muscat, unless we tender some pecuniary equivalent, supported by naval protection, against the neighbouring Muslim powers interested in the continuance of the Slave Trade. . . . I am, however, of opinion that His Highness would be happy to meet our views, even on this subject, so far as is consistent with the maintenance of his power and the financial revenues of his Government; but to entirely shut the ports of His Highness' African possessions against the export of slaves could, in my opinion, only be effected by a pecuniary equivalent for the loss of revenue.

Seyyid Said was nevertheless persuaded by Captain Hennell, the British Resident in the Persian Gulf, to add three additional articles to the Moresby Treaty of 1822. This supplementary treaty was signed on December 17, 1839. The early treaty had in effect sanctioned an 'internal' trade in slaves by restricting the right of British vessels to search and detain suspect vessels to the eastward of a line drawn from Cape Delgado, passing sixty miles east of Socotra to Diu Head in the Gulf of Cambay. Under the new treaty that line was pushed back to a line drawn east of Cape Delgado, passing two degrees seaward Socotra, and ending at Pasni on the Makran coast of what is now Pakistan and British cruisers were allowed to search and detain vessels carrying slaves beyond that line, unless they had been driven there by stress of weather. In the final article Seyyid Said solemnly declared that 'the selling of slaves, whether grown up or young, who are *hoor* or free, is contrary to the Muslim religion', and that Somalis were included in this definition of 'hoor'. He further declared that the sale of Somalis of any age or sex, was to be considered as piracy, any of his subjects convicted of being concerned in such act should be punished as pirates. It was a small concession, which was not likely to cause much disaffection amongst his subjects or any serious diminution of his revenue. It still left the enforcement of the treaty mainly to the British Navy.

One of the articles of Captain Cogan's treaty with Seyyid Said acknowledged the right of each contracting party to appoint Consuls to reside in each other's dominions, 'wherever the interests of commerce may require the presence of such officers'. After signing and sealing the treaty Seyyid Said wrote to Lord Palmerston begging him of his kindness 'to send us a steady wise man and a genuine Englishman; may your other men also, who are to reside in our country either at Zanzibar or Muscat or in any other places, be all true pure Englishmen and not of other nations'. The choice of the British Government fell upon Captain Atkins Hamerton of the 15th Regiment of Bombay Native Infantry, who was instructed to reside at the court of Seyyid Said in the dual capacity of Her Britannic Majesty's Consul and Agent of the East India Company. He proceeded in the first place to Muscat, where Seyyid Said happened to be at the time. On November 10, 1840, the Sultan, who had been greatly perturbed by news which he had received regarding French activities in East Africa, sailed from Muscat for Zanzibar. In due course Hamerton received instructions from Bombay to follow him there. On May 4, 1841, he reached Zanzibar. In reporting his arrival to Bombay, he gave an account of his voyage which well indicates the difficulties of navigation in the Indian Ocean in the days before steam.

On the 18th of April last we made the north-west coast of the island of Zanzibar, which the *nahoda* (captain) and *maalims* (pilots) unfortunately mistook for the island of Mafia on the coast of Africa, and the brig lay to all night and in the morning we were off the south-east coast of the island of Pemba or Hathera to the north of the island of Zanzibar, but which the people of the vessel still thought was the island of Zanzibar; and in the evening of the 19th of April the boat was sent ashore to ascertain whereabout the brig was, and we then learnt we were on the north-east point of the island of Pemba or Hathera and that we could not reach Zanzibar unless we stood out to sea for about eight degrees to the eastward, and that even then we were not likely to reach Zanzibar under twenty or five and twenty days. To do this at this season of the year the equipment of the brig was quite unfit, the sails were split and much damage done to the rigging and, in fact, the crew were afraid to undertake the voyage. I then procured small boats to take my things round the northern point of the island, and walked across the island to the western coast at Chake Chake, where I procured with the assistance of the *Wali* or governor a boat, in which I proceeded to Zanzibar, and on 4th instant anchored opposite to the Imam's house (at Mtoni) about a mile (three miles) to the north of the town and immediately went ashore and had an interview with His Highness, who I found dejected and broken spirited in consequence of his having a few days before received authentic information of the occupation of the island of Nossi Bé by the French.

I beg leave to state that I received every possible assistance from the Wali of Pemba, Nasser bin Kheluf (el Mauli), and, indeed, I know not what I should have done without his aid; it rained incessantly during the time I was walking across the island and the heat was very great; all my people were sick and knocked up.

Hamerton's instructions were to furnish the governments in London and Bombay with information regarding the extent of the slave trade which was being carried on in Seyyid Said's African dominions and also regarding the alleged aggressions of the French within those territories. The Arab population quickly sensed the former part of his instructions. Hamerton's arrival was accordingly regarded by them with the utmost suspicion. On July 13, he reported to Bombay that

His Highness told me while riding out with him some days ago that the people troubled him much about my coming here, (and) that they constantly asked if I was come to emancipate the slaves and stop the trade. I turned the subject by replying that I was astonished to observe how little people regarded his authority. He replied that I know well how he was situated. I then said, 'If Your Highness would keep even one ship efficient, you would find it to your advantage', He said that the people he required must be had from India, but that they would be too expensive for him.

Hamerton was to be in close association with Seyyid Said until the latter's last return from Zanzibar to Muscat in 1854. He was to end his days in Zanzibar without ever once visiting his mother country. During their long and intimate acquaintance it was inevitable that the relations between the two should at times have become somewhat strained – and in particular on those occasions when Hamerton, as the mouthpiece of the British Government, urged Seyyid Said to adopt sterner measures for the suppression of the slave trade or insisted upon a strict adherence to the terms of the anti-slavery and commercial treaties into which the Sultan had entered with the same government. Once indeed in 1844 Seyyid Said wrote to Lord Aberdeen to complain 'that we are constantly perplexed by annoyances from your Consul, Captain Hamerton'.

Hamerton's reply was that he had never intentionally shown any disrespect to Said.

Setting aside what I know to be my public duty, the kindness which I have ever experienced from the Imam would have restrained me or any other man of proper feeling from intentionally offering to His Highness the slightest possible disrespect. . . . I am aware that His Highness the Imam has told his authorities that free effect must and shall be given to all treaties without subterfuge or evasion; had we, my Lord, only the Imam himself to deal with in these matters, we should find no trouble.

The rift between the two was eventually closed. When a few months later, Hamerton presented a letter addressed by Aberdeen to the Sultan, 'His Highness said, swearing by Almighty God, that he from that instant considered that all that was said regarding me had been buried in the sea and His Highness has certainly behaved towards me as if he did so'. In 1849 Hamerton reported to Bombay that he had been seriously ill for nine weeks, and that 'it is impossible for me to express my sense of gratitude for the extraordinary kindness I have received during my illness from His Highness the Imam. He almost constantly visited me or sent some of his family to see me'. When in February 1853, Hamerton returned to Zanzibar after several months of convalescence in Bombay, he reported that on landing he 'was most honourably received by the Imam. His Highness came down to the beach, accompanied by all his sons and the principal Arabs, and embraced me after the Arab fashion, and took me to his palace, and sent his sons to accompany me to the Consulate'.

The two had not a few things in common. Both were horse lovers and from time to time raced their rival steeds against each other at low tide on the sand of the dried up creek at the back of the town of Zanzibar. Each also was quick to realize the good points in the other. Hamerton's opinion of the Sultan has already been given. Unlike his American colleagues Hamerton had no commercial interests at stake in Zanzibar. He belonged to a service which had already acquired very high traditions. He could understand and sympathize with many of the difficulties besetting the ruler to whom he was accredited. Whilst he was resolute in his insistence on the observance by the Sultan of his treaty obligations, he also respected those obligations which the treaties imposed upon British subjects. In so doing he more than once incurred the displeasure of the British community in Zanzibar. Seyyid Said, who himself had an innate love of justice and fair play, clearly appreciated this last mentioned fact and came to realize that Hamerton's advice, unlike that of the Consul Waters, was disinterested advice and had no ulterior motive behind it. Fourteen years of constant association had led him and many of the leading Arabs to appreciate Hamerton's character so well that in 1854, when Seyyid left Zanzibar for Muscat, he publicly entrusted his son Khalid, whom he was leaving in charge of his African dominions, to Hamerton's care and tutelage. When two years later he was lying on his death bed, he was heard in his delirium or semi-consciousness to call again and again for Hamerton.

To revert, however, to the early days of their association Hamerton reported to Bombay on July 13, 1841, that he estimated the number of slaves annually imported into Zanzibar and Pemba at from 8,000 to 9,000 and that the customs master received in respect of each such slave a duty of one dollar. He went on to say that

in no part of the world is the misery and suffering these wretched slaves endure, whilst being brought here and until they are sold, exceeded. They are in such a wretched state from starvation and disease that they are sometimes not considered worth landing, and are allowed to expire on the boats to save the dollar a head duty.

On January 2, 1842, Hamerton further reported to Bombay that

the Arabs from the pirate coast in the Persian Gulf yearly take a number of slaves by force from Zanzibar; yet the Imam is unable to prevent them; he fears to do so. With respect to the suppressing – even the amelioration – of the Slave Trade which is carried on by the subjects of His Highness the Imam and other chiefs of the coast of Africa, nothing can ever be effected by negotiation. The Imam has not the power to interfere in this matter, even if he were willing to do so, but he is not. Should the Government determine to stop the Slave Trade by sea, it can easily be done; but little or no assistance can be expected from the Imam.

Early in 1842 Hamerton presented a letter to the Sultan from Lord Aberdeen urging him to abolish the slave trade. He later reported that he had found the Sultan most reluctant to do anything in the matter and that at one stage 'he muttered about one thing and another and behaved in a way I had never seen him do before'. Hamerton then 'assumed a high tone with him' and eventually Seyyid Said announced that he would send his ship *Sultani* to convey his agent Ali bin Nasser to England to lay his case before Lord Aberdeen, exclaiming,

This letter is enough for me. It is the same as the orders of Azrael (the angel of death) – nothing but to obey. Even I will write to the Queen and her *wazirs*. Will you translate the letters so that I may be certain they will be understood? I said of course I would and have done so.

Seyyid Said accordingly wrote on February 11 of that year informing the noble lord that the result of such a measure would be

that these countries will be totally and entirely ruined, and no revenue nor any income, saving and except a trifle, will remain with me; the loss of the whole world is as one shore, while to the people of these countries the loss will be as ten shores; my hopes and expectations were that, should loss or oppression happen to me from any other nation, I could look to Her Most Gracious Majesty and her Government for refuge and protection. Now the thing your friend hopes for, without troubling you and not as a matter of right, is that you would take my case into consideration, and to what may be for my benefit.

When Ali bin Nasser reached England, he found Lord Aberdeen in no way disposed to reduce his demands. On July 12, 1842, he was told that

neither the duty of Her Majesty's Government, nor the feelings of the British nation, will allow them to rest satisfied with an imperfect execution of this great work. . . . It is most desirable that Her Majesty should receive the co-operation of His Highness. . . . If in the first instance some sacrifice of revenue will be necessary, the loss will be speedily compensated by the establishment of a legitimate commerce far more profitable to the revenue and beneficial to the population of His Highness' dominions than the inhuman one which now occupies its place.

The only extent to which Lord Aberdeen was prepared to relent was by expressing the British Government's willingness

to assist the Imam in meeting the first deficiency which may arise from the loss of duties hitherto levied upon the slave trade; and they invite His Highness to communicate without delay the terms upon which he would be willing to take a share in the proposed measures, both as regards the amount of payment to be made to His Highness and the time during which it is to continue.

Seyyid Said realized that, like the commands of Azrael, the will of the British Government would sooner or later inevitably have to be obeyed for reasons of policy, but he was resolved to temporize and to yield as little ground as possible. The offer of pecuniary compensation made little or no appeal to him, but he instructed Ali bin Nasser to inquire whether the British Government would consent to his retaking possession of the Island of Bahrain, which had thrown off its allegiance to Oman. At the same time he expressed the hope that the defence of that island 'against the sects of Islam' should rest with the British Government. Aberdeen was ready to give his consent, but on political grounds the Government of India vetoed the plan. Later still, Said suggested to Aberdeen that he might be allowed to annex the East African coast from Ras Hafun to Berbera. In due course he was informed that Her Majesty's Government would have no objection to the proposal.

This concession emboldened Seyyid Said to ask for another. On August 8, 1844, he sent and entrusted a letter for Lord Aberdeen to Captain Robert Cogan, who had negotiated the commercial treaty with him in 1839. Once again, he pointed out that the total abolition of the slave trade would throw 'great difficulty upon the whole commerce of our dominions and will stop a great portion of the trade which now exists, and consequently the loss to us in our revenue will be most serious, (but) this loss we will sacrifice to your wishes'. Nevertheless, he asked for two concessions.

First, we desire an agreement with you that the free sale and transit of slaves on the coast between the ports of Lamu and Kilwa, including the islands of Zanzibar, Pemba and Mafia, shall be continued as it now is with those places and that this agreement shall be confirmed to our heirs and successors. Secondly, if any person be guilty of breaking the agreement to be made, by stealing slaves unknown to us, we must not be answerable for this. And should false wicked informers report that slaves have been so taken and sold, without their reports are corroborated by good authority, or by officers of ships-of-war, do not pay attention to such reports.

On December 31, 1844, Aberdeen wrote to inform Said that these two concessions would be granted and that a treaty containing them was being sent to Hamerton to submit to Said for his signature. 'Her Majesty greatly regrets', wrote Aberdeen, 'that you anticipate serious loss to your revenue from this further restriction of the export of slaves from your African dominions. But Her

Majesty confidently trusts that loss will be speedily compensated by the establishment of legal commerce.'

Having obtained these concessions, Seyyid Said tried to obtain a few more. He once again stressed the loss of revenue which the treaty would entail and desired Hamerton to inform Aberdeen that he felt 'quite certain' that this was a matter which the British Government would take into consideration. He further asked Hamerton to say that he trusted that explicit orders would be issued to British men-of-war 'not to search or interfere with any of his vessels which may from time to time have any of his family on board, in going from his dominions in Africa to Arabia, and also coming from thence to his African possessions'. He also hoped that the same treatment would be accorded to 'vessels coming from the Red Sea bringing to his African possessions slaves, particularly Abyssinians, girls and eunuchs'. Both these concessions, if granted, would have reduced the terms of the treaty more or less to a nullity. Even if the members of the Sultan's family were to observe meticulously the terms of the treaty the exemption of their vessels from being searched would have provided a cloak for the smuggling of slaves by others. As Hamerton told Aberdeen, considerable numbers of Abyssinian concubines and eunuchs had hitherto been imported annually from Mocha and other Red Sea ports. Hamerton also reported to Aberdeen that he had informed the Sultan that the articles of the proposed treaty and the contents of Aberdeen's letter of December 31, 1844, 'contain the meaning of the additional articles which he requires'. Except, however, for the addition of a clause postponing the coming into operation of the treaty until January 1, 1847, the terms thereof were not amended.

At length on October 2, 1845, the new Slave Trade Treaty was signed by Seyyid Said personally and by Hamerton on behalf of the British Government. By the first article the Sultan undertook to prohibit the export of slaves from his African dominions and to issue to his officers the necessary orders to prevent and suppress the trade. In the second article he undertook to prohibit the importation of slaves from any part of Africa into his possessions in Asia and also 'to use his utmost influence with all the chiefs of Arabia, the Red Sea and the Persian Gulf' to enforce the like prohibition from Africa into their respective territories. The third article empowered men-of-war of Her Britannic Majesty and of the East India Company to seize and detain any vessels belonging to himself or his subjects which were carrying the slaves, with the exception of those engaged in the transport of slaves from one part to another of his African dominions between Lamu and Kilwa, including the islands of Zanzibar, Pemba and Mafia.

During the negotiations Hamerton was instructed by the Governor of Bombay to point out that the Moresby Treaty of 1822 omitted to state that Seyyid Said was to bind himself, his heirs and successors to afford assistance, when required by persons authorized to demand it, in the apprehension of British subjects engaged in the slave traffic. On August 18, 1845, Said wrote to inform Hamerton that he was prepared to give that undertaking, but was unwilling to make any alterations or additions to the treaty in question. On March 12, 1847, after the new Slave Trade Treaty had come into force, the Governor of Bombay wrote to inform Said that they would not press their request to have the Moresby Treaty amended, but that they would treat his letter as having the force of a treaty.

After conclusion of this supplemental treaty Hamerton pointed out the difficulties which would have to be encountered in attempting to enforce it. On September 28, 1846, he reported to Lord Aberdeen that

His Highness will have great difficulties to encounter, but he will do all in his power and make every sacrifice; and he is entitled to and well deserves every possible consideration from the people and Government of England. He has been looked up to not only by his own subjects, but by all the Arabs generally, as the person who should protect and guarantee to them what they all consider as their dearest interest – the right to carry on the Slave Trade.

Now his subjects, almost without exception, would declare that he had betrayed them. In the circumstances it was not surprising that Seyyid Said was 'in great distress of mind on this slave question'.

By the time this despatch reached England Palmerston had replaced Aberdeen at the Foreign Office. He was a lifelong and uncompromising enemy of the slave trade. He had little sympathy with or understanding of the difficulties of a ruler, who had just declared to his subjects that a commerce, which they had carried on for centuries and which they had always regarded as lawful, had become unlawful and punishable as a criminal offence. He addressed a letter to Said, which was distinctly brusque in tone,

R

informing him that 'Your Highness' subjects may not as yet all of them have understood that slave trading is a criminal act, deserving of severe punishment; but it is so considered in England, and the British Government is only following out its unavoidable destiny by employing all the means in its power to put an end to the Slave Trade'.

Hamerton was treated to a somewhat sententious homily.

You will take every opportunity of impressing upon these Arabs that the nations of Europe are destined to put an end to the African Slave Trade, and that Great Britain is the main instrument in the hand of Providence for the accomplishment of this purpose; that it is in vain for these Arabs to endeavour to resist the consummation of that which is written in the book of fate; that they ought to bow to superior power, to leave off a pursuit which is doomed to annihilation, and a persever-ance in which will only involve them in pecuniary losses and in various other evils; and that they should hasten to betake themselves to the cultivation of the soil and to lawful and innocent commerce.

Official records do not indicate how far (if at all) Hamerton carried out the above instructions. He may well have doubted their efficacy. On the other hand, Rigby, his successor in office, subsequently made a point of reading Lord Aberdeen's homily, at frequent intervals to Said's son and successor on the throne.

In 1849 Seyyid Said made at least one effort to stop the export of slaves from the mainland, when he sent a combined military and naval force under the command of the Governor of Kilwa to destroy a village in Kiswara Bay for having dealings with a Portu-guese slave ship. But it was out of the question for him to undertake frequent operations on this scale. As in the case of the earlier Moresby Treaty, so also in the case of this more recent treaty it was out of the question to expect the Sultan to make any long sustained or large scale attempt to enforce the terms thereof. Once again this had to be left to the vigilance of British men-of-war, which could not be expected to intercept anything more than a tithe of the vessels carrying slaves from Africa to Southern Arabia and Oman. British agents in the Persian Gulf were constantly reporting the landing of slaves at Muscat. In 1849 one of these vessels was reported to be the property of Seyyid Said himself. On August 23, 1849, the Bombay Government instructed Hamerton 'to enter into a friendly remonstrance with His Highness the Imam on these glaring violations of the provisions of his Treaty'.

As Hamerton reported, he had more than once remonstrated with Seyyid Said. As often as not he was met with the reply that the British Government had similar treaties with European nations, yet the slave trade was carried on by the subjects of those nations; and that it was difficult for him to do what other people found it impossible to do with means far superior to anything he could command; that the measure was a new thing and not yet well understood by the Arabs and that time was required. 'When they saw the British Government was determined to suppress the Slave Trade, the people would be obliged to give it up, as they (the Arabs) could not contend against the wishes of the Government, like the Portuguese and Spaniards.'

Hamerton then said to him,

But suppose the *Wazir* (Prime Minister), or the Governor of Bombay, or the Governor-General were to write to me saying report what measures the Imam of Muscat has taken to carry out the stipulations of the Treaty, I would be obliged to answer none at all further than to issue orders to forbid his people carrying on the slave trade; he has not punished anyone for not obeying his orders.

The Sultan replied that he had not thought of that 'but that *Inshallah* this season he would do something'.

Subsequently to this conversation Hamerton reported that the Sultan

has certainly done more than he ever was known to do before; he has had the slave traders severely flogged for selling slaves for export to the Northern Arabs and also taken the slaves from the Arabs and imprisoned many of them; he has sent guards of Baluchis (but such guards, every man of them, are slave dealers) to various places to prevent slaves being embarked.

But, as Hamerton added,

notwithstanding all this, I can assure the Government (that) a great number of slaves will be taken this year from this (island). The Imam of Muscat has not the power to prevent it; he has not a faithful man about him and, be his wish ever so great to meet the views of the British Government – and he certainly does wish to do so – he has not one man in his dominions to render him any zealous assistance to stop the Slave Trade; even his own children are against him.

Later that year Commodore Christopher Wyvill, commanding on the Cape Station, reported that there were a number of slave barracoons, owned by Banyans, on the coast between Kilwa and Tungwe Bay, just to the south of Cape Delgado. When Hamerton asked for permission for the Navy to enter all creeks, rivers and harbours between those two places and seize all vessels and destroy all barracoons, that permission was readily granted. Accordingly, Captain Bunce of H.M.S. *Dee* proceeded to Masani, about five miles to the north of Cape Delgado, where he found barracoons capable of holding a thousand slaves, which he destroyed. Other barracoons in Tungwe Bay to the south of Cape Delgado were likewise destroyed and three Banyans, who had been left in charge by a compatriot, were taken as prisoners to Zanzibar, whence Hamerton had them deported to India. As Hamerton informed Wyvill, the result of these operations was that 'the Arab boats in the north, which have been in the habit of proceeding south of Zanzibar, have this season returned without being able to procure slaves'. Seyyid Said's personal comment to Hamerton on learning of H.M.S. *Dee's* operation was, 'All has been well done and meets with our entire approval . . . and we all hope in God that these proceedings will lead to opening the eyes of the brute animals who do these things'.

Nevertheless, as Hamerton once again had to stress,

to expect or hope that the Imam of Muscat will ever suppress the Slave Trade is out of the question. His Highness most positively does not possess the means to do it; his authority on the coast of Africa, particularly to the southward is merely nominal; he has no force at his disposal (either land or sea) to enforce his orders and, even if he had, I do not believe he has one officer in his service who would do his duty, and carry the Imam's orders fully into effect, if sent upon any service for the suppression of the slave trade.

In the following year Seyyid Said showed that he had not wearied of well-doing. On April 9, 1851, Hamerton reported that 'the Slave Market always held here was discontinued from the 3rd of February last and will not be opened until all the Northern Arabs have left Zanzibar and no slaves have been imported into this island since February'. At the same time Hamerton was well aware that slaves had been exported from Zanzibar during previous months.

It was beyond the Sultan's power to prevent this. Every man in his dominions is against him in this affair, but much for the suppression of the trade in slaves has been done; certainly there is not one fourth the number of slaves imported to or exported from the Imam's dominions which there were a few years ago.

Hamerton fully realized that he could not expect the Sultan to enforce the anti-slavery treaties against his own subjects, unless he insisted upon British subjects likewise conforming to the terms thereof. As there was a strong suspicion that planters in Mauritius might endeavour to obtain slave labour for their sugar plantations, he induced Sir Lionel Smith, governor of that island, to prohibit the importation of labourers from East Africa.

His insistence on the observance by his compatriots of the terms of the treaty naturally did not make him very popular. In 1849 Captain Robert Cogan, who had concluded the commercial treaty with Seyyid Said in 1839, had obtained a concession for working the guano deposits on Latham Island about fifty miles S.W. of Zanzibar. But the Sultan prohibited the shipping of 'native' labourers on the ground that none but slaves were available. Hamerton supported him and Cogan thereupon complained to the Foreign Office. Aberdeen replied that the ban applied only to 'natives' of East Africa and that 'free foreign labourers' could be shipped, provided that Cogan gave security for the return of each such person to his place of engagement. This apparently put a stop to the guano enterprise. About the same time Cogan also went into partnership with Seyyid Said in connection with a sugar plantation. On March 29, 1844, Cogan asked if he could be per- mitted to recruit labour by obtaining slaves from dealers and manumitting them after they had worked for a term of years. Hamerton told him that he 'could not consider the business (between God and my own conscience) in any other light than aiding and abetting the slave trade'. In 1847 the firm of Cogan & Co. went out of business and Hamerton no longer encountered difficulties in that quarter.

Indians caused Hamerton far more trouble than his own com- patriots. Inquiries showed that they were one and all not only owners of slaves but also interested in the slave trade.

At the time of Hamerton's first arrival in Zanzibar slave holding was still quite lawful in India. It was not until 1843 that the status was abolished. Soon after he learnt that slaves were being regularly shipped from India to East Africa. They were shipped as servants of persons on board the vessels and were landed as such at Zanzibar.

As only a very small number could be borne on the ship's papers as servants, their number was not very large, but the traffic was a steady one and many of the victims were young Indian girls who had been kidnapped in their own country. Usually, commissions had been previously given to members of the crew or intending passengers to obtain the slaves for some person resident in Zanzibar, but sometimes they were put up for sale in the slave market.

The story of Jafran, a native of Hyderabad, was probably a typical one. When she was about ten or eleven years old, she was kidnapped near her village and conveyed to Bombay. She was sold to an Arab, who took her to Mukalla in Southern Arabia. There she was sold to another Arab, who brought her to Zanzibar. Arrived there, she changed hands no less than three more times. In September, 1844, her last master decided to put her up for sale in the slave market. Thereafter, to use her own words,

one day when I was exposed for sale in the market, the Imam of Muscat came there; he stopped his horse and spoke to me. He asked me the name of my country and the manner in which I was reduced to slavery. I told him. He then sent me to the house of the British Agent who sent me to Bombay.

It was not the only time in which Seyyid Said intervened in this manner. In 1846 he learnt that another Indian woman had been sent by a slave dealer from Kilwa to Zanzibar and he at once ordered her release and handed her over to Hamerton for repatriation.

His Highness the Imam [reported Hamerton] has a constant lookout kept that he may be informed if natives of India, whether British subjects or not, are offered for sale which is in general done by Bohoras and Khojas, natives of Bombay, Surat and the protected states; these people are rich and possess considerable influence in the territories of the Imam and to procure evidence to convict them in a court of law is almost impossible.

As said already, this particular branch of the traffic was conducted on a relatively small scale. What greatly concerned Hamerton was the extent to which Indians were directly and indirectly engaged in the African slave trade. On January 2, 1842, he reported to the Bombay Government that the number of slaves imported into Zanzibar from the mainland averaged 15,000 yearly.

'They are procured chiefly by Banyan brokers from the chiefs coming to the coast. The brokers go to the different ports under the dominion of His Highness the Imam and procure slaves in the following manner'.

The tribes from the interior who bring down the ivory and gum copal have it all carried by the people they from time to time take in war, and they always barter the slaves along with the articles they have carried from the interior to the coast. Money is not given either for the slaves or for the articles they bring. It is a barter trade . . . , and the business is chiefly carried on by Banyans and Indian Mohammedans. The slaves from the time they come into the hands of the brokers are kept at the least possible expense, barely receiving so much food as will keep them alive until they reach the market at Zanzibar. . . .

On December 9, 1843, he wrote again to Bombay asking for instructions as to how to deal with the natives of Cutch and Kathiawar

who are all concerned in the slave trade; indeed many of them, particularly the Cutch Banyans and Mohammedans, are most extensive slave dealers, and as these people smuggle slaves into India and bring girls from India into the Imam's dominions, every British subject or native of India will call himself a subject of the Rao of Cutch.

In addition to being slave dealers these people were also slave owners. In another letter of February 15, 1851, to the Bombay Government Hamerton reported that

there is not a Banyan or an Indian Mussulman, who had resided for any length of time in any part of the Imam's dominions, who has not purchased African females with whom they cohabit during their stay in the Imam's countries and, if they leave, they generally make them over or sell them clandestinely to a friend. The Banyans never bring their wives with them to the Imam's dominions, either to Arabia or to Africa, nor do they take these women away with them, when they leave for their own country, but the Indian Mohammedans frequently do.

The destruction in 1850 by H.M.S. *Dee* of a number of slave barracoons in the vicinity of Cape Delgado revealed the extent of the participation of a number of Banyans in the traffic. Three of their number were killed in attempts to resist the work of destruction and three more were made prisoners.

For the time being this measure acted as a useful deterrent to Indians who had hitherto engaged in the slave trade, but Hamerton realized that their participation in the traffic would be revived as soon as vigilance was relaxed. When therefore in 1851 Seyyid Said was proposing to return to Muscat and Hamerton himself received instructions to follow him there, the last named informed Commodore Wyvill in a letter of March 13 that

Ibji Siwji, the Customs Master here, has, I understand, large outstanding debts for property sent by him to slave dealers all along the coast south of Songo Manara (near Kilwa Kisiwani) down to Ibo. I have learned that he has been trying to induce some of the Banyans to go from here as his agents to collect his debts, but they have declined to do so, saying they are afraid. I am well aware (that) when I am gone from this, and the Imam (is) away, this man Ibji Siwji will do much mischief and undo many things for the suppression of the slave trade. This man, Ibji Siwji, a Banyan, is not at present Customs Master; it is his brother. Jairam Siwji, is a fair, honourable sort of man, but the brother Ibji is most insidious, intriguing, dishonest man. He has caused me a lot of trouble ever since I have been here. He detests our government and will spread all sorts of reports regarding us.

On August 29, 1851, Hamerton informed the Bombay Government that, whilst the recent activities of the Navy had induced almost all the Banyans to withdraw for the time being from the slave trade,

unless some severe measures are adopted to punish the Cutch Banyans trading in the Imam's territories in East Africa, when fairly found carrying on the slave trade, I am quite certain they will again soon have recourse to it in consequence of the very considerable profit to be derived from it – from three to five hundred per cent. . . . The Banyans are and always have been, from what I can learn, much more engaged in the slave trade than the Indian Mohammedans and they chiefly purchase slaves as domestic servants, but the Banyans deal in them in thousands.

When Hamerton endeavoured to check the French attempts to recruit so called indentured labour for service in Réunion, he was met with the retort that British subjects and British protected persons from India were allowed to indulge in the traffic in slaves with impunity. In 1855 a report was actually disseminated that Banyans, Khojas and Bohoras were going to be allowed to carry on the trade with impunity. On September 3, 1855, Hamerton reported to Bombay that he had availed himself

of a very fair and favourable opportunity which offered lately to induce the authorities here to publicly contradict this report and to make known by public proclamation the consequences certain to happen to any Banyans, Khojas or Bohoras convicted of dealing in slaves or carrying on the slave trade in the dominions of His Highness the Imam of Muscat.

The Prince Majid, now in the absence of his father administering the Government of Zanzibar, rose in open durbar in presence of the chief Arabs here told me he had a letter from his father, the Imam, desiring him to consult me on all matters of difficulty regarding treaties or differences which might arise between him and anyone whomsoever and to consider my advice as his, the Imam's orders; and many of the Arabs then said: 'Thus have we heard Seyyid Said, the Imam and our sovereign lord, and Inshallah! it shall be. Majid is young and the nature of treaties we do not understand. 'I told them a treaty was a sacred bond and I hoped their love for their Imam would cause them to support Majid and enable him to carry out the engagement entered into by his father with Her Majesty . . . in preventing the slave trade from being carried on by natives of India, to which all present responded: 'Please God we will do so'.

It was accordingly agreed that all such persons should have their property confiscated, be publicly flogged and then imprisoned until opportunity offered for their deportation.

Such drastic measures obviously required the active co-operation of the Sultan's authorities. Only four days after the Arabs had thus professed lip service to their ruler's treaty obligations, a dhow sailed for Cutch carrying a slave and Hamerton was assured that 'the Indians here declare they can send as many slaves to Cutch as they please by putting them on board the *bagalas* as sailors'. As Hamerton has said on May 14, 1853, 'with the exception of the Imam himself every man in these countries is a slaver and ready to aid and abet any man who requires their assistance to carry on the trade'. It was therefore to be many years before the Indian connection with the African slave trade could finally be stamped out.

There was one reform which Hamerton induced the Sultan to carry out at a very early date. If a slave died, the disposal of his mortal remains was not the concern of his owner. If the dead man's fellow slaves did not bury him, it was nothing to all those who passed by. Writing to the Indian Government on January 2, 1842, Hamerton said,

they were always thrown out on the beach when they died and were devoured by the dogs of the town, but on my continually talking to the Imam on the shameful practice contrary to the law of God and men, as I used to tell him, he has caused all dead bodies to be buried. I have seen fifty dead Africans, men and women, lying on the beach and the dogs tearing them to pieces as one sees the carrion eaten by the dogs in India.

He was, however, able to add that Seyyid Said had prohibited the practice in future.

CHAPTER XIII

SEYYID SAID BIN SULTAN'S
LATTER DAYS

THOUGH he left no heirs by any of his lawful wives, Seyyid Said had no less than twenty-five sons by his many *surias*. These *surias* stood to him in much the same relation as Hagar stood to Abraham. They were chosen by him from amongst his slaves and their offspring were recognized as legitimate and entitled to share in their deceased father's estate in the same manner as the children begotten of his lawfully wedded wives. When it was a question of lands, goods and chattels, each son took an equal share thereof at his father's death, but for obvious reasons this rule could not be applied in the case of succession to a throne. Strictly speaking, there was no recognized law of succession in Oman, unless it were what one of Said's sons described at a later date as 'the law of the longest sword'. There was no law of primogeniture or of entail. A Sultan might give public expression to his wishes regarding his successor, but such wishes were not necessarily carried out. Public opinion or the longest sword might set somebody else on the throne in place of his nominee. Needless to say, such nominee was not inevitably the eldest son of the Sultan.

Hilal, the eldest son of Seyyid Said, was born in about 1811. Unfortunately for him, his mother, an Abyssinian, died either at the time of his birth or else during his early childhood. He was thereafter left to be brought up by other members of his father's harem, where he became the victim of the intrigues and jealousies of many of the mothers of Said's other numerous progeny. According to information given later to Hamerton, Kurshit, a Circassian *suria*, who was the mother of Khalid, a boy four years younger than Hilal, made a particular point of bringing her child to the notice of his father. A half-sister of the two boys has described Kurshit as

a very unusual woman. Of heroic bodily stature, she combined extraordinary will power with a highly developed intelligence, and I do not remember encountering her equal among the members of my sex. . . . Her two eyes were so sharp and observing that they saw as much as Argus's hundred eyes. . . . Small children found her repulsive and gladly avoided her.

The motherless Hilal was doubtless as guilty of peccadillos as other boys of his age and one feels that this lynx-eyed female was quick to discover them and to bring them to the notice of his father, with whom she undoubtedly had considerable influence which was used largely to advance the cause of her own son.

In a country, where rulers could be as quickly unmade as they were made, there was an almost natural tendency for the ruler for the time being to look upon his eldest son as his potential supplanter and therefore not to entrust him with any posts in which he might have an opportunity of intriguing against him. It was often asserted that Seyyid Said, who had the general reputation of being a most affectionate parent, never treated Hilal as fairly as he treated his other children. It would appear certain that at a very early date he began to show his preference for Khalid at the expense of Hilal. When in 1828 he first came to Zanzibar, it was Khalid, and not his eldest brother, who was left behind in nominal charge of the government. Khalid was again left in charge when at later dates his father was recalled from Zanzibar to Muscat by affairs in the Persian Gulf. Everything pointed to the fact that, in so far as Zanzibar was concerned, Khalid was intended by his father to be his successor.

On the occasion of Seyyid Said's first visit to East Africa in 1828 Hilal had been left in ostensible charge at Muscat. During Said's absence a kinsman, named Saud bin Ali, had organized a rebellion and had succeeded in making a prisoner of Hilal and a nephew of Said, named Muhammad bin Salim. It was this rising which had caused Seyyid Said's return to Oman. On arrival he had to ransom his son and nephew for the sum of 30,000 dollars and to patch up a reconciliation with his rebel kinsman. Said blamed Hilal for this serious set back to his prestige in Oman. As Hilal was at the time little more than seventeen years old, such censure could hardly have been deemed just. The upshot of the incident was that thereafter Hilal was relegated to the less important governorship of Barkah.

Some time before 1840 Hilal was recalled from Barkah to Muscat. According to Guillain the reason for recall was because his father no longer trusted him and wanted to keep him under closer observation. As in the following year Hilal accompanied his father to Zanzibar, this may well be true.

Guillain met Hilal at Muscat for the first time in 1840. He described him as

a man of middle height, but well proportioned; his features were quite regular, but they were neither as noble or as marked as are ordinarily found in the typical Arab; his face showed no lack of intelligence, but had an expression of sadness, which betrayed the fact that his heart was troubled by grief or his pride was wounded.

After his arrival in Zanzibar Hamerton was very favourably impressed by Hilal. On June 4, 1842, Hamerton informed the Bombay Government that he was 'more friendlily disposed towards us than any of the Imam's family'. Very possibly the reason for this friendly disposition was because Khalid, under the tutelage of Suleiman bin Hamed, was known to be a notorious francophile and Hilal was anxious to enlist English support for himself in any contest there might be hereafter between himself and Khalid. Writing again to Bombay on July 31, 1844, Hamerton reported that Hilal was

the greatest favourite of the Imam's Arab subjects. . . . When His Highness himself is not present, this prince, Seyyid Hilal, is the most shrewd and energetic of all the Imam's sons, and has the good will and sympathy of all his Highness' Arab subjects; they always say in talking of him as 'the model of what Seyyid Said was'.

When later on Hilal visited England, he created a similar impression in high circles.

But relations between father and son gradually worsened. On July 23, 1844, Seyyid Said wrote to Lord Aberdeen informing him that he had directed that after his death Khalid should be ruler of his African possessions and that his third son, Thuwein, should become ruler of Oman. From Hamerton's covering letter to Aberdeen one learns that

the object His Highness has in making this communication is to ascertain whether he may look to Her Majesty's Government to guarantee the succession to his sons Khalid and Thuwein, as it is the intention of the Imam to set aside his eldest son, Seyyid Hilal, and disinherit him altogether; but in so doing considerable difficulty is likely to arise

owing to the great popularity of Hilal and the intense unpopularity of Khalid with the people of Zanzibar. One infers from what

Hamerton said that Seyyid Said's communication was purely for Aberdeen's private ear and that it was not publicly proclaimed to the people of Zanzibar. But it showed which way the wind lay.

Hamerton tells us that matters came to a head on the following October 5 when Seyyid Said banished Hilal from his dominions:

telling him to go where he listed, but never to return or on any account enter any part of His Highness' dominions. . . . When the prince went to take final farewell of his father, the Imam was greatly distressed. His women rushed out of the house and wanted to give what little property they possessed to the exiled prince and a state of melancholy was observed throughout the town generally. The Id of Ramadan, which happened some days after the expulsion of the Prince Seyyid Hilal, was not celebrated in the usual manner at the Imam's palace; nor did his Highness appear in the *durbar* to receive the congratulations of his people. His Highness' wife (the only married and lawful one now alive) told the people that feasts and rejoicing were not to be expected in a house of mourning. The Id was celebrated in the house of the Prince Seyyid Khalid, but His Highness did not attend. He is now much distressed and frequently says, 'I have no friends in the hour of need; they come not around me'. The Imam certainly thought his people would intercede for the Prince at the last moment; and many of the Arabs thought the Imam would not exile his son.

Both at the time of Hilal's banishment, and subsequently, there was much speculation as to the cause thereof. As Hamerton says, that cause was probably known only to the parties and to a few members of the family and household. Naturally, rumour was rife at the time. An early one which reached Hamerton's ears was that he had debauched one or more of his father's *surias*. Another told to Guillain a little later was that, during a dispute with Khalid, Hilal had been on the point of drawing his dagger, when his father struck him in the face. Many years later Khalid's half-sister, who was only a month old when he left the country, referred to 'a sad report' that, 'seduced by Christians and in particular by the then French Consul', Hilal had become a heavy drinker. When Said wrote about the affair in 1846 to Lord Aberdeen, he said

the thing that made me angry was the conduct of Hilal (his own doing) which neither God nor men could approve of; and although I often and often reprimanded him, he would not hearken; no effect was produced on him; and he at last said he would go to Mecca. I told him it would be well, perhaps he would repent and mend his ways.

On more than one occasion Seyyid Said told Hamerton that 'the offences of his son against him were such as he would not mention; that they were such as violated the laws of God and men'. These veiled references to Hilal's iniquity or alleged iniquity tend to suggest that the final rupture between father and son was due to the accusation reported to Hamerton at the time of Hilal's departure in 1844. If so, it was a terrible scandal which could not be discussed outside the immediate family circle. The story may have been only too well founded or it may be that the middle-aged Sultan gave an over-ready ear to malicious and untrue tales told by members of his harem. The truth of the whole story of this unhappy quarrel has long been buried with those few who knew it and no useful purpose can be served by trying to disinter it today.

Hilal left Zanzibar ostensibly for Mecca, but actually made his way to Egypt. Hamerton believed that the young man had not been fairly treated by his father. He also feared that Hilal's supplanter, Khalid, would be inclined to favour the French interest and to adopt a reactionary policy regarding the slave trade. He may therefore have hinted to Hilal that an appeal to London might procure that justice was done to him. In any event he gave Hilal a letter addressed to all British Agents requesting them to give every facility to the bearer. On the strength of this letter, which was later to be the subject of a rebuke to Hamerton from the Foreign Office, the British Agent and Consul-General in Egypt gave Hilal a passage to England in one of the Oriental Steam Company's vessels.

Hamerton was later informed that,

the Prince having arrived at Southampton, Her Majesty's Government decided to receive the son of the Imam of Muscat with hospitality and kindness, and Captain Cogan was immediately requested to go to Southampton to meet the Prince and to take charge of him during the time he shall remain in England. Her Majesty's Government decided upon this course out of the respect and the regard which they entertain for the character of the Imam.

On November 15, 1845, Lord Aberdeen wrote a letter to Seyyid Said, which he entrusted to Hilal. It informed Said that,

notwithstanding the private character in which the Prince has appeared in this country, Her Majesty the Queen has nevertheless been graciously pleased to waive the etiquette which is usually observed on such occasions at the British Court and has deigned to receive His Highness in a private audience at Her Majesty's country palace of Windsor Castle. This gracious condescension on the part of Her Majesty can scarcely fail to prove to Your Highness the great estimation in which Her Majesty holds the relations of friendship which have so long subsisted between Her Majesty's dominions and those of Your Highness, as well as the interest which Her Majesty has taken in the welfare and happiness of Your Highness' family.

Hamerton was at the same time informed that

the Prince Hilal has been received and treated with the respect and hospitality befitting the son of the Imam of Muscat. His Highness and his suite have visited several of the commercial and manufacturing towns in England, and Her Majesty's Government trust that their anxious desire to render the Prince's sojourn in this country agreeable has been successful, and that he will return to his own country with a sincere wish to cement the good understanding which has so long existed between Her Majesty's Government and the Imam of Muscat.

Hilal was provided with a passage back to Zanzibar and Hamerton was instructed 'to take a convenient opportunity to explain to the Imam the anxiety felt by Her Majesty's Government for the restoration of his son, Prince Hilal, to his confidence and kindness, whereby the two probable evils of a disputed succession and a civil war may be averted from His Highness' dominions'.

In his already cited letter to Seyyid Said, Lord Aberdeen likewise stressed the desirability of a reconciliation between father and son.

Her Majesty's Government do not feel competent nor would it be respectful to your Highness, to enter upon the merits of this un-happy misunderstanding; but Her Majesty's Government would most earnestly call Your Highness' attention to the deep responsibility which Your Highness would incur by disregarding the rights of your eldest son, thereby exposing Your Highness' subjects and the traders to your dominions to the danger of anarchy and bloodshed, which would but too probably ensue from a disputed succession. . . . In conclusion, I beg to assure Your Highness that during my intercourse with Prince Hilal I could not fail to observe his intelligence and amiability, and partic-ularly the deep desire he evinces to obtain the confidence of Your Highness, to effect which he is prepared to make any sacrifice.

The noble Lord accordingly expressed the hope that Seyyid Said would restore his son to favour and that 'you will treat him with such confidence and kindness, as shall fit him for the high station which he may be required to fulfil'.

The exile's return on February 6, 1846, has been vividly described by Hamerton.

The guns of the Honourable Company's war schooner *Mahe* (from Aden) announced the arrival of His Highness the Imam's son, the Prince Seyyid Hilal. . . . His Highness . . . sent off to the *Mahe* a message to his son saying that he would receive him immediately at his palace in the town or in the evening at Mtoni; to which the prince replied that he was anxious to see his father directly. I then told the Imam I would go off to the schooner and have her got under weigh and bring the Prince at once up to the town; at which His Highness the Imam appeared greatly pleased. I had my boat ready and landed with the Prince Hilal, the schooner *Mahe*, and the French steamer *Crocodile* and the Imam's frigate *Shah Allum* all saluting with twenty-one guns from each vessel and the Imam's flag at the fore. The excitement in the town was extraordinary; all hands were on the beach and, before the boat could reach the shore, the people ran into the sea and put their hands upon the prince, and almost all weeping. His Highness the Imam came out to receive his son and took him by both hands without saying a word; he could not speak; he appeared greatly affected; and when we entered the palace, His Highness made a sign for every person to retire and gave vent to his feelings and, after the Arab fashion, embraced him and wept from his very soul.

For reasons best known to himself, Hilal never handed Lord Aberdeen's letter to his father, but Hamerton had been supplied with a copy and supplied Seyyid Said with a translation thereof. Three days later Said penned a reply to it.

My dear friend [he wrote] you know that none could rejoice or be pleased that harm should happed to his own child. . . . You sent him back to me. I have forgiven him all that he did, (and) all that was in my mind against him even for your sake. Now he is my eldest son; yet amongst Arabs this is of no consequence; but the ornament and dignity of a man is (to be judged) by his conduct, be he the elder or the younger; and, should it please God, my son Hilal shall see nothing from me but what is good. If he wishes to stay with me and be respected, he shall do so or I will make him governor in any part of my dominions.

It is to be noted that Seyyid Said gave no intimation that he was ready to reconsider the question of the succession to his dominions. He firmly, but courteously, insisted that primogeniture did not

s

enter into the matter. He was ready to forgive Hilal for the past and to restore him to his paternal affection, but the son would be judged by his works. He might be given a governorship, but no hope was definitely held out that he would ever become successor to his father's throne. The scenes which took place at the time of Hilal's exile and at the time of his return must have clearly shown to Said how intensely popular his son was and that, if he disputed Khalid's claim to Zanzibar, civil war might well ensue with disastrous results to Khalid. Apart from this, whatever may have been the young man's past misdeeds, Hilal was his son and he still had some lingering affection for him. Said may therefore have greatly desired to reconsider his previous disherison of Hilal, but influences behind the scenes were clearly too strong for him. Khalid was his favourite son and Khalid's mother was a very strong minded and determined woman. He may have made no public declaration regarding his successor, but back in the harem he had evidently made a promise, for which his better judgment might afterwards have made him sorry, but for the sake of that promise and for the sake of domestic peace and quiet he could not go back upon what he had said.

Said's first instinctive emotion at the time of his eldest son's return did not last for long. For some six months past differences appear to have been patched up, but it was really little more than a sort of armed truce in which each party was watching the other with an exceedingly jealous eye. On September 9, 1846, Hamerton had to report 'that matters do not go well between His Highness the Imam and his son, the Prince Seyyid Hilal; some unfortunate disputes and angry discussions have lately taken place between the parties'. Once again friends managed to effect a temporary reconciliation, but the peace could not last for ever. Doubtless the fault lay on both sides, but it appears evident that Hilal had returned from England under the distinct impression that, if there was once more an open breach between himself and his father, the British Government would come down on his side. As already said, he had not delivered to his father the letter which had been entrusted to him by Lord Aberdeen. The letter was in a sealed envelope addressed to Seyyid Said. On November 5, 1849, Hamerton reported that Hilal was in the habit of producing it and 'telling all persons that Captain Cogan had told him not to deliver this letter to his father unless in the case of the utmost need; and that on his delivering the same to his father, the Imam, all differences would be instantly settled'. Hamerton was aware of the contents of that letter and told Hilal that the contents were not what he believed them to be, at the same time advising him to deliver the letter to his father.

On November 9, 1849, Seyyid Said addressed a long letter to Lord Palmerston, telling him that Hilal had once again left Zanzibar

When [he wrote] my son Hilal arrived from London, I received him in a friendly way – even more than he deserved, because he had come, as it were, from your Lordship and the Government; but at the same time I did not feel pleased at his return. . . . We said to him, at your wish, that we should give him a place in any situation, or 'Do you wish to remain with us and be as we are?' He said, 'I wish to remain with you' and he remained for some time with us. *But I was overwhelmed by the thoughts of what he might do* – things not approved of by either God or the Prophet.

Several persons returned here from the pilgrimage to Mecca and informed us that his son and wives were in distressed circumstances at Mecca. We said to him, 'It is impossible for your son and wives to remain at Mecca; we will bring them from thence that they may be with us'. He replied, 'It is not possible to bring them, until they are established in some place'. We said to him, 'If you wish to remain with us, we will build a house for you and furnish for you and them all the expenses.' He said, 'Such is not possible'. We replied, 'Never mind. Do you wish for Bandar Abbas and Ormuz and their dependencies?' He replied, 'If you give with it an equivalent to the revenue of Muscat, I will accept it'. We replied, 'We could not, but we will give you as much as your brothers'. He replied, 'If you give me thirty thousand dollars, I will take Lamu'. We replied that if we had thirty thousand dollars we would not remain in Zanzibar. We offered him Pemba. He refused it. He wished to be placed in the government of Muscat or Zanzibar and that we and all others should be placed under him. We told him, 'This is difficult for all of us,' (and) that it was impossible, and, moreover that Arabs do not acknowledge the right of the eldest son to be the successor.

The letter was of course a purely *ex parte* indictment, but reading between the lines thereof one can see that not all the fault lay with Hilal. Whatever Hilal might have done before his previous exile, there had been no repetition of the offence. An over suspicious father, whose mind was doubtless being constantly poisoned by others, was 'overwhelmed by thoughts' that his son might repeat his offence or alleged offence. He did not want to have his son near him. Furthermore it is clear that he was keeping Hilal on very short commons. Hamerton reported that he was in a state of destitution.

His Highness the Imam has not given him anything for the support of himself or family, and, while here, he took from him his horses and slaves, and degraded him in every way possible. There is a strong feeling on the part of the Arabs here in favour of the Prince Hilal, but all agree that a reconciliation between His Highness the Imam and his son, the Prince Hilal, cannot take place.

At the same time Hamerton saw that the blame did not rest entirely on one side.

Since the return of the Prince Hilal from England he has not in any way tried to conciliate his father, the Imam; nor indeed, in so far as I could learn, did His Highness the Imam wish him to do so; he always appears to me not to wish to be reconciled to his son. He offered to place him as governor in several places but, without furnishing him with the means to support his dignity, such offers were of course useless.

The final rupture between father and son was, according to Hamerton brought about in circumstances which certainly did not redound to the credit of the former.

His Highness the Imam wished to induce his son, the Prince Hilal, to go to Mecca and had written to the Sharif to keep the Prince Hilal a prisoner there, but he (the Sharif) refused to do so and informed the Prince of his father the Imam's wish that he should be made a prisoner and assured him that, if he came there, he might rest satisfied that he should not be molested in any way.

In the circumstances it became clear to Hilal that the sooner he left Zanzibar the better. He called on Hamerton and stated that he wished to go to Aden and thence to London. He asked the Consul to give him letters to Queen Victoria's Minister, but Hamerton, who had received an official rebuke for his action on the occasion of Hilal's previous exile, had to tell him that he could not do so without first writing for instructions on the subject. The Consul advised him to go and take up his residence at Lamu or some other place and that no good could be expected to result from his wandering from place to place.

Hilal accordingly proceeded to Lamu. His arrival was greeted

with the utmost enthusiasm. Eight days later the inhabitants of
that place as well as those of Pate, Siu and Faza assembled and
took an oath on the Koran to stand by Hilal and to see that his
wrongs were redressed. In furtherance of this resolution they
expelled the garrison from the fort of Lamu and replaced them by
more reliable men. The former garrison was sent back to Zanzibar
together with the collector of customs, who was not allowed to
take the customs receipts with him. Hilal then addressed a letter
to his kinsman, Suleiman bin Hamed el-Busaidi, knowing full
well that the latter would show it to his father. He disclaimed any
responsibility for the acts of his supporters and asked to be
admitted once more to his father's favour and to be treated like
his brothers. He said he was ready to return and submit all differences between them to either the French or the British Consul.
The result was not what he expected. Both the French and the
British Consul declined to intervene in a family quarrel without
Seyyid Said's consent and Said announced his intention of dealing
with Hilal and his supporters as rebels. If in the past Hilal had not
shunned to smite his father in worse way, yet he had the grace of
courtesy left in him and he spared to raise his hand against his
father and ruler. Accordingly he left Lamu for Aden, where he
arrived on December 10, 1850. Five days later the Political Agent
at Aden reported to Bombay that Hilal was sick and apparently
destitute. The Bombay Government wrote to Hamerton telling
him that, 'whenever you may see reason for a favourable result,
you will mention to His Highness the Imam the destitute state of
his son, Seyyid Hilal'. But there is no record of any assistance
coming to the dying man from that quarter.

Hilal's malady was declared to be consumption. He lingered on
for six months. A fortnight before his death he was joined by his
youngest son, Faisal, and the boy's mother, a Georgian *suria*, who
constantly attended him in his last days. On June 24, 1851, the
Political Agent went to see Hilal. He asked him if he could do
anything for him. The dying man replied, 'No, I wish to live but,
if I go, I leave my family to God.' He did not want to write to his
father, but the Agent believed that 'he has a hope that his family
will be received by him with kindness, when he is no more'. The
end came four days later.

News of Hilal's death reached Zanzibar on July 19. Hamerton
reported that

His Highness did not make any public demonstration of grief or the usual mourning for the death of his son, but he did not hold a public *baraza* or *durbar* for three days, but remained in private. I paid him a visit on the day after the receipt of the news of Seyyid Hilal's death and saw the Imam in private. His Highness was in great distress and frequently said, while I was with him, 'God help me. As I become older, my misfortunes increase. Praise be to God, these things will make me better pleased to go when the Angel of Death comes'.

Hilal's last hope was fulfilled. His father did receive his grandchildren with kindness and bring them up as his own.

Thus ended an unhappy story of differences between father and son, which has frequently had its counterpart in many lands and in many walks of life. Spiteful and malicious tongues in the harem would appear to have played a large part in bringing this tragedy about. But after this lapse of time there is no need to moralize or to seek to apportion blame. Like Duncan, Hilal in his grave, after life's fitful fever, sleeps well and malice domestic cannot touch him further.

Hilal's death removed one potential source of danger to Khalid's peaceful succession to his father's African dominions. In his early days in Zanzibar Hamerton formed a poor opinion of Khalid mainly because he appeared to be well disposed towards the French. On March 3, 1842, he reported that the young man was 'beyond doubt ill disposed towards us'.

When in 1844 Seyyid Said announced his intention of making Khalid his successor in Zanzibar, Hamerton wrote to the Foreign Office reporting that Khalid was 'unfortunately not esteemed by the Imam's Arab subjects; he is parsimonious and grasping to a degree which will always prevent his being beloved or respected by the Arabs'. His parsimony, which was in distinct contrast to the lavishness of Hilal, earned him the nickname of 'the Banyan'. When his father was absent in Oman, he stood in *loco parentis* to his younger half-brothers and half-sisters and one of the latter afterwards declared that 'he was very strict, and we often had reason to complain of his harsh measures'. The same half-sister (Salme) also said that, when Khalid represented his father during the latter's absence from Zanzibar, his mother Kurshit was said to have 'governed our country with Khalid as her puppet'.

Certainly Kurshit was a very strong-minded woman and doubtless her son was upon occasion considerably influenced by her opinions, but it would be slandering him to say that he submitted to petticoat rule. His upbringing had been entrusted by his father to his kinsman, Suleiman bin Hamed el-Busaidi, and there can be no doubt that in his early days he had been very much under his tutor's influence. As Captain Guillain tells us Suleiman bin Hamed was well disposed towards the French and disliked the English because of their anti-slavery campaign. Hamerton alleged in 1845 that he had instilled into Khalid's mind 'a rancorous hatred of the English nation'. Khalid certainly had at one time a strong pre-dilection for the French and things French, as was evidenced by his calling his principal country estate Marseilles and by his large purchases of French goods. But neither he nor his preceptor Suleiman ever bound themselves hand and foot to the French cause. When in 1840, during Seyyid Said's absence in Oman, the French tried to establish a French Consulate in Zanzibar, Khalid, presumably acting with the advice and approval of his mentor, 'declined to receive Mr. Noel as Consul, or to consent to the French settling at Zanzibar, without the sanction of his father, and in consequence the corvette proceeded to Muscat', where its commanding officer, Captain Guillain, met with no greater success than at Zanzibar.

Seyyid Said was well aware of Suleiman bin Hamed's anglo-phobia and of the influence he had with Khalid. On several occasions he spoke to Hamerton about it. On October 25, 1845, Hamerton was able to report to Lord Aberdeen that 'the Imam has broken off almost all connexion between this man and his son, but he was not at present in a position openly to displease him'. Thenceforward Khalid's attitude to the British appears to have changed. He evidently had become a man very much after his father's own heart and pre-eminently suited to continue his father's plans and policy when the time came.

This was clearly proved in 1851, when his father was again absent in Oman and Khalid was in charge at Zanzibar. Before leaving Zanzibar, Seyyid Said gave his son stringent orders to prevent in every way possible any violation of the slave trade treaties with Great Britain. After the Sultan's departure a French merchant brig arrived at the island, ostensibly for the purpose of recruiting 'free labourers' for work on the plantations in Bourbon (Réunion). An attempt was made to give a semblance of legal colour to the transactions by offering the slave owner a 'bonus' for each slave engaged for this purpose. After payment of the bonus the owner made a formal pronouncement in the following words or words to the like effect, 'This man was my slave. I make him free. He is at liberty to serve the French merchant or anyone else, if he accepts the terms offered'. The terms in question were that the slave should work for his French master for five years and would thereafter be at liberty to go where he pleased.

As Hamerton explained to the Foreign Office the cloak could not conceal what the transaction really was. The so-called volunteer was as often as not a

slave bought from a slave dhow just arrived from the (mainland) coast of Africa, and paraded once or twice in the slave bazaar, (and then) being told by the person, the slave dealer, who buys him that he is a free man, but must consent to go with this person or that, and that after five years he may go where he please. *He must go:* he understands not his position. It is not optional with him to refuse. He only considers it a change from one owner to another.

Khalid not only sternly prohibited any dealings of this nature, but also sent a boat to search the French brig, which he believed had on board twelve slaves who were being conveyed to Bourbon against their will. Monsieur Belligny, the French Consul, was at once up in arms. He sent a formal protest to Muscat. He then departed for Bourbon, announcing 'that he will not return until some measures are taken by the Government of the French Republic to vindicate what he considers to be an outrage to the French flag'. Khalid became somewhat uneasy at the turn which events had taken. Hamerton had accompanied Seyyid Said to Muscat and was therefore not at hand to advise him and to lend him moral support. Fortunately, John Francis Webb, the American Consul, stepped into the breach and sent a report to Hamerton in which he laid the true state of the facts before him. Hamerton passed on the information to the British Government, urging that representations should be made in Paris against this barefaced attempt by a Christian nation to revive the slave trade. The affair eventually blew over. In France the days of the Second Republic were rapidly drawing to a close and, until the Second Empire became firmly established, no French Government had either the time or the inclination to take a stand upon a matter which might embroil it with the British Government. Monsieur Belligny had to swallow his pride and return to Zanzibar without receiving any satisfaction.

Shortly after the close of this incident Seyyid Said returned to Zanzibar. On December 4, 1853, Admiral la Guerre arrived in the frigate *Jeanne d'Arc* and remained anchored off Zanzibar for a whole month. He and Belligny renewed the question of allowing the recruitment of labour for Bourbon (Réunion). According to Hamerton the proposed method of recruitment was to be as follows:

The French dealer says to the slave broker or other proprietor of slaves, 'I wish to engage this slave or these slaves; for how much will you consent to make him or them over to me as a freeman or freemen?' The price being agreed on, the slave is to be taken before the Kathi or judge, when the proprietor says, 'I make this man or these men free; therefore I want you to give a certificate of his or their freedom'; which being granted, the slave or slaves are made over to the French dealer to be taken away as a free labourer or labourers, to be sent to Bourbon or elsewhere, to labour for the space of five years, or whatever term the dealer stipulates for; at the end of the term he is to be a freeman to do as he pleases, and during the time of his servitude he is to be paid two dollars per month, and to receive rations.

Whilst Seyyid Said was perfectly ready to allow genuinely free men to go to Bourbon on such terms, he said he could not allow the French dealers to buy a slave who had just been imported from the main continent and who had not the slightest idea of what his position was after his so-called emancipation. He told Hamerton that 'such is contrary to the Muhammadan law' as well as at variance with the spirit of his treaty obligations to Great Britain.

He took up this attitude during the course of the interviews which he had with the French Admiral and Consul. He was told

that if he would not consent to the French dealers obtaining labourers as they wished to do . . . , the French Government would force him to comply; to which His Highness answered, that he was of course unable to resist the force of France, but that the Government with which he had a treaty for the prevention of the sale of slaves to Europeans would perhaps prevent France buying slaves in his territories. The admiral told the Imam if they could not procure the labourers as they wished at Zanzibar, that French ships would go to the coast of Africa within his (the Imam's) dominions to procure them, supported by French ships-of-war. The Imam replied, 'I have told you, if you threaten to use force, I cannot resist; but I do not consent'.

Whilst the French flagship was still anchored off Zanzibar, a brig arrived from Bourbon and eventually sailed, having on board 170 slaves recruited in the manner above mentioned. Another brig arrived on March 27, 1854, to collect 400 more labourers. Hamerton reported that he had heard that 'the French intended establishing agencies on the coast of Africa within the Sultan of Zanzibar's dominions for the purchase of the numbers of the slaves which they required'. He accordingly wrote on April 13 to Lord Clarendon at the Foreign Office to report the matter and to ask for instructions as to how Seyyid Said had best act.

I see plainly [he wrote] the French are seeking a cause of quarrel with the Imam; and they will seize upon some of the ports on the coast of Africa within his dominions, saying they have been forced to do so to protect French interests; and I most respectfully beg leave to assure your Lordship that something of this kind is most positively in contemplation by the French, and expected by the Imam.

Clarendon instructed the British ambassador in Paris to make the necessary representations to the French Government and in due course it was announced that the Governor of Bourbon had been instructed 'to put a stop to every undertaking having for its object the indirect trade in negroes'. But all this took time and on April 18, 1854, Hamerton informed the Bombay Government that 'exceeding great fear of the French has come over the people here'. It so chanced that affairs in the Persian Gulf were calling Seyyid Said back to Muscat. In accordance with his standing instructions Hamerton was due to accompany him there. It may have been no more than a coincidence but, as these pages have shown, French attempts to force the hand of the Zanzibar Government had on several occasions occurred whilst Seyyid Said was away in Muscat. There might well be a repetition of such attempts after Said had set sail from Zanzibar.

On April 15, 1854, Hamerton received a visit from Seyyid Said, his son Khalid and 'all the principal Arabs of the town'. In the presence of this assemblage Said told Hamerton that, when he himself left Zanzibar, neither Khalid nor any of the leading Arabs would remain there, unless Hamerton stayed behind. The Sultan then

placed his son's hand in mine and desired him in all difficulties to be guided by my advice and to do nothing without consulting me. The

Arabs then rose and came and kissed my hand, saying, 'we are now satisfied through the favour of the Almighty and the powerful destiny of Her Majesty Queen Victoria all will go well with us'. Said then asked to be allowed to speak to Hamerton in private. The two went into an inner room where Said told Hamerton that his son and the notables had for three days past asked him to persuade the British Consul not to go to Muscat because they were so much afraid of the French. Writing on June 6, 1854, to the Bombay Government, Said once more repeated that he had asked Hamerton to remain behind in Zanzibar because he believed that the French were 'pressing a quarrel on him'.

On April 18, 1854, Seyyid Said bin Sultan embarked upon his frigate *Queen Victoria* and left Zanzibar to a salute of twenty-one guns. He and Hamerton were destined never to meet again. During their fourteen years of close association they had had their differences of opinion and even quarrels. Hamerton had not always been wise in some of the things which he had said and done; neither had Said. But in the course of years they had come to know each other well and to learn each other's worth. Their parting therefore was not the formal parting between a ruler of a state and the agent of a foreign government. It was a parting between friends, but Said hoped that it would not be for long and that in November he would be able to make his way back to his beloved Zanzibar. This, however, was not to be.

Khalid fell ill shortly after his father's departure. His malady was diagnosed, like that of his former rival Hilal, as being consumption. He died on November 7, 1854, just about the time that his father was expected to return. He had grown in wisdom and in stature during the twenty odd years which had elapsed since the day when as a mere boy he had first landed in his father's newly found dominion. He does not appear ever to have made himself popular with his father's subjects, but they had perforce to recognize his strength of character and general ability. Although there had been a time when Hamerton had been strongly disposed in favour of Hilal to the disparagement of Khalid, latterly he came to recognize that, of all the Sultan's many sons, Khalid took nearest after his father and would have been the most fit and proper person to succeed him. In reporting his death the Governor of Bombay, Hamerton described him as 'a prince of excellent character, both public and private, and in no way addicted whatever to the vices usual with Asiatic princes. He was determined and upright in the administration of justice, and respected by all classes, and exceedingly courteous towards Europeans'.

It would appear that Seyyid Said had made no provision for the contingency of Khalid predeceasing him. It so chanced that, with the exception of Majid, all the Sultan's elder sons were with him in Muscat. His remaining five sons, of whom the eldest was no more than thirteen, were all of them too young to be likely to stir up trouble of their own accord against Majid, who was then eighteen years old and marked out as being the most likely successor to Khalid. But there was always the likelihood that one or other of them might be thrust forward as the nominee of the el-Harthi clan or some other rival of the Busaidi dynasty. Khalid's death in fact was the signal for a certain section of the el-Harthi, whom Hamerton describes as 'a drunken cowardly set of scoundrels, a sort of half-caste Arabs', to bring in a large band of slaves from the plantations with a view to fishing in troubled waters. There was considerable alarm in the town of Zanzibar, especially amongst the Indian traders, who feared that the plantation slaves would take to looting. But none of the Seyyid Said's sons was prepared to become the tool of the would be trouble makers. All came in considerable alarm to Hamerton and asked for his advice, telling him that their father had told them to come to him to seek his advice in case any difficulty arose. Hamerton sent for the Baluchi Jemadar commanding the few Sultan's troops in the island, a certain Din Mahomed, 'a civil good sort of man' with a record of twelve years' exemplary service, who rose to the occasion. On Hamerton's advice an order was issued for all plantation slaves to leave the town before nightfall. A warning also went forth that all persons assembling or walking about the town after dark armed with weapons would be shot at sight. Guards were posted at all strategic points and troops patrolled the town at uncertain hours of the night to see that all these orders were carried out. The result was that the potential trouble makers rapidly dispersed and peace prevailed until such time as Seyyid Said's instructions regarding Khalid's successor arrived from Muscat.

Lastly, but by no means least, the Nestor of the family, Suleiman bin Hamed el-Busaidi, who had been consistently a loyal and faithful servant of his kinsman, was at hand to pilot the ship of state until Seyyid Said's wishes could be known.

In due course an order came from Muscat appointing Majid 'to be governor of Zanzibar, the mainland of Africa, and its islands'. Letters to the like effect went out 'to all the chiefs of Africa and the islands, as also to the commanders of troops' directing them to submit to the new governor and to obey his orders. It was also proclaimed to all the chief Arabs in Zanzibar in open *baraza* that Majid 'was to be regarded in exactly the same position as Prince Khalid had held, that he had succeeded to all his rights and the future sovereignty of Zanzibar and the African dominions'. At the same time the foreign consuls in Zanzibar were notified as to the appointment. In Majid's own words, 'from that time the consuls visited me in uniform and the principal persons of these dominions were aware that I was their ruler; moreover, by the aid of God, the country and the people were obedient to me'.

In appointing Majid as governor of and heir to his African dominions, Seyyid Said had passed over his three eldest surviving sons, Thuwein, Muhammad and Turki. But the choice was not unexpected. Next to Khalid, Majid was his father's favourite son. As already seen, Thuwein, had been nominated in 1844 by his father to succeed him in Oman. He was in 1854 Governor of Muscat and had recently been causing his father great trouble and anxiety by his quarrels with the chiefs and tribes of Oman. Muhammad and Turki were governors of Sumail and Sohar in Oman and, like Thuwein, were not at the moment in a position to dispute Majid's appointment. Another potential trouble maker, Barghash, a youth of seventeen, had accompanied his father from Zanzibar to Muscat and at that distance was quite unable to intrigue against his brother.

Though he was only nineteen, Hamerton was favourably impressed by Khalid's successor. Two years later he reported that

the Prince Majid has given the fairest possible promises from the way in which he has acted on various occasions and under some very trying circumstances of his perfect fitness and aptitude for the duties it was his father's intention should devolve upon him. He has frequently shown a sense of justice and fair dealing in his decisions in difficult cases which has elicited the admiration and astonishment of all. His administration has given particular satisfaction to the foreign residents.

Seyyid Said's wisdom in urging Hamerton to remain in Zanzibar whilst he was in Muscat was amply proved not only by the threatened crisis which occurred at the time of Khalid's death but also later on. The matters which had taken Said back to Oman not only prevented him from availing himself of the north-east monsoon of 1854 to return to Zanzibar; they also prevented his return in the following year. On 10 Safar, 1272, (October 22, 1855) Seyyid Said wrote what appears to have been his last letter to Hamerton. Affairs were not going as he could have wished in the Persian Gulf, but in a fortnight's time 'the matter will be decided one way or the other, and whatever happens thereafter, we shall inform your Honour'. He concluded the letter in the following words: 'What I want from you is that you should not omit your oversight of our son Majid and I am sure you will not be unmindful of this. Our son Majid is utterly and extremely grateful to you.'

At last news reached Zanzibar from Muscat that Seyyid Said was on his way to his beloved island and should arrive there in October 1856. On the afternoon of October 25 his frigate *Queen Victoria* and man-of-war *Artemise* were sighted off Chumbe, an island seven miles to the south of the town of Zanzibar. His daughter, Salme, then a girl of twelve years, has described what followed.

In the courtyard commenced butchering and boiling and baking, the apartments were sprinkled with perfumes, and everything was arranged to look perfect. . . . Majid hastened with an escort to meet his father. They went in two cutters, fighting the storm which threatened their destruction, and expecting to be in our midst again that evening accompanied by Seyyid Said.

Night fell. Not a ship was seen. The town, and especially our house, began to show disquietude and then loud alarm. It was supposed that Majid and his escort had perished in the tempest, but this apprehension grew into a fear that the whole fleet had sunk to the bottom. . . .

Suddenly a rumour sprung up, which at first obtained no credence, to the effect that the palace was surrounded and guarded by soldiers. We all rushed to the windows to ascertain the truth. The night was dark as pitch, but you could occasionally see the barrel of a gun glisten. . . . We were given to understand that the soldiers had established a blockade of the house, allowing neither entrance nor departure. . . . Majid, as far as we knew, was not back; moreover, people were hasting to and fro uneasily in his house, which was guarded like ours.

. . . A few of the bravest women betook themselves to the hall on the ground floor, where they could speak to the soldiers through the windows. The troops, however, proved obdurate, abiding by their instructions to give no information. . . .

Morning dawned, and still we were left in ignorance as to why we had been imprisoned; nor did we hear anything of Majid. But as we were dispersing at the regular hour for prayer, someone exclaimed that the fleet lay anchored in the harbour with mourning flags displayed. Then our brothers came – without the Sultan.

On November 10 Atkins Hamerton wrote to the Foreign Secretary to report the death of Seyyid Said bin Sultan. It was not just the formal letter of the British representative at a foreign court reporting the demise of the sovereign to whom he was accredited. It was the letter of a man mourning the loss of a real friend.

I have the honour, but with the profoundest distress and the sincerest sorrow, to communicate for your Lordship's information the melancholy intelligence of the death of His Highness the Imam of Muscat, which sad event took place at half-past 8 o'clock in the morning of the 19th October last at sea on board His Highness' frigate the *Queen Victoria* in Lat. 7° 12' South and Long. 36° 12' East whilst on the voyage from Muscat to Zanzibar.

His Highness was taken ill on the 18th September last while at sea, shortly after his departure from Sur, at which place he touched to transact some business on his way down; the illness increased with the swelling of the legs and thighs, when dysentery set in on the 13th October, which terminated his existence at the hour above mentioned.

His Highness appeared to be aware before leaving Muscat of his approaching end; he took final leave of his aged mother and said he felt confident he would see her no more and, what is exceeding strange, he had a number of planks prepared at Muscat, which he took on board with him and gave orders that in the event of any one dying on board the frigate a coffin should be made, and that the body of whoever might die on the voyage should be placed therein and conveyed to Zanzibar, but under no circumstances should the burial take place at sea, and from the moment that he became seriously ill he ordered his grave clothes to be brought to him, which he placed under his head and used as a pillow until he died.

On the afternoon of the 25th ultimo His Highness' frigate *Queen Victoria* and ship of war *Artemise* have in sight off the island of Chumbe, to the southward of Zanzibar, distance five miles, when they came to an anchor without any flags hoisted. It was at once known that some unfortunate circumstance had occurred in consequence of the ships hoisting no flags, which with the Arabs is the same as with us hoisting half-mast high in case of death on board any vessel. Several persons put off in boats, but no one succeeded in boarding the vessels as the night closed in dark. Between 9 and 10 o'clock the body of His Highness in the coffin was brought to town in one of the quarter boats of the *Queen Victoria*, where it was immediately buried in a new cemetery close to the palace and alongside that of his son, the Prince Khalid. It was not publicly known until the next morning what body was in the coffin.

William Ashton Shepherd, an American who visited Seyyid Said at Muscat shortly before he set out on his last voyage, wrote this description of him:

One of the noblest looking men I have seen in the East. There is not a feature on his face that would indicate the possibility of his being guilty of a tithe of the deeds that report lays at his door, excepting perhaps the firm light mouth and the large grey eyes; but there is much that is mild and kind, gentle and loving, that you would endeavour to excuse and shield him under the plea of necessity.

It had not been an altogether blameless life. It needed no thousand peering littlenesses to blacken more than one of the dark spots appearing therein. But there was, as Shepherd says, another and more attractive side to his character which must be set in the scales to weigh against his failings and his faults. When this has been done, I venture to think that history must say that, when weighed in the balance, Seyyid Said cannot be found wanting. The people of Zanzibar must for ever look back on his reign with gratitude. To use the words of Samuel Pepys writing of a European governor of another part of Africa, 'he went all ways to make this place great'. His subjects knew this and they trusted him. At times – and more particularly in matters relating to the slave trade – he had introduced measures which were extremely unpopular, but their confidence in him never wavered. They realized, as Hamerton had once reported, that he aspired to be 'most truly every man's friend; he wishes to do good to all'. Perhaps the most striking evidence of this confidence was the unswerving loyalty displayed towards him by many of his officers at times when the temptation to go over to the other side must have been very great indeed. If it had been permitted to him once more to land alive on his beloved island, Seyyid Said bin Sultan might well have spoken to those who came to welcome him home in the words of the first Elizabeth of England. 'Though God hath raised me high, yet count I this the glory of my crown, that I have reigned with your loves.'

AUTHORITIES

CHAPTER I

INTRODUCTORY

Printed Authorities

Africa Pilot, Part III.
CHRISTIE, pp. 268, 269 (description of Zanzibar *c*.1870).
COUPLAND, *East Africa*, pp. 162–7 (Blankett's voyage in 1799).
CROFTON, pp. 1, 2 (Hamerton's voyage to Zanzibar in 1841).
LYNE, pp. 1–2 (Blankett's voyage in 1799).
RUSSELL, p. 331 (Rigby's description of the creek at Zanzibar).
STOCKLEY, *Geology of the Zanzibar Protectorate*.

CHAPTER II

EARLY HISTORY OF ZANZIBAR AND PEMBA

Manuscripts

(1) *British Museum*

Or. 2666, 'Notes on the History of Kilwa, by Sheikh Moheddin of Zanzibar'.

(A transcript in Arabic of part of an earlier Arab MS. history of Kilwa. Contains a number of references to Zanzibar. The English translation by S. A. Strong (*q.v.*) calls for revision in a number of respects.)

(2) *Peace Memorial Museum, Zanzibar*

(Photostats of transcripts of the following original MSS.)

(*a*) Deed of sale of land at Ndagoni between Shirazis, dated 1st Muharram, 910 (June 13, 1504).

(*b*) MS. dated 27th Shaban, 1267 (July 3, 1851) recording a Shirazian immigration to Pemba ten years before the arrival of the Portuguese and the revolt against the Mazrui in Pemba in 1822.

(*c*) Genealogy of Shirazis of Pemba (no date).

T

(*d*) MS. dated 22 Safar, 1255, (May 3, 1839) giving an account of Shirazi immigrations to Pemba, Tumbatu and Zanzibar. (A variant of the Kilwa MS. in the British Museum.)

(3) *Zanzibar Archives*

Letter of J. T. Last to W. Lloyd Mathews, February 5, 1898.

Printed Authorities

BAUMANN, *Pemba* (description of ancient monuments).

——, *Zanzibar* (description of ancient monuments).

BAXTER, (wars of Wadebuli on mainland).

BUCHANAN, *The Ancient Monuments of Pemba.*

BURTON, *Zanzibar*, ii. 361 (Wadebuli at Kilwa).

DALE, *The Peoples of Zanzibar.*

DAMMAN, ERNST, *Beitrage auf Arabischer Quellen.*

DEVIC, *Les Pays des Zendjs . . . aprés les écrivains arabes.*

FLURY, *The Kufic Inscriptions of Kizimkazi Mosque.*

GOES, Chapter XXXVII (use of cannon by people of Zanzibar in 1503).

GRAY, *Nairuzi or Siku ya Mwaka.*

——, *Wadebuli and Wadiba.*

——, *Claim to land at Vitonguji, Pemba.*

GUILLAIN, ii. 107 (Celebration of Nairuzi in Zanzibar).

HORNELL, *The Sea-going Mtepe and Dhau.*

HOURANI, *Arab seafaring in the Indian Ocean.*

INGRAMS, *Zanzibar:* Introductory (Zanzibar and the People); Part I, A (early history and external influences) B (later history of the native tribes); Part II, B (native tribes of Zanzibar).

——, *Chronologies*, p. 3 (including early rulers of Pemba, Tumbatu and Zanzibar).

JOHNSTON, *Comparative Study* (story of first arrival of Hadimu in Zanzibar, Hadimu Vocabulary).

KIRKMAN, J. S., *Excavations at Ras Mkumbuu.*

KRUMM, *Words of Oriental Origin in Swahili.*

LYDDEKER, *Mtepe Dhau.*

PAKENHAM, pp. 6, 7 (refers to the Wadebuli).

PEARCE, Chapters I–V (Zanzibar and Pemba before the advent of the Portuguese), XVI (the Swahili), XXIII–XXVIII (ruins in Zanzibar and Pemba).

RIGBY, *See* Russell.

ROBINSON, *Shirazi Colonisation of East Africa.*

——, *Shirazi Colonisation of Vumba.*

ROLLESTONE, *The Watumbatu of Zanzibar*.
RUSSELL, pp. 341, 348 (the Hadimu and first settlement of El Harthi in East Africa).
SCHOFF, *The Periplus*.
SELIGMAN, Chapters VIII, IX (the Bantu in Africa).
STIGAND, pp. 29–109 (early relations between Pate and Zanzibar).
STORBECK, (Yakut's description of Zanzibar and Tumbatu).
STRANDES, Chapters I (history of East Africa before advent of the Portuguese), V (Muslim culture in East Africa).
STRONG, S. A., *History of Kilwa* (together with its early relations with Zanzibar).
STUHLMANN, p. 854 (gives theory as to original habitat of Wadebuli being SW. Arabia).
THEAL, iii. 67–142 (translation of Goes *q.v.*), vi. 147–306 (translation of Barros *q.v.*).
VELTEN, pp. 253, 254 (Wadebuli colonization of Kilwa).
VOELTZKOW, p. 250 (well on Mnemba Island constructed by Wadebuli).
WALKER, *History and Coinage of Sultans of Kilwa*.
——, *Some New Coins from Kilwa*.
WERNER, *Wahadimu of Zanzibar*.

The author is also grateful to the following gentlemen for information supplied personally, namely, Dr. A. G. Mathew (resemblances between Kilwa and Bahmani cultures), Mr. J. S. Kirkman (archaeology of Zanzibar and Pemba) and Dr. G. S. P. Freeman-Grenville (ancient coins discovered in Zanzibar).

CHAPTER III

THE PORTUGUESE IN ZANZIBAR, 1498–1698

Manuscripts

British Museum

Add. MSS. 20, 883, f. 173, King of Portugal to Viceroy of India March 13, 1700 (Queen of Zanzibar to be thanked for assistance rendered to besieged garrison at Mombasa).
——, f. 204, Same to same, February 23, 1701 (censures Francisco Pereira da Silva for proceeding to Zanzibar without attempting to relieve or retake Mombasa).
Sloane MS. 197, Livro do Estado da India compiled in about 1634 by Antonio Bocarro and Pedro Barreto de Rezende.

Printed Authorities

ASTLEY, Vol. I, Part I, Book I, Chapters III to IX (Voyages of Vasco da Gama, João de Nova, Cabral and Almeida).

AXELSON, *South-East Africa 1486–1530.*

——, *Portuguese in South-East Africa 1600–1700.*

BARROS, *Da Asia* (*see also* Theal).

BERNARDINO, p. 26 (Zanzibar in 1606).

BOXER, C. R. and AZEVEDO, C. DE, *Fort Jesus.*

CASTENHEDA, *Descobrimentos e. conquistas da India* (*see also* Litchfield and Theal).

CORREA, *Lendas da India* (*see also* Stanley and Theal).

COUPLAND, *East Africa*, Chapter III (the Portuguese Conquest).

DALRYMPLE, *Plan of the Island of Zanzibar. From Manuel Pimentel Chart of the East Coast of Africa. From a Portuguese MS.*

DANVERS, i. 252 (visit of *Union* to Zanzibar).

FARIA DE SOUSA, *Asia Portuguesa* (*see also* Stevens and Theal).

FOSTER, *Voyage of Sir James Lancaster.*

GAMA, VASCO DA, *Diario da Viagem.*

GIBBS, *History of . . . the reign of Emmanuel* (a translation of Osorio *q.v.*).

GOES, *Chronica . . . do Emmanuel* (*see also* Theal).

GRAY, *Sir John Henderson and the Princess of Zanzibar.*

GUILLAIN, Vol. I pp. 395–472.

HAKLUYT, Vol. IV pp. 242–59 (voyage of Sir James Lancaster).

KERSTEN, *Tabellarische Uebersicht* (contains useful chronological tables).

LAFITAU, *Historia des Descobertos e Conquistas dos Portugueses.*

LANCASTER, *See* Foster.

LITCHFIELD, *Historie of the Discovery and Conquest of East India* (a translation of Castenheda).

MARMOL, *L'Afrique.*

MONCLAROS, *Relacão da Viagem . . . com Francisco Barretto* (*see also* Theal).

OSORIO, *De Rebus Emmanuelis* (*see also* Gibbs).

PURCHAS, *His Pilgrimes* (voyage of *Union* to Zanzibar).

PYRARD DE LAVAL, (voyage of *Union* to Zanzibar).

QUINTELLA, *Annaes da Marinha Portuguesa.*

RAVENSTEIN, *First Voyage of Vasco da Gama.*

SANTOS, Book V Chapter XIII (witchcraft at Zanzibar).

STANLEY, *The Three Voyages of Vasco da Gama.*

STEVENS, *Portuguese Asia* (translation of Faria de Sousa *q.v.*).

STRANDES, Chapters II–XVIII.

STRONG, *History of Kilwa.*

THEAL, *Records of South-Eastern Africa* (contains translations of the following Portuguese writers, namely, Castenheda (Vol. V), Couto (Vol. VI), Faria de Sousa (Vol. III), Osorio (Vol. V)).

VEIGA, *Relacão do . . . Estado da India Oriental* (description of Zanzibar before 1634).

CHAPTER IV

THE PORTUGUESE IN PEMBA, 1505–1695

Manuscripts

(1) *British Museum*

(a) Letters from King of Portugal to Viceroy of India relative to the rebellion and expulsion of King Philip from Pemba as under.
Add. MS. 20,863, f. 127, February 26, 1605,
Add. MS. 20,860, f. 96, December 28, 1613.

(b) Letters from same to same regarding claims to Pemba of Estavão, son of King Philip to throne of Pemba.
Add. MS. 20,863, f. 172, January 2, 1607,
Add. MS. 20,863, f. 265, January 16, 1607.

(c) Letters from same to same regarding claims of King of Malindi to Pemba.
Add. MS. 20,866, f. 97, January 29, 1614,
Add. MS. 20,868, f. 70, March 17, 1619,
Add. MS. 20,873, f. 228, April 12, 1632.

(d) Letters from same to same regarding complaints of oppression received from King of Pemba.
Add. MS. 20,877, f. 66, December 3, 1645.

(e) Letter from same to same regarding donation by Queen of Pemba of her kingdom.
Add. MS. 20,880, f. 219, March 20, 1682.

(f) Letters from Viceroy of India to King of Portugal regarding rebellion in Pemba.
Add. MS. 20,903, f. 248, December 6, 1694,
Add. MS. 20,904, f. 182, September 18.

(g) Sloane MS. 197, Livro do Estado da India compiled in 1646 by Pedro Barretto Rezende, Antonio Bocarro and Pedro Barreto Rezende.

(2) *Transcript in the Peace Memorial Museum, Zanzibar*
Jambangome MS., An account of the Portuguese in Pemba commencing 4 El Haj, 1041, corresponding to April 18, 1606.

(3) *Fort Jesus, Mombasa*
Inscription over gateway, dated 1639, describing the subjugation by the Portuguese of the rebellion in Pemba.

Printed Authorities (in addition to those mentioned as authorities for Chapter III)

ASTLEY, Vol. I pp. 339–41 (visit of *Ascension* in 1607 to Pemba).
BERNARDINO, (visit to Pemba of the writer in 1607).
BOCARRO, Chapters XXVI, LIII, LV, LVI (dispute between Portuguese and Sultan of Malindi, 1614).
Documentos remittidos, Vol. I pp. 78, 113–4, 144, 258, 260, Vol. II pp. 39, 162 (claims of Sultan of Malindi to Pemba); Vol. I p. 78 (Dutch threat to Pemba); Vol. II p. 35, Vol. III pp. 187, 448, Vol. IV p. 375 (reign of Sultan Hassan bin Ahmed of Malindi).
JOURDAIN, pp. 30–45 (visit of *Ascension* to Pemba).
PURCHAS, *His Pilgrimes*, I. 228, 229 (visit of *Ascension* to Pemba).
SANTOS, Part I, Book II Chapter VII and Book V Chapter VIII (expulsion of the Portuguese from Pemba c.1589).
WELCH, *Some Unpublished Documents*, pp. 38, 39 (revolt of Pemba in 1694).

CHAPTER V

ZANZIBAR UNDER THE ARABS OF OMAN, 1698–1815

Manuscripts

(1) *British Museum*

Add. MS. 8950, Capt. Thomas Smee to Bombay Marine Department, Zanzibar, April 6, 1811.
Add. MS. 19,419, f. 7, (as to French trade with Zanzibar and Pemba in 1809).
——, f. 8, 'Extracts from a remark [*sic*] by Capt. J. Tomkinson of the *Caledon* brig'.

(2) *Public Record Office, Chancery Lane, London*

Adm. 1/62, Report of Capt. Fisher of H.M.S. *Racehorse* on visit to Pemba in 1809.
Adm. 1/63, Report of Capt. Tomkinson of H.M.S. *Caledon* on visit to Zanzibar in 1809.

(3) *Rhodes House Library, Oxford*

Afr. R. 6, Morice MS. (Zanzibar and East Africa in 1776).

(4) *Mauritius Government Archives, Port Louis*

Vol. G.A. 11 No. 119, 'Reflections' of P. Dallons (Zanzibar and East Africa in 1803).

Printed Authorities

BISSEL, pp. 31–7 (visit of Commodore Blankett to Zanzibar in 1794).

BURTON, *Zanzibar*, Vol. II App. III (visit of Capt. Smee to Zanzibar in 1811).

——, *Lacerda* pp. 37, 95 (trade between Zanzibar and interior of Africa in 1798).

COUPLAND, *East Africa*, Chapters IV, VI.

GREY, *Pirates of the Eastern Seas* (at Zanzibar *c.*1700) pp. 182, 226, 227.

GUILLAIN, Vol. I, pp. 533–8.

JACKSON, pp. 99–100, 108 (English trade with Zanzibar in eighteenth century).

JEFFREYS, pp. 22, 44–7, 139–41 (Dutch trade with Zanzibar in eighteenth century).

MANSUR, Sheikh, p. 29 (revenue of Zanzibar from slave trade in early nineteenth century).

MILES, p. 233 (pirates at Zanzibar *c.*1700).

OWEN, Vol. I pp. 421 *seq.* (*Mombasa Chronicle*).

PRIESTLEY, *France Overseas* (in eighteenth century) p. 216.

RIVARA, Vol. II pp. 207–14, 231–8, 255–62, Vol. III pp. 11–16, 32–40, 81–90 (temporary recovery of Mombasa by Portuguese in 1728).

SALT, pp. 90, 91 (offer of cession of Pemba to Great Britain in 1810).

STIGAND, pp. 56, 66 (Mazrui occupation of Pemba and invasion of Zanzibar).

STRANDES, pp. 273–96 (temporary recovery of Mombasa by Portuguese in 1728).

THEAL, *South-Eastern Africa*, Vol. IX pp. 1–3 (visits of British men-of-war to Zanzibar and Pemba in 1809 and 1810).

——, *Cape Colony*, Vol. VI p. 504 (ditto).

THOMAS and SCOTT, p. 6 (trade between Uganda and coast in eighteenth century).

CHAPTER VI

THE COMING OF SEYYID SAID BIN SULTAN
TO EAST AFRICA, 1814–29

Manuscripts

(1) *Peace Memorial Museum, Zanzibar*

Ndagoni Chronicle (written on 12 Shaaban 1267, corresponding to July 13, 1851; sets out treaty between Seyyid Said and Diwan Ngwachani *c.*1821).

Letter of Kirk to Earl Granville, December 10, 1873 (Obituary of Suleiman bin Hamed El Busaidi-Zanzibar Archives).

'Reflections of P. Dallons (Mauritius Government Archives, Vol. G.A. 11 No. 119 (earliest reference to cloves being imported into Zanzibar in 1803).
Letters of Edmund Roberts to Senator Levi Woodbury, December 19 and 26, 1828 (Library of Congress, Washington, D.C.).
Letter of Edmund Roberts to Seyyid Said, January 27, 1828 at Zanzibar (*ibid.*).

(2) *Public Record Office, Chancery Lane, London*

Adm. 52/3,940, Journal of Lieut. J. B. Emery (contains many references to the disputes between the Mazrui and Busaidi).

Printed Authorities

BALL, *Zanzibar Treaties*, pp. 7–9.
BURTON, *Zanzibar*, Vol. I p. 362 (introduction of cloves into Zanzibar).
COUPLAND, *East Africa*, Chapters IV–VI, VIII, IX.
FARSY, *Seyyid Said bin Sultan*, p. 29 (introduction of slaves into Zanzibar), pp. 33–5 (particulars regarding Suleiman bin Hamed El Busaidi).
FITZGERALD, p. 554 (introduction of cloves into Zanzibar, where, however, he misnames the introducer).
GUILLAIN, Vol. I pp. 557–9 (struggle between Mazrui and Busaidi), Vol. II pp. 26–7 (particulars of Suleiman bin Hamed El Busaidi).
HAMERTON, *Brief Notes*, B.R. XXIV. 237–8 (Suleiman bin Hamed El Busaidi).
HOLMAN, Vol. III pp. 44–50 (visit of H.M.S. *Jaseur* to Zanzibar in 1829).
RUSCHENBERGER, Vol. I pp. 23–77 (return of Seyyid Said to Zanzibar in 1832).
STIGAND, pp. 79–91 (struggle between Mazrui and Busaidi).
WERNER, *History of Pate*, J.A.S., Vol. XIV, No. LV pp. 291–5 (struggle between Mazrui and Busaidi).

CHAPTER VII

SEYYID SAID BIN SULTAN IN ZANZIBAR, 1833–56

Manuscripts

(1) *Zanzibar Archives*

'Report on the Affairs of the Imaum of Muscat, 1856' (by Atkins Hamerton).
Letters of Atkins Hamerton to Bombay Government, September 8, 1844 (sugar industry); January 2, 1844 (clove industry); September 9, 1846 (Imamate of Muscat); April 24, 1847

(Northern Arabs); March 24, 1855 (administration of justice); October 25, 1849 (Suleiman bin Hamed). Mauritius Government, August 26, 1843 and October 10, 1844 (sugar industry). Resident, Persian Gulf, June 27 and July 7, 1843 and January 10, 1854 (piracy).

Letter of C. P. Rigby to Bombay Government, March 30, 1860 (Northern Arabs).

Administrative report of R. L. Playfair for 1864 (revenue and customs of Zanzibar).

Administrative report of John Kirk for 1870 (revenue and customs of Zanzibar).

(2) *Rhodes House Library, Oxford*

Afr. 6, 'Projet d'un Etablissement' by Morice (trade with interior of Africa).

(3) *Mauritius Archives, Port Louis*

Vol. G.A. 11 No. 119 'Reflections' of P. Dallons (importation of cloves into Zanzibar in 1803).

(4) *Library of Congress, Washington, D.C.*

Letters of Edmund Roberts to Senator Levi Woodbury, December 19 and 26, 1828 (trade with interior of Africa).

Published Authorities (in addition to those mentioned in Chapter VII)

BALL, pp. 11, 22 and 27 (references to piracy in treaties).
BISSELL, pp. 31–7 (Northern Arabs).
BURGESS, *Missionary Herald*, Vol. 86 pp. 119, 120 (trade with interior of Africa).
BURTON, *Lake Regions*, Vol. I p. 125 (slave revolt in Zanzibar).
——, *Zanzibar*, Vol. I pp. 361–3 (clove industry), Vol. II pp. 405, 406, 501 (currency).
——, *Lacerda*, pp. 37, 95 (trade with interior of Africa in 1793).
COGHLAN, p. 98 (El Harthi clan).
COUPLAND, *East Africa*, p. 366 (piracy).
FARSY, *Seyyid Said*, p. 29 (clove industry).
——, *Tarehe*, pp. 19–25 (administration of justice).
FITZGERALD, pp. 553, 554 (clove industry).
GUILLAIN, Vol. II pp. 49–51 (clove industry), 146–7 (indigo industry), 237–8 (administration of justice).
HAMERTON, *Brief Notes*, B.R. XXIV. 237–41 (clove industry, administration of justice, and local government).

HART, B. R. XXIV. 274–80 (Seyyid Said's embassy to Madagascar, clove industry, and visit to Zanzibar in 1833).

HUME, *Missionary Register*, Vol. 86 p. 60 (currency).

JIDDAWI, A. M., T.N.R. No. 31 pp. 25–31 (Seyyid Said's mercantile marine).

LIVINGSTONE, pp. 501–8 (trade with interior of Africa).

RUSSELL, pp. 227, 228 (trade with interior of Africa), 331–2 (administration of justice).

State Papers, xxi. 343 (trade with interior of Africa).

STEERE, p. 499 (administration of justice).

WARDEN, B.R. XXIV. 207 (piracy).

CHAPTER VIII

SEYYID SAID AND THE AFRICAN INHABITANTS OF
ZANZIBAR AND PEMBA

Manuscripts

(1) *Zanzibar Archives: Correspondence*

J. T. Last to Lloyd Mathews, September 21, 1901 (Mwenyi Mkuu and office of Sheha).

Col. Pelly to Bombay Government July 10, 1862 (Muhammad bin Ahmed, Mwenyi Mkuu).

Col. Playfair to Bombay Government, June 25, 1865 (death of above named).

(2) *Rhodes House Library, Oxford*

Afr. 6, Morice MS. (Mwenyi Mkuu in 1776).

(3) *Library of Congress, Washington, D.C.*

Letters of Edmund Roberts to Senator Levi Woodbury, December 19 and 26, 1828 (Mwenyi Mkuu).

Published Authorities

BARROS, Decade IV, Book V, Chapter III (Utondwe in 1528).

BAUMANN, *Die Insel Sansibar*, pp. 16, 17, 30 (Sakalava raid on Mafia and Segeju immigrations into Zanzibar).

BELLEVILLE, *Trip round the Island of Zanzibar*, (in the Hadimu country in 1875) P.R.G.S. XX. 69–73.

BURTON, *Zanzibar*, Vol. I pp. 410–11 (Muhammad bin Ahmed, Mwenyi Mkuu).

ELTON, pp. 65–7 (Mwenyi Mkuu).

FRERE, *Correspondence*, pp. 32 (Tumbatu), 109–10 (Hamadi bin Muhammad).

GUILLAIN, Vol. II p. 275 (Hadimu).
INGRAMS, *Zanzibar*, Chapters II, X, XI, XL.
——, *Chronology*, p. 3.
JOHNSTON, *Comparative Study* (first Hadimu settlement in Zanzibar).
KIRK, *Annual Report for 1873–4 – S.T. No. 4 (1876)* p. 58 (death of Hamadi bin Muhammad, last Mwenyi Mkuu).
LYNE, pp. 239–41 (Muhammad bin Ahmed, Mwenyi Mkuu).
PAKENHAM, *Land Tenure amongst the Wahadimu.*
PEARCE, pp. 91 (Utondwe), 154–85 (Hadimu), 184–6 (Queen Fatuma binti Bakari), 250–2 (Tumbatu).
ROLLESTONE, *The Watumbatu* (T.N.R. No. 8 pp. 85–97).
RUSSELL, p. 341 (Muhammad bin Alawi, Mwenyi Mkuu).
STEERE, pp. 491–3 (Hadimu).
STRANDES, pp. 275–6 (Queen Fatuma), 287 (Hassan bin Abdulla, Mwenyi Mkuu).
VELTEN, pp. 249, 250 (Sakalava raid on Mafia).
WERNER, *The Wahadimu.*

CHAPTER IX

RELATIONS OF SEYYID SAID WITH PORTUGAL,
FRANCE AND GERMANY

Manuscripts

(1) *British Museum*

Add. MS. 20,887, f. 42, King of Portugal to Viceroy of India, April 4, 1731 (provisional appointment of Governor of Mombasa).
Add. MS. 20,890, f. 155, Same to same, March 22, 1745 (same subject).

(2) *Rhodes House Library, Oxford*

Afr. 6, Morice MS. (relations between France and Zanzibar in 1776).

(3) *Mauritius Archives, Port Louis*

Vol. G.A. 11 No. 119 'Reflections' of P. Dallons (relations between France and Zanzibar, 1722–1803).

(4) *Zanzibar Archives*

Hamerton to Bombay Government, July 7 and August 25, 1840 and March 23, 1843 (abortive attempt of French to conclude treaty).

Same to same, October 2, 1843 (treaty with Governor of Mozambique).

Bombay Government to Hamerton, July 16, 1840 (proposed treaty with France).

Draft agreement for recruitment of labour for Bourbon, April 20, 1843.

J. L. Krapf to D. Coates, February 18, 1844 (French attempts to recruit labour for Bourbon).

Hamerton to Bombay Government, November 22, 1844 (conclusion of treaty with France).

Directors of H.E.I.C. to Hamerton, January 21, 1846 (Imam to be thanked for assistance given to Krapf).

Hamerton to Foreign Office, October 20, 1845 (French party in Zanzibar); December 15, 1848 (French trade with Zanzibar); January 3, 1849 (visit of *Caroline* to Marseille).

Hamerton to Bombay Government June 3, 1853 (complaint against Krapf).

Hamerton to Foreign Office, February 16, 1854 (complaint against Krapf).

Rigby to Bombay Government, October 30, 1861 (Tungwi Bay).

Pelly to Bombay Government, November 23, 1861 and January 10, 1862 (Tungwi Bay).

Playfair to Bombay Government, November 15, 1863 (Tungwi Bay).

Kirk to Foreign Office, October 1, 1877 (Tungwi Bay).

Petre to Lord Salisbury, October 14, 1889 (enclosing Portuguese memo on claims to Tungwi Bay).

Printed Authorities

BALL, pp. 3–4, 7–9, 18–23, 25–8 (treaties and early relations between Portugal, France and Hanseatic Republics).

BISSELL, (relations between France and Zanzibar in 1798).

BOTELHO, J. J. T., *Historia Militar*, i. 491–5, ii. 288–300 (relations between Zanzibar and Mozambique).

BURTON, *Lake Regions*, i. 6, 73 (murder of Maizan).

——, *Zanzibar*, i. 313–28 (French trade in Zanzibar in 1859), ii. 458–493 (relations between France and Zanzibar in 1810).

COUPLAND, *East Africa*, pp. 73–107, 115–28, 133–52, 421 (relations with France), 333, 422, 425, 438–49, 457 (French activities in Madagascar), 353–7 (murder of Maizan), 382–6 (German trade with Zanzibar), 387–426 (C.M.S. Missionaries in East Africa).

——, *Exploitation*, pp. 388, 415, 446–54, 475, 482 (Portuguese claims to Tungwi).

CROFTON, *Old Consulate*, pp. 8 (treaty with Portugal), 16 (treaty with France).

GUILLAIN, Vol. I pp. xiv, xv (French activities in Madagascar), Vol. II pp. 15–21, 91–3 (murder of Maizan).

JACKSON, pp. 236, 237 (Portuguese relations with Seyyid Said).

KELLER, pp. 124, 126 (French annexation of Mayotte and Nossi Bay).

KERSTEN, *Von der Decken*, Vol. II pp. 201–12, 225–30 (French annexation of Mayotte and Nossi Be).

KRAPF, *Travels*, pp. 121–7, 166, 368, 498, 538.

——, *Journals*, C.M. Rec. XVI, 12–14, 39; XVIII. 1–2.

MANSUR, p. 30 (early relations between France and Muscat).

MILES, II. 268–74, 301, 302, 323, 341 (early relations between France and Muscat).

O'Swald, The House of, (relations between Hamburg and Zanzibar).

PARKINSON, p. 72 (seizure of Muscat ship by French).

SILLERY, T.N.R. No. 10 pp. 89–91 (murder of Maizan).

SPEKE, pp. 29, 30 (murder of Maizan).

STRANDES, pp. 299, 305 (Portuguese efforts to recover Mombasa).

TEXUGO, p. 58 (visit to Zanzibar in 1838).

CHAPTER X

SEYYID SAID AND THE UNITED STATES OF AMERICA

Manuscripts

(1) *Zanzibar Archives*

Hamerton to Bombay Government, July 8 and 13, August 17, September 6, October 10 and December 12, 1841; February 9, 1842; September 21, 1843; March 26, 1847 and December 15, 1848.

Hamerton to Foreign Office, December 15, 1848.

Director of H.E.I.C. to Hamerton, February 22, 1843.

R. B. Norsworthy to Hamerton, s.d. (*c.*1841).

Said bin Sultan to Hamerton, 24 Rabi el Awal, 1263 (March 12, 1847).

(2) *Library of Congress, Washington, D.C.*

Edmund Roberts to Said bin Sultan, January 27, 1828.

Edmund Roberts to Senator Levi Woodbury, December 19 and 26, 1828.

Despatches from U.S.A. Consuls in Zanzibar, Vols. I–III (1836–1857).

(3) *Peabody Museum, Marine Hall, Salem, Mass.*

38.25A. to 38.25G.H., Said bin Sultan to R. P. Waters, 1846.
38.25G.I., Seif bin Said to R. P. Waters, June 22, 1845.
38.25J., Suleiman bin Hamed to R. P. Waters, El Haj, 1256
    (corresponding to January–February 1841.)
Charles Ward to Said bin Sultan, July 5, 1850.
Said bin Sultan to Charles Ward, July 6, 1850.
Said bin Sultan to Michael Shepherd, February 24, 1851.
C. C. Jewett to Michael Shepherd, May 14, 1851.

Printed Authorities

BALL, pp. 9–12 (treaty with U.S.A.).
BENNET, N. R., *Americans in Zanzibar.*
BURGESS, *Missionary Herald*, Vol. 36, pp. 118 *seq.* (visit to Zanzibar in 1839).
BURTON, *Zanzibar*, i. 144–5, 313, 318.
——, *Lake Regions*, i. 22, 73–7, 148–9, 386.
COUPLAND, *East Africa*, Chapter XII.
CROFTON, *Old Consulate*, pp. 3, 4.
HAMERTON, *Brief Notes*, B.R. XXIV. 238.
HART, B.R. XXIV. 280, 281 (visit to Zanzibar in 1833).
HUME, *Missionary Herald*, Vol. 36 pp. 60–2 (visit to Zanzibar in 1839).
JACKSON, pp. 159–60, 164, 213, 214–27.
JIDDAWI, T.N.R. No. 31 pp. 25–31 (visit of Zanzibar ship to U.S.A. in 1840).
MILES, p. 536 (supply of cannon by U.S.A. to Said bin Sultan).
MORIS, S. E., *Maritime History of Massachusetts.*
NORTHWAY, (trade between Salem and Zanzibar, R. P. Waters).
OSGOOD, C. S. and BATCHELDER, pp. 163–6 (trade between Salem and Zanzibar).
PAINE, R. D., *Sailors and ships of Old Salem.*
PHILLIPS, J. D., *Salem and the Indies.*
PUTNAM, R. D., *Salem Vessels and their Voyages.*
ROBERTS, E., *Embassy to . . . Muscat.*
ROBOTTI, E. D., *Chronicles of Old Salem.*
——, *Whaling and Old Salem.*
ROSS BROWNE, J., *Etchings of a Whaling Cruise with Notes of a Sojourn in the island of Zanzibar.*
RUETE, R. S., pp. 125–7 (connections between Zanzibar and Salem).
State Papers, xxix. 1207–8, xxxii. 175–6, xxxiii. 674–5.
TALBOT SMITH, *Early Records of the (United States) Consulate at Zanzibar.*

TOUSSAINT, *Early American Trade with Mauritius.*

The author is also indebted to Mr. Ernest E. Dodge, Director of the Peabody Museum, Marine Hall, Salem, Massachusetts, for information supplied to him personally.

CHAPTER XI

SEYYID SAID AND THE SLAVE TRADE

Manuscripts

(1) *British Museum*

Add. MS. 41,265, Fairfax Moresby to Sir Robert Farquhar, April 4, 1821.

(2) *Public Record Office, Chancery Lane, London*

C.O. 167/58 (a duplicate copy of the above).

Printed Authorities

AFRICAN INSTITUTION, *Reports*, Nos. xvi (1822), xvii (1823), xix (1825) (Moresby Treaty and Owen's reports on Slave Trade).

BALL, *Zanzibar Treaties*, pp. 5–8.

COGHLAN, *Proceedings*, pp. 35–36 (will of Seyyid Said).

COUPLAND, *East Africa*, Chapter VII (Britain and the Slave Trade).

HUGHES, *Dictionary of Islam* (article of slavery).

INGRAMS, *Mauritius and East Africa* (local appointments of British representatives at Zanzibar).

LLOYD, Chapters XIII (East African Slave Trade), XIV (Moresby and Owen).

MORESBY, Two Admirals, pp. 20–24 (Moresby Treaty and capture of *Le Succes*).

NORTHWAY, *Salem and the Zanzibar-East African Trade* pp. 144–5 (plantation slaves).

OWEN, *Voyage* Vol. I Chapters XVIII (interview with Seyyid Said at Muscat), XIX (visit to Mombasa), XXII (visit to Pemba and Zanzibar).

Vol. II Chapters XIII (second visit to Mombasa), XV (visit to Pemba and Zanzibar).

SLAVE TRADE PAPERS, *Return to an Address of the House of Commons* (1824).

——, *Copies or Extracts . . . relative to the Slave Trade* (1826).

——, *Minutes of Evidence taken before the Select Committee appointed to inquire into* (1827).

——, *Correspondence relating to* (1828).

State Papers, x. 616–18, xi. 630–8 (Moresby Treaty).

THEAL, *South-East Africa*, ix. 11–14 (letter of Earl of Caledon to Vansittart, June 1810), 49–54 (letter of Moorsom to Christian, May 24, 1825).

CHAPTER XII

THE BRITISH CONSULATE AT ZANZIBAR

Manuscripts

Zanzibar Archives

'Political Department 1840–1846' (Bombay Government to Hamerton).

'Inward from Bombay 1840–1852.'

'Hamerton's Letters 1840–1842' (to Bombay Government).

Miscellaneous letters written by Hamerton (no title).

'Letters from Foreign Office – Inwards 1843–1846.'

'Colonel Hamerton's Outward Letters from 31st July, 1844, to 10th November, 1856.'

Bundle of unlabelled letters written by Hamerton, 1845–54.

'Political Department from Bombay Government, 1846–1852.'

'Outward letters to Bombay, 1846–1851.'

'Letters to the Bombay Government for 1849.'

'Letters to Zanzibar, 1855–1856.'

Printed Authorities

BALL, *Zanzibar Treaties*, p. 23.

BUXTON, *African Slave Trade and the Remedy*.

COGHLAN, *Proceedings*, pp. 62, 65, 106, 113 (revenues of Zanzibar).

COUPLAND, *East Africa*, Chapters VII (Britain and the Slave Trade), XV (The British at Zanzibar).

CROFTON, *Old Consulate*, pp. 1, 2 (Hamerton's first arrival in Zanzibar), 20 (friendship of Seyyid Said and Hamerton).

GUILLAIN, ii. 52, 53, 124.

HART, B.R. XXIV. 276 (request by Seyyid Said for presence of a British Resident).

KRAPF, *Travels*, pp. 424 (evasions by slave traders), 427 (punitive expedition against Kiswara).

LLOYD, Chapters XIII (East African Slave Trade), XIV (Moresby and Owen), XV.

OWEN, Vol. I Chapters XVIII (interview with Seyyid Said at Muscat), XIX (visit to Mombasa), XXII (visit to Pemba and Zanzibar).

Vol. II Chapters XIII (second visit to Mombasa), XV (visit to Pemba and Zanzibar).

Ross Browne, Chapter XIX (horse racing at Zanzibar).

State Papers

xxvii. 807–9 (treaty of 1839), 885–6 (Capt. Cogan on slave trade).

xxxi. 640–52 (letters of Said bin Sultan, Ali bin Nasir, Hamerton and Aberdeen).

xxxii. 175–88 (letters of Said bin Sultan, Queen Victoria, Hamerton and Palmerston), 564–5 (letters of Sir Charles Forbes and Cogan).

xxxiii. 349–54 (letters of Slave Trade Commissioners, Cape of Good Hope to Aberdeen), 674–8 (letters of Said bin Sultan, Hamerton and Aberdeen).

xxxiv. 993 (letter of Said bin Sultan, dated June 29, 1845, to Aberdeen regarding Bahrein).

xxxv. 628–32 (letters of Said bin Sultan, Hamerton and Aberdeen Treaty of 1845 – instructions issued by Said bin Sultan regarding slave trade), 633–6 (correspondence between Henderson & Co. and Foreign Office), 636–9 (letters of Said bin Sultan, Hamerton, Aberdeen and Palmerston).

xxxvii. 450–2 (letters of Said bin Sultan, Hamerton and Palmerston).

xxxviii. 481, 482 (letter of Palmerston to Hamerton, February 12, 1850).

xl. 245, 246 (letter of Slave Trade Commissioner, Cape of Good Hope, to Aberdeen, January 1, 1851), 267–9 (letters of Said bin Sultan, Commodore Wyvill, Hamerton and Admiralty), 411–13 (correspondence between Hamerton and Palmerston), 451, 452 (Letters of Said bin Sultan, Hamerton and Palmerston).

CHAPTER XIII

SEYYID SAID BIN SULTAN'S LATTER DAYS

Manuscripts

   Zanzibar Archives

(1) Correspondence relating to Hilal bin Said

    Aberdeen to Consul-General, Egypt, October 27, 1845.
    Hamerton, October 6 and No. 17, 1845.
    Said bin Sultan, November 18, 1845.
    Aden, Political Agent at, to Bombay Government, June 24, 1851.
    Bombay Government to Hamerton, August 15, 1845 and July 7, 1846.

U

Hamerton to Bombay Government June 4, 1842; April 14, 1845; February 2, March 3 and September 9, 1846; November 5, 1849; September 10, 1850; July 23, 1851.
Hamerton to Foreign Office, July 31, 1844, February 10, 1846 and November 2, 1849.
Rigby to Bombay Government, April 14, 1859.
Said bin Sultan to Aberdeen, February 9, 1846.
Said bin Sultan to Palmerston, November 9, 1849.

(2) Correspondence relating to Khalid bin Said

Hamerton to Bombay Government, February 3, 1842, November 29, 1843, October 25, 1849, September 10, 1850, April 18 and November 15, 1854, March 24, 1855.
Hamerton to Foreign Office, July 31, 1844, October 25, 1845.
Rigby to Bombay Government, February 17, 1859.
Said bin Sultan to Hamerton, July 3, 1841.

(3) Correspondence relating to Majid bin Said

Hamerton to Bombay Government, November 15, 1854, March 24 and September 5, 1855.
Said bin Sultan to Hamerton, October 2, 1855.

(4) French attempts to recruit labour for Réunion

Hamerton to Foreign Office, September 20 and 24, 1851, March 16, 1855.

(5) Said bin Sultan's final departure from Zanzibar and death

Hamerton to Bombay Government, April 15, 1854 and November 10, 1856.

Printed Authorities

BADGER, p. 353 (Hilal bin Said in Oman).
BURTON, *Zanzibar*, Vol. I Chapter VII.
COGHLAN, pp. 29, 58, 116 (Khalid bin Said and Majid bin Said).
COUPLAND, *British Anti-Slavery Movement*, pp. 304–6 (French attempts to recruit labour for Réunion).
——, *East Africa*, pp. 274, 322, 324, 439, 453, 454 (Hilal bin Said), 293, 326, 440, 453–6 (Khalid bin Said), 296, 322, 350, 434, 456, 554 (Majid bin Said), 553, 554 (death of Said bin Sultan), 453–8 (French attempts to recruit labour for Réunion).
FARSY, *Seyyid Said bin Sultan*, pp. 9–18 (family of Said bin Sultan), 87–9 (death of Said bin Sultan).

GUILLAIN, Vol. II pp. 226, 227 (Hilal bin Said), 228, 229, 237 (Khalid bin Said).

HOLMAN, Vol. III Chapter III (Khalid bin Said).

INGRAMS, *Zanzibar*, Chapter XIII.

——, *Said bin Sultan*.

——, *Chronology*.

LYNE, Chapter II.

MILES, pp. 345, 346 (Hilal bin Said in London), 347 (Khalid bin Said), 350–2 (departure of Said bin Sultan from Zanzibar and death).

RUETE, E., Chapters I, II (Hilal and Khalid aulad Said); X (death of Said bin Sultan).

RUETE, R. S., pp. 79–82 (Hilal bin Said), 69, 80, 81, 87 (Khalid bin Said), 89, 90 (death of Said bin Sultan).

RUSCHENBERGER, Vol. I pp. 36, 56 (Khalid bin Said).

SHEPHERD, pp. 46–54 (Said bin Sultan in his latter years).

U*

BIBLIOGRAPHY

Abbreviations

B.R.: *Selections from the Records of the Bombay Government.*
H.M.S.O.: Her Majesty's Stationery Office.
J.R.G.S.: *Journal of the Royal Geographical Society.*
N.C.: *Numismatio Chronicle.*
P.R.G.S.: *Proceedings of the Royal Geographical Society.*
T.N.R.: *Tanganyika Notes and Records.*

Africa Pilot: Part III. South and East Coasts of Africa (London, 1929).
African Institution: Reports Nos. XV (1821), XVI (1822), XVII (1823), XVIII (1824) and XIX (1825).
Albuquerque, Affonso *de: Cartas de . . . sequidos de documentos que das elucidam.* 7 Vols. (Lisbon, 1834–1935).
Annaes da Marinha: cf. Quintella.
Anon.: *England's East African Policy* (London, 1875).
Anti-Slavery Reporter: Vol. I (N.S.) No. 3 (1853).
Annual Register: (1823) Part II. p. 90.
Archivo Portuguez Oriental: 8 Vols. Edited by J. H. da Cunha Rivara (Nova Goa, 1857–76).
Arquivo Portugues Oriental (Nova edicao): 11 Vols. (Bastora, Goa, 1936–40). (Edited by A. B. de Braganca Pereira. Contains many misprints.)
Assentos do Consilio: See Pissurlencar, P.
ASTLEY, THOMAS: *A New General Collection of Voyages* (London, 1745), Vol. I.
AXELSON, ERIC: *South-East Africa, 1488–1530* (Aberdeen, 1940).
——: *Portuguese in South-East Africa, 1600–1700* (Johannesburg, 1960).
BADGER, G. P.: *Imam and Seyyids of Oman* (Haklyut Society, 1871).
BALL, N.: *Zanzibar Treaties* (London, 1910).
BARNARD-LIEUT, F. L.: *A Three Years' Cruise in the Mozambique Channel for the Suppression of the Slave Trade* (London, 1848).
BARROS, JOÃO DA: *Da Asia* (Decade I, Coimbra, 1930), Decades II, III and IV. 7 Vols. (Lisbon, 1777–8).
BAUMANN, O.: *Die Insel Zanzibar* (Leipzig, 1897).
——: *Die Insel Pemba* (Leipzig, 1897).
BAXTER, H. C.: *Pangani. The Trade Centre of Ancient History* (T.N.R. xvii. 33–7).

BENNET, N. R.: *Americans in Zanzibar* 1825–45 (T.N.R. No. 56 and Essex Institute Historical Collections XCV).

BERNARDINO, G. DE ST.: *Itinerario da India ate este reino de Portugal* (Lisbon, 1607).

BIKER, J. F. J.: *Collecção de Tratadas e concertos de pazes.* 14 Vols. (Lisbon, 1881–7).

BIRDWOOD, Sir GEORGE: *Report on the Old Records of the India Office* (London, 1891).

BISSELL, Lieut. AUSTIN: *A Voyage from England to the Red Sea,* 1795–9. (Published by A. Dalrymple at the expense of the East India Company, 18 – –.)

BOCCARO, ANTONIO: *Decada XIII* (Lisbon, 1876).

BOMBAY GOVERNMENT: *Selections from Records of.* (*New Series*) Nos. XXIV (1856) and LIX (1861).

BOTELER, THOMAS: *Narrative of a Voyage of Discovery in Africa and Arabia.* 2 Vols. (London, 1835).

BOTELHO, Gen. J. J. T.: *Historia Militar e Politica dos Portugueses em Mocambique de descoberta a* 1833 (Lisbon, 1934).

BOTELHO, SEBASTIÃO XAVIER: *Memoria Estatica sobre os Dominios Portugueses na Africa Oriental.* 2 Vols. (Lisbon, 1835 and 1837).

BOXER, C. R.: *The Portuguese in the Land of Zanj* (*History today,* November 1959). *From the Maghgreb to the Moluccas* (*History today,* January, 1961).

BOXER, C. R. and AZEVEDO, CARLOS DE: *Fort Jesus and the Portuguese in Mombasa* (London, 1960).

BRODY, C. T.: *Commerce and Conquest in East Africa* (Salem, 1950).

BRUCKS, Capt. G. B.: *Navigation of the Gulf of Persia* (B.R. XXIV. 587–635).

BUCHANAN, L. A. C.: *The Ancient Monuments of Pemba* (Zanzibar, 1933).

BURGESS, EBENEZER: *Probable Openings for Missionaries at Zanzibar.* (Printed in the *Missionary Herald* of the American Board of Commissioners for Foreign Missions, Vol. 31 (1840) pp. 118 *seq.*)

BURTON, R. F.: *The Lake Regions of Central Africa.* 2 Vols. (London, 1860).

——: *Zanzibar: City, Island and Coast.* 2 Vols. (London, 1872).

——: *Lacerda's Journey to Cazembe in 1798* (R.G.S. 1873).

BUXTON, Sir THOMAS FOWELL: *The African Slave Trade* (London, 1839).

——: *The Remedy* (London, s.d.).

CASTANHEDA, F. L. DE: *Extractos do Descobriments e Conquista de India* (Coimbra, 1551). (English translations by Litchfield and Theal.)

CHARPENTIER DE COSSIGNY, J. F.: *Moyens d'Amélioration et de Restauration proposés aux Gouvernment et aux Habitants des Colonies* (Paris, 1803).

CHRISTIE, JAMES: *Cholera Epidemics in East Africa* (London, 1869).

COGHLAN, Brig.-Gen. WILLIAM M.: *Proceedings connected with the Commission appointed by Government to investigate and report on the Disputes between the Rulers of Muscat and Bombay* (Bombay, 1861).

COLE, SONIA: *The Prehistory of East Africa* (London, 1954).

CORREA, GASPAR: *Lendas da India* Vols. I–IV (Lisbon, 1858–61). (Translated in part by E. S. Stanley.)

CORTESÃO, J.: *A Expedicão de Pedro Alvares Cabral* (Lisbon, 1922).

COUPLAND, R.: *East Africa and its Invaders* (Oxford, 1938).

——: *The Exploitation of East Africa, 1856–90* (London, 1939).

——: *The British Anti-Slavery Movement* (London, 1932).

COUTO, DIOGO DE: *Extractos da Asia* (Lisbon, 1777–8). (A continuation of Barros *supra*. Translated partly into English by Theal.)

CROFTON, R. H.: *Zanzibar Affairs* (London, 1953).

——: *The Old Consulate at Zanzibar* (Oxford, 1935).

——: *A Pageant of the Spice Islands* (London, 1936).

CUNHA RIVARA, J. H. DA: *Archivo Portugez Oriental.* 8 Vols. (Nova Goa, 1857–76).

——: *Chronista de Tissuary.* 4 Vols. (Nova Goa, 1866–9).

DALE, VEN. GODFREY: *The Peoples of Zanzibar* (London, 1920).

DALRYMPLE, ALEXANDER: *Plan of the Island of Zanzibar near the East Coast of Africa. From a French MS.* (May 31, 1796).

——: *Plan of the Road or Harbour of Zanzibarra or Zanzibar. From an English MS.* (February 5, 1774).

——: *Plan of the Island of Zanzibar on the East Coast of Africa. From a French MS.* (April 17, 1784).

——: *Plan of the Island of Zanzibar from Manuel Piementel* (March 18, 1782).

——: *Chart of the East Coast of Africa. From a Portuguese MS. received from Capt. Robert Holford* (s.d.).

——: *Chart of the Coast of Zanzibar on the East Side of Africa. From M. D'Apres* (s.d.).

——: *Chart of the Coast of Aethopia from Cape Delgado to Bombass. From an English MS.* (s.d.).

DAMMAN, ERNST: *Beitrage auf Arabischen Quellen Zur Kenntniss des Negerischen Afrika* (Bordesholm, 1929).

DANVERS, C. F. and FOSTER, W.: *Letters received by the East India Company.*

DECKEN, C. C. VON DER: *See* Kersten.

DEVIC, L. MANUEL: *Les Pays des Zendjs . . . apres les écrivains arabes* (Paris, 1833).

Documentos remettidos da India: 5 Vols. (Lisbon, 1880–1935).

ELTON, J. F.: *Travels and researches in the Lake Regions of East and Central Africa* (London, 1879).

FARIA DE SOUSA, M. DE: *Asia Portuguesa* (Vols. I–IV. Oporto, 1947). (Translated by Stevens and Theal.)

FARLER, J. P.: *Slavery Report* in *Africa* (*No.* 6), 1895.

FARSY, A. S.: *Wafalme wa Kibusaidy wa Unguja* (printed serially in *Mazumgumzo* (*q.v.*)).

——: *Tarehe ya Imam Shafi* (Zanzibar s.d.).

——: *Seyyid Said bin Sultan* (Zanzibar s.d.).

FERRAND, G.: *Relation des Voyages at Textes Geogrophiques Arabes, Persans et Turks* (Paris, 1914).

FINDLAY, A. G.: *A Directory for the Navigation of the Indian Ocean* (London, 1882).

FITZGERALD, W. W. A.: *Travels in the Coastlands of British East Africa and the Islands of Zanzibar and Pemba* (London, 1898).

FOSTER, Sir WILLIAM: *The Voyage of Sir James Lancaster* (Hakluyt Society, 1940).

——: *The English Factories in India.*

——: *See also* Danvers and Jourdain.

FRERE, Sir BARTLE: *Zanzibar and its Sultan* (MacMillan's Magazine, June 1875).

——: *Zanzibar: A Commercial Power* (MacMillan's Magazine, July 1875).

——: *Eastern Africa as a Field for Missionary Labour* (London, 1874).

——: *Correspondence relating to . . . Mission to the East Africa* 1872–3 (H.M.S.O. 1873).

GAMA, VASCO DA: *Diario do Viagem* (Oporto s.d.).

——: *See also* Ravenstein and Stanley.

GIBBS, JAMES: *The History of the Portuguese during the reign of Emmanuel* (London, 1752). A translation of Osorio *q.v.*

GOES, DAMIANO DE: *Chronica . . . do Emmanuel.* Vols. (Coimbra, 1790).

GRANDIDIER, A.: *Notice sur l'Ile de Zanzibar* (Réunion, 1869).

GRAY, J. M.: *East Africa and America* (T.N.R. No. 22 pp. 55–86).

——: *Report on . . . claims to certain Land at or near Ngezi, Vitongoji . . . Pemba* (Zanzibar, 1956).

——: *The Wadebuli and the Wadiba* (T.N.R. No. 51).

——: *Early Portuguese Missionaries in East Africa* (London, 1958).

——: *Sir John Henderson and the Princess of Zanzibar* (T.N.R. No. 60).

——: *Zanzibar Local Histories.*

GREENLEE, W. B.: *The Voyage of Pedro Alvares Cabral.* (Translation of an anonymous narrative for the Hakluyt Society, 1933.)

GRENVILLE, G. S. P. FREEMAN: *Medieval Evidences for Swahili* (Journal of East Africas Swahili Committee, January 1959).

——: *Some Problems of East Africa Coinage. From Early Times to* 1890 (T.N.R. No. 53).

——: *A New Hoard and some unpublished Variants of the Coins of the Sultans of Kilwa* (N.C. 1954 and T.N.R. No. 45).

GRENVILLE, G. S. P. FREEMAN: *Coinage in East Africa before Portuguese Times* (N.C. 1957).

GREY, CHARLES: *Pirates of the Eastern Seas* (1618–1723). (London, 1933.)

GROVES, C. P.: *The Planting of Christianity in East Africa.* 3 Vols. (London, 1948–53).

GUILLAIN, M.: *Documents sur l'Histoire, la Geographie, et le Commerce de l'Afrique Occidentale.* 3 Vols. (Paris, 1856).

HAKLUYT, RICHARD: *The Principal Navigations, Voyages, Traffiques and Discoveries of the English Nation* (8 Vols. Everyman edition, London, 1907).

HAMERTON, Lt-Col. ATKINS: *Brief Notes containing information on various points connected with His Highness the Imam of Muscat* (B.R. XXIV. 235).

HARRIS, JOHN: *Navigantium atque Itinerarium Bibliotheca: or Complete Collection of Voyages and Travels.* 2 Vols. (London, 1705).

HART, Captain: *Extracts from Brief Notes of a visit to Zanzibar* (B.R. XXIV. 274–83).

HERTSLET, Sir E.: *The Map of Africa by Treaty.* 3 Vols. Maps (London, 1909).

HICHENS, WILLIAM: *Khabar al Lamu: A Chronicle of Lamu* (Bantu Studies Vol. XII, March 1938).

HOLMAN, JAMES: *Voyage round the World.* 4 Vols. (London, 1834–5).

HORNELL, J.: *The Sea-going Mtepe and Dau of the Lamu Archipelego* (T.N.R. XIV. 27–37).

HORSBURGH, JAMES: *The India Directory: or Directions for sailing to and from the East Indies.* 2 Vols. 6th Ed. (London, 1852).

HOURANI, G. F.: *Arab Seafaring in the Indian Ocean* (Princetown, 1951).

HUGHES, T. P.: *Dictionary of Islam* (London, 1885).

HUME, ROBERT WILSON: *Extracts from Journal of.* (Printed in *The Missionary Herald* of the American Board of Commissioners for Foreign Missions Vols. 36 (1840) pp. 60–2.)

HUMMERICH, FRANZ: *Vasco da Gama and die Entdeckung des Seewegs nach Ostinden* (Munich, 1898).

HUTCHINSON, EDWARD: *The Slave Trade of Africa* (London, 1874).

INGRAMS, W. H.: *Zanzibar: Its History and its People* (London, 1930).

——: *Some points of contact between Mauritius and East Africa* (Trans. of the Royal Society of Arts and Science, Mauritius, 1929–32).

——: *Said bin Sultan: An Appreciation* (Zanzibar, 1926).

——: *Chronology and Genealogies of Zanzibar Rulers* (Zanzibar, 1926).

——: *Zanzibar: An Account of its People, Industries and History* (Zanzibar, 1924).

——: *Arabia and the Isles* (London, 1942).

INGRAMS, W. H. and HOLLINGSWORTH, L.: *A School History of Zanzibar* (London, 1925).

JACKSON, MABEL V.: *European Powers and South-East Africa* (London, 1941).

JEFFREYS, K. M.: *Kaapse Archiefstukken* (Capetown, 1926).

JIDDAWI, A. M.: *Extracts from an Arab Account Book, 1850–1854* (T.N.R. No. 31 pp. 25–31).

JOHNSTON, Sir HARRY: *The Colonisation of Africa* (Cambridge, 1899).

——: *Comparative of the Bantu and Semi-Bantu Languages* (Oxford, 1919).

JOURDAIN, JOHN: *The Journal of.* (Edited for Hakluyt Society by William Foster, 1905.)

KELLER, C.: *Die Ostafrikanischen Inseln* (Berlin, 1898).

KEMBALL, Lieut. A. B.: *Papers relating to the Measures adopted by the British Government between the Years 1820 and 1844 for effecting the Suppression of the Slave Trade in the Persian Gulf* (B.R. XXIV. 637–650). *See also* Warden.

KERSTEN, OTTO: *Tabellarische Uebersicht der Geschichte Ostafrikas* (Leipzig and Heidelberg. c.1862).

——: *Baron Carl Claus von der Dackens Reisen in Ost-Afrika.* 2 Vols. (Leipzig and Heidelberg, 1869).

KIRKMAN, J. S.: *Excavations at Ras Mkumbuu on the Island of Pemba* (T.N.R. No. 53).

KIRK, J.: *Annual Report on Zanzibar,* 1873–4 (S.T. (No. 4) 1876 pp 55–86).

KRAPF, J. L.: *Travels, Researches and Missionary Labours during Eighteen Years' Residence in Eastern Africa* (London, 1860).

——: *Journals.* (Extracts printed in the *Church Missionary Record* Vols. XVI to XVIII (1845–7).

KRUMM, B.: *Words of Oriental Origin in Swahili* (London, 1940).

LAFITAU, P.: *Historia das Descobertas e Conquistas dos Portuguessas* (Lisbon, 1848).

LANCASTER, Sir JAMES: *The Voyage of.* (Edited for Hakluyt Society by C. R. Markham (1877) and Sir William Foster (1940).)

LEO AFRICANUS: *The History and Description of Africa.* (Translated by John Pory in 1600 and edited for Hakluyt Society (2 Vols.) by Robert Brown, 1896.)

LIMA, J. J. S.: *Ensaios sobre e Estatica das Possessoes Portugueses.* 4 Vols.

LITCHFIELD, N. L.: *The First Book of the Historie of the Discoverie and Conquest of the East Indies* (London, 1551). Translated from Castenheda.)

LIVINGSTONE, D.: *Journeys and Researches in South Africa* (London, 1851).

LYDDEKER, C. J. W.: *Mtepe Dhau* (*Man*, 1919, p. 46).

LYNE, R. N.: *Zanzibar in Contemporary Times* (London, 1905).

McQUEEN, JAMES: *A Geographical Survey of Africa* (London, 1820).
——: *Notes on African Geography: Visit of Leif bin Said to the Great African Lake* (J.R.G.S. (1845) XV. 371–6).
——: *Notes on the Geography of Central Africa* (J.R.G.S. (1856) XXVII. 109–30).

MANSUR, SHEIKH: *History of Seyd Said, Sultan of Muscat* (London, 1819).

MARMOL: *L'Afrique.* 3 Vols. (Paris, 1762).

Mazumgumzo ya Walimu wa Unguja: A monthly periodical formerly issued under the aegis of the Zanzibar Education Department.

MILES, Col. S. B.: *The Countries and Tribes of the Persian Gulf.* 2 Vols. (London, 1919).

Missionary Register for 1821, 1823, 1824 and *1827.*

MONCLAROS, F.: *Relacão da Viagem . . . do Francisco Barretto.* (Translated by Theal in *Records of South Africa* Vol. III.)

MORESBY, Admiral JOHN: *Two Admirals: Admiral of the Fleet Sir Fairfax Moresby and his son John Moresby* (Edinburgh, 1909).

NORTHWAY, P. E.: *Salem and the Zanzibar – East African Trade, 1825–1845* (Essex Institute Historical Collections, Vol. xc, April, July, October, 1954).

NUNEZ, ANTONIO: *Livro dos Pesas da Yndia e assy Medidas e Monedas escripto em 1554.* (Printed in *Subsidios para a Historia da India Portugueza* Vol. I (Lisbon, 1863).) (Gives weights and measures for Malindi, Mombasa and Zanzibar.)

OLIVER, ROWLAND: *The Missionary Factor in East Africa* (London, 1952).

OSGOOD, C. S. and BATCHELDER, H. M.: *Historical Sketch of Salem 1626–1879* (Salem, Essex Institute, 1879).

OSGOOD, J. B. F.: *Notes of Travel* (Salem, Mass., 1854).

OSORIO, H.: *De Rebus Emmanuelis* (Coimbra, 1781).
——: *Da Vida E Feitos de el Rei D. Mannuel.* (Vols. I and II, Oporto, s.d.). (English Translation by Gibbs.)

O'Swald, *The House of:* (Hamburg, 1931).

OWEN, Capt. W. F. W.: *Narrative of Voyages to explore the Shores of Africa, Arabia and Madagascar.* 2 Vols. (London, 1833). (Edited by Heaton Boustead Robinson.)

PAINE, R. D.: *The Sailors and Ships of Old Salem* (London, 1924).

PAKENHAM, R. H. W.: *Land Tenure amongst the Wahadimu at Chwaka, Zanzibar Island* (Zanzibar, 1947).

PARKINSON, C. N.: *War in the Eastern Seas* (London, 1954).

PAULITSCHKE, P.: *Die Afrika: Literatur in der Zeit von 1500 ins 1750* (Vienna, 1882). A useful bibliography.

PEARCE, Major F. B.: *Zanzibar: The Island Metropolis of Eastern Africa* (London, 1920).

PERRY, Sir ERSKINE: *Cases illustrative of Oriental Life and the Application of English law to India, decided in H.M. Supreme Court of Bombay* (Bombay, 1852).

PHILIPS, J. D.: *Salem and the Indies* (Cambridge, Mass., 1947).

PISSURLENCAR, PANDUROGA (ed.): *Assentos do Conselho do Estado du India*, 1618–1750. 5 Vols. (Bastora – Goa, 1953–8).

PRIESTLEY, H. I.: *France Overseas through the Old Regime: A Study of European Expansion* (New York and London, 1939).

PRINS, A. H. J.: *The Coastal Tribes of the North-Eastern Bantu* (London, 1952).

PRIOR, JAMES: *Narrative of a Voyage in the Indian Seas in the Nisus Frigate . . . during the years 1810 and 1811* (London, 1820).

PULLICINO, P.: *Aulad el Imam* (Zanzibar, 1954).

PURCHAS, SAMUEL: *His Pilgrimes*. 5 Vols. (London, 1625).

——: *His Pilgrimage* (London, 1617).

PUTNAM, G. G.: *Salem Vessels and their Voyages* (Salem, Mass., 1924).

PYRARD DE LAVAL, FRANCOIS: *The voyage of.* 2 Vols. (Translated by A. Gray for Hakluyt Society 1887–90.)

QUINTELLA, Vice-Admiral IGNACIO DA COSTA: *Annaes da Marinha Portuguesa* 2 Vols. (Lisbon, 1839 and 1840). (Gives a brief account of each voyage from Portugal to India between 1498 and 1638.)

RAVENSTEIN, E. G.: *A Journal of the First Voyage of Vasco da Gama.* (A translation of the *Diaris de Viagem* for the Hakluyt Society 1898.)

REINHARDT, C.: *Ein Arabischer Dialekt gesprochen in Oman und Zenzibar* (Stuttgart, 1894).

RIGBY, Lt-Col. C. P.: *Report on the Zanzibar Dominions* (B.R. LIX (1861). Also printed as an appendix in Russell *q.v.*).

RIVARA, J. H. DA CUNHA: *Archivo Portugez.* 8 Vols. (Goa, 1861).

ROBERTS, E.: *Embassy to the Eastern Courts of Cochin-China, Siam and Muscat in the U.S. Sloop of War Peacock 1832–34* (New York, 1837).

ROBINSON, ARTHUR E.: *The Shirazi Colonisation of East Africa* (T.N.R. No. 3).

——, *The Shirazi Colonisation of East Africa: Vumba* (T.N.R. No. 12).

ROBINSON, H. B.: *See* Owen.

ROBOTTI, F. D.: *Whaling and Old Salem* (Salem, Mass., 1950).

——: *Chronicles of Old Salem* (Salem, Mass., 1948).

ROLLESTON, I. H. O.: *The Watumbatu of Zanzibar* (T.N.R. No. 8).

ROSS BROWNE, JAMES: *Etchings of a Whaling Cruise with Notes on a sojourn in the Island of Zanzibar* (London, 1846).

RUETE, RUDOLPH SAID: *Said bin Sultan* (London, 1929). (The author was a grandson of Said bin Sultan.)

RUSCHENBERGER, W. S. W.: *Narrative of A Voyage round the World* (London, 1838).

RUSSELL, Mrs. C. E. B.: *General Rigby, Zanzibar and the Slave Trade* (London, 1935).
SACLEUX, P. CH.: *Grammaire des Dialectes Swahilis* (Paris, 1909).
SALT, HENRY: *A Voyage to Abyssinia* (London, 1814).
SANTOS, JOÃO DOS: *Ethiopia Oriental* (Lisbon, 1809).
SCHMIDT, K. W.: *Sansibar: ein Ostafrikanisches Culturbild* (Leipzig, 1888).
SCHOFF, W. H.: *The Periplus of the Erythaean Sea* (London, 1912).
SELIGMAN, C. G.: *Races of Africa* (London, 1930).
SHELSWELL-WHITE, G. H.: *A Guide to Zanzibar* (London, 1932).
SHEPHERD, W. A.: *From Bombay to Bushire and Bussors* (London, 1857).
SILVA REGO, ANTONIO DA: *Documentacão para a historia des missoes do padraodo português do Oriente India.*
Slave Trade: Return to an Address of the House of Commons (1824).
——: *Copies or Extracts received by His Majesty's Government relative to the Slave Trade at the Mauritius and Bourbon and the Seychelles from the time of their capture to the Present Time* (1826).
——: *Correspondence relating to.* (1828).
——: *Minutes of Evidence taken before the Select Committee appointed to inquire into.* (1827).
SMEE, Captain T.: *Observations during a Voyage of Research on the East Coast of Africa from Cape Guardafui South to Island of Zanzibar.* (Reprinted in Burton: *Zanzibar, City, Island and Coast II*, 458–93 *q.v.*).
SPEKE, J. H.: *Journal of the Discovery of the Source of the Nile* (London, 1863).
STANLEY, E. G.: *The Three Voyages of Vasco da Gama.* (Translated from Correa for Hakluyt Society, 1869.)
STANLEY, H. M.: *How I found Livingstone* (London, 1872).
State Papers: Vol. X (1822–3) to Vol. XIII (1825–6); Vol. XXVIII (1839–40) and Vol. XXIX (1840–1); Vol. XXXI (1842–3) to Vol. XXXIV (1845–6); Vol. XXXVI (1847–8) to Vol. XXXVIII (1849–50); Vol. XLI (1850–1) and Vol. XLII (1852–3).
STEERE, E.: *Swahili Tales as told by the Natives of Zanzibar* (London, 1869).
STEVENS, JOHN: *The Portuguese Asia* (London, 1695). (A translation of Faria y Sousa.)
STIGAND, C. H.: *The Land of Zinj* (London, 1913).
STOCK, EUGENE: *The History of the Church Missionary Society.* 3 Vols. (London, 1890).
STOCKLEY, G. M.: *Report on the Geology of the Zanzibar Protectorate* (Zanzibar, 1920).
STORBECK, FRIEDRICH: *Die Berichte der arabischen Geographen des Mittelalters über Ost-Afrika.* (Published in *Mitt. des Seminars für Orintalische Sprachen* (1914) XVII, Part II, Berlin.)

STRANDES, JUSTUS: *Die Portugiesenzeit von Deutsch-und-Englisch Ostafrika* (Berlin, 1899).

STRONG, S. A.: *The History of Kilwa* (*Journal of the Royal Asiatic Society* (1895).

STUHLMANN, F.: *Beitrage zur Kulturgeschichte von Ostafrika* (Berlin, 1909).

SYKES, Colonel: *Notes on the Possessions of the Imaum of Muskat, on the Climate and Productions of Zanzibar, and on the prospects of African Discovery* (J.R.G.S. (1853) pp. 101–19).

TALBOT SMITH, E.: *Early Records of the Consulate at Zanzibar*, (Printed in *The American Foreign Service Journal*, May, 1940.)

TAYLOR, W. E.: *African Aphorisms or Saws from Swahililand* (London, 1891).

TEXUGO, F. TORRES: *A Letter on the Slave Trade still carried on along the Eastern Coast of Africa . . . addressed (by permission) to T. Fowell Buxton, Esquire* (London, 1839).

THEAL, G. M.: *Records of South-Eastern Africa.* 9 Vols. (London, 1898–1902). Contains (*inter alia*) translations of extracts from de Castanheda (Vol. V), Correa (Vol. II), de Couto (Vol. VI), Faria y Sousa (Vol. I), Monclaros (Vol. III), Osorio (Vol. V) and dos Santos (Vol. VII).

——: *Records of Cape Colony.* Vol. VI.

THOMAS, H. B. and SCOTT, R.: *Uganda* (London, 1935).

TOUSSAINT, A.: *Early American Trade with Mauritius* (Port Louis, Mauritius, 1954).

VELTEN, C.: *Prosa und Poetrie der susheli* (Berlin, 1907).

VEIGA, A. B. DA COSTA: *Relacão das Plantas, e Dezcripsoes de todas as Fortelezas, Cidades, e. Povaçoes qu as Portuezas tem no Estado da India Oriental* (Lisbon, 1936).

VOELTZKOW, ALFRED: *Reise in Ostafrika in den Jahren, 1903–1905.* 2 Vols. (Stuttgart, 1923).

WALKER, JOHN: *History and Coinage of the Sultans of Kilwa.* (Reprinted from *Numismatic Chronicle* 5th Ser. Vol. XVI (1936).)

——: *Some New Coins from Kilwa.* (Reprinted from same *Chronicle*, 5th Ser. Vol. XIX (1939).)

WARDEN, FRANCIS, HENNEL, Lieut. S., KEMBALL, Lieut. A. B. and DISBROUGH, Lieut. H. F.: *Historical Sketch of the Rise and Progress of the Government of Muskat* (B.R. XXIV 168–234).

——: *Historical Sketch of the Joasmee Tribe of Arabs* (B.R. XXIV. 300–6).

WELCH, S. R.: *Some Unpublished Documents relating to South and East Africa* (Pretoria, 1930).

WERNER, ALICE: *Article on Zanzibar in Encyclopaedia of Islam.*

——: *The Wahadimu of Zanzibar* (*Journal of African Society*, 1916).

——: *A Swahili History of Pate* (*Journal of African Society*, 1915).

Zanzibar Gazette: 1892 to date.

INDEX

Aberdeen, Earl of, 245–50, 261–5
Abdulmalik, 11, 12
Abri, el—
    Khalfan b. Suleiman, 127, 142
    Saleh b. Haramili, 129, 130
Alawi, el—
    Ahmed b. Hassan, 160, 161
    Ahmed b. Muhammad, 168, 169
    Hassan b. Abdulla, 159
    Muhammad b. Ahmed, 162, 170
    Sultan b. Hassan, 160
    See also Mwenyi Mkuu
Acland, Capt. C. D., 121, 123
Ali b. Nasser, 246, 247
Almeida, F. J. de Lacerda, 107
Amar b. Sultan el Habshi, 142
America, see United States
Amerikani cloth, 196
Arnold, surgeon, 40
Athmani, Diwan, 114, 115, 173
Augustinians, 45, 46, 50, 51, 83
Aulick, Commodore James, 222, 223
Ave Maria, Manoel de, 46, 52
Azevedo, Jeronimo de, 71

Bahmani dynasty, 26
Barbosa, Duarte, 30
Barker, Edmund, 39
Barreto, Francisco, 36–8, 56
Barroso, José, 53
Barwani, Abdulla b. Juma el, 142
Bernardino, G. de St., 41, 64
Bissell, Lt. A., 97–9, 137, 179
Blankett, J., 2, 97–9
Bocarro, Antonio de, 43, 73, 74
Booth, George, 82
Botelho, Pedro, 50, 73
Bourbon, 90, 91, 99, 129, 153, 179–88, 256, 257, 271–4
Brito, Antonio de, 53
Browne, J. Ross, 211–13
Brucks, Capt. G. B., 149
Bumbwini, 130
Bunce, Capt., 178
Burgess, Ebenezer, 159, 203
Burnham, Capt., 197
Burton, Sir R. F., 7, 164, 197
Busaidi, el—
    Ahmed b. Said, 93, 94, 135, 160, 179
    Barghash b. Said, 179, 277
    Bedr b. Seif, 111
    Hamed b. Ahmed, 115
    Hilal b. Said, 213, 259–70, 277

Busaidi, el (continued)—
    Khalid b. Said, 127–31, 134, 181, 182, 213, 245, 259–60, 270–5, 280
    Majid b. Said, 257, 278–80
    Muhammad b. Salim, 128
    Nasser b. Hamed, 127
    Said b. Sultan, arrived in East Africa, 109–31; early days in Zanzibar, 132–55; relations with African inhabitants, 156–73; with Portugal, 174–9; with France, 170–88; with Germany, 188–93; with U.S.A., 194–223; attitude to Slave Trade, 224–38; relations with British Consul, 239–58; latter days, 239–78; death, 278
    Salim b. Sultan, 111
    Seif b. Ahmed, 93, 94, 110, 143
    Suleiman b. Hamed, 127–9, 134–6, 150, 181–2, 271, 276
    Sultan b. Ahmed, 94, 110, 143

Cabreira, Francisco Seixas de, 51, 73, 74, 76, 77
Castro, Martin Affonso de, 63
Cavaco, Vas, 53
Cazembe, 107
Chande, 44
Chake Chake, 4
Chanoca, Lopes, 34
Chingulia, see Yusuf b. Hassan
Christian, Commodore H. H., 123
Christie, James, 6
Churchman, Edward, 67
Chwaka (Pemba), 25, 26, 115 (Zanzibar), 32, 158
Clonard, M. de, 92
Cloves, 96, 97, 129
Cogan, Robert, 240, 241, 247, 253, 266
Cole, Sir Lowry, 123
Conçeição, Manoel de, 52
Coutinho, Fernando, 55
    Thomé de Sousa, 58
Cunha, André de, 45
    Nuno da, 34, 35, 38

Dabhol, 26
Dale, Archd. Godfrey, 23
Dallons, 94–6, 126, 153
Damman, Ernst, 18
Deccan, 26
Dutch in E. Africa, 61, 66, 89, 91

Printed in Great Britain by
NEILL & CO. LTD., EDINBURGH

WITHDRAWN